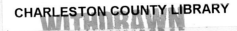
LOVE IN FOCUS

3

Yoko Nogiri

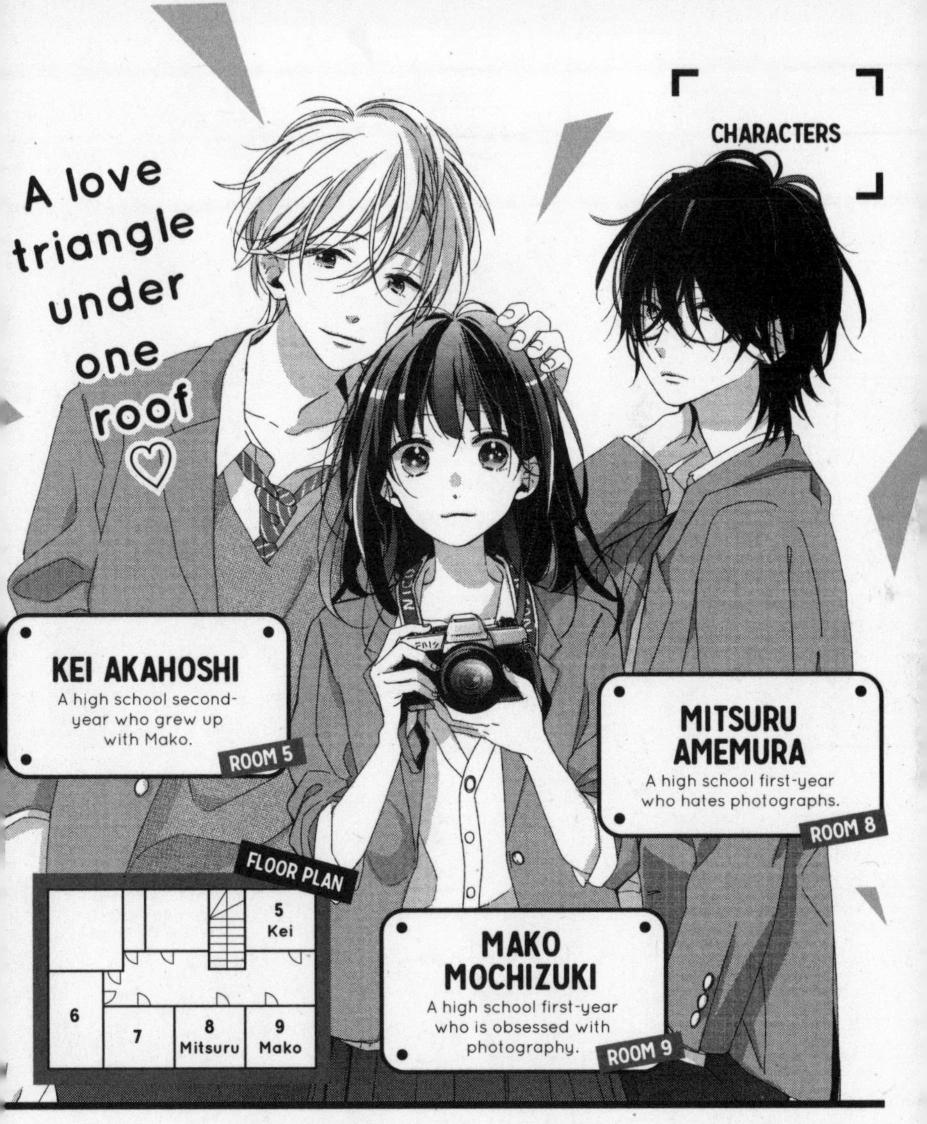
A love triangle under one roof
CHARACTERS
KEI AKAHOSHI
A high school second-year who grew up with Mako.
ROOM 5
MITSURU AMEMURA
A high school first-year who hates photographs.
ROOM 8
MAKO MOCHIZUKI
A high school first-year who is obsessed with photography.
ROOM 9
FLOOR PLAN
5
Kei
6
7
8
Mitsuru
9
Mako

STORY

Mako is a high school girl who is obsessed with photography. At the invitation of her childhood friend Kei, she enrolls in a school that is famous for its photography club and starts her new life in a boarding house with a triangle roof.

There she meets Mitsuru, who hides his face and insists, "I don't like pictures." Mako manages to convince Mitsuru to be her model, and through their first photo shoot, Mako and Mitsuru gradually grow closer.

Sensing a crisis of his own as he watches things develop, Kei tells Mako, "I really like you." This sudden confession is so startling to Mako that she comes down with a fever!

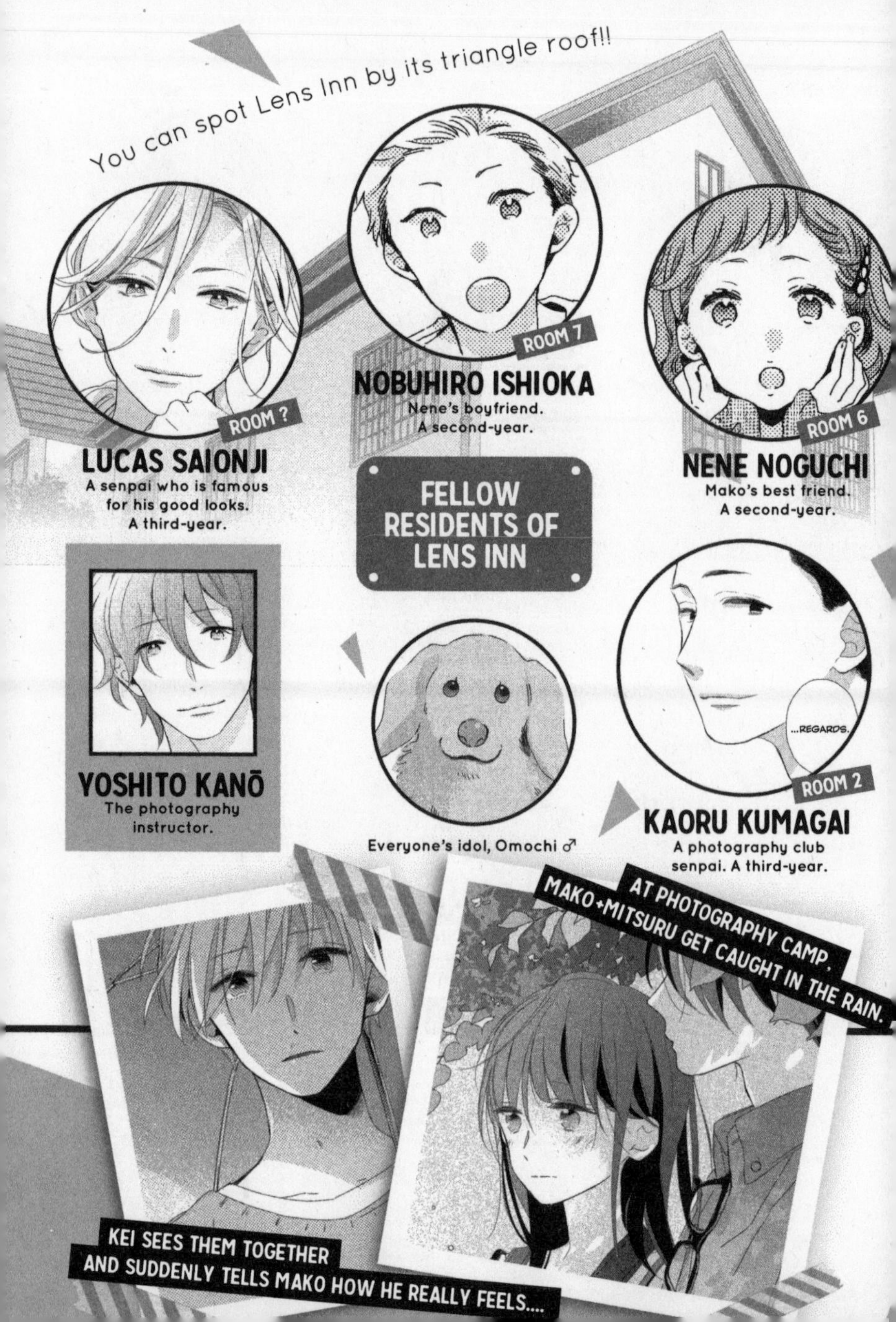

You can spot Lens Inn by its triangle roof!!
FELLOW RESIDENTS OF LENS INN
ROOM ?
LUCAS SAIONJI
A senpai who is famous for his good looks. A third-year.
ROOM 7
NOBUHIRO ISHIOKA
Nene's boyfriend. A second-year.
ROOM 6
NENE NOGUCHI
Mako's best friend. A second-year.
YOSHITO KANŌ
The photography instructor.
Everyone's idol, Omochi ♂
...REGARDS.
ROOM 2
KAORU KUMAGAI
A photography club senpai. A third-year.
AT PHOTOGRAPHY CAMP, MAKO+MITSURU GET CAUGHT IN THE RAIN.
KEI SEES THEM TOGETHER AND SUDDENLY TELLS MAKO HOW HE REALLY FEELS....

CONTENTS

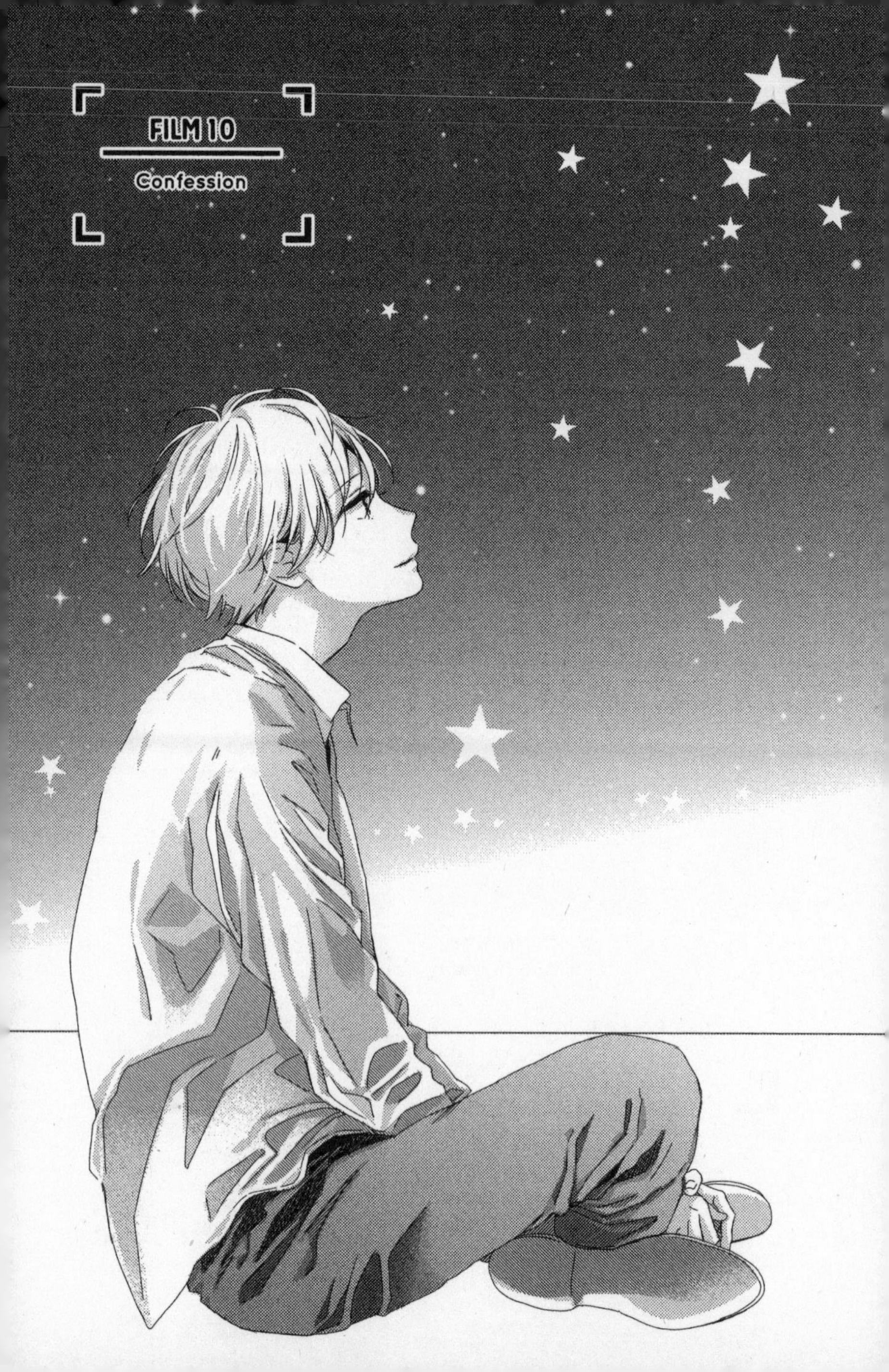
FILM 10
Confession

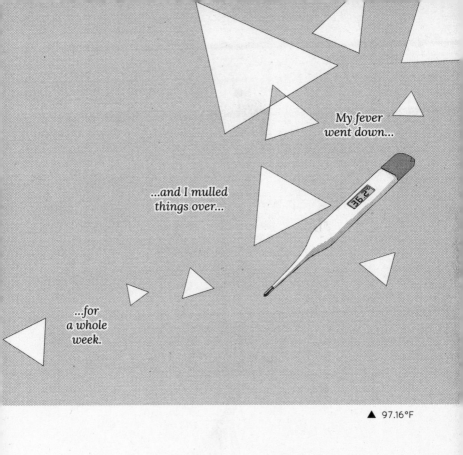

My fever went down...

...and I mulled things over...

...for a whole week.

▲ 97.16°F

LOVE in FOCUS

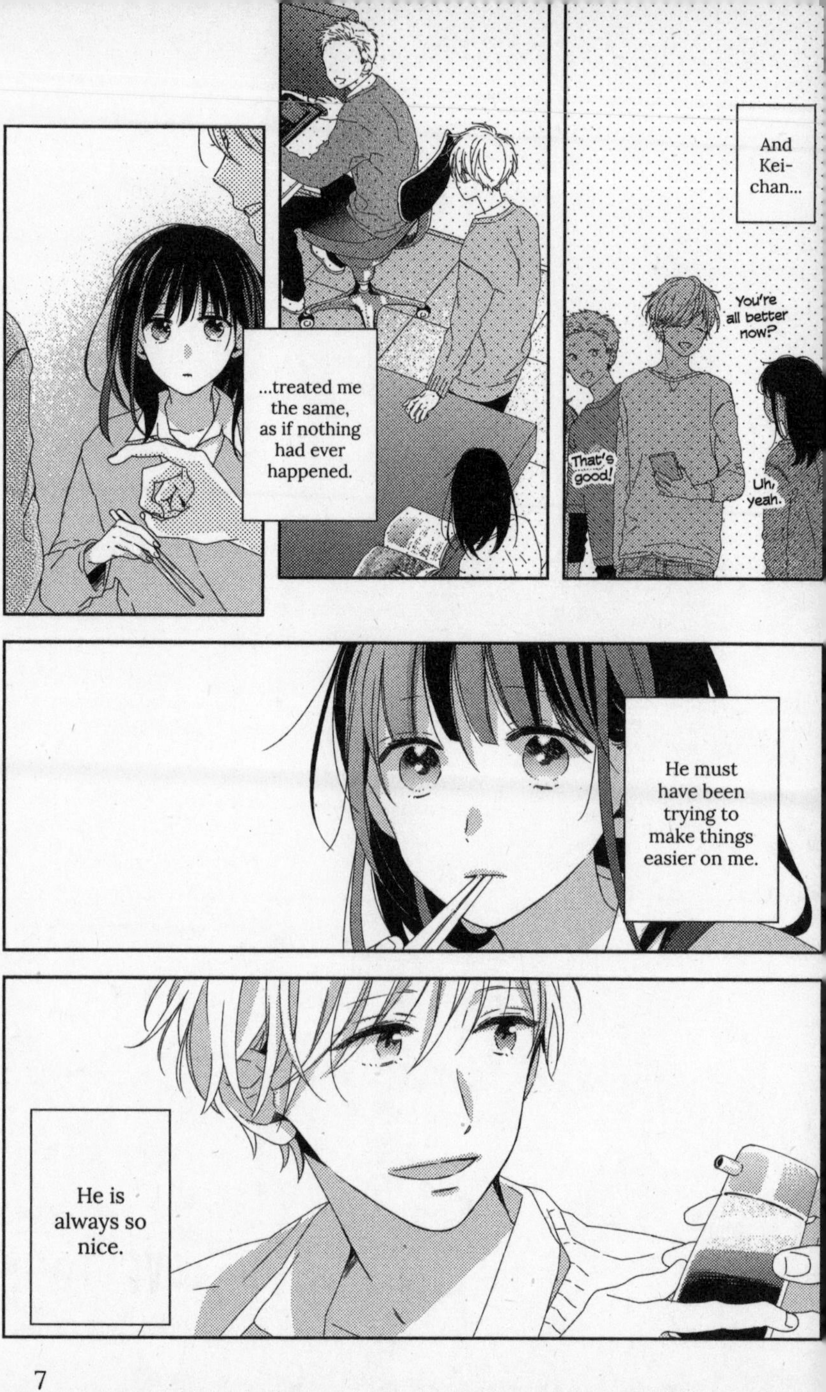
And Kei-chan...
You're all better now?
Uh, yeah.
That's good!
...treated me the same, as if nothing had ever happened.
He must have been trying to make things easier on me.
He is always so nice.

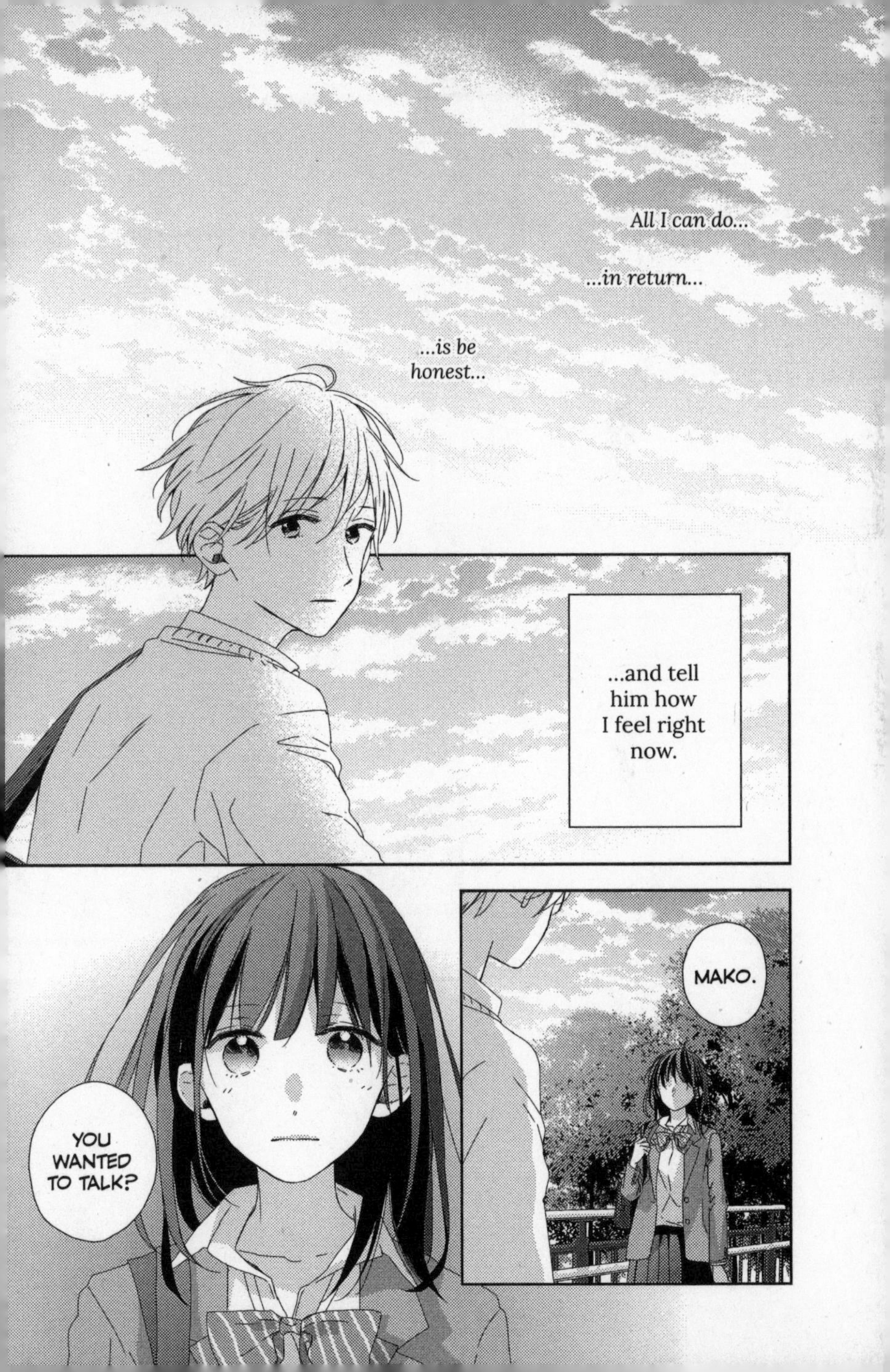
All I can do...
...in return...
...is be honest...
...and tell him how I feel right now.
MAKO.
YOU WANTED TO TALK?

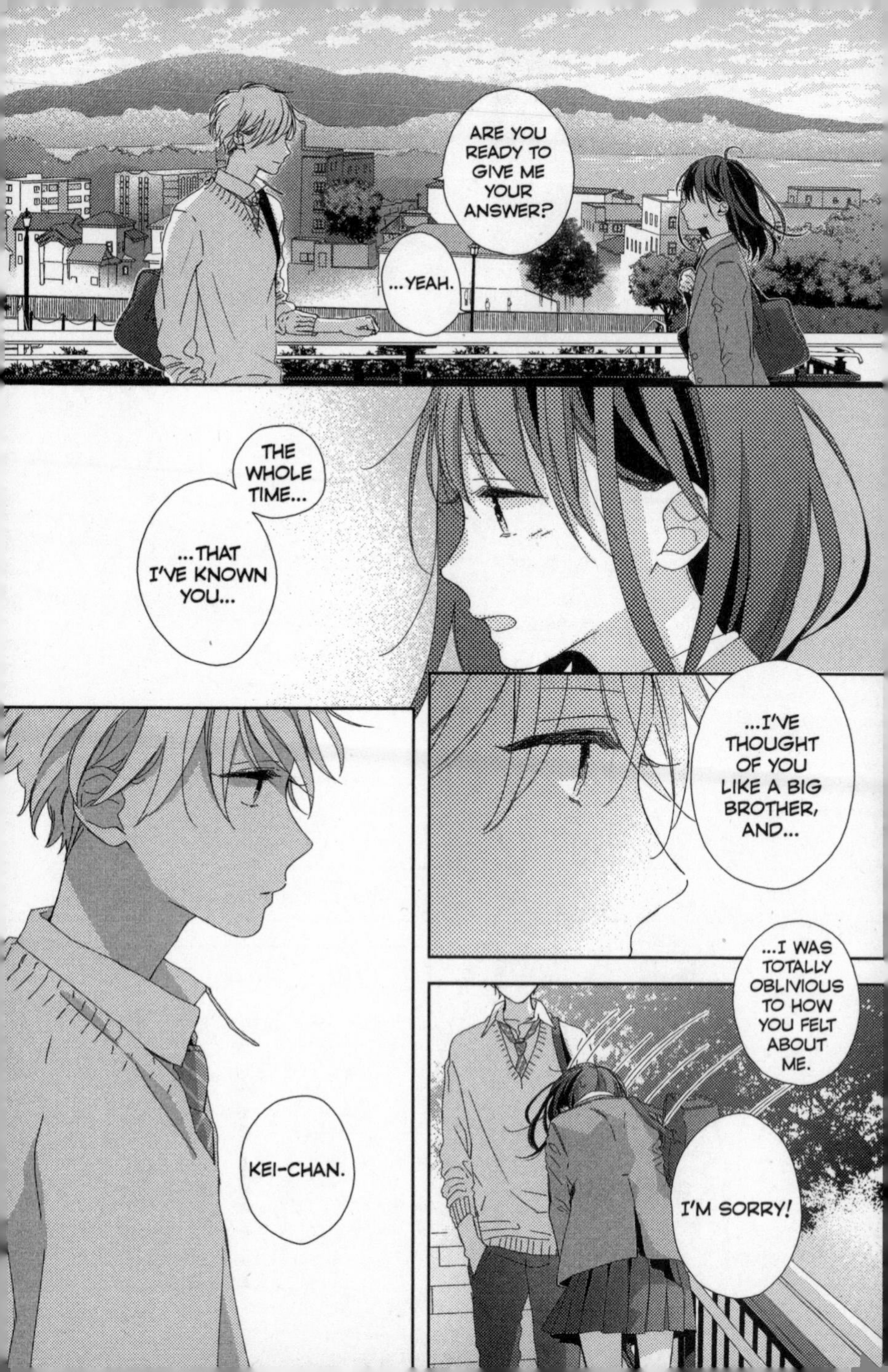
ARE YOU READY TO GIVE ME YOUR ANSWER?
...YEAH.
THE WHOLE TIME...
...THAT I'VE KNOWN YOU...
...I'VE THOUGHT OF YOU LIKE A BIG BROTHER, AND...
...I WAS TOTALLY OBLIVIOUS TO HOW YOU FELT ABOUT ME.
I'M SORRY!
KEI-CHAN.

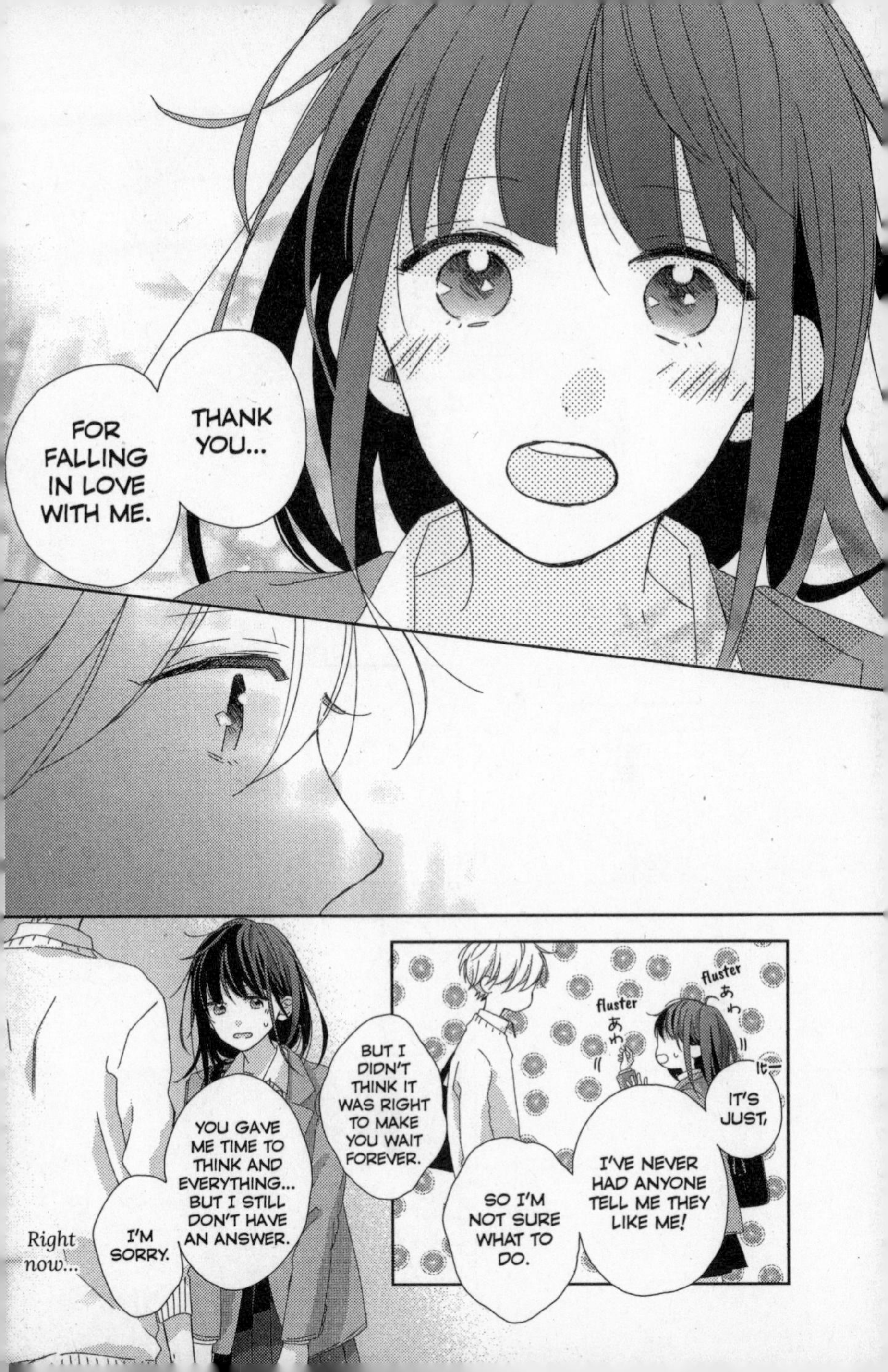
THANK YOU...
FOR FALLING IN LOVE WITH ME.
fluster
あわ
fluster
あわ
IT'S JUST,
I'VE NEVER HAD ANYONE TELL ME THEY LIKE ME!
SO I'M NOT SURE WHAT TO DO.
BUT I DIDN'T THINK IT WAS RIGHT TO MAKE YOU WAIT FOREVER.
YOU GAVE ME TIME TO THINK AND EVERYTHING... BUT I STILL DON'T HAVE AN ANSWER.
I'M SORRY.
Right now...

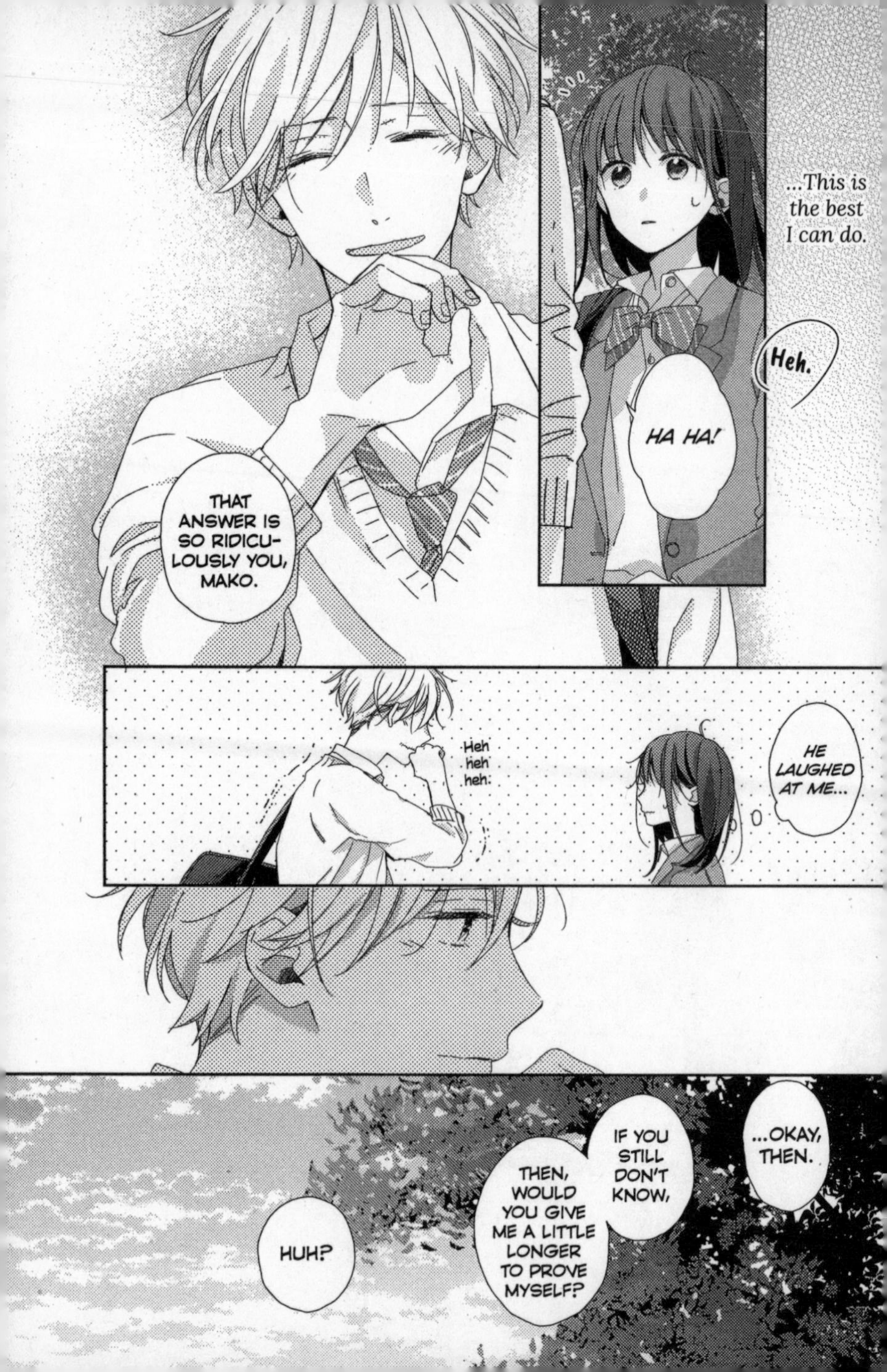
...This is the best I can do.
Heh.
HA HA!
THAT ANSWER IS SO RIDICULOUSLY YOU, MAKO.
HE LAUGHED AT ME...
Heh heh heh.
...OKAY, THEN.
IF YOU STILL DON'T KNOW,
THEN, WOULD YOU GIVE ME A LITTLE LONGER TO PROVE MYSELF?
HUH?

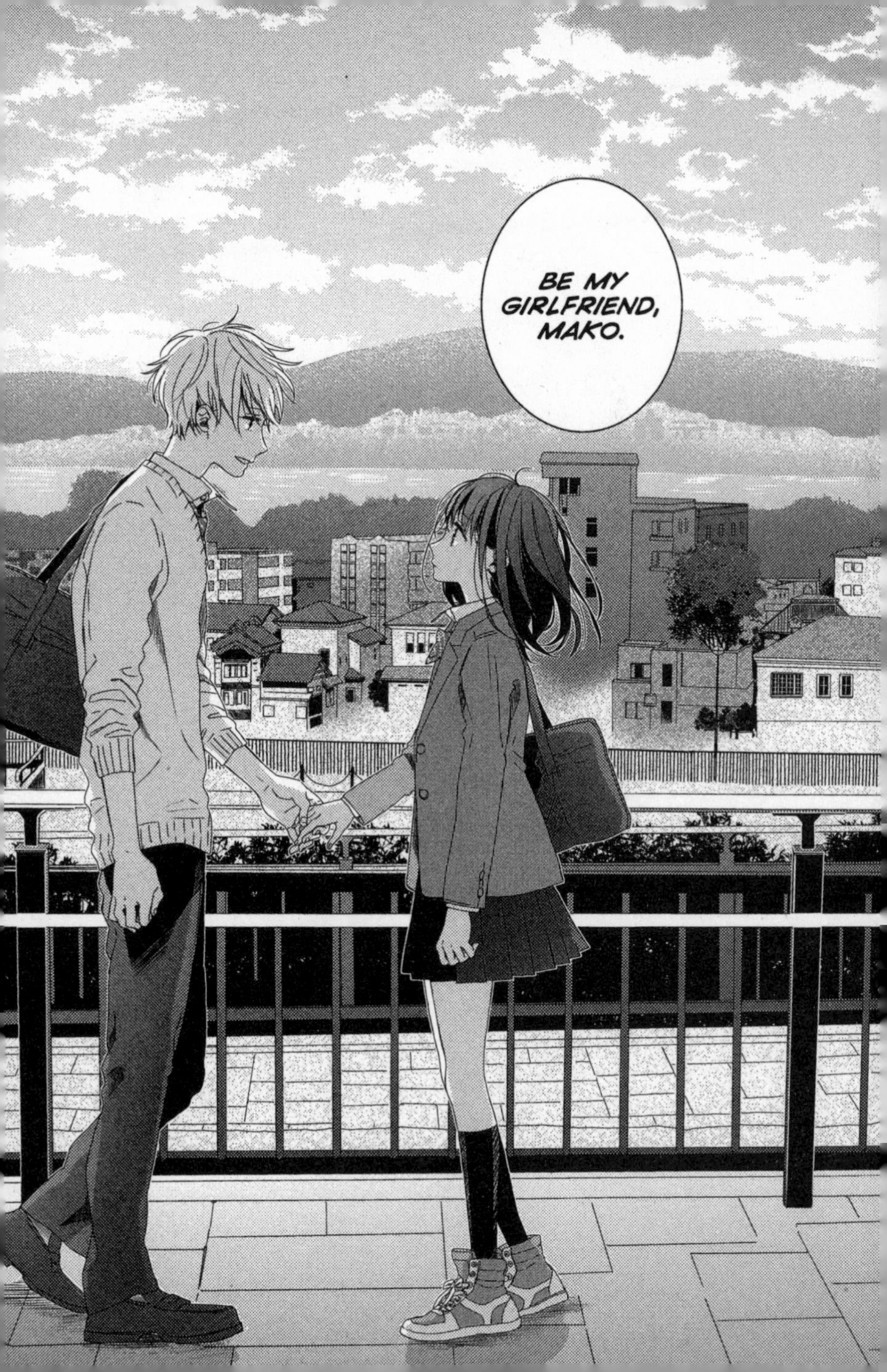
BE MY GIRLFRIEND, MAKO.

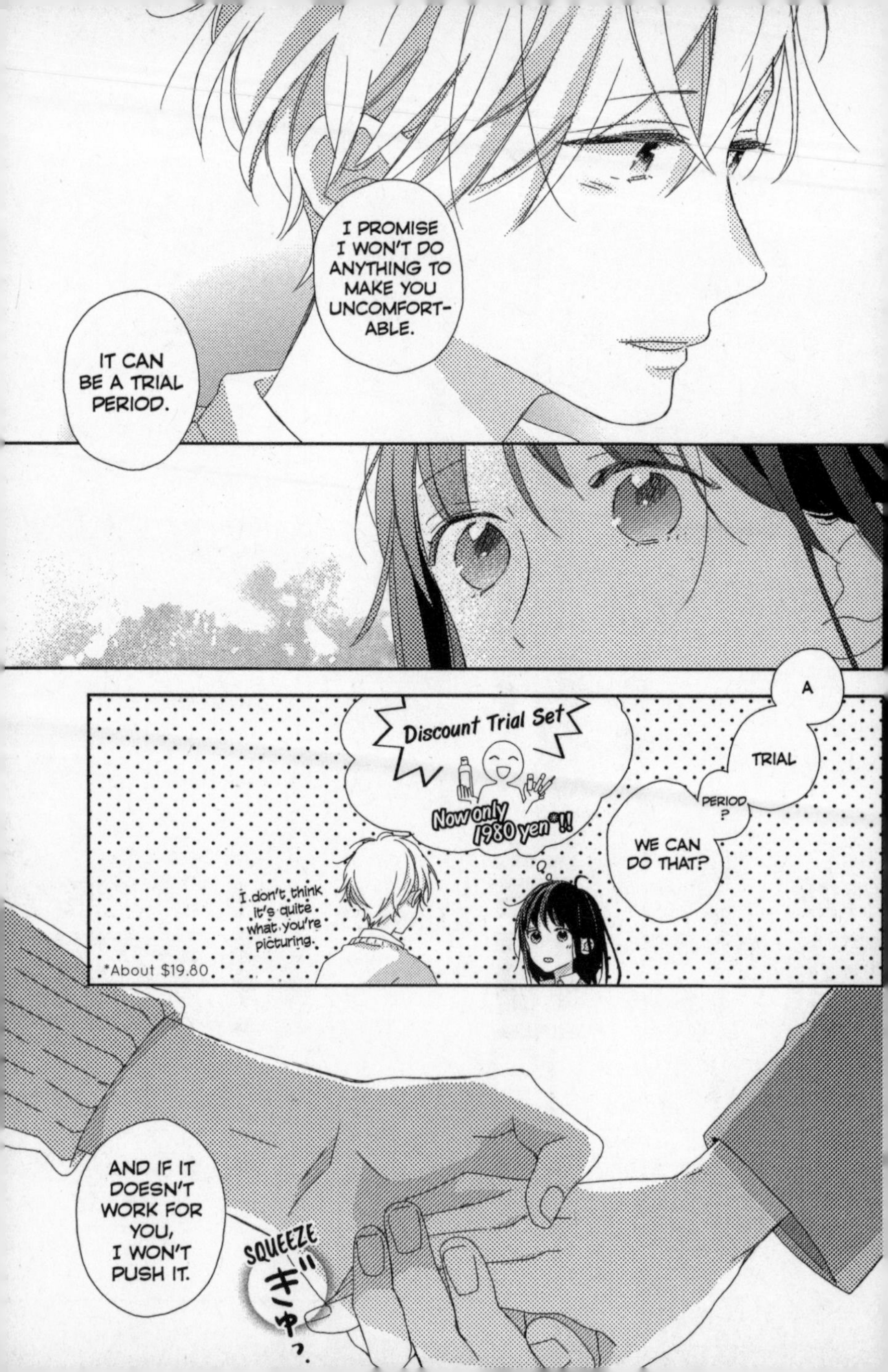
I PROMISE I WON'T DO ANYTHING TO MAKE YOU UNCOMFORTABLE.
IT CAN BE A TRIAL PERIOD.
A
TRIAL
PERIOD?
WE CAN DO THAT?
Discount Trial Set
Now only 1980 yen*!!
I don't think it's quite what you're picturing.
*About $19.80
AND IF IT DOESN'T WORK FOR YOU, I WON'T PUSH IT.
SQUEEZE
ぎゅっ

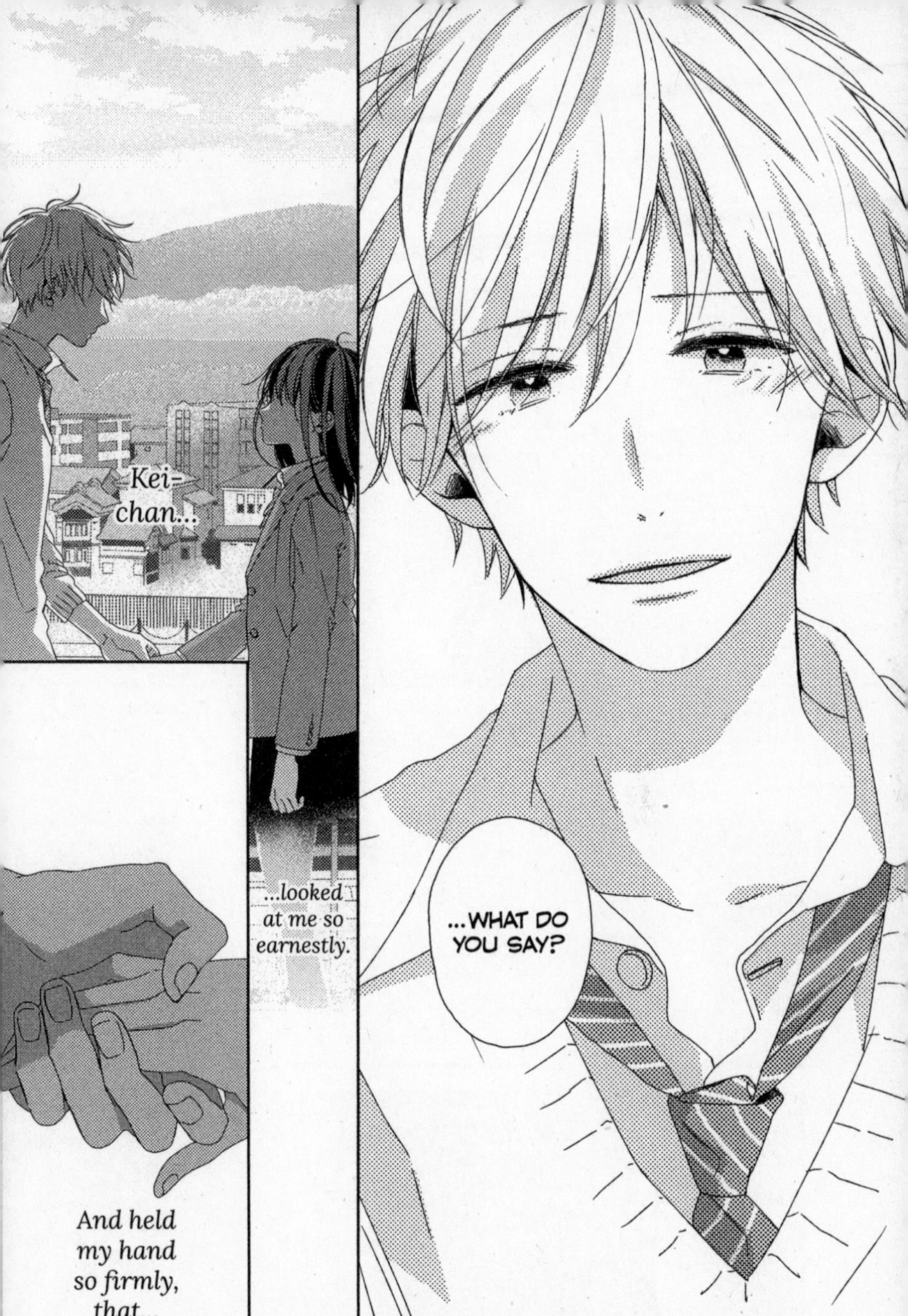
...WHAT DO YOU SAY?
Kei-chan...
...looked at me so earnestly.
And held my hand so firmly, that...

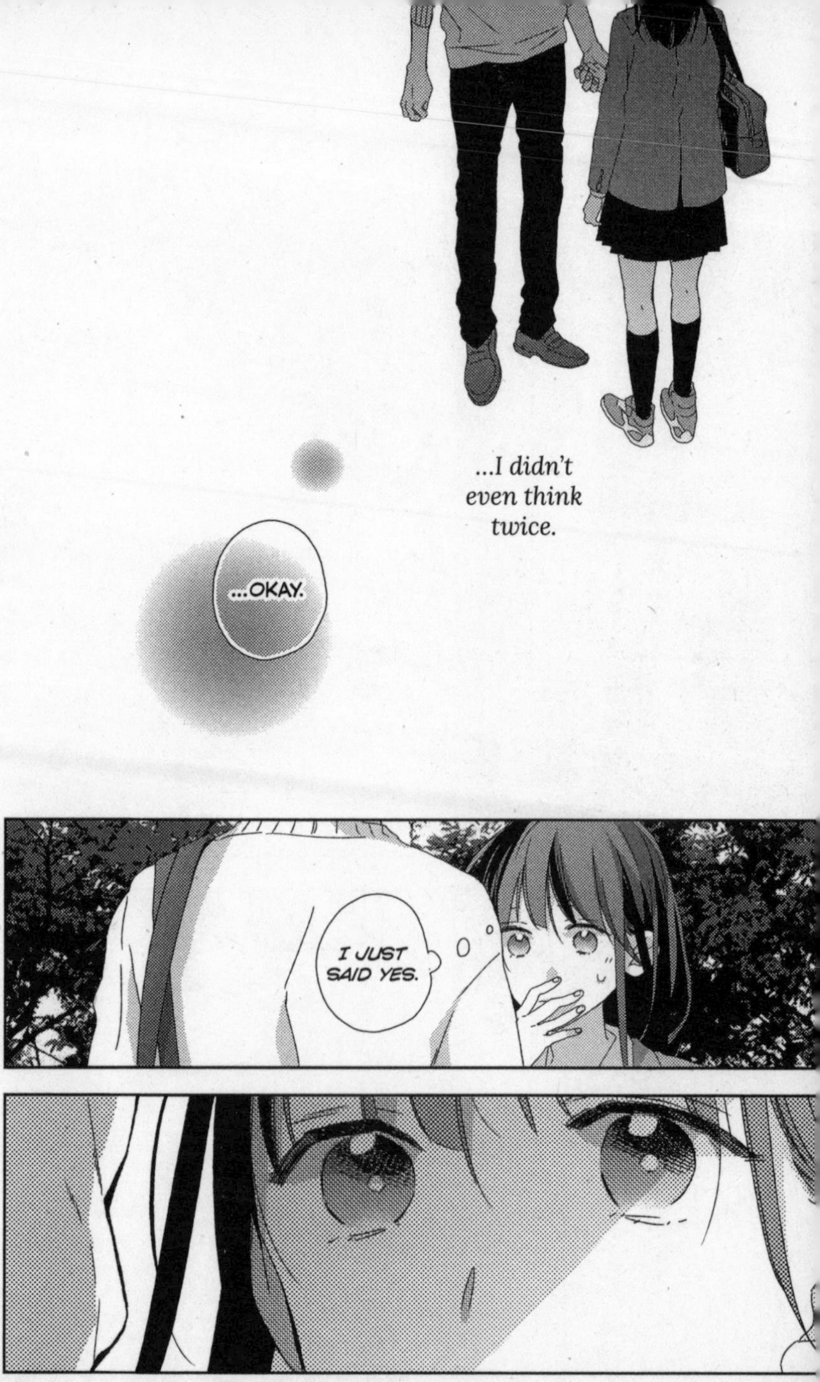
...I didn't even think twice.
...OKAY.
I JUST SAID YES.

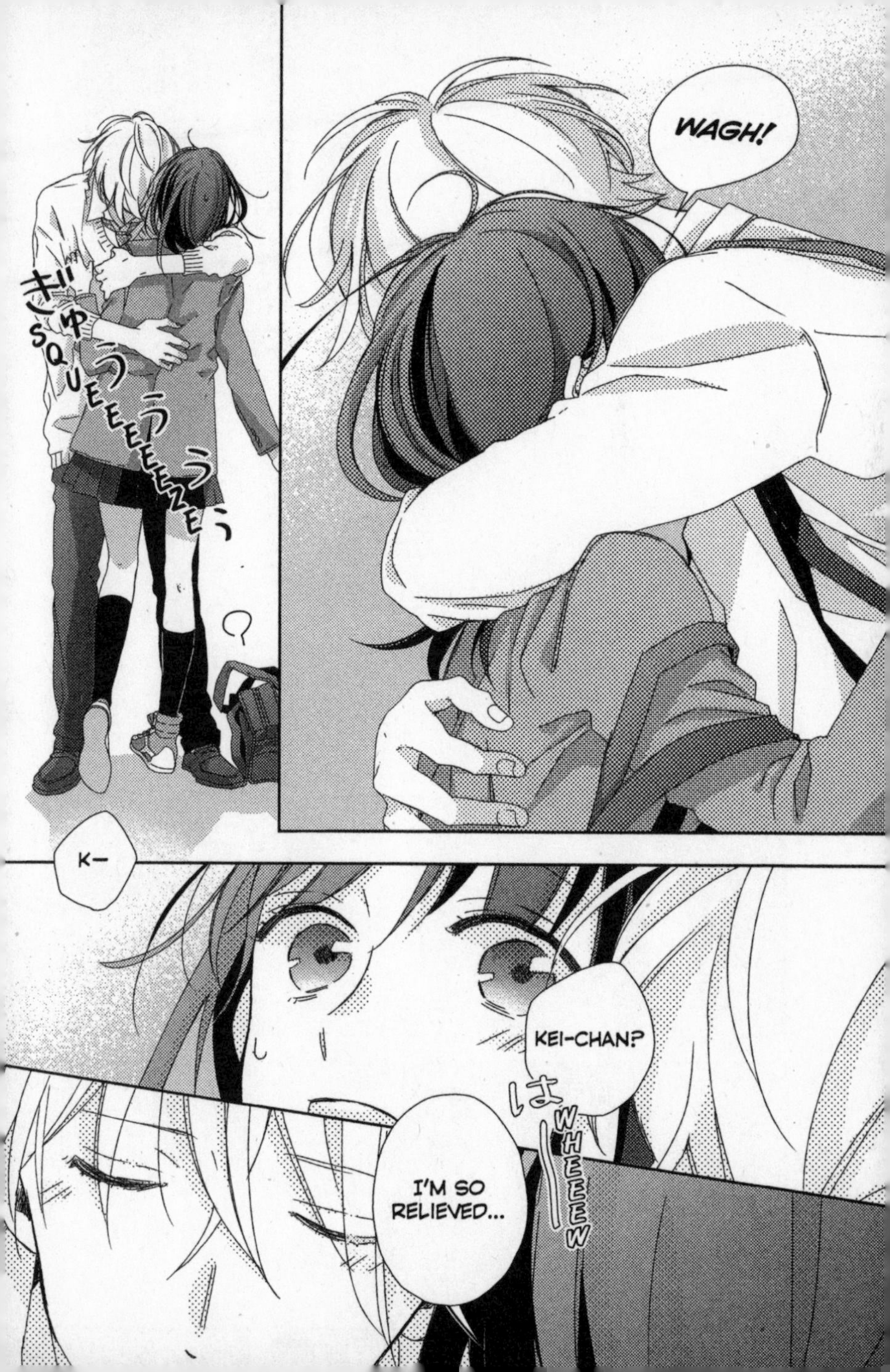
WAGH!
ぎゅううう
SQUEEEEEEZE
K—
KEI-CHAN?
I'M SO RELIEVED...
は WHEEEEW

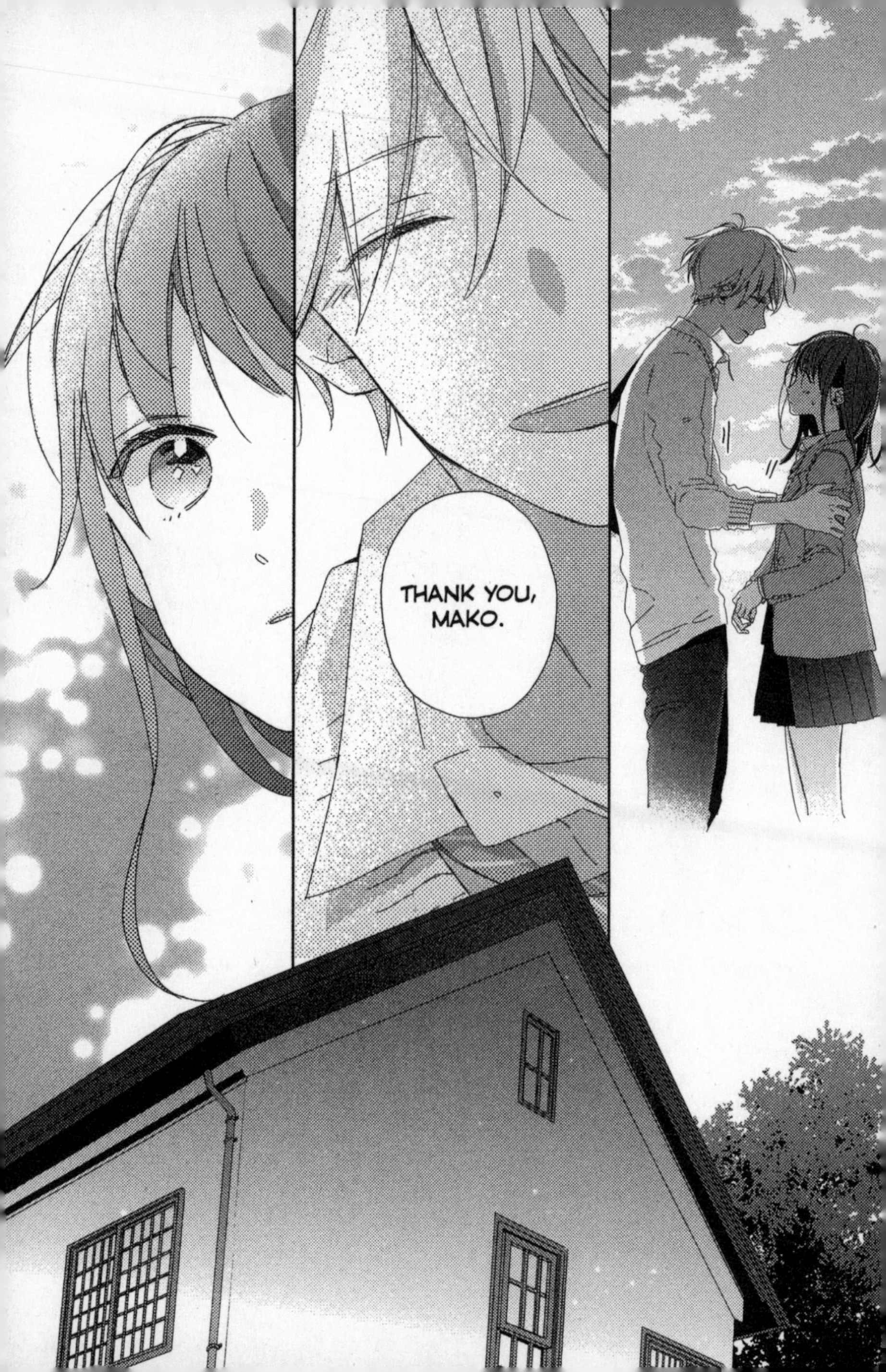
THANK YOU, MAKO.

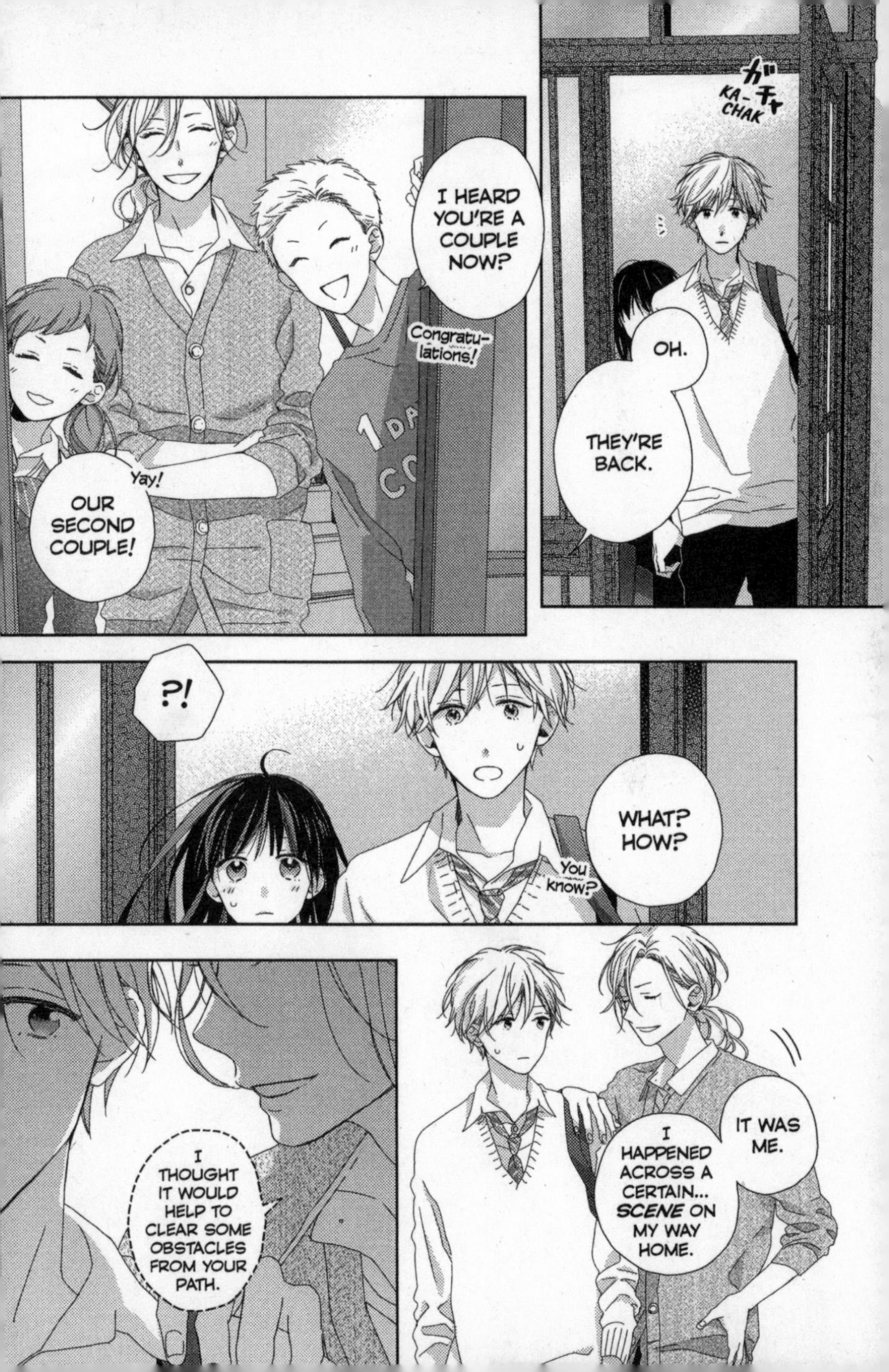
ガチャ
KA-CHAK
...
OH.
THEY'RE BACK.
I HEARD YOU'RE A COUPLE NOW?
Congratu-lations!
Yay!
OUR SECOND COUPLE!
?!
WHAT? HOW?
You know?
IT WAS ME.
I HAPPENED ACROSS A CERTAIN... *SCENE* ON MY WAY HOME.
I THOUGHT IT WOULD HELP TO CLEAR SOME OBSTACLES FROM YOUR PATH.

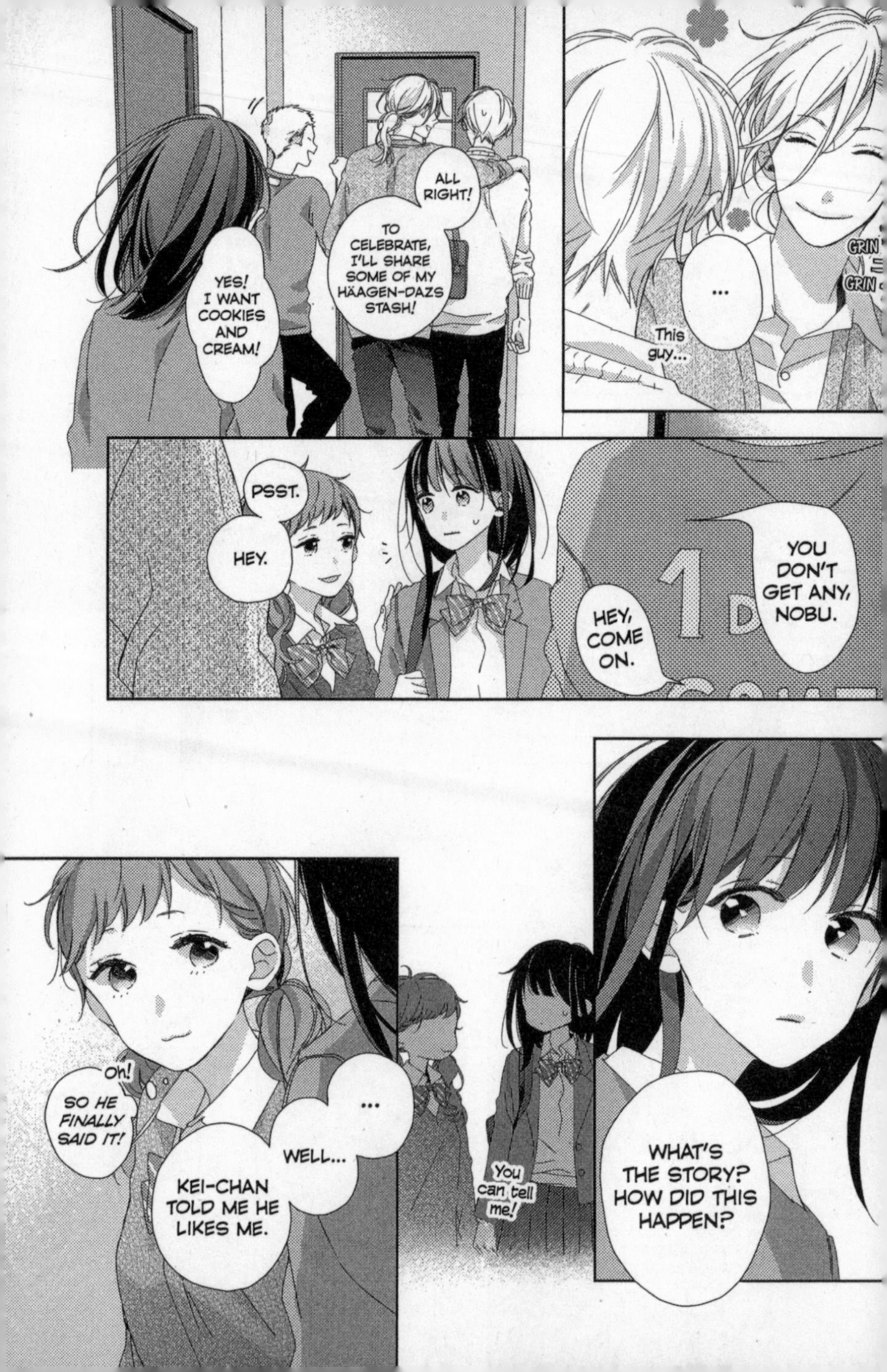
GRIN GRIN
...
This guy...
ALL RIGHT!
TO CELEBRATE, I'LL SHARE SOME OF MY HÄAGEN-DAZS STASH!
YES! I WANT COOKIES AND CREAM!
YOU DON'T GET ANY, NOBU.
HEY, COME ON.
PSST.
HEY.
WHAT'S THE STORY? HOW DID THIS HAPPEN?
You can tell me!
...
WELL...
KEI-CHAN TOLD ME HE LIKES ME.
Oh! SO HE FINALLY SAID IT!

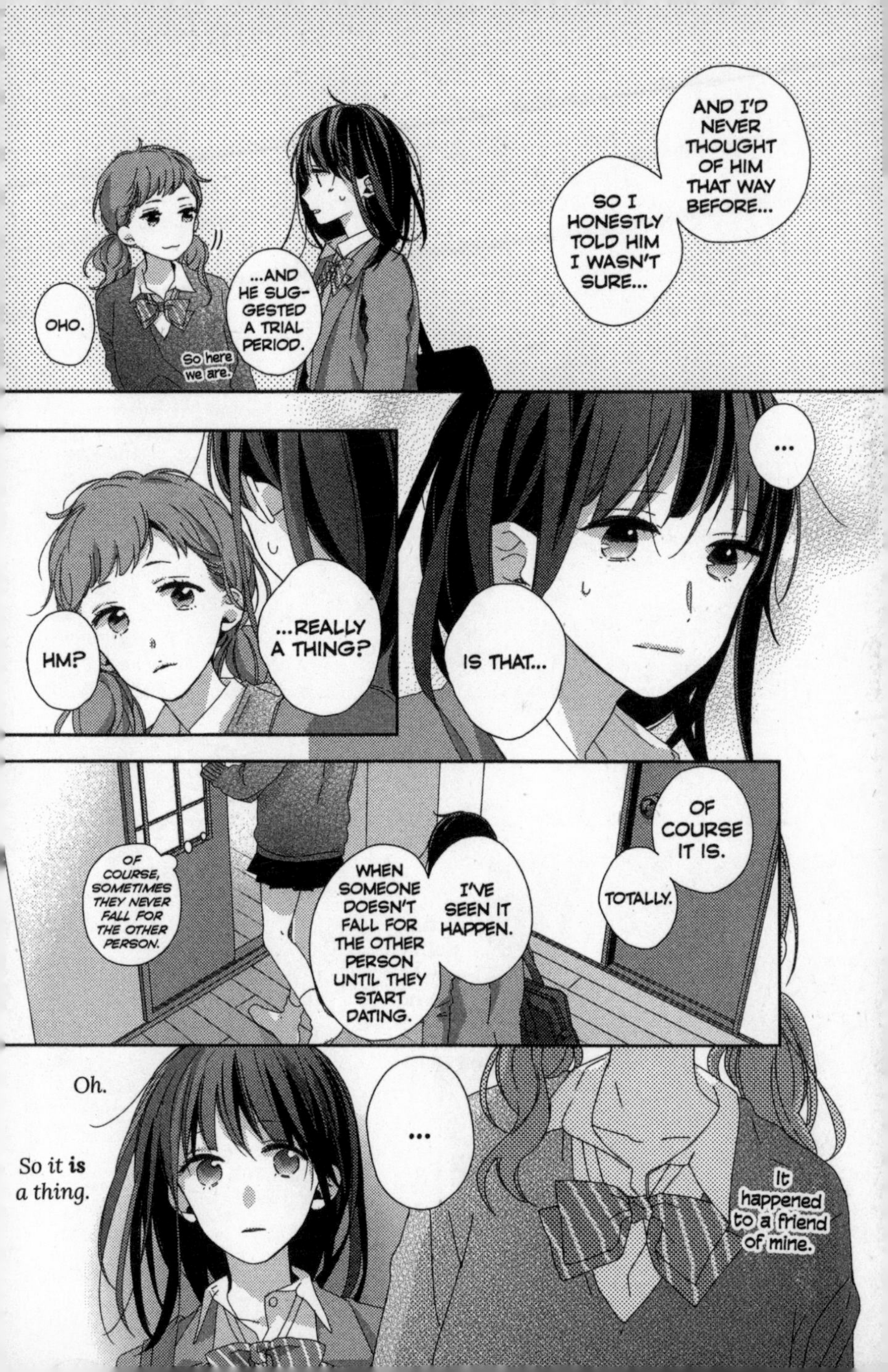
AND I'D NEVER THOUGHT OF HIM THAT WAY BEFORE...
SO I HONESTLY TOLD HIM I WASN'T SURE...
...AND HE SUG-GESTED A TRIAL PERIOD.
So here we are.
OHO.
...
IS THAT...
...REALLY A THING?
HM?
OF COURSE IT IS.
TOTALLY.
I'VE SEEN IT HAPPEN.
WHEN SOMEONE DOESN'T FALL FOR THE OTHER PERSON UNTIL THEY START DATING.
OF COURSE, SOMETIMES THEY NEVER FALL FOR THE OTHER PERSON.
It happened to a friend of mine.
...
Oh.
So it **is** a thing.

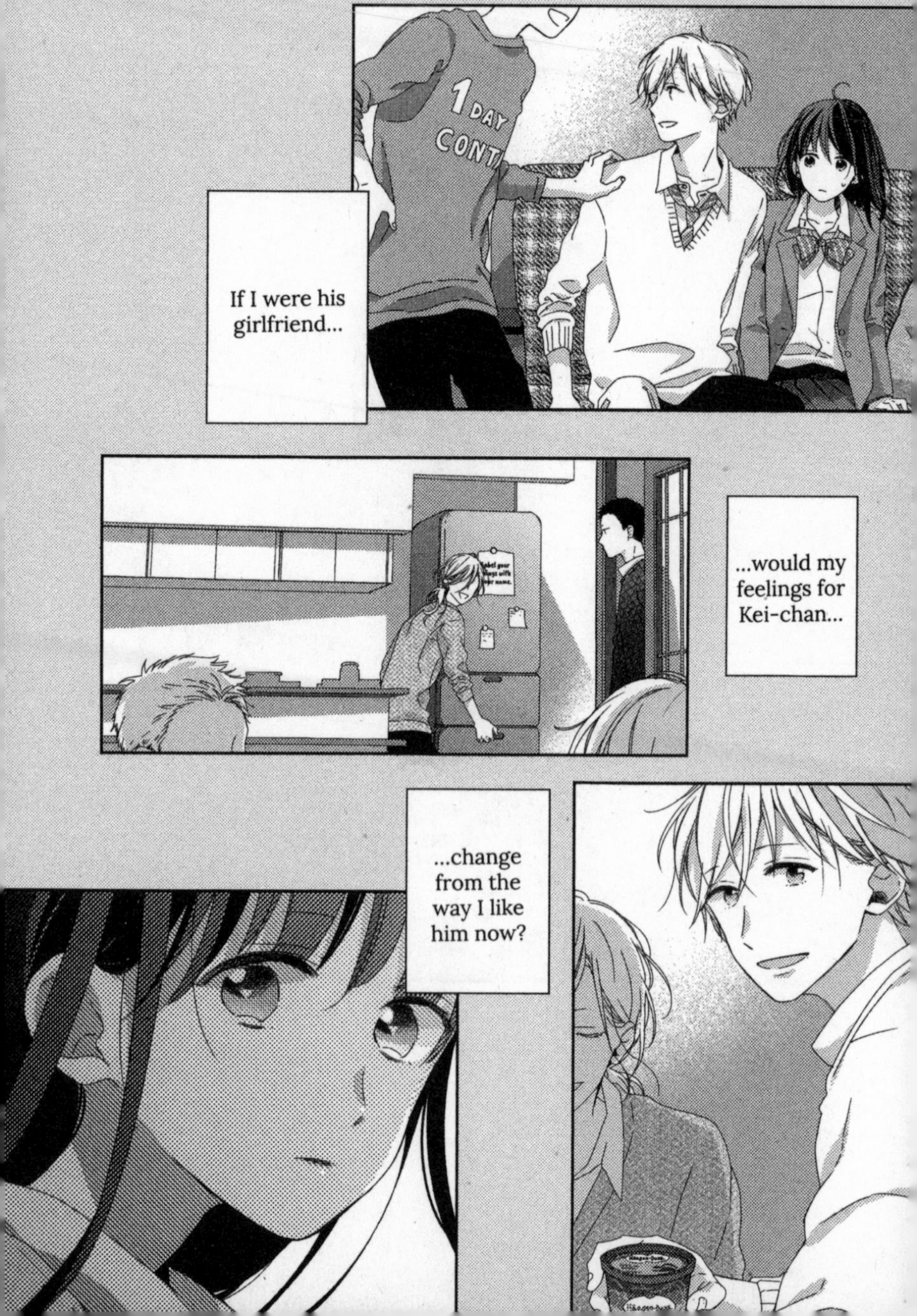
If I were his girlfriend...
...would my feelings for Kei-chan...
...change from the way I like him now?

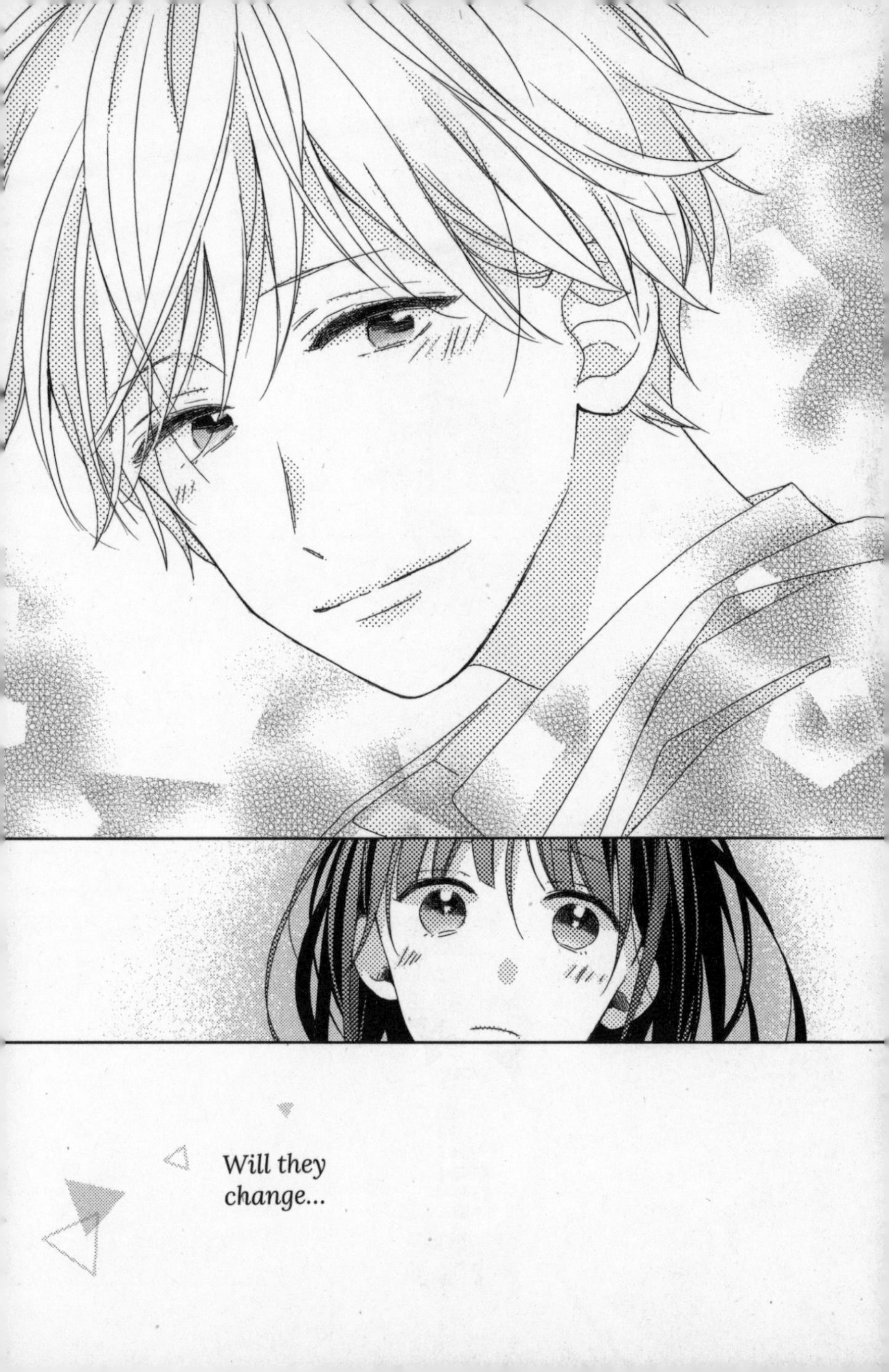
Will they change...

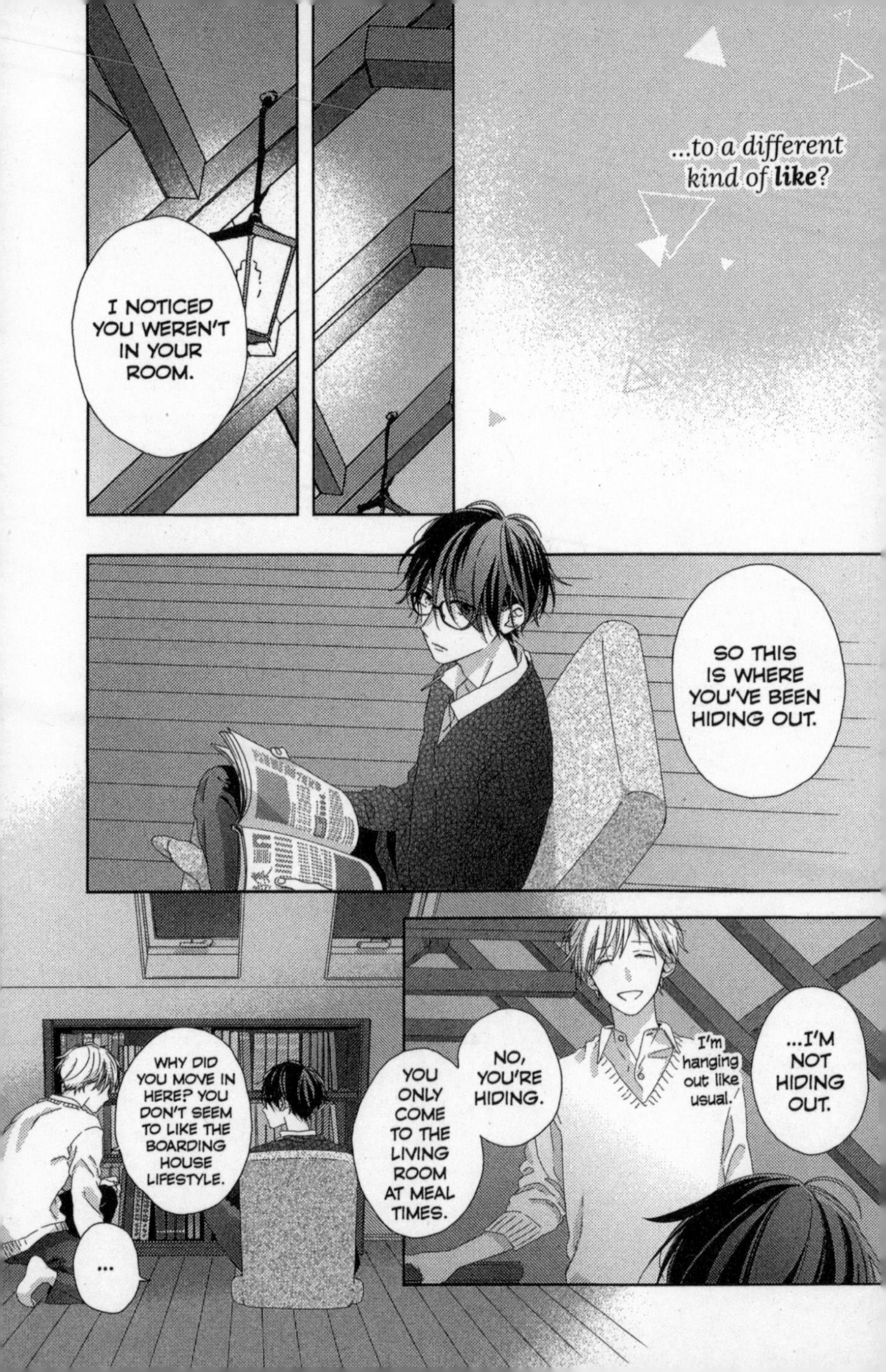
...to a different kind of **like**?
I NOTICED YOU WEREN'T IN YOUR ROOM.
SO THIS IS WHERE YOU'VE BEEN HIDING OUT.
...I'M NOT HIDING OUT.
I'm hanging out like usual.
NO, YOU'RE HIDING.
YOU ONLY COME TO THE LIVING ROOM AT MEAL TIMES.
WHY DID YOU MOVE IN HERE? YOU DON'T SEEM TO LIKE THE BOARDING HOUSE LIFESTYLE.
...

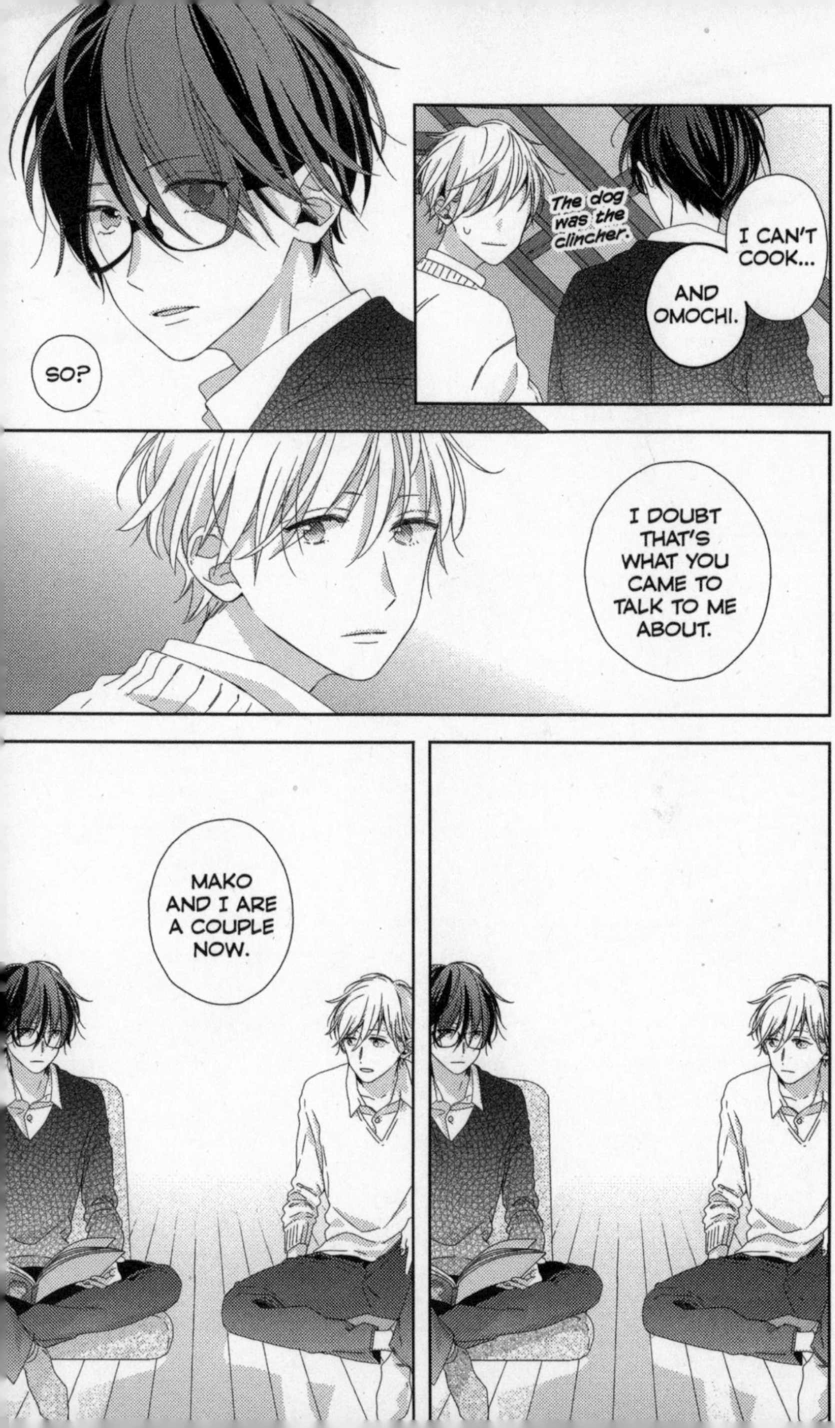
I CAN'T COOK...
AND OMOCHI.
The dog was the clincher.
SO?
I DOUBT THAT'S WHAT YOU CAME TO TALK TO ME ABOUT.
MAKO AND I ARE A COUPLE NOW.

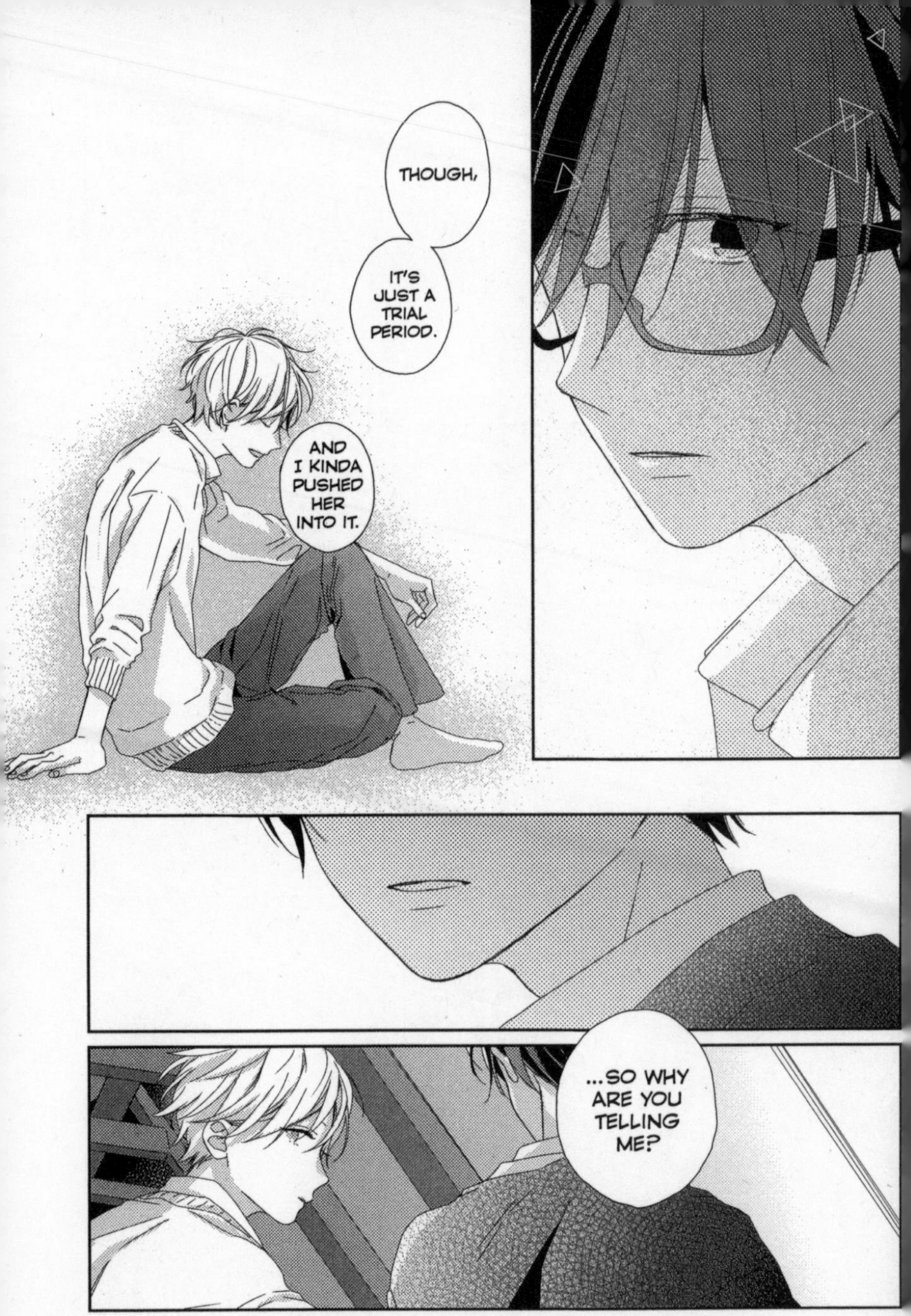
THOUGH,
IT'S JUST A TRIAL PERIOD.
AND I KINDA PUSHED HER INTO IT.
...SO WHY ARE YOU TELLING ME?

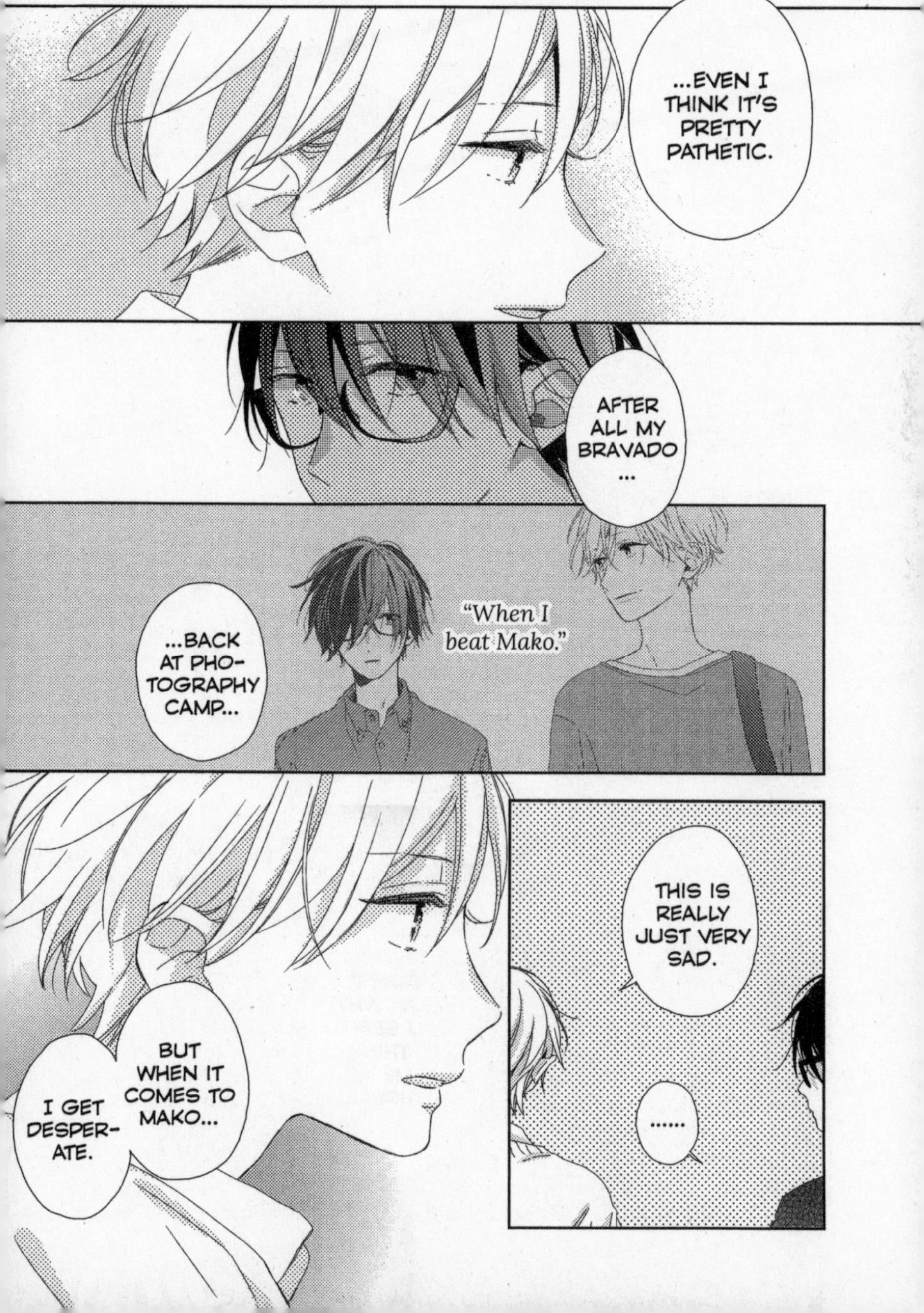
...EVEN I THINK IT'S PRETTY PATHETIC.
AFTER ALL MY BRAVADO ...
"When I beat Mako."
...BACK AT PHOTOGRAPHY CAMP...
THIS IS REALLY JUST VERY SAD.
......
BUT WHEN IT COMES TO MAKO...
I GET DESPERATE.

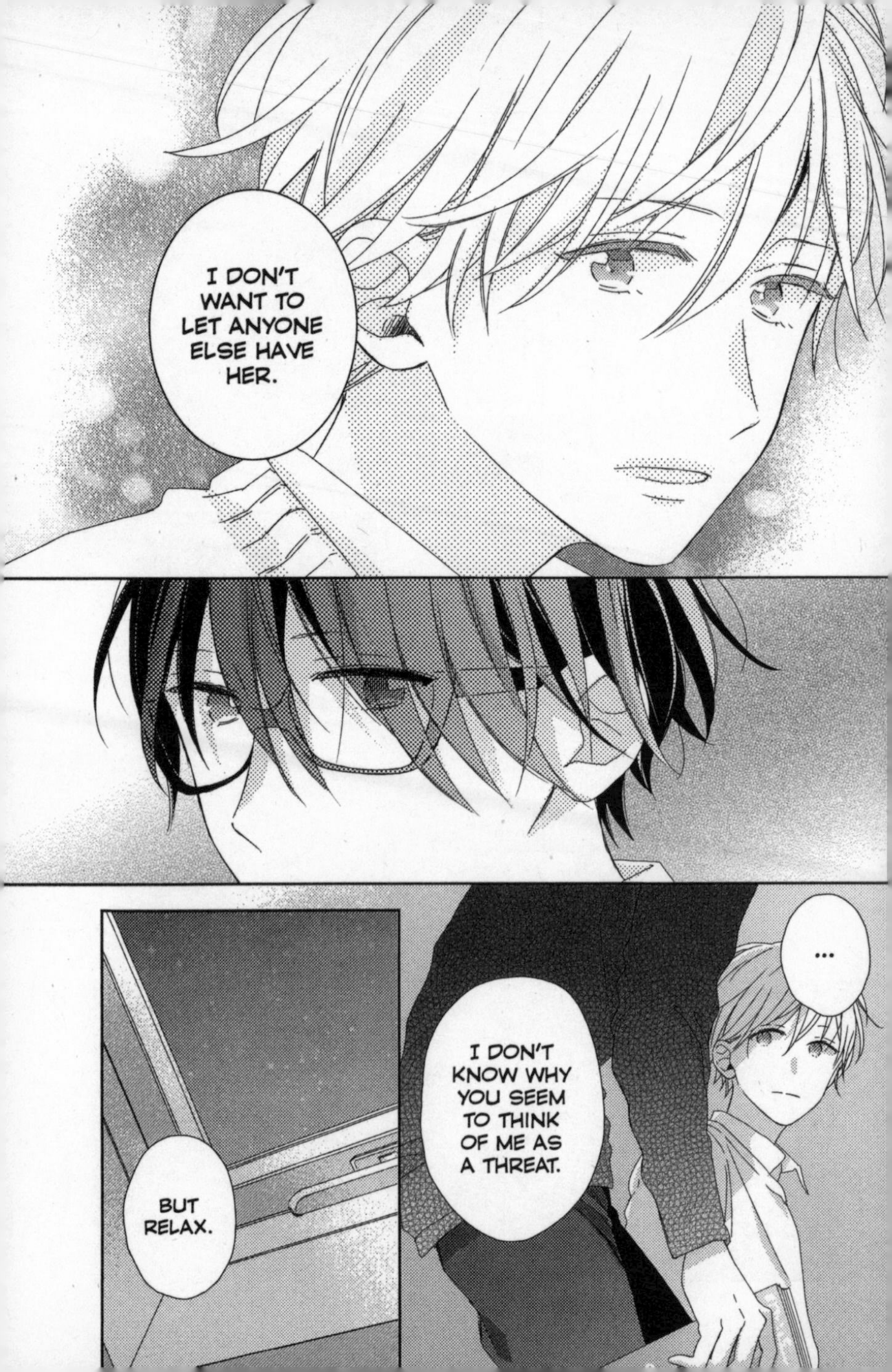
I DON'T WANT TO LET ANYONE ELSE HAVE HER.
...
I DON'T KNOW WHY YOU SEEM TO THINK OF ME AS A THREAT.
BUT RELAX.

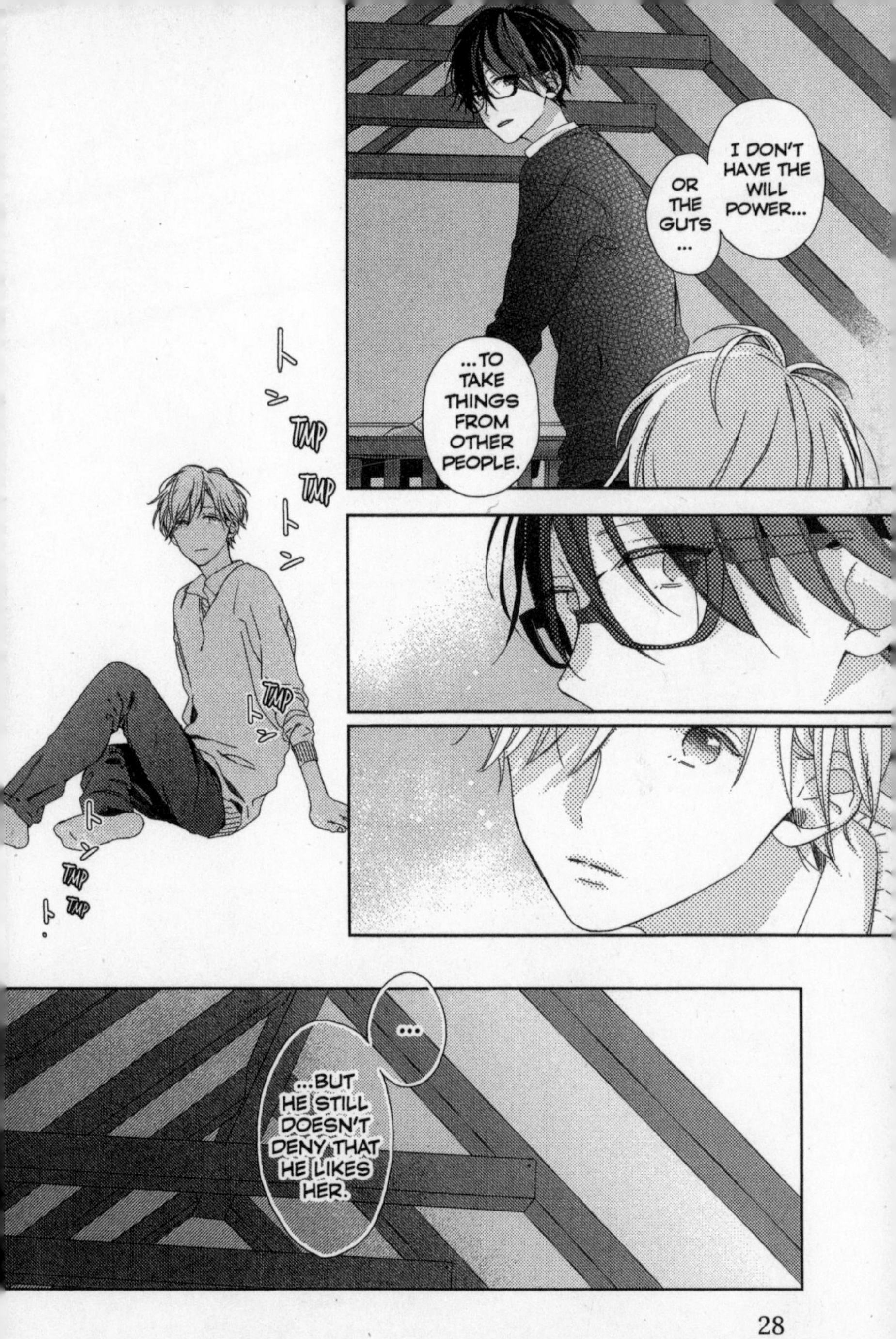
I DON'T HAVE THE WILL POWER...
OR THE GUTS ...
...TO TAKE THINGS FROM OTHER PEOPLE.
TMP
TMP
TMP
TMP
TMP
...
...BUT HE STILL DOESN'T DENY THAT HE LIKES HER.

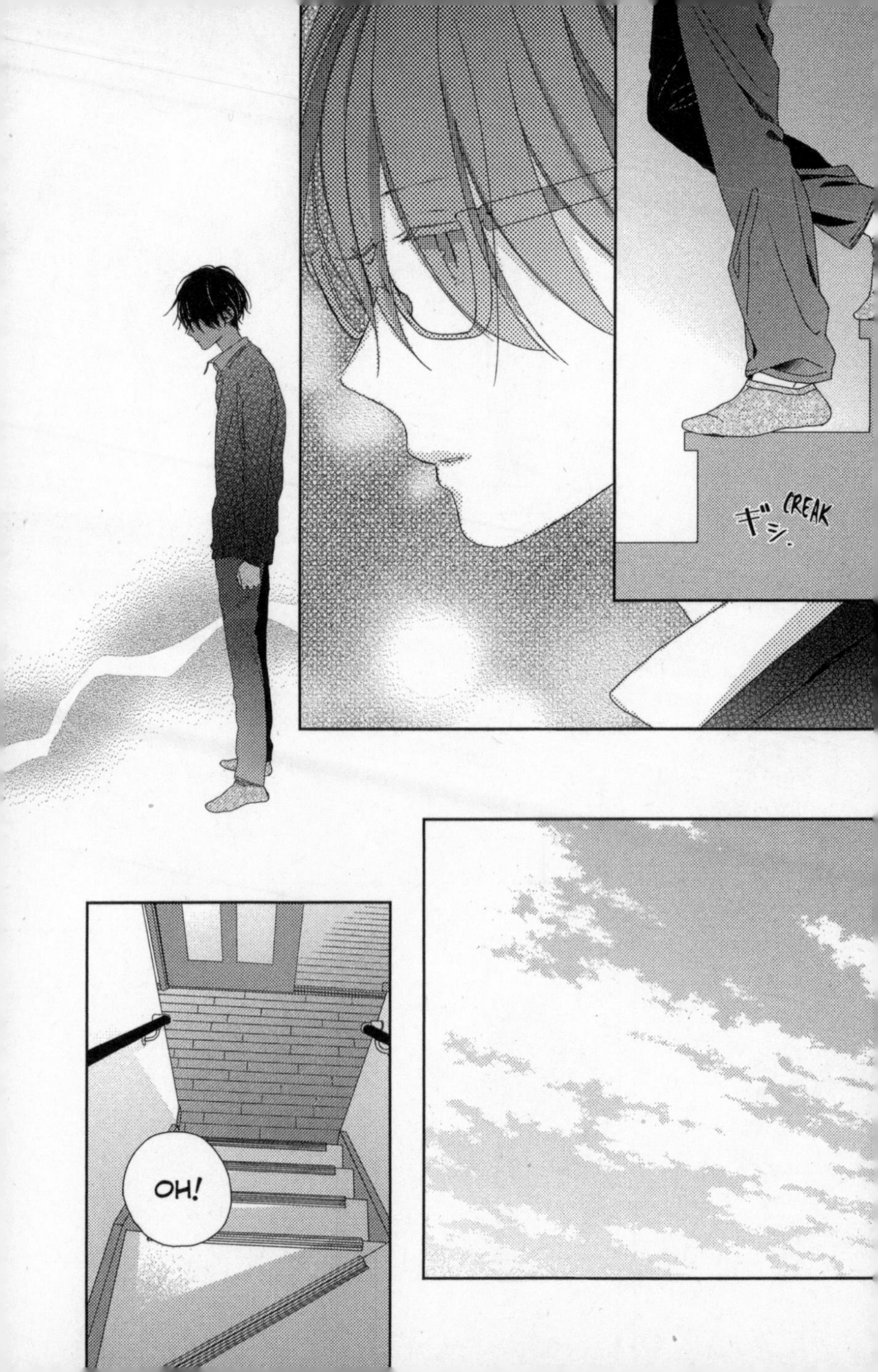
ギシ
CREAK
OH!

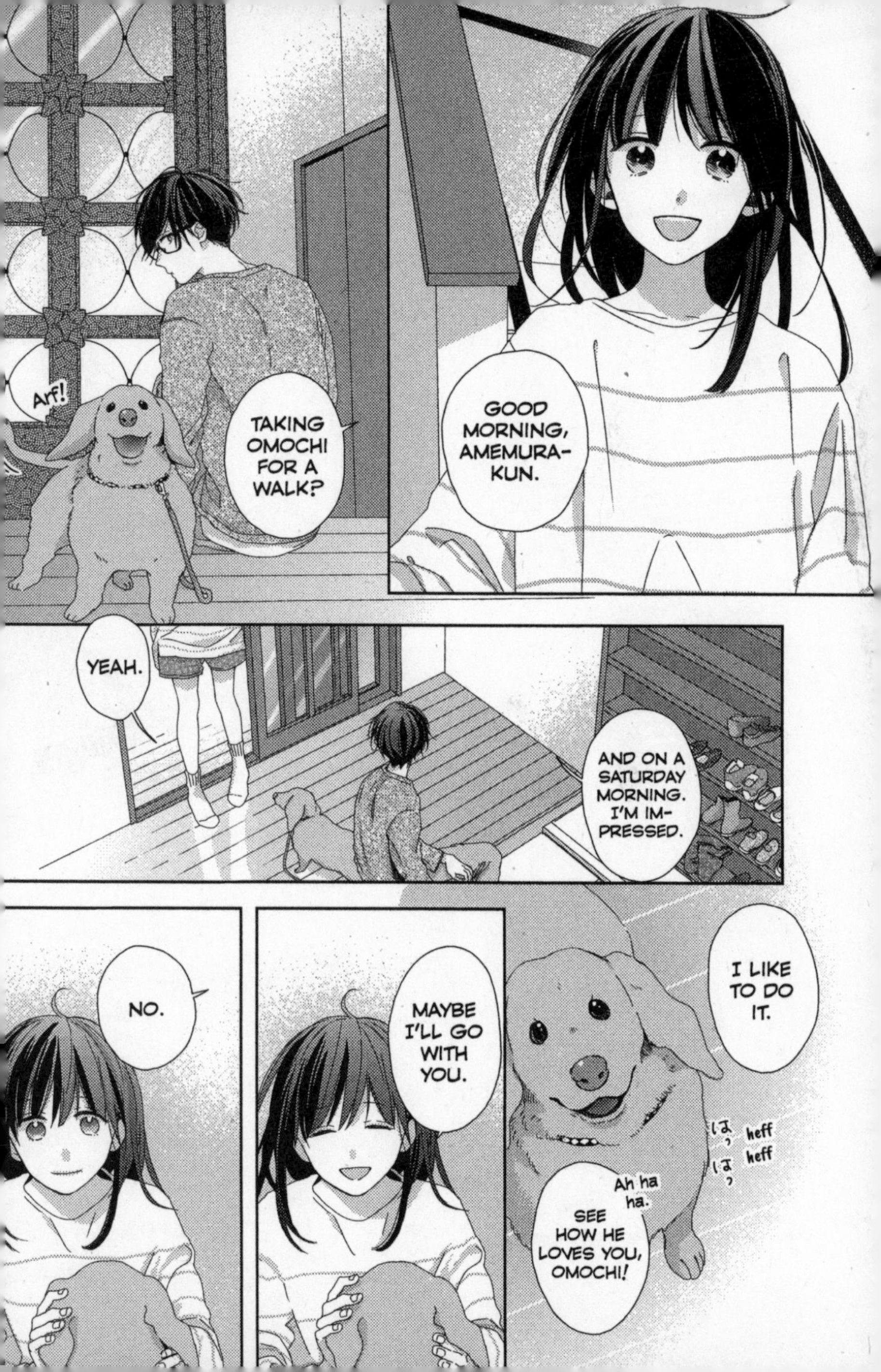
GOOD MORNING, AMEMURA-KUN.
TAKING OMOCHI FOR A WALK?
Arf!
AND ON A SATURDAY MORNING. I'M IM-PRESSED.
YEAH.
I LIKE TO DO IT.
はっ heff
はっ heff
Ah ha ha.
SEE HOW HE LOVES YOU, OMOCHI!
MAYBE I'LL GO WITH YOU.
NO.

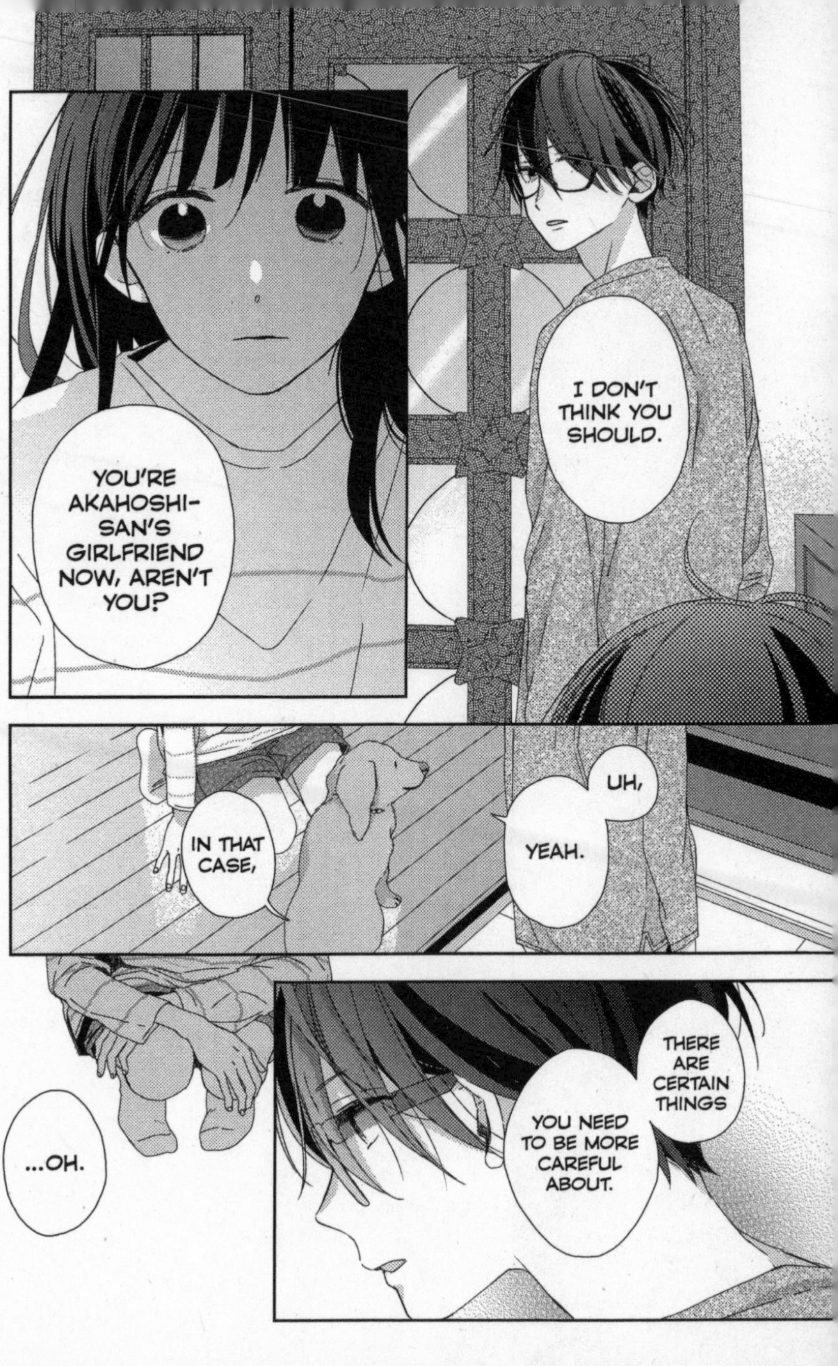
I DON'T THINK YOU SHOULD.
YOU'RE AKAHOSHI-SAN'S GIRLFRIEND NOW, AREN'T YOU?
UH,
YEAH.
IN THAT CASE,
THERE ARE CERTAIN THINGS
YOU NEED TO BE MORE CAREFUL ABOUT.
...OH.

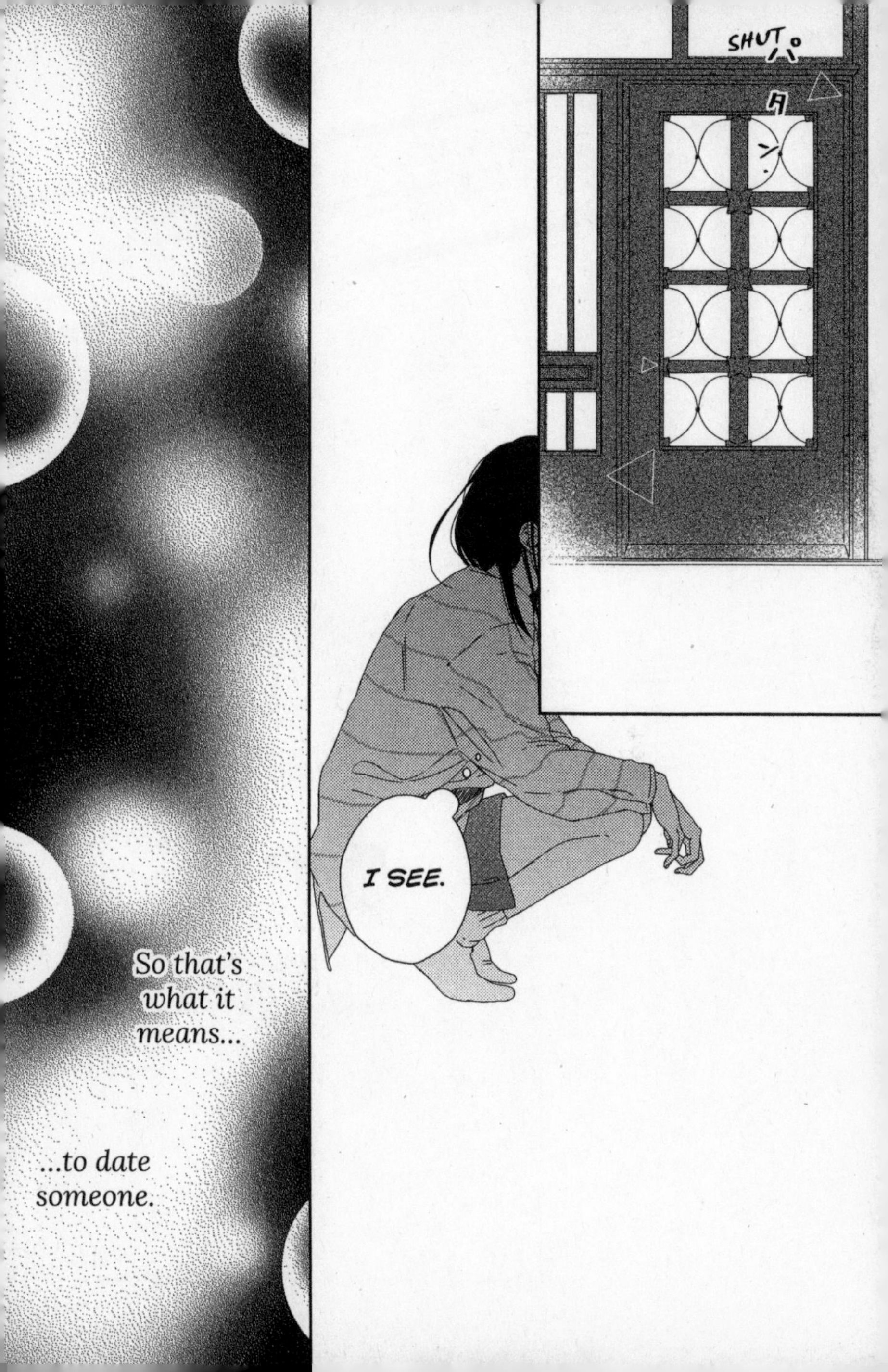
SHUT
I SEE.
So that's what it means...
...to date someone.

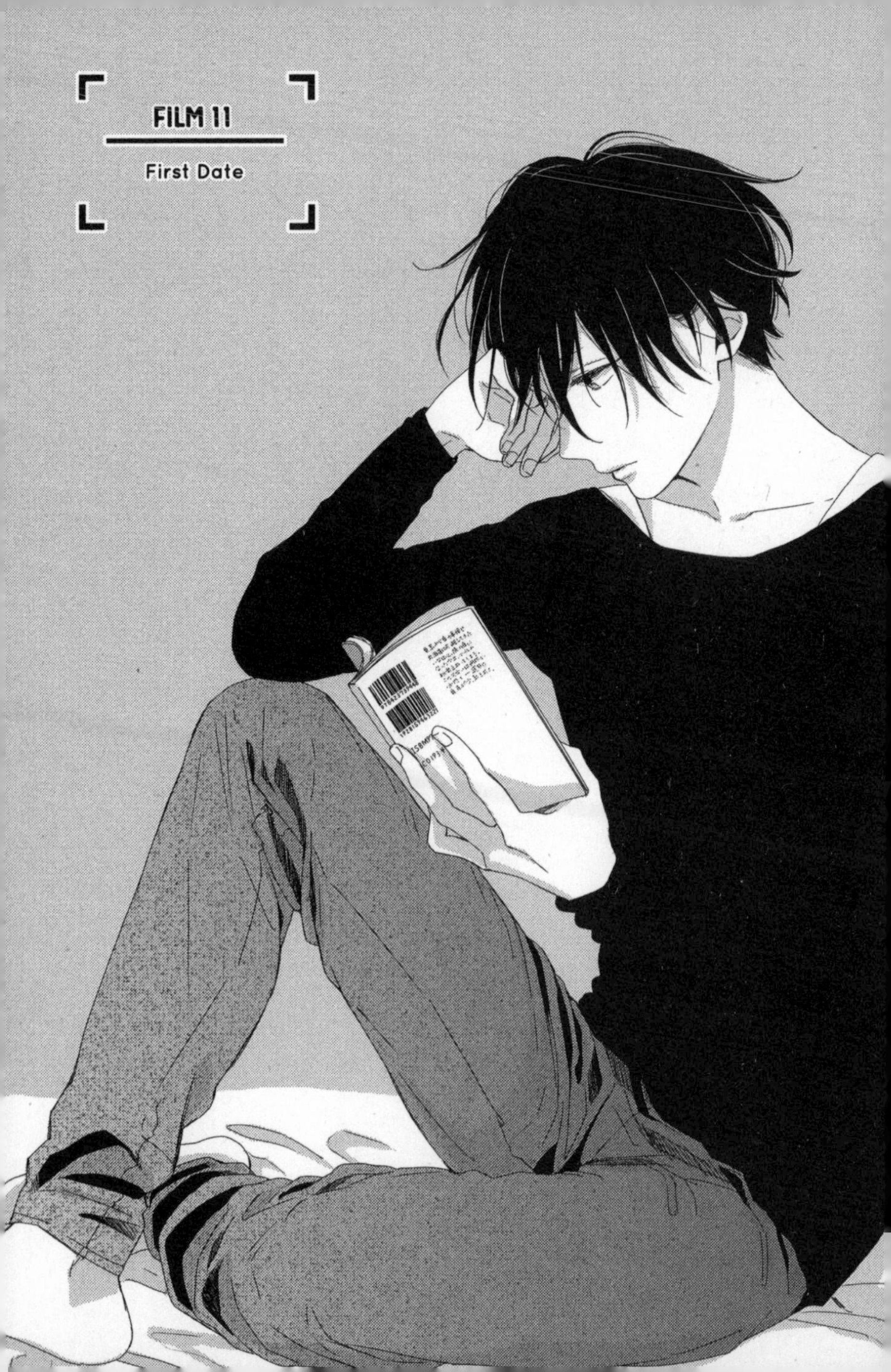
FILM 11
First Date

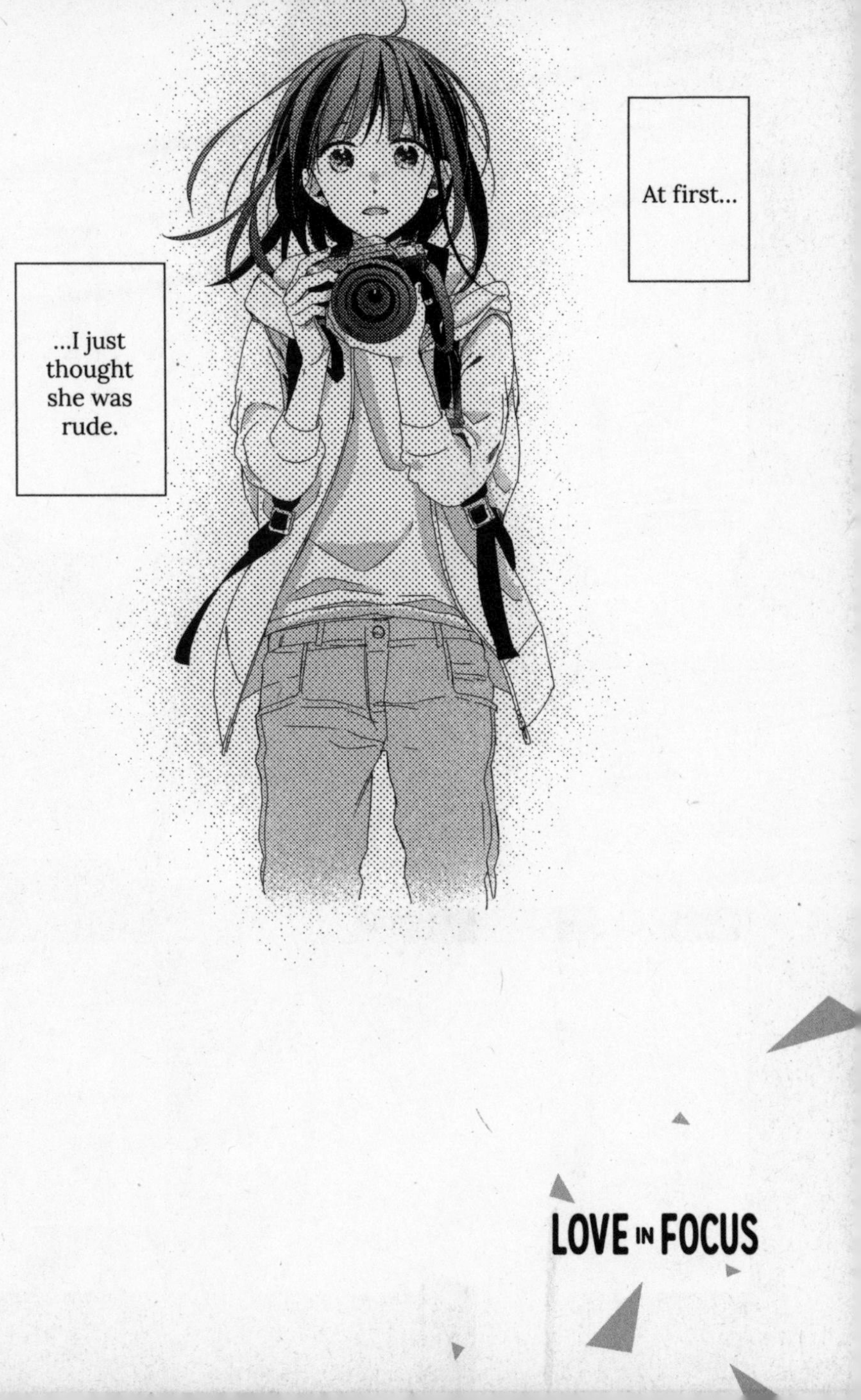
At first...
...I just thought she was rude.
LOVE IN FOCUS

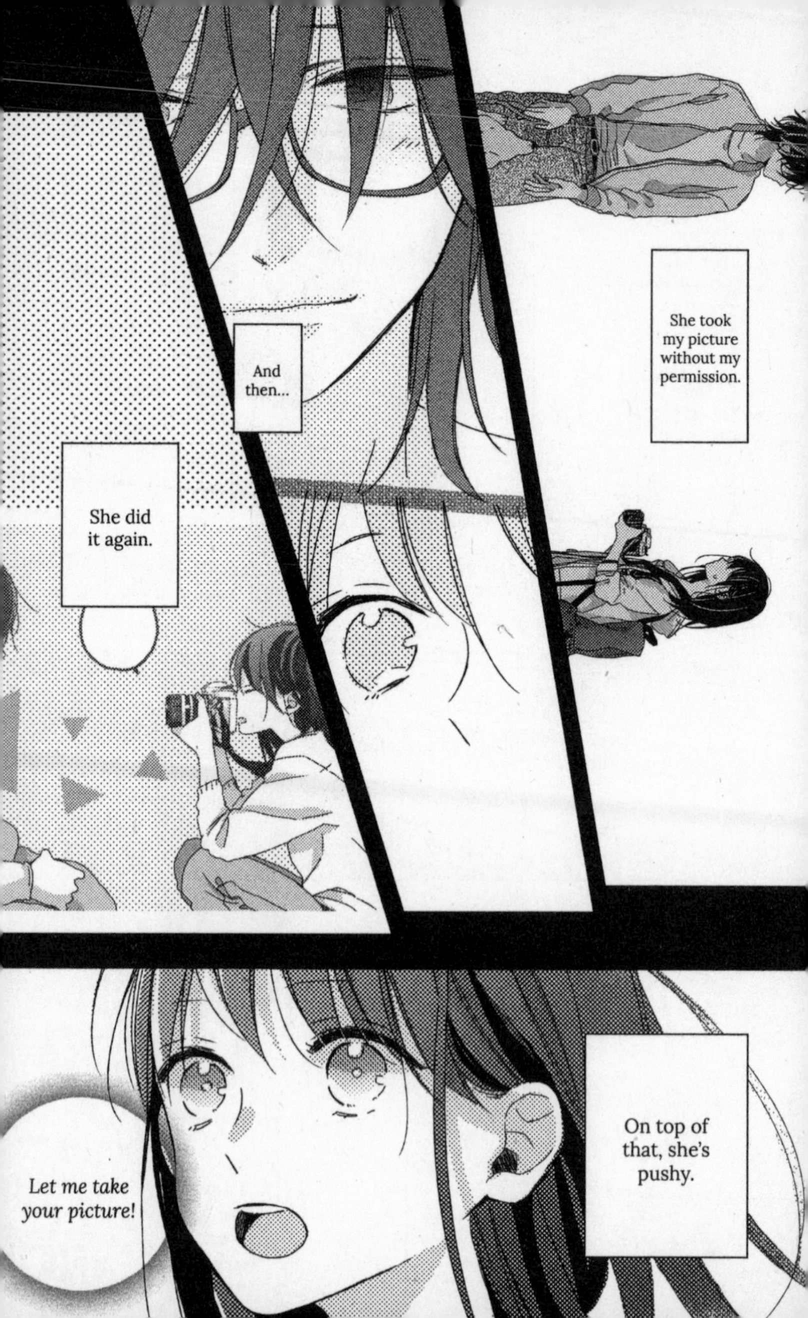
She took my picture without my permission.
And then...
She did it again.
On top of that, she's pushy.
Let me take your picture!

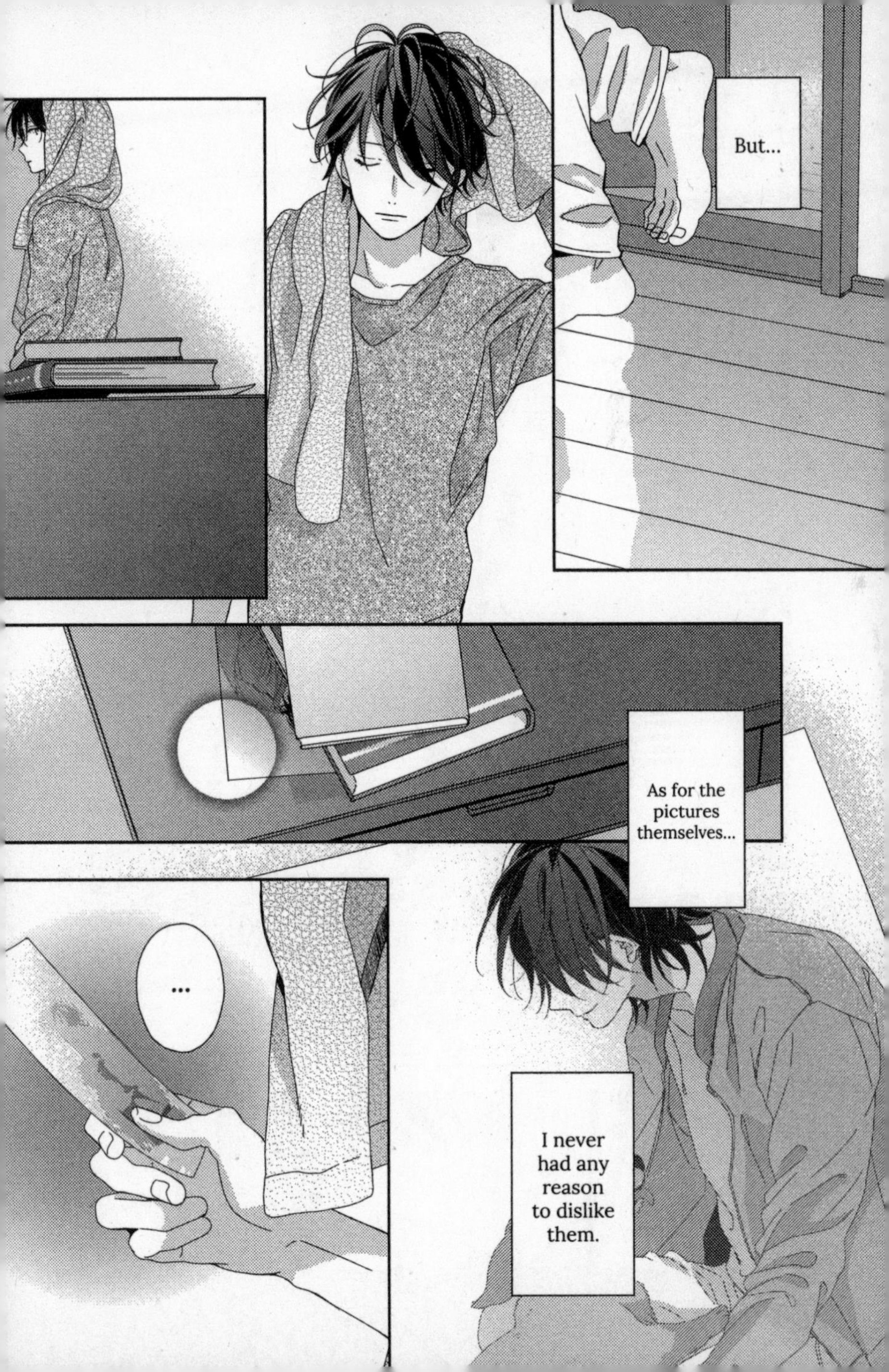
But...
As for the pictures themselves...
I never had any reason to dislike them.
...

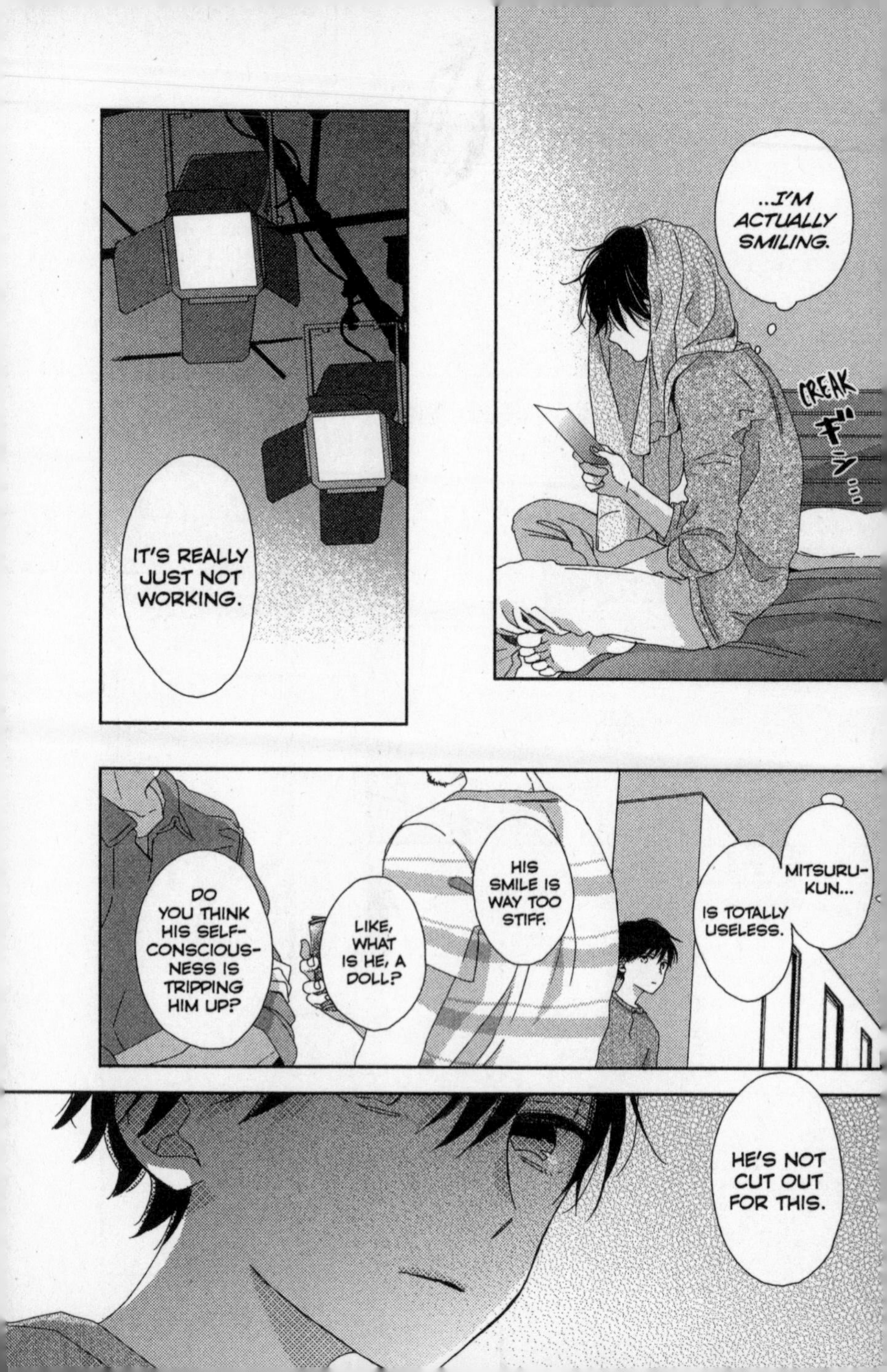
...I'M ACTUALLY SMILING.
CREAK
IT'S REALLY JUST NOT WORKING.
MITSURU-KUN...
IS TOTALLY USELESS.
HIS SMILE IS WAY TOO STIFF.
LIKE, WHAT IS HE, A DOLL?
DO YOU THINK HIS SELF-CONSCIOUSNESS IS TRIPPING HIM UP?
HE'S NOT CUT OUT FOR THIS.

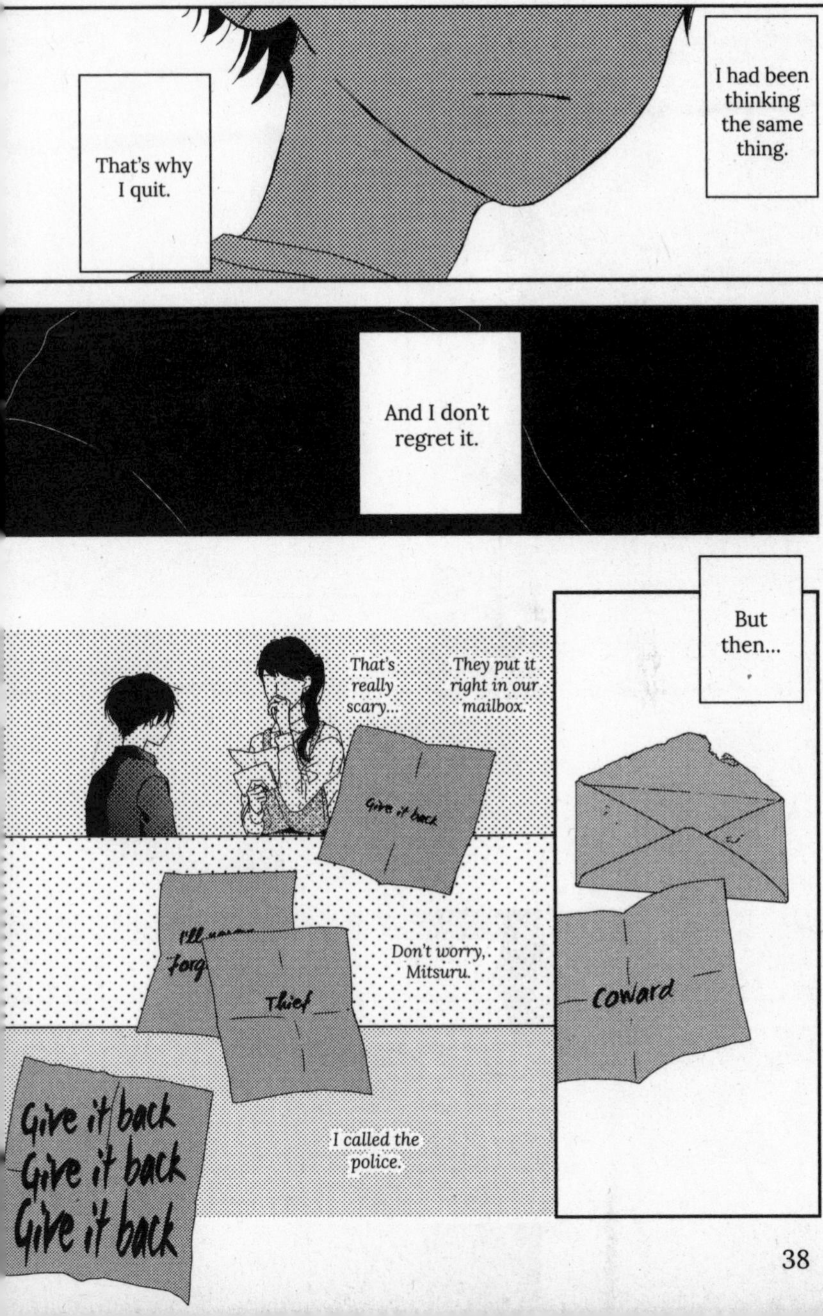

I had been thinking the same thing.
That's why I quit.
And I don't regret it.
But then...
Coward
They put it right in our mailbox.
That's really scary...
Give it back
Thief
Don't worry, Mitsuru.
Give it back
Give it back
Give it back
I called the police.

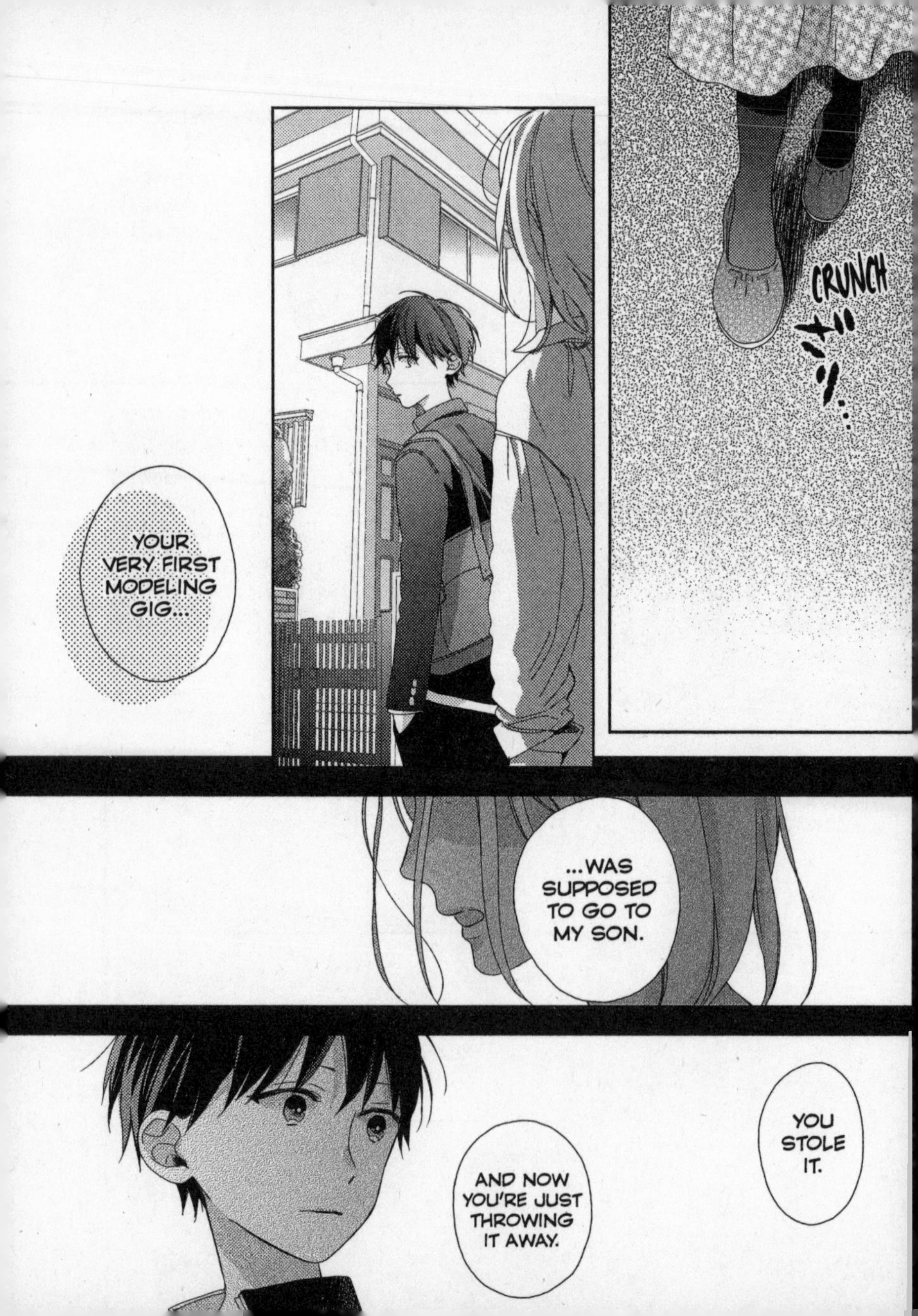
CRUNCH
ザッ…
YOUR VERY FIRST MODELING GIG...
...WAS SUPPOSED TO GO TO MY SON.
YOU STOLE IT.
AND NOW YOU'RE JUST THROWING IT AWAY.

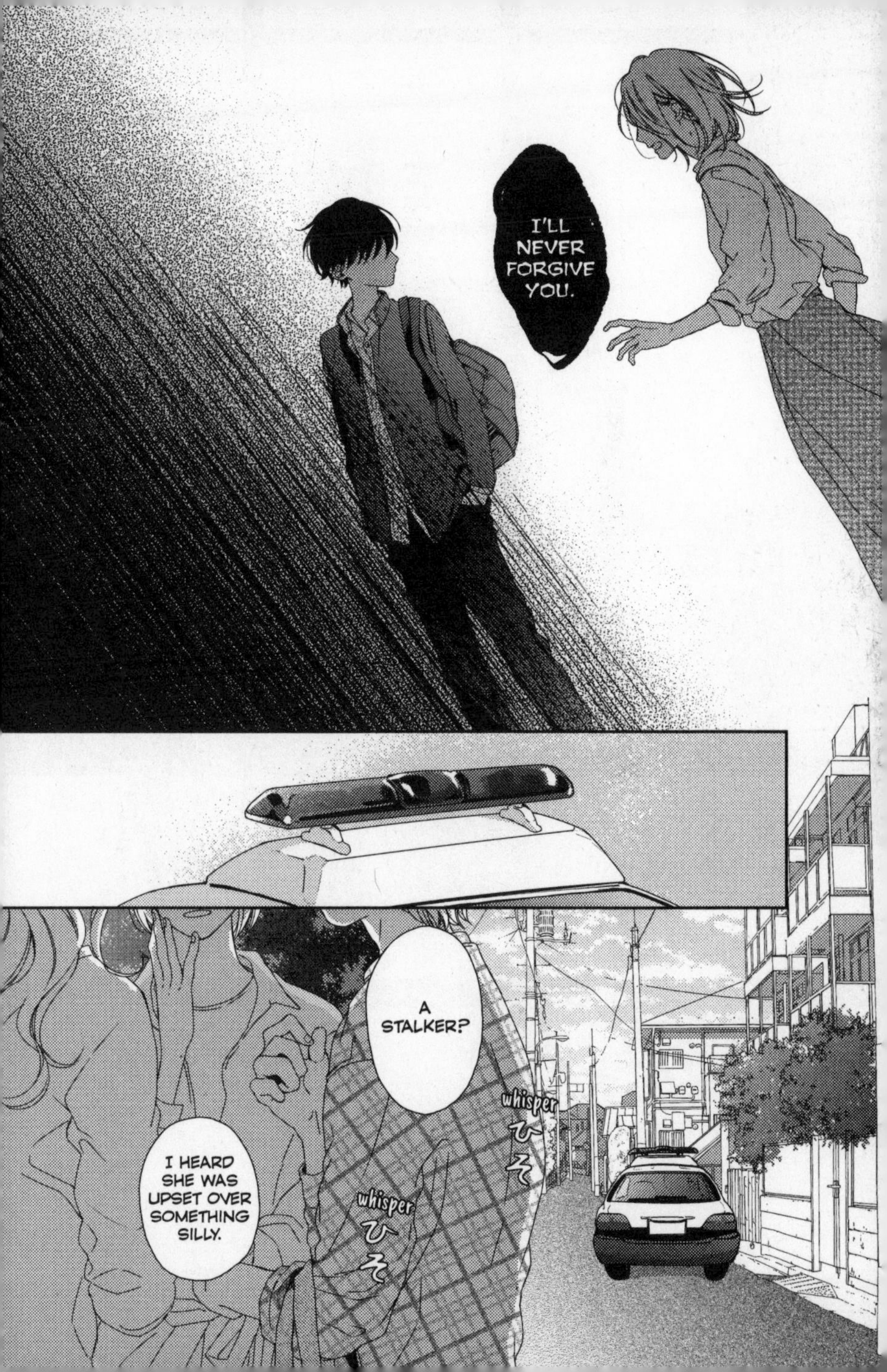
I'LL NEVER FORGIVE YOU.
A STALKER?
whisper
ひそ
whisper
ひそ
I HEARD SHE WAS UPSET OVER SOMETHING SILLY.

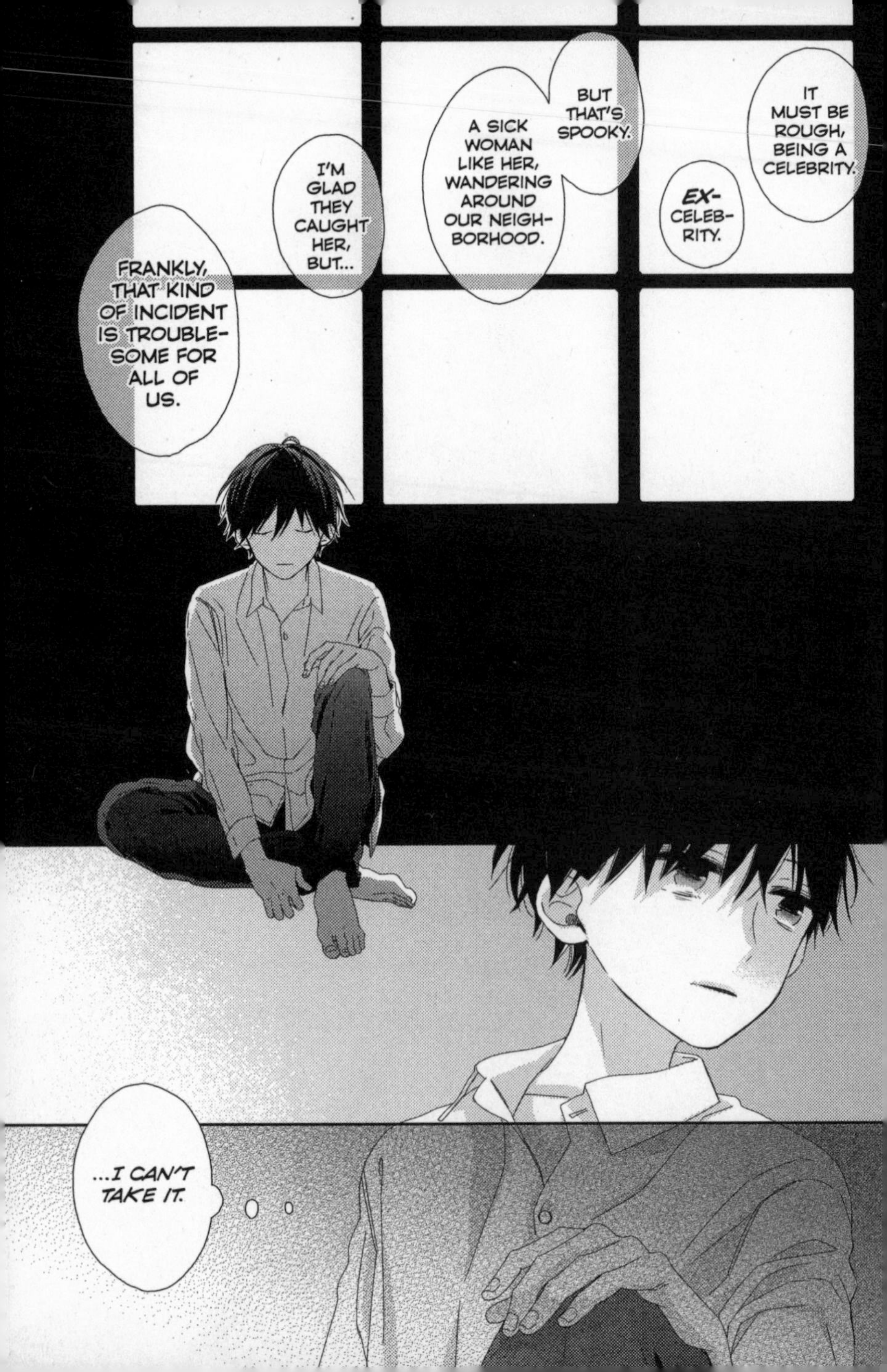
IT MUST BE ROUGH, BEING A CELEBRITY.
EX-CELEBRITY.
BUT THAT'S SPOOKY.
A SICK WOMAN LIKE HER, WANDERING AROUND OUR NEIGHBORHOOD.
I'M GLAD THEY CAUGHT HER, BUT...
FRANKLY, THAT KIND OF INCIDENT IS TROUBLESOME FOR ALL OF US.
...I CAN'T TAKE IT.

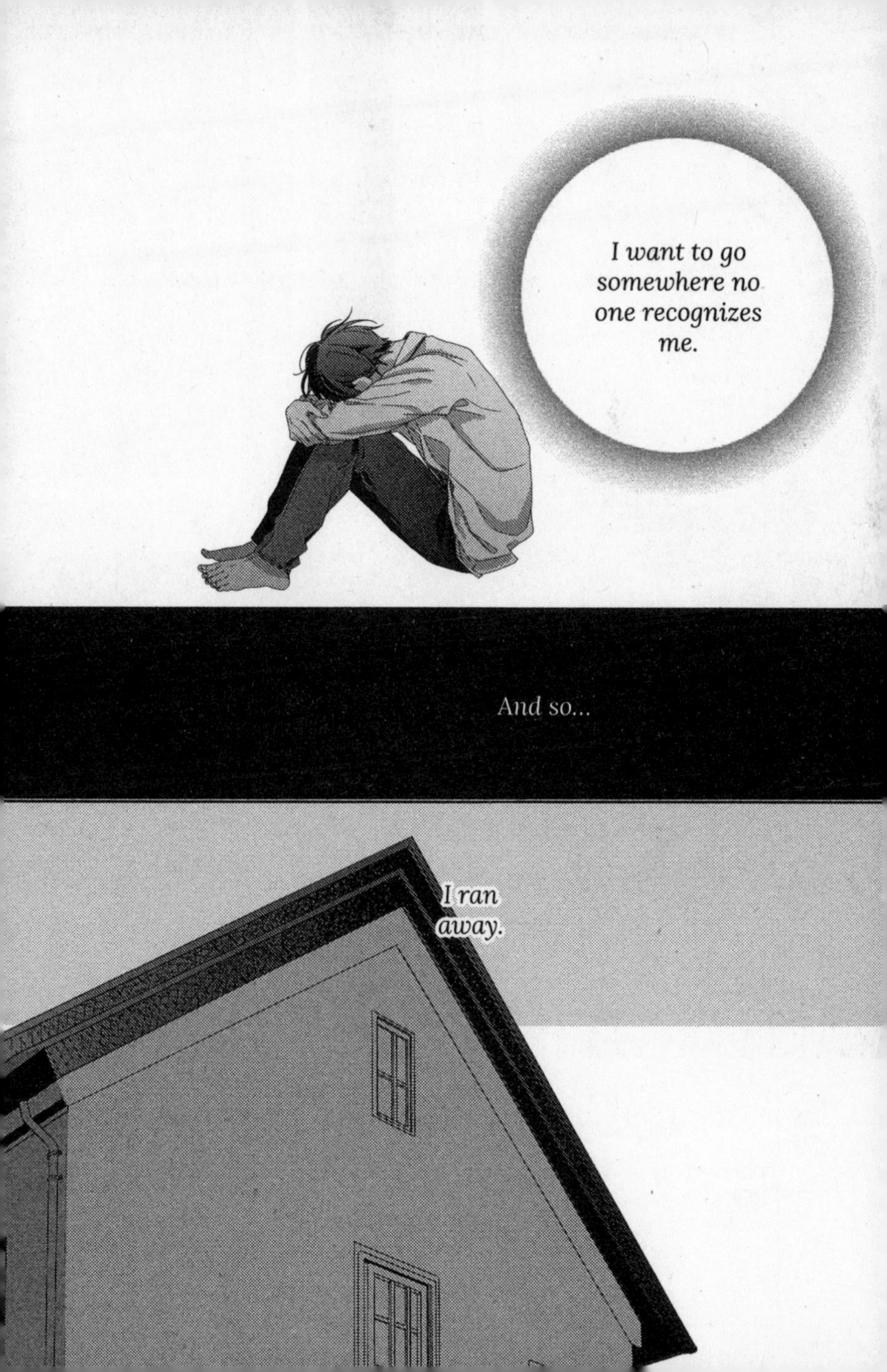
I want to go somewhere no one recognizes me.
And so...
I ran away.

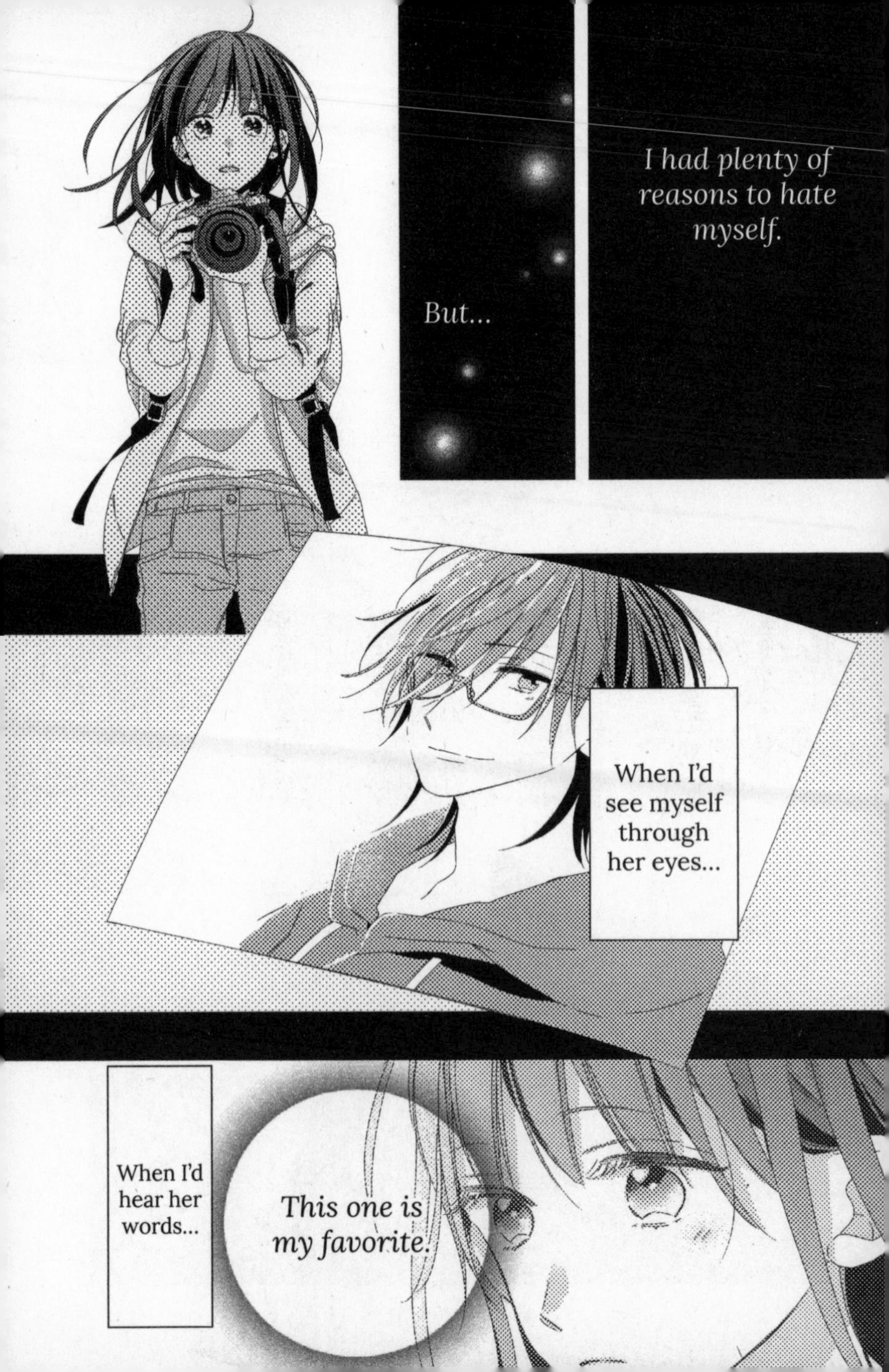
I had plenty of reasons to hate myself.
But...
When I'd see myself through her eyes...
This one is my favorite.
When I'd hear her words...

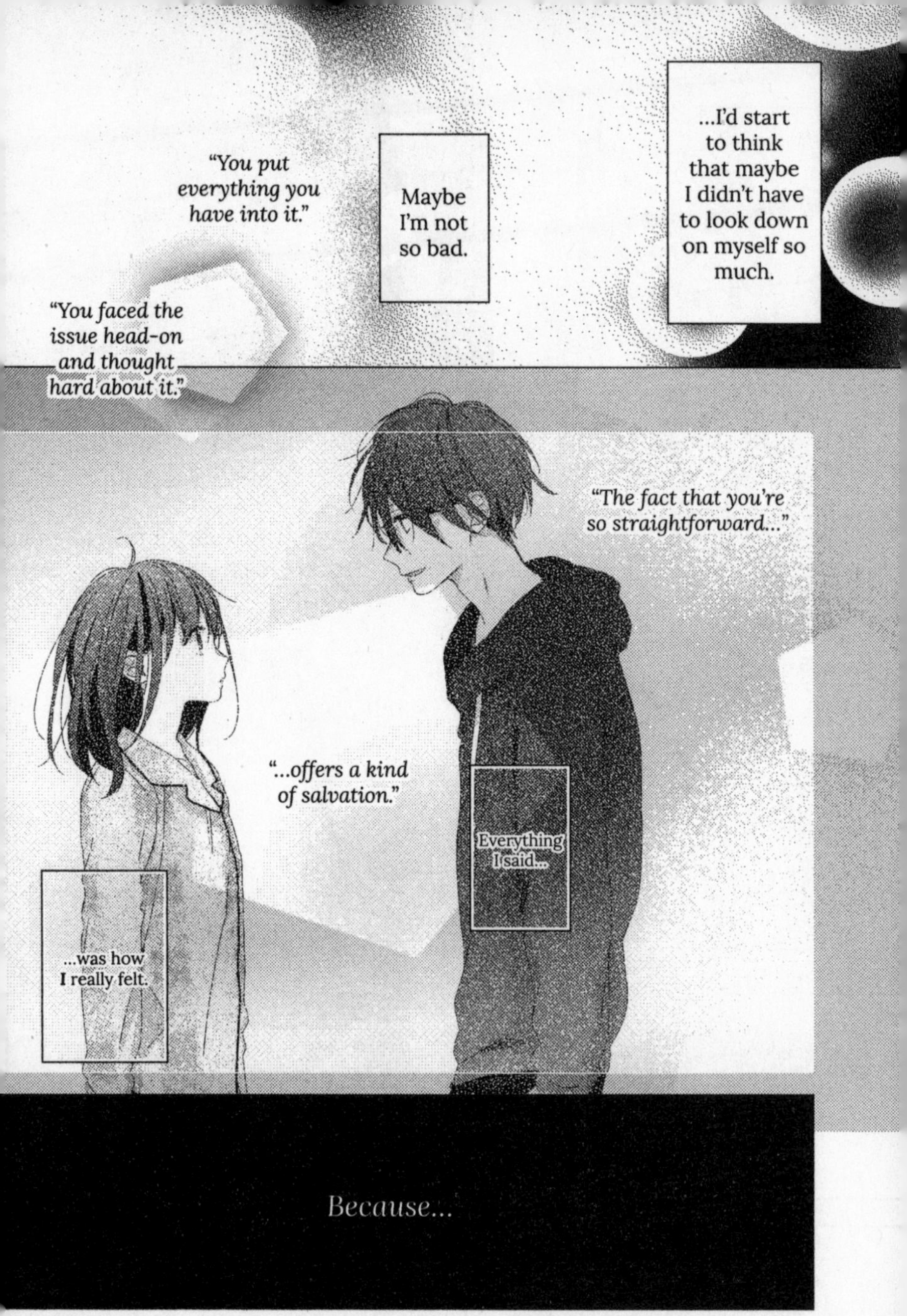
...I'd start to think that maybe I didn't have to look down on myself so much.
Maybe I'm not so bad.
"You put everything you have into it."
"You faced the issue head-on and thought hard about it."
"The fact that you're so straightforward..."
"...offers a kind of salvation."
Everything I said...
...was how I really felt.
Because...

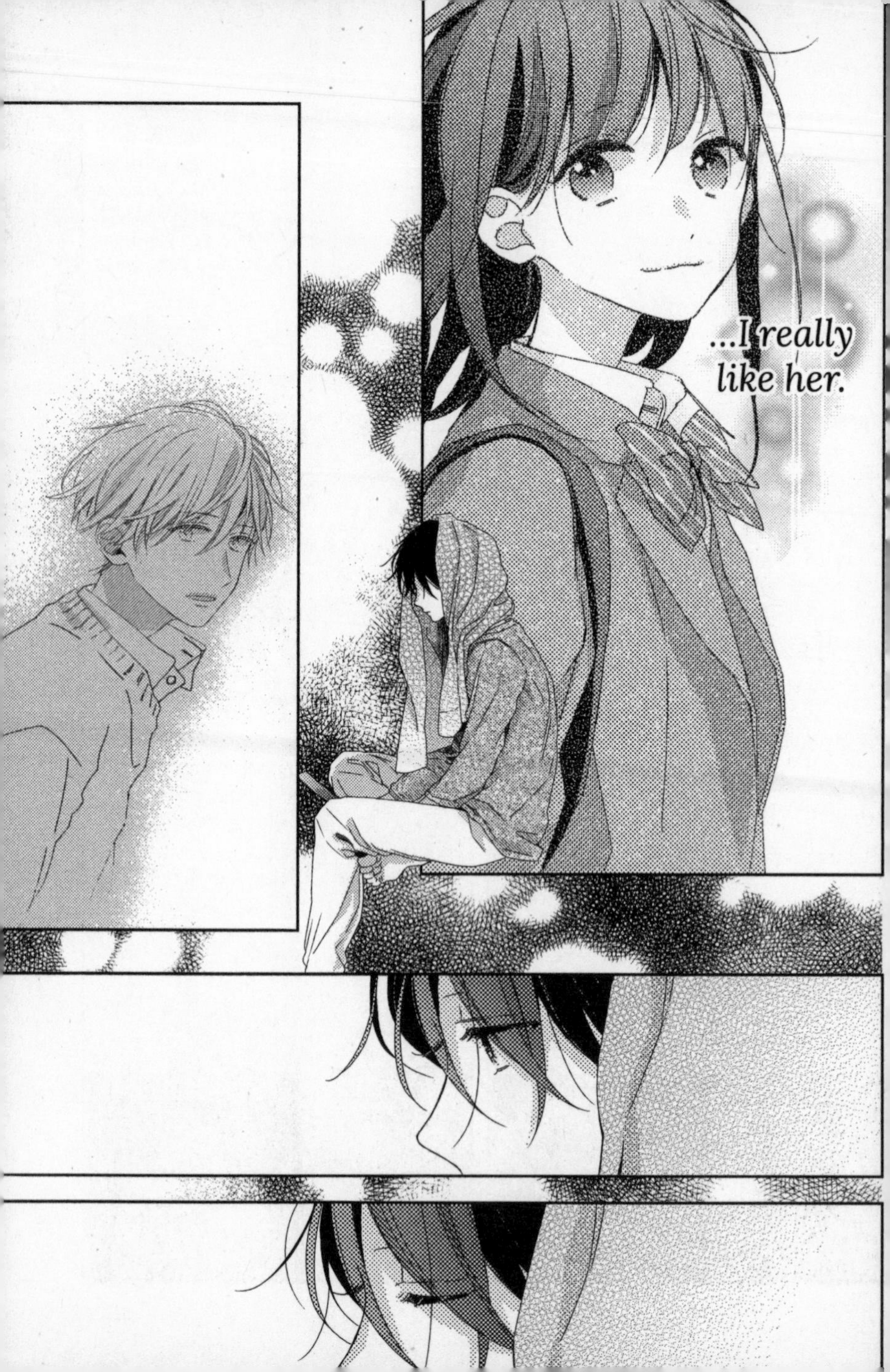
...I really like her.

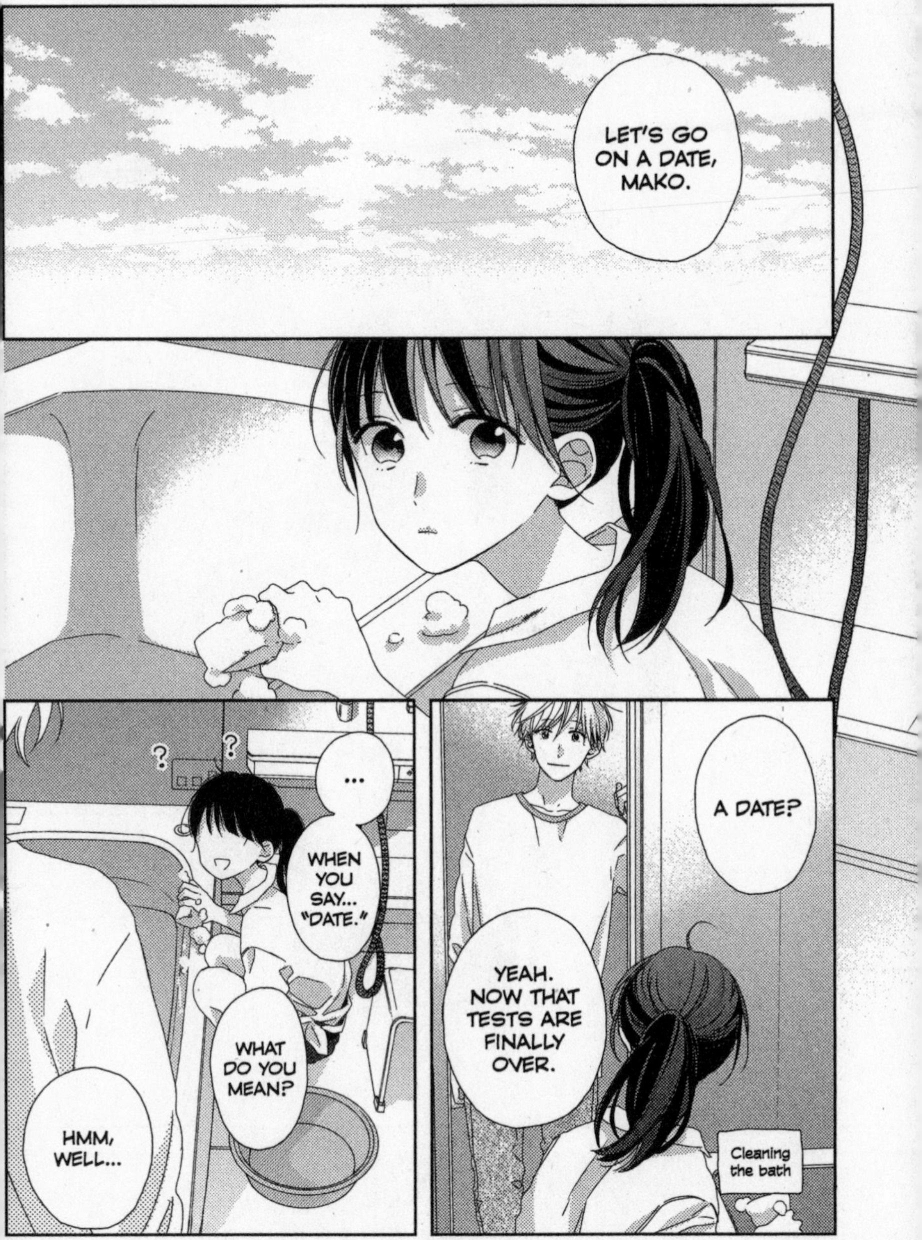
LET'S GO ON A DATE, MAKO.
A DATE?
YEAH. NOW THAT TESTS ARE FINALLY OVER.
Cleaning the bath
? ?
...
WHEN YOU SAY... "DATE."
WHAT DO YOU MEAN?
HMM, WELL...

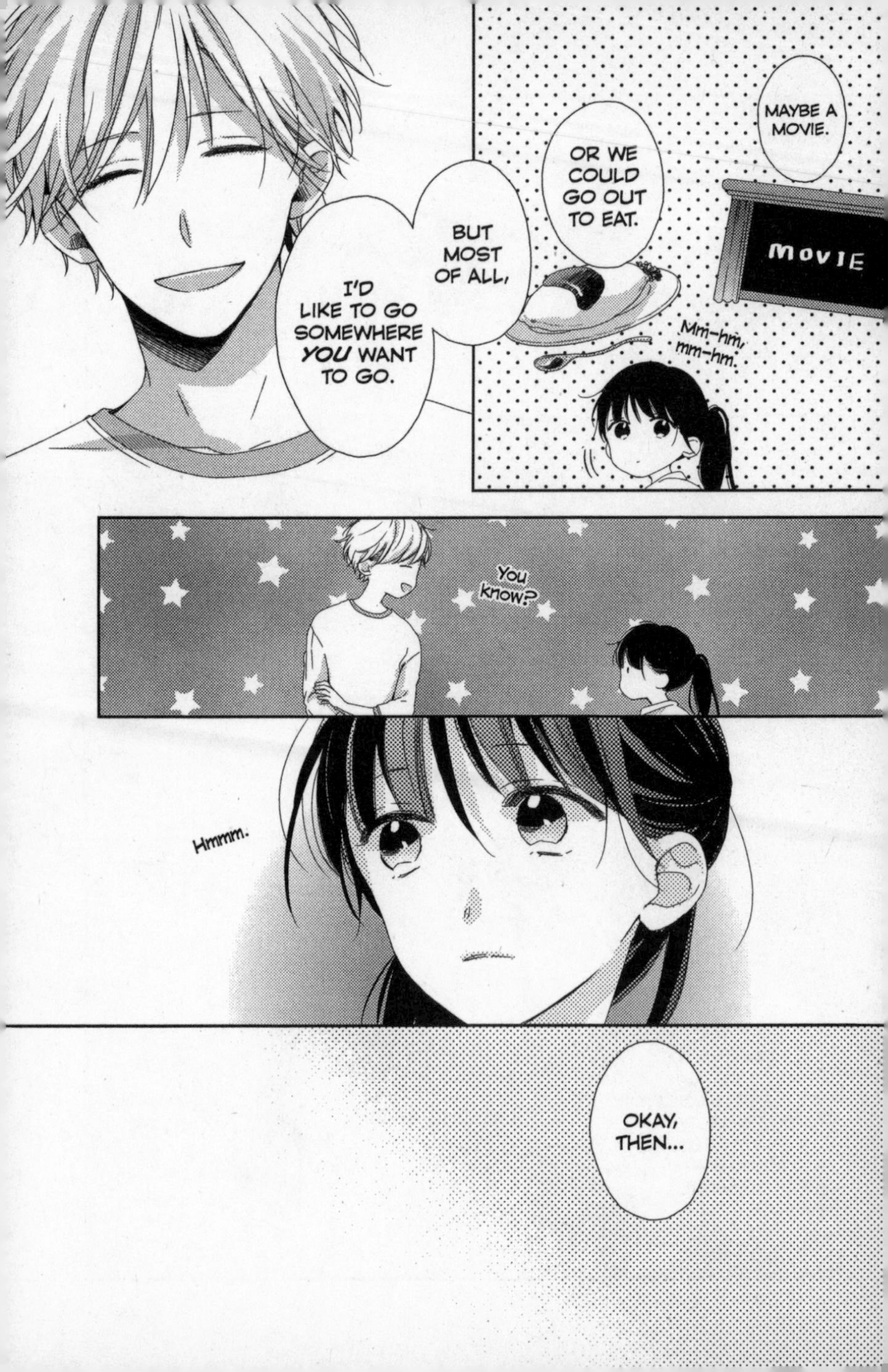
MAYBE A MOVIE.
OR WE COULD GO OUT TO EAT.
MOVIE
Mm-hm, mm-hm.
BUT MOST OF ALL,
I'D LIKE TO GO SOMEWHERE YOU WANT TO GO.
You know?
Hmmm.
OKAY, THEN...

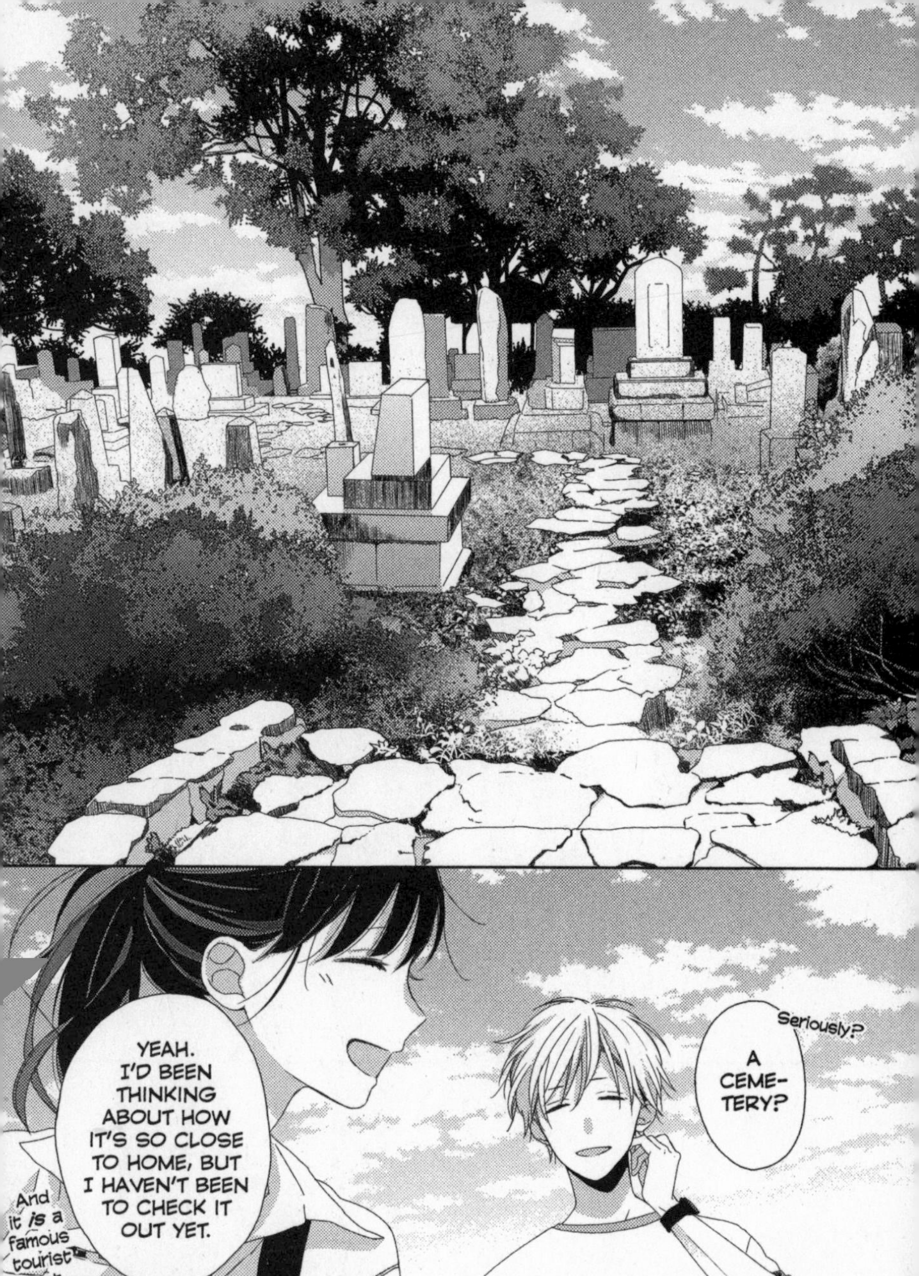
Seriously?
A CEMETERY?
YEAH. I'D BEEN THINKING ABOUT HOW IT'S SO CLOSE TO HOME, BUT I HAVEN'T BEEN TO CHECK IT OUT YET.
And it *is* a famous tourist spot.

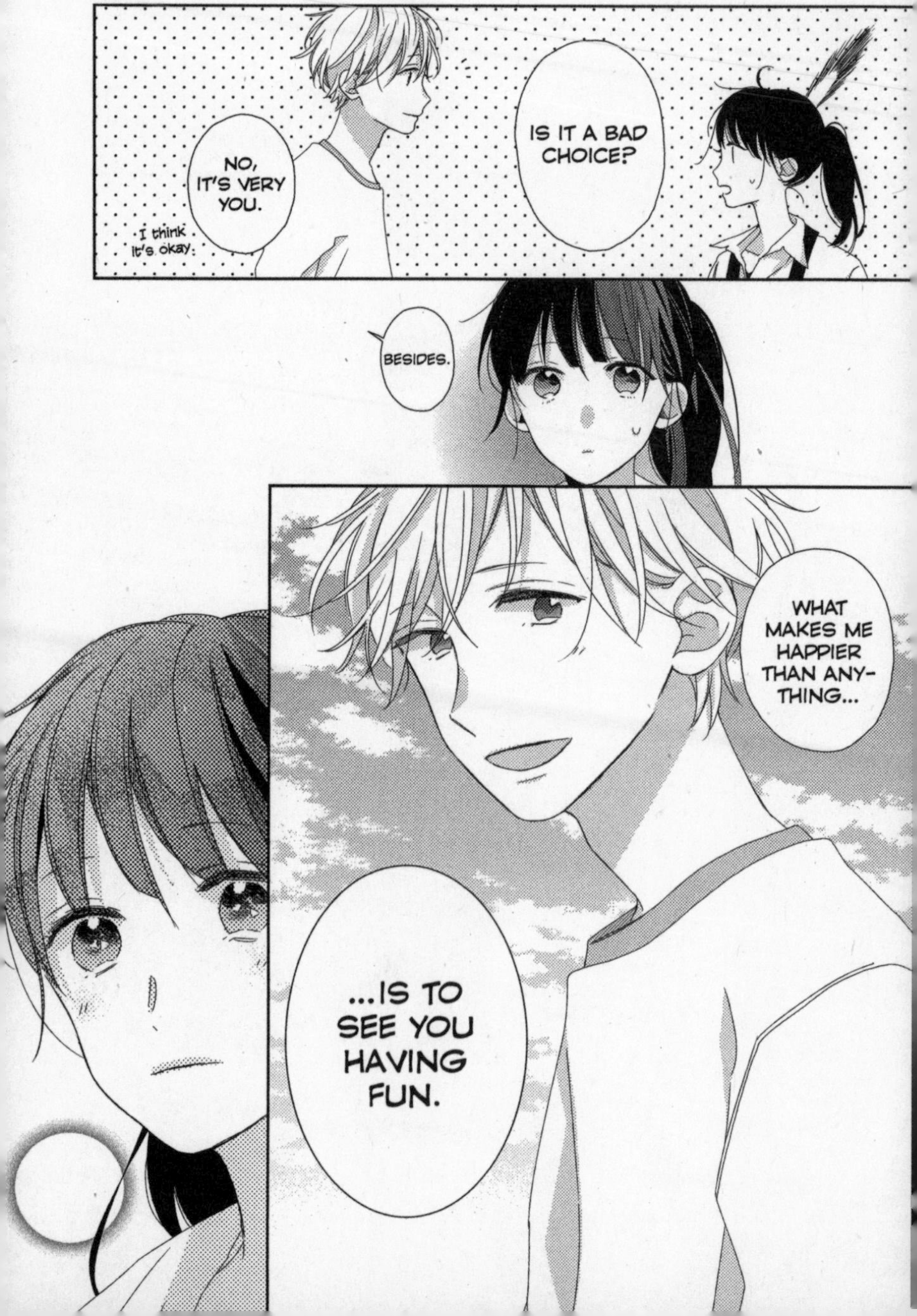
IS IT A BAD CHOICE?
NO, IT'S VERY YOU.
I think it's okay.
BESIDES.
WHAT MAKES ME HAPPIER THAN ANY-THING...
...IS TO SEE YOU HAVING FUN.

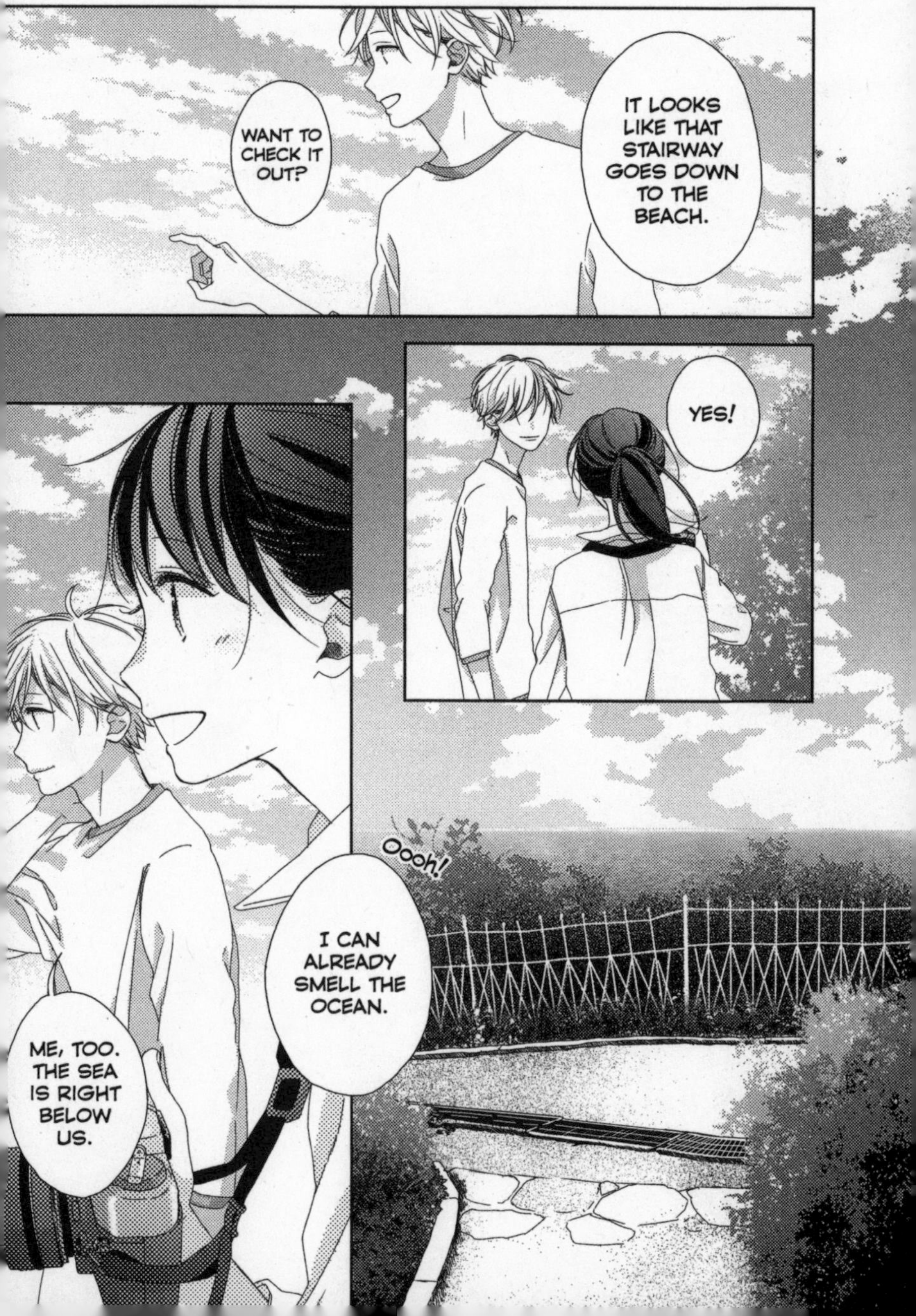
IT LOOKS LIKE THAT STAIRWAY GOES DOWN TO THE BEACH.
WANT TO CHECK IT OUT?
YES!
Oooh!
I CAN ALREADY SMELL THE OCEAN.
ME, TOO. THE SEA IS RIGHT BELOW US.

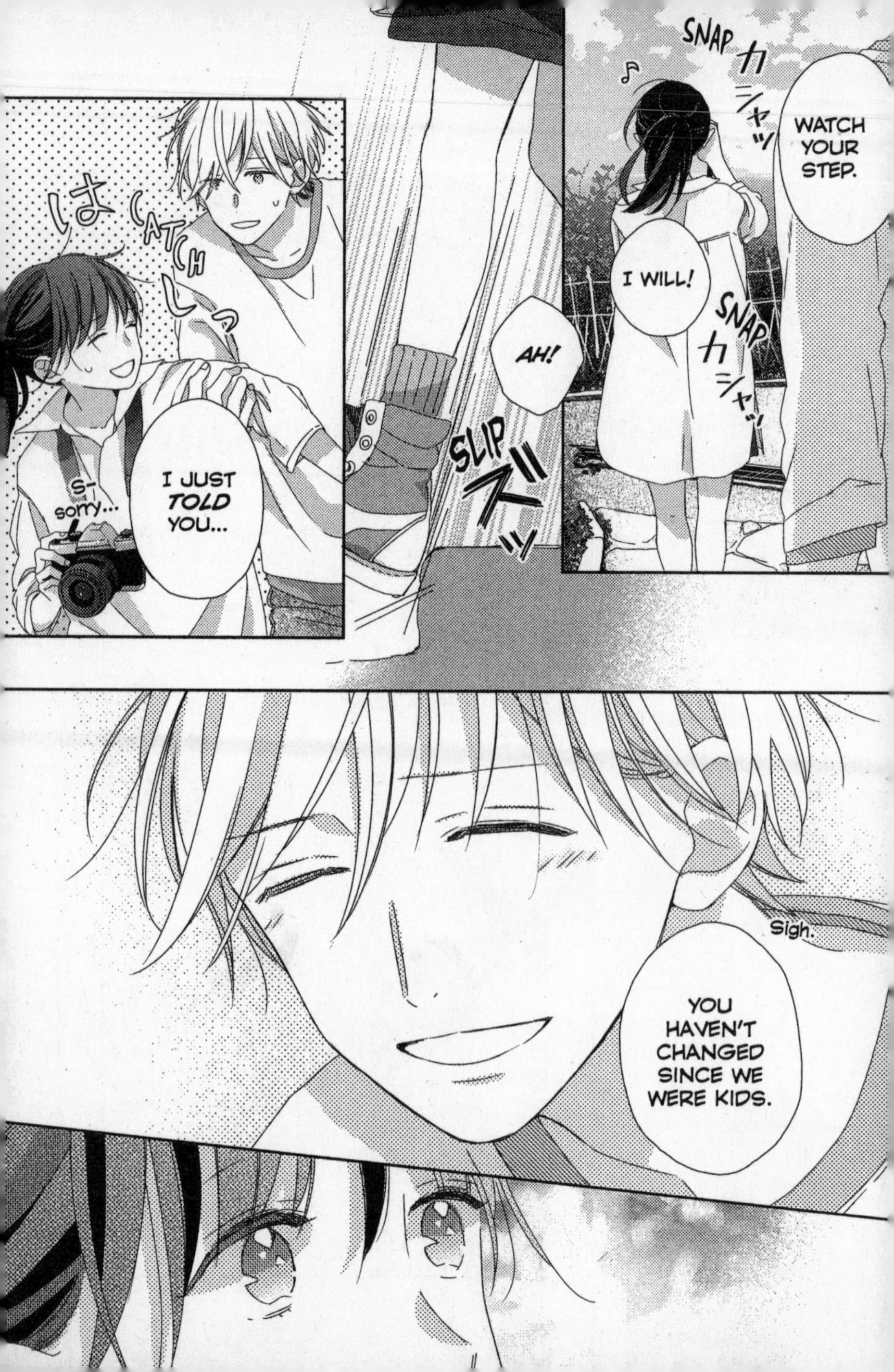
SNAP カシャッ
♪
WATCH YOUR STEP.
I WILL!
SNAP カシャッ
AH!
SLIP ズルッ
CATCH はしっ
I JUST *TOLD* YOU...
S-sorry...
Sigh.
YOU HAVEN'T CHANGED SINCE WE WERE KIDS.

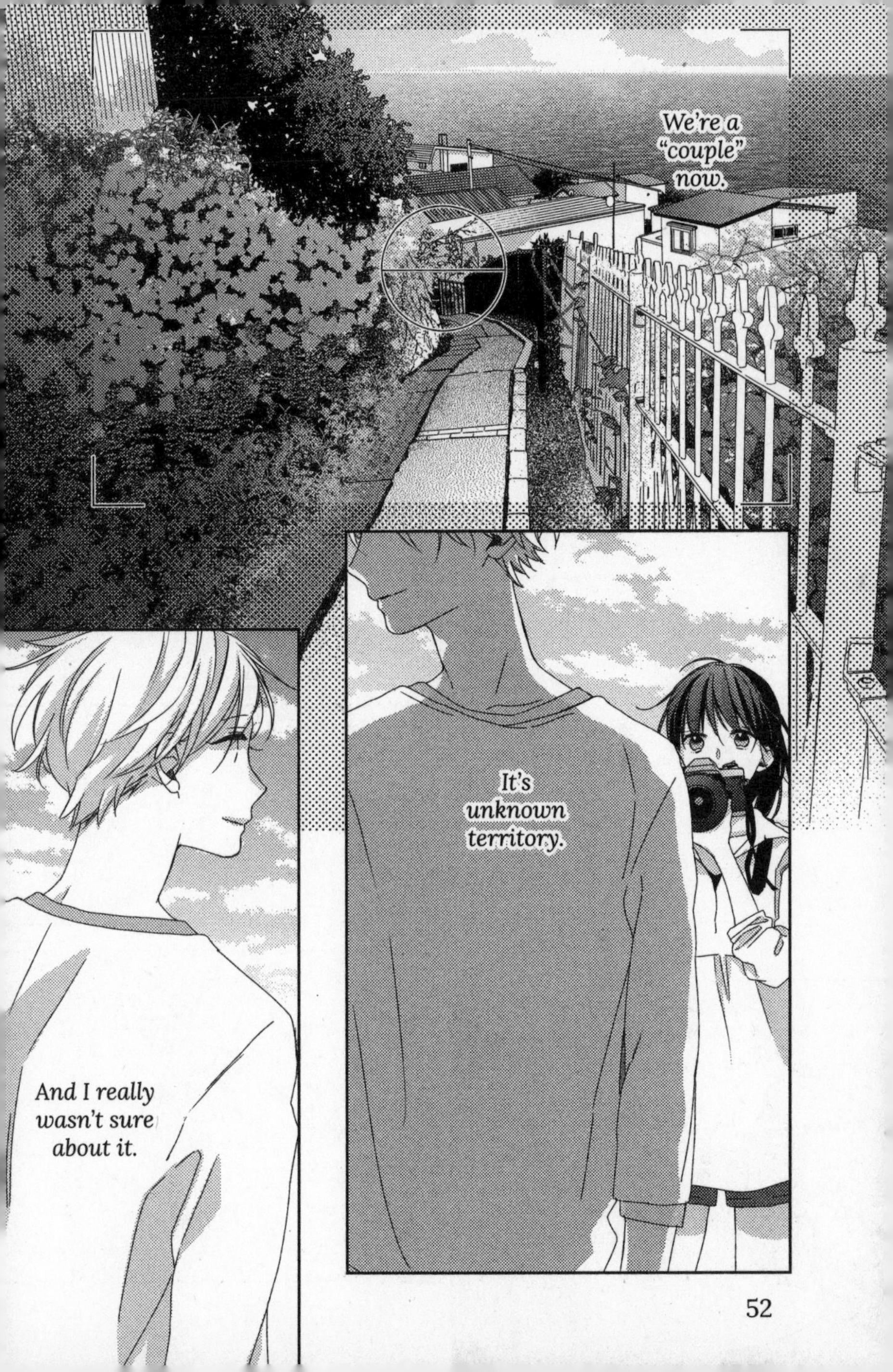
We're a "couple" now.
It's unknown territory.
And I really wasn't sure about it.

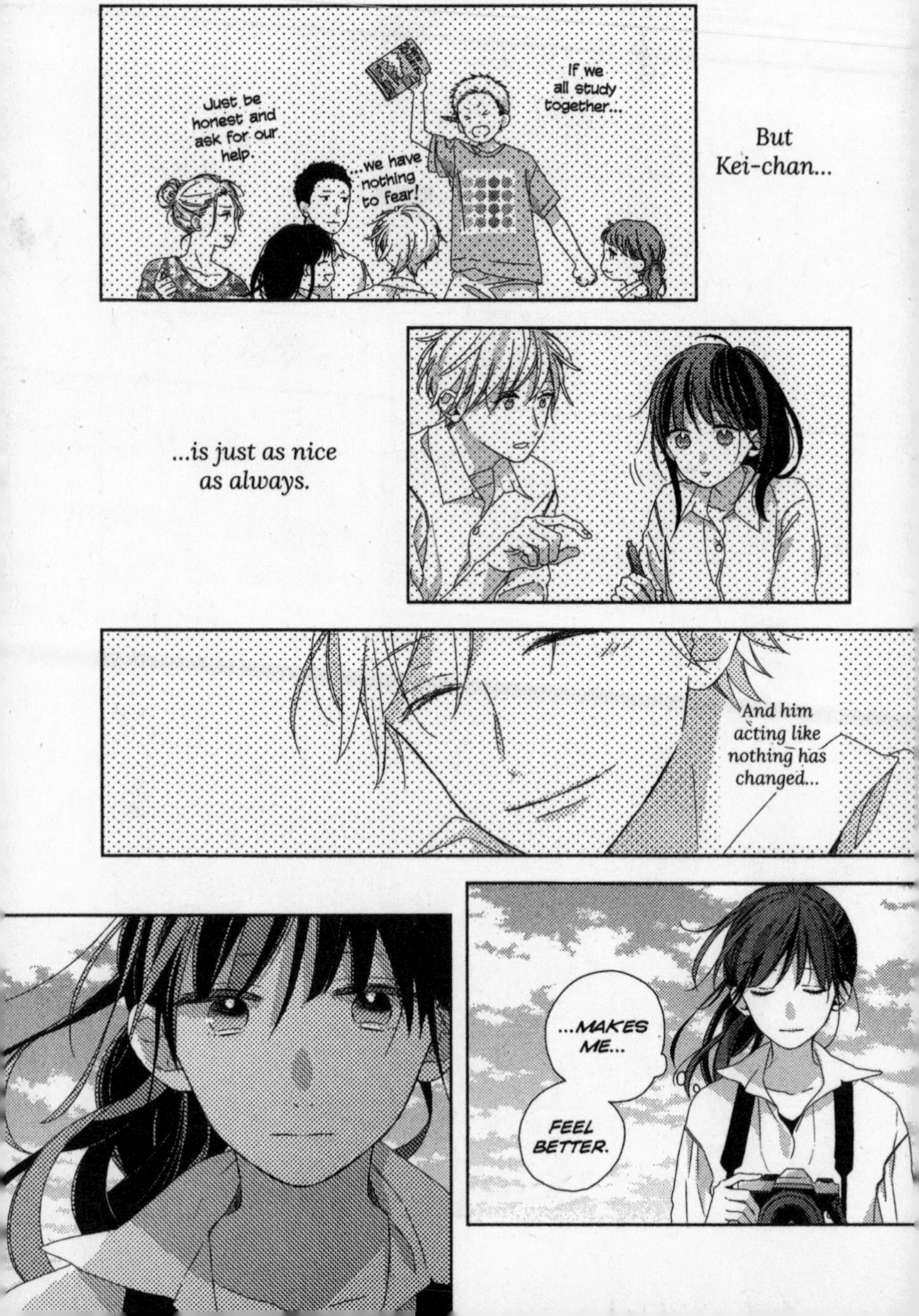
If we all study together...
...we have nothing to fear!
Just be honest and ask for our help.
But Kei-chan...
...is just as nice as always.
And him acting like nothing has changed...
...MAKES ME...
FEEL BETTER.

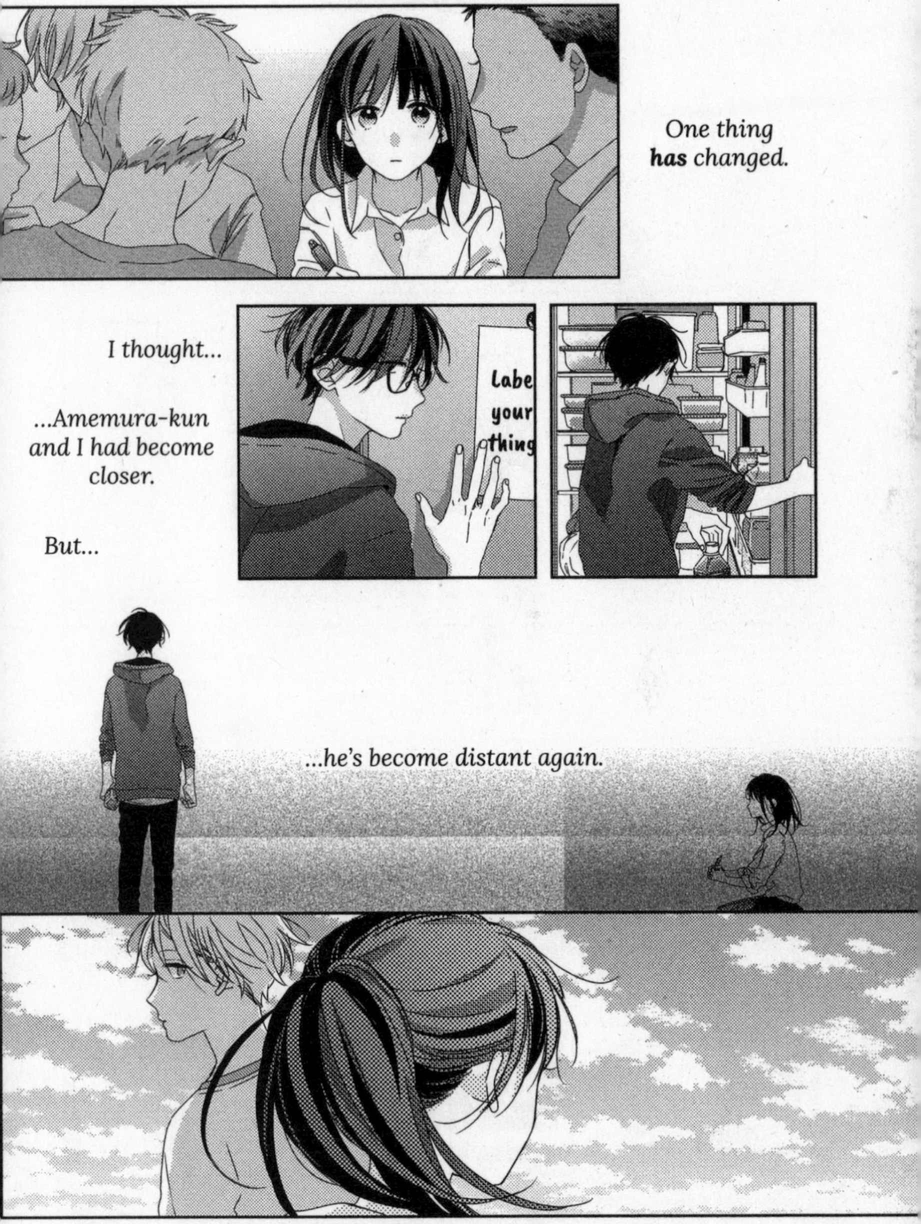
One thing **has** changed.
Labe
your
thing
I thought...
...Amemura-kun and I had become closer.
But...
...he's become distant again.

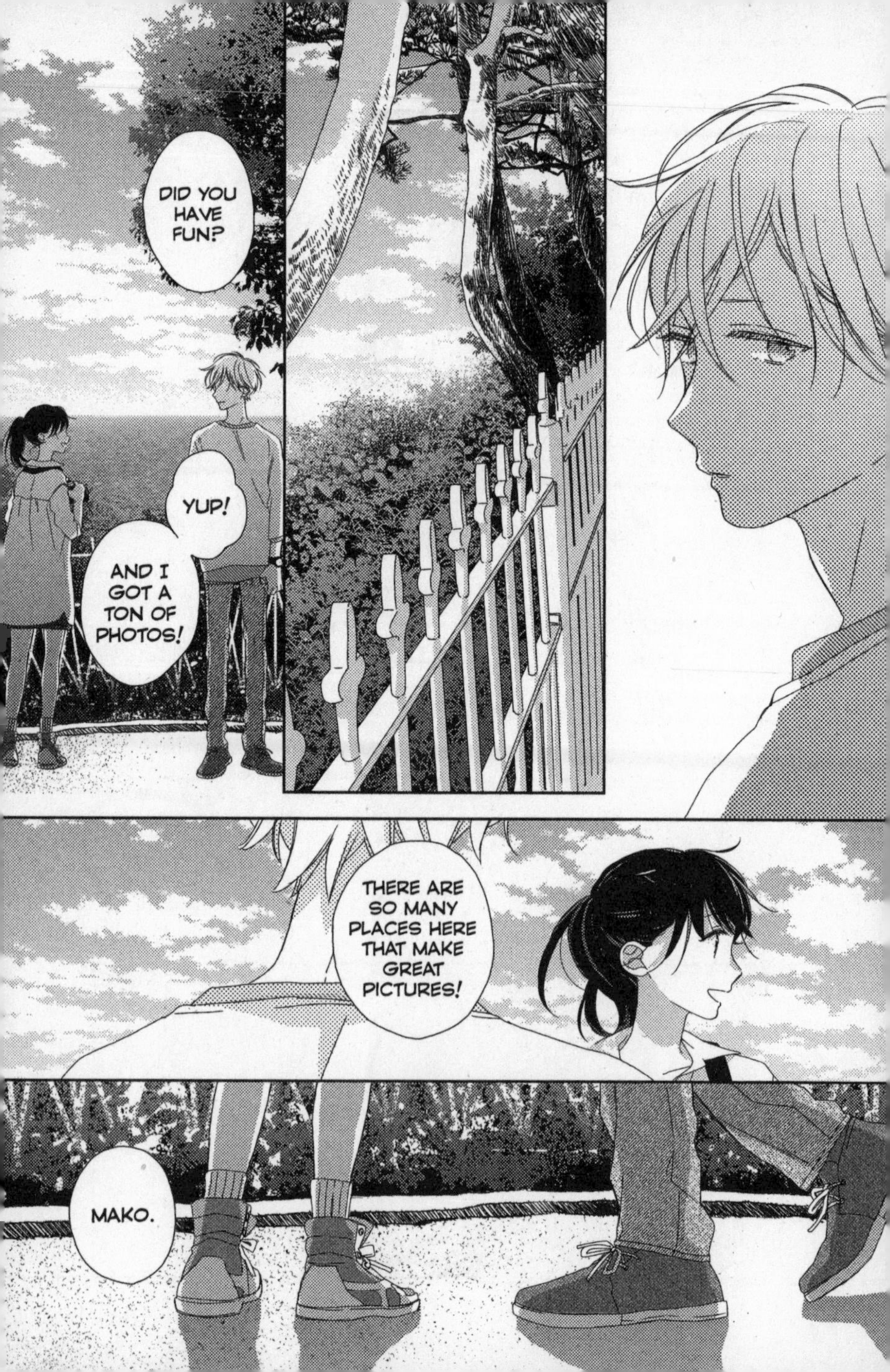
DID YOU HAVE FUN?
YUP!
AND I GOT A TON OF PHOTOS!
THERE ARE SO MANY PLACES HERE THAT MAKE GREAT PICTURES!
MAKO.

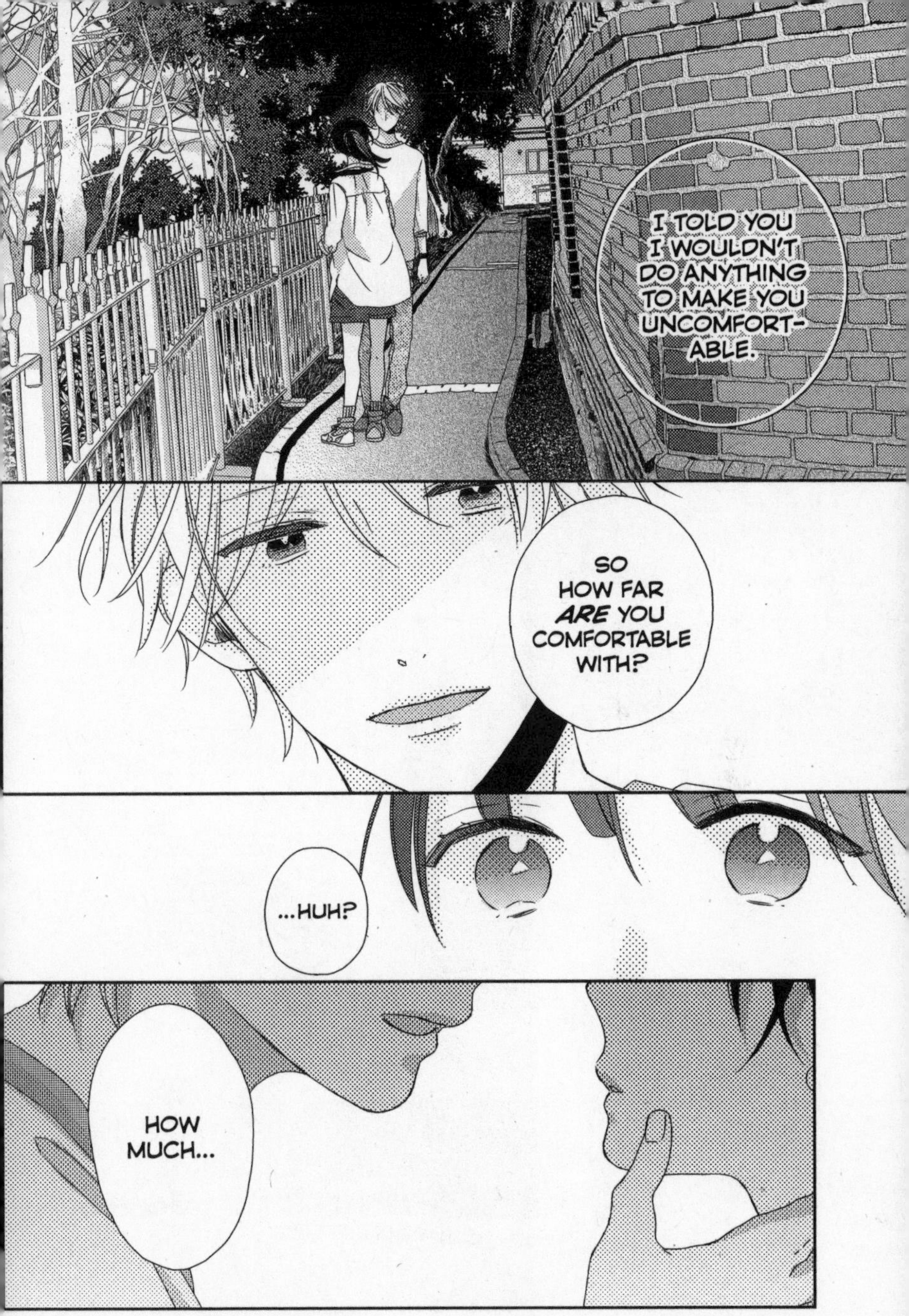
I TOLD YOU I WOULDN'T DO ANYTHING TO MAKE YOU UNCOMFORT-ABLE.
SO HOW FAR *ARE* YOU COMFORTABLE WITH?
...HUH?
HOW MUCH...

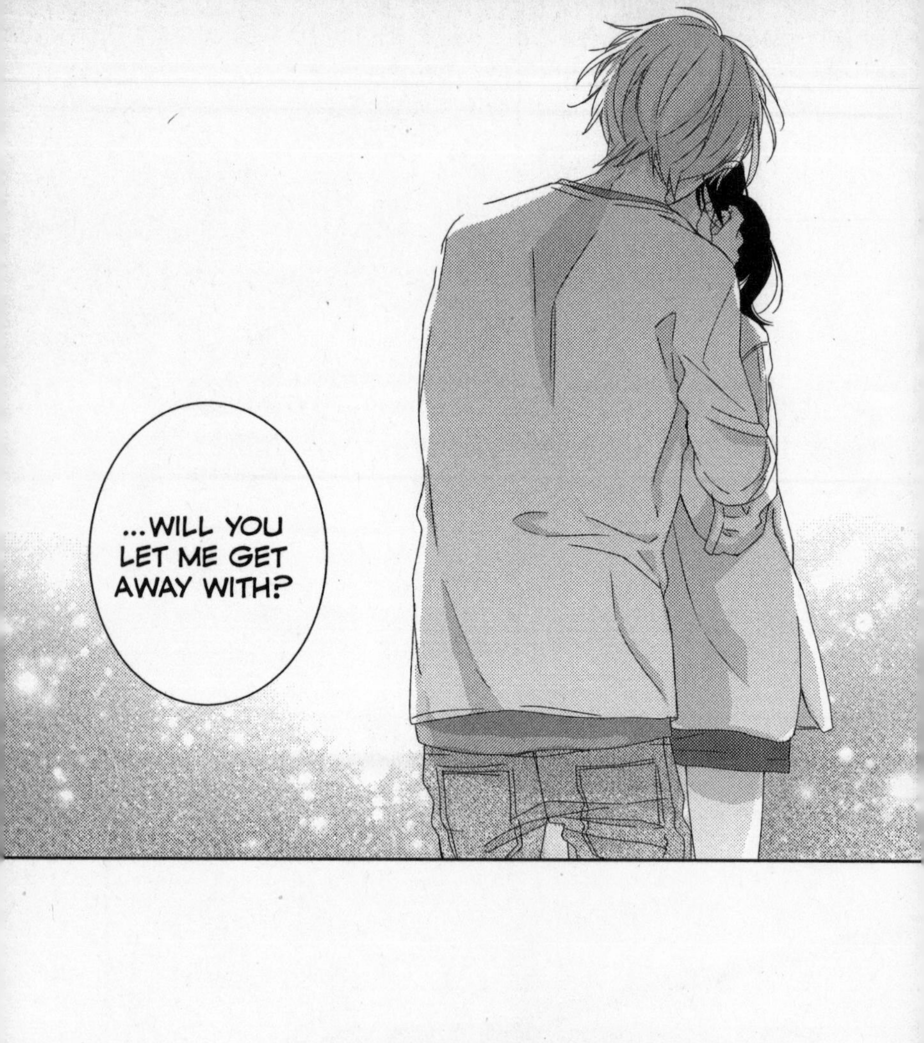
...WILL YOU LET ME GET AWAY WITH?

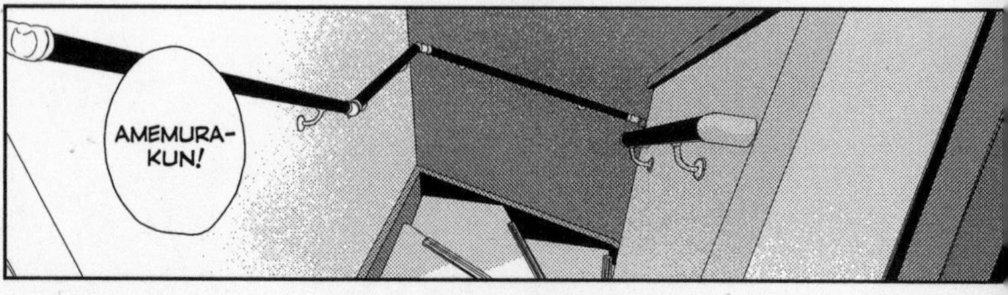
AMEMURA-KUN!

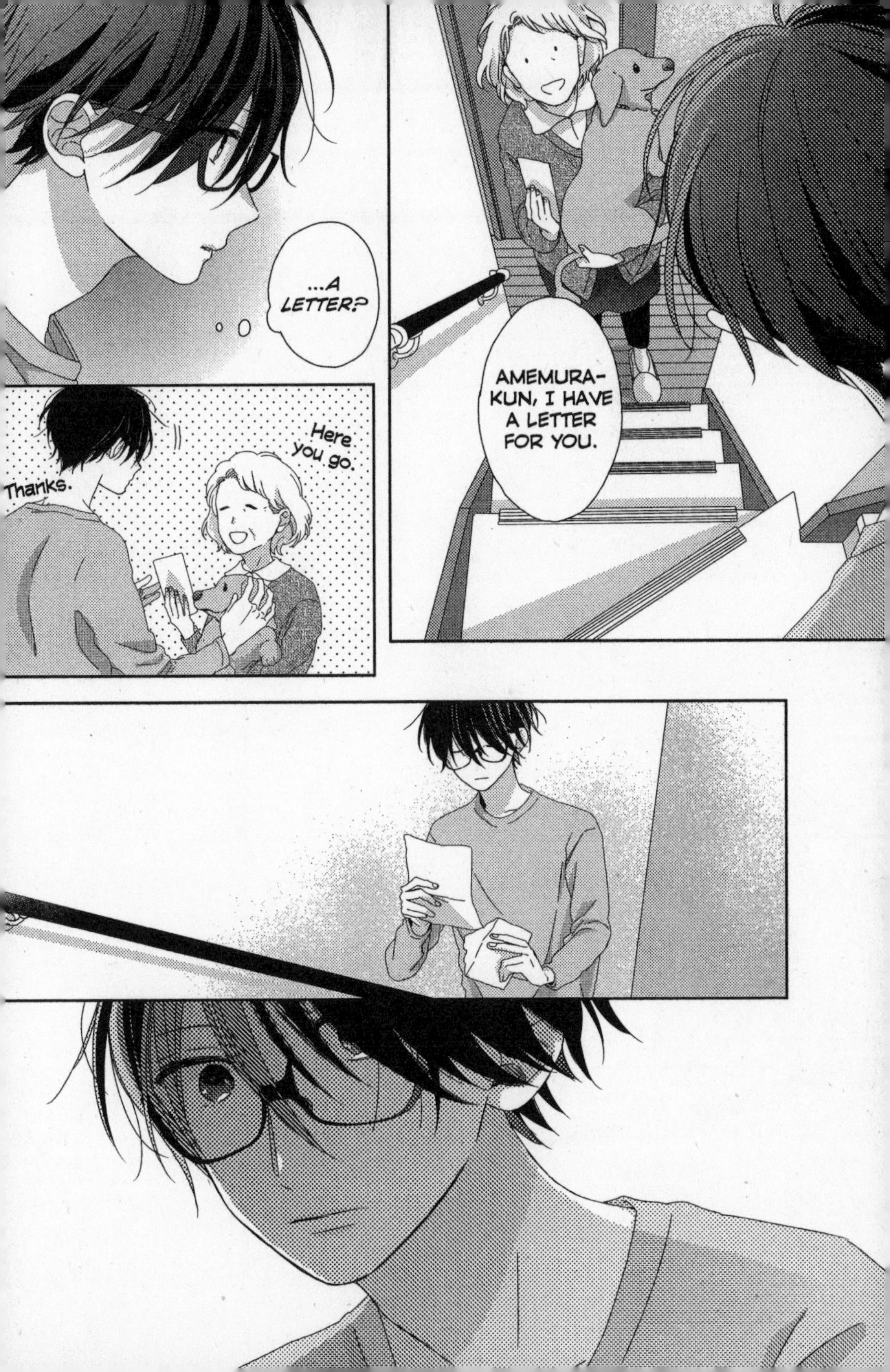
AMEMURA-KUN, I HAVE A LETTER FOR YOU.
...A LETTER?
Here you go.
Thanks.

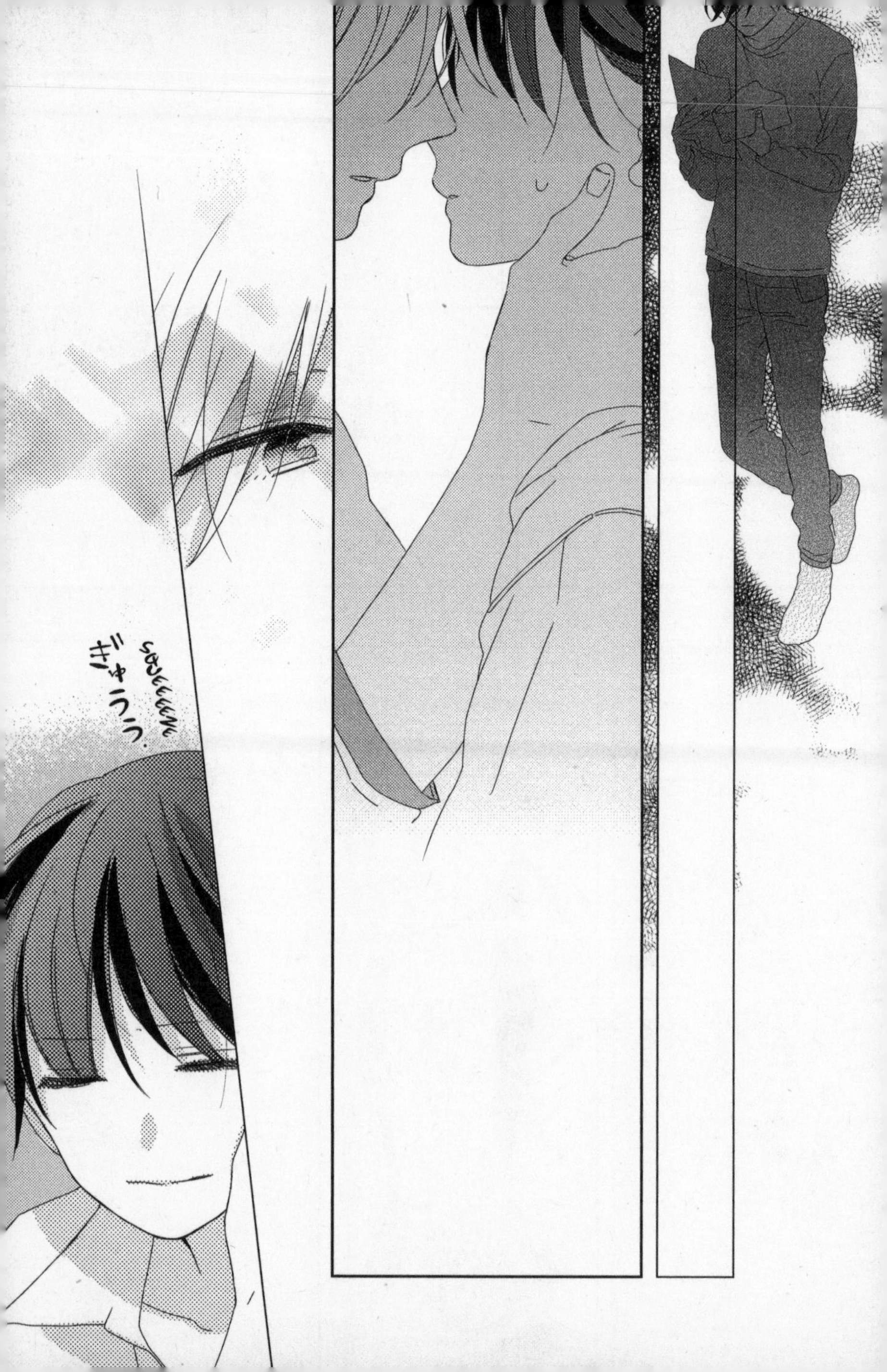

ぎゅうう
SQUEEEEZE

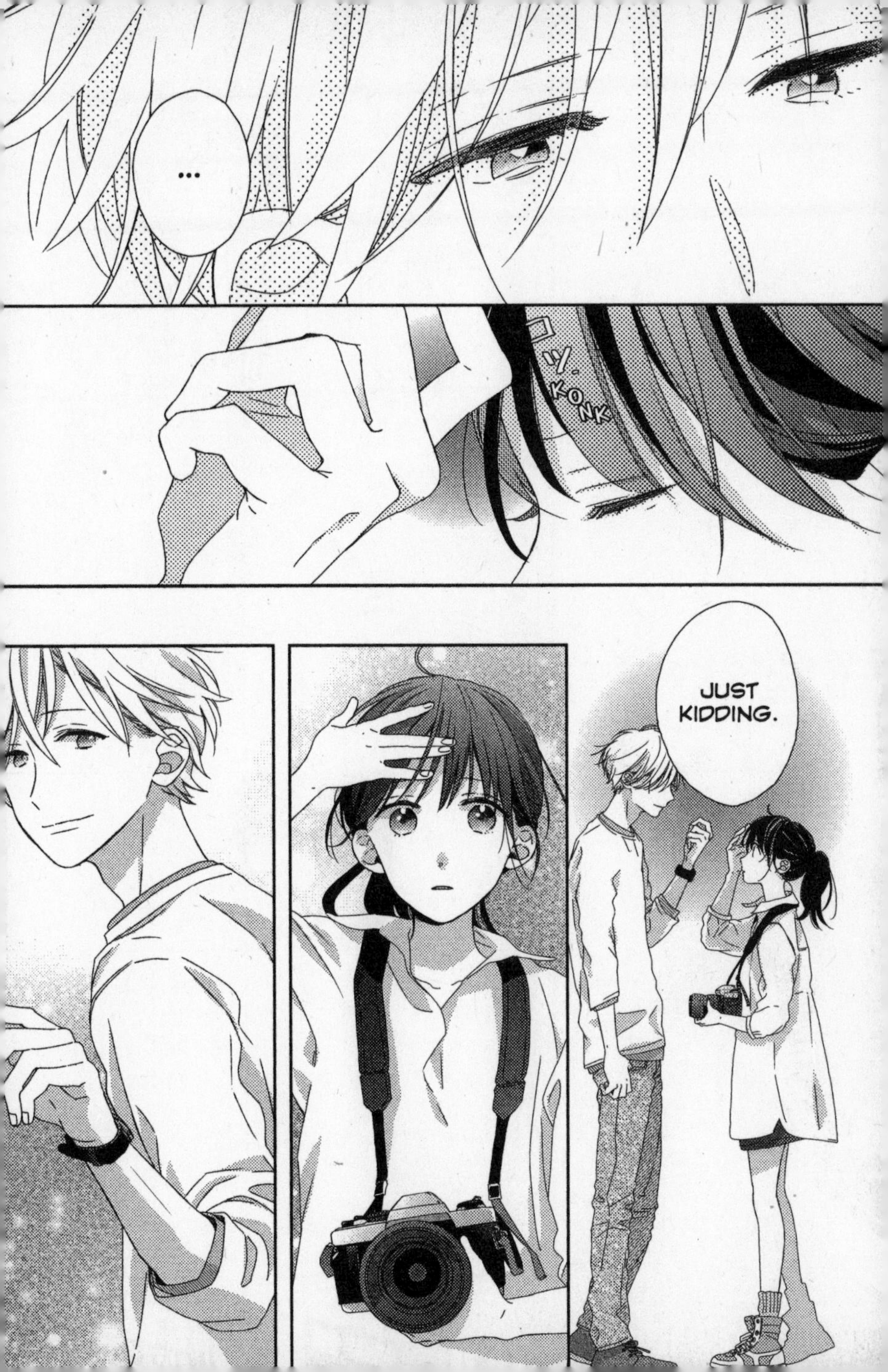
...
KONK
JUST KIDDING.

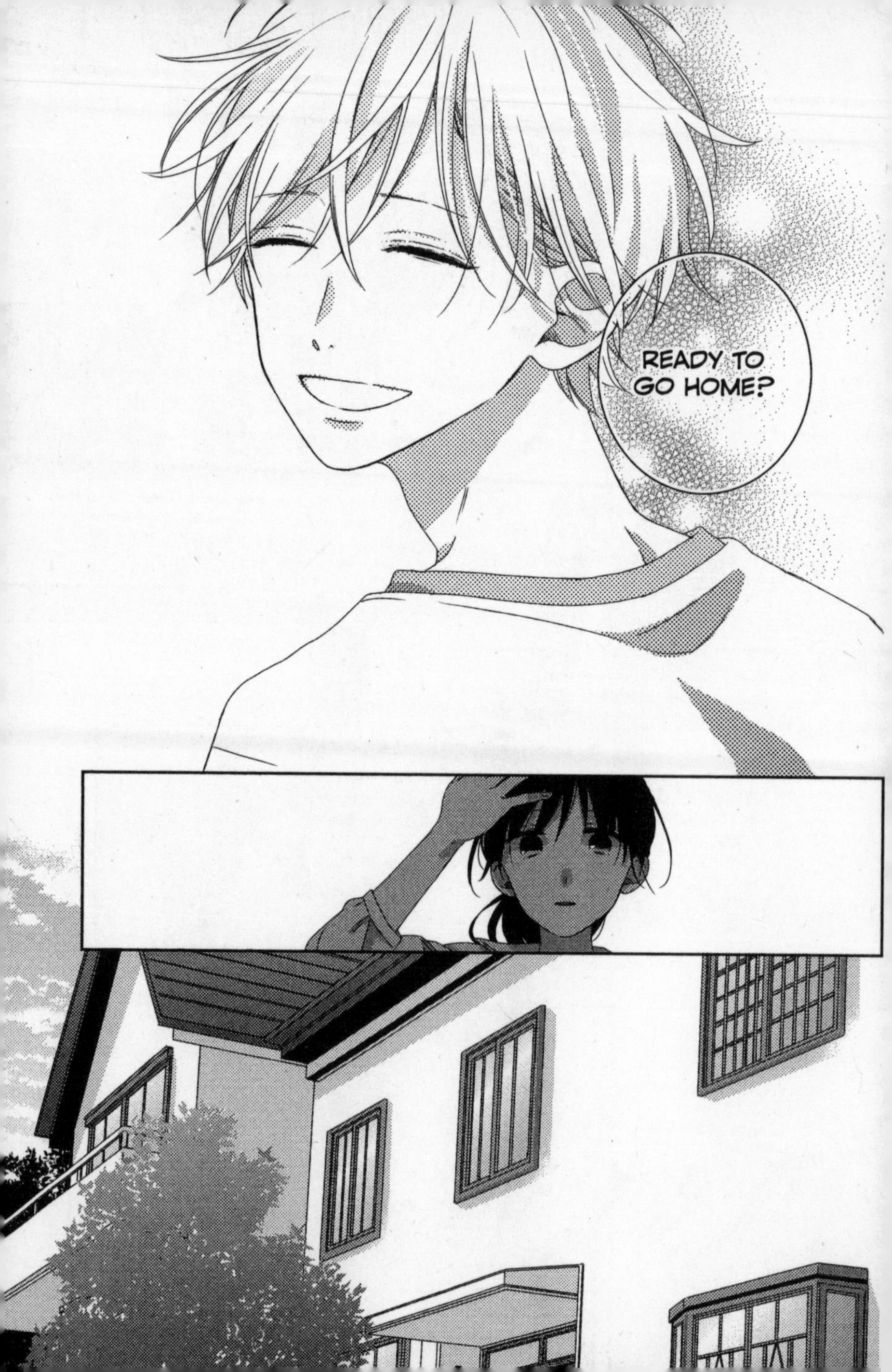
READY TO GO HOME?

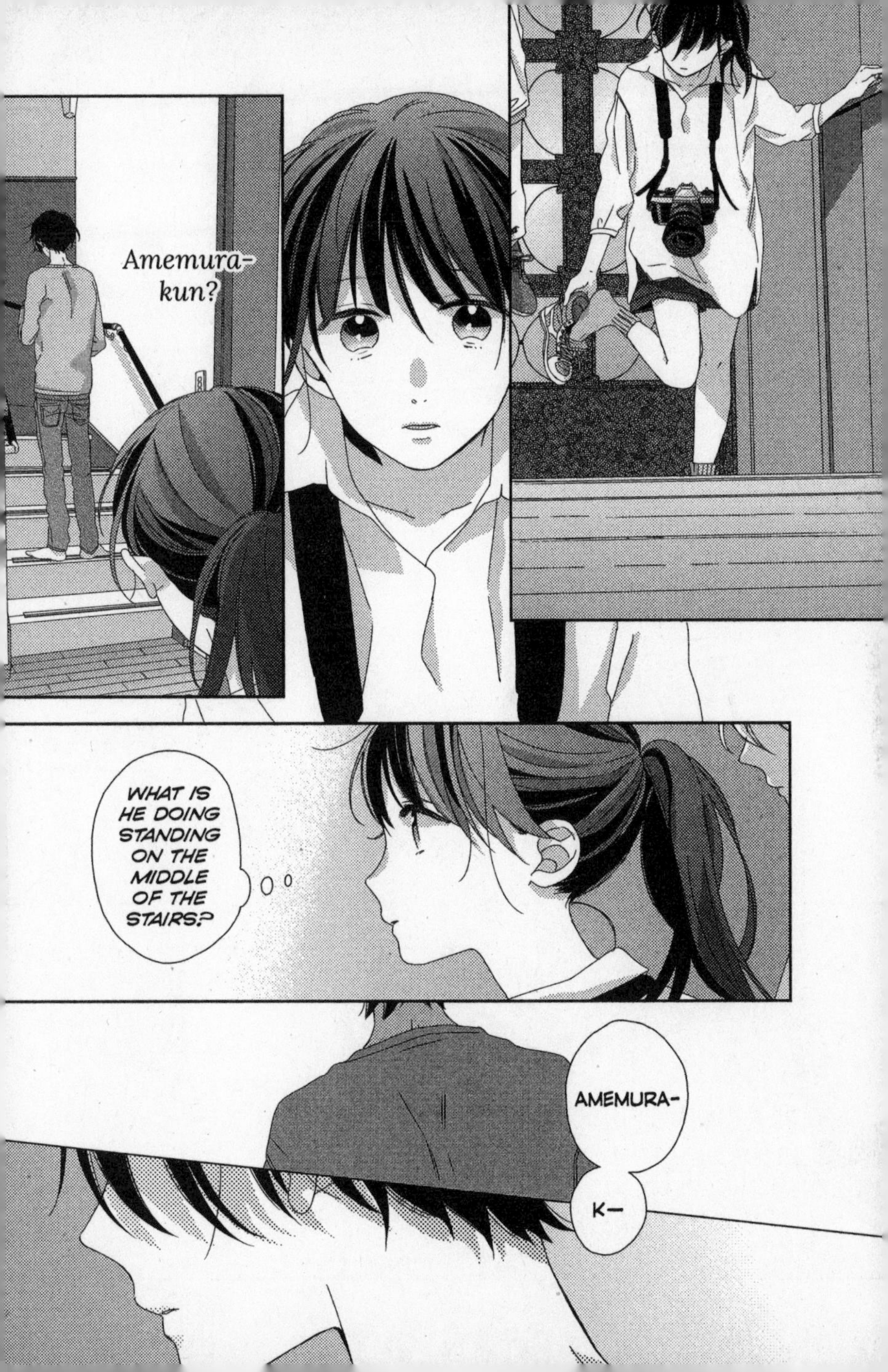

Amemura-kun?
WHAT IS HE DOING STANDING ON THE MIDDLE OF THE STAIRS?
AMEMURA-
K—

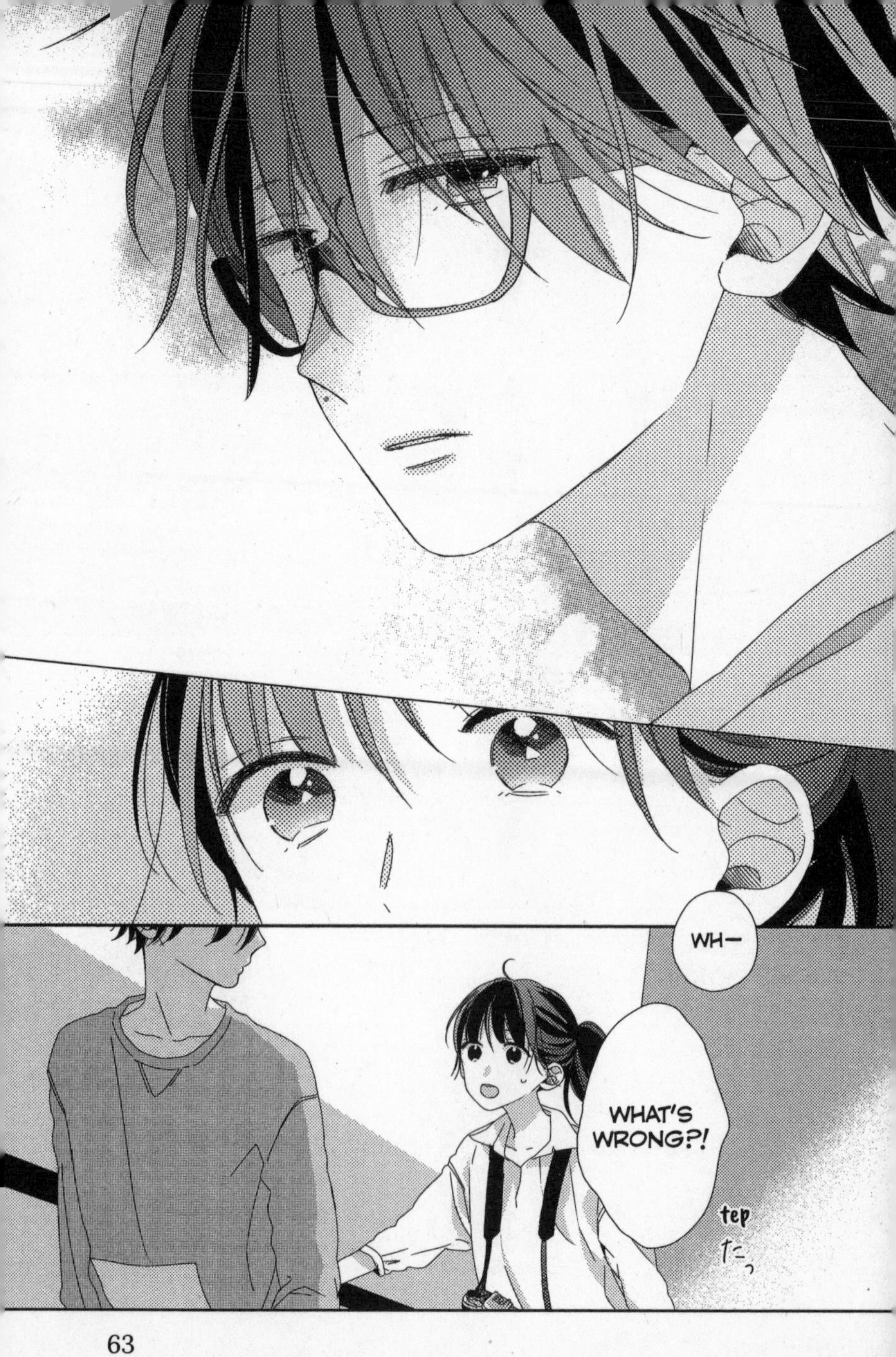
WH—
WHAT'S WRONG?!
tep
たっ

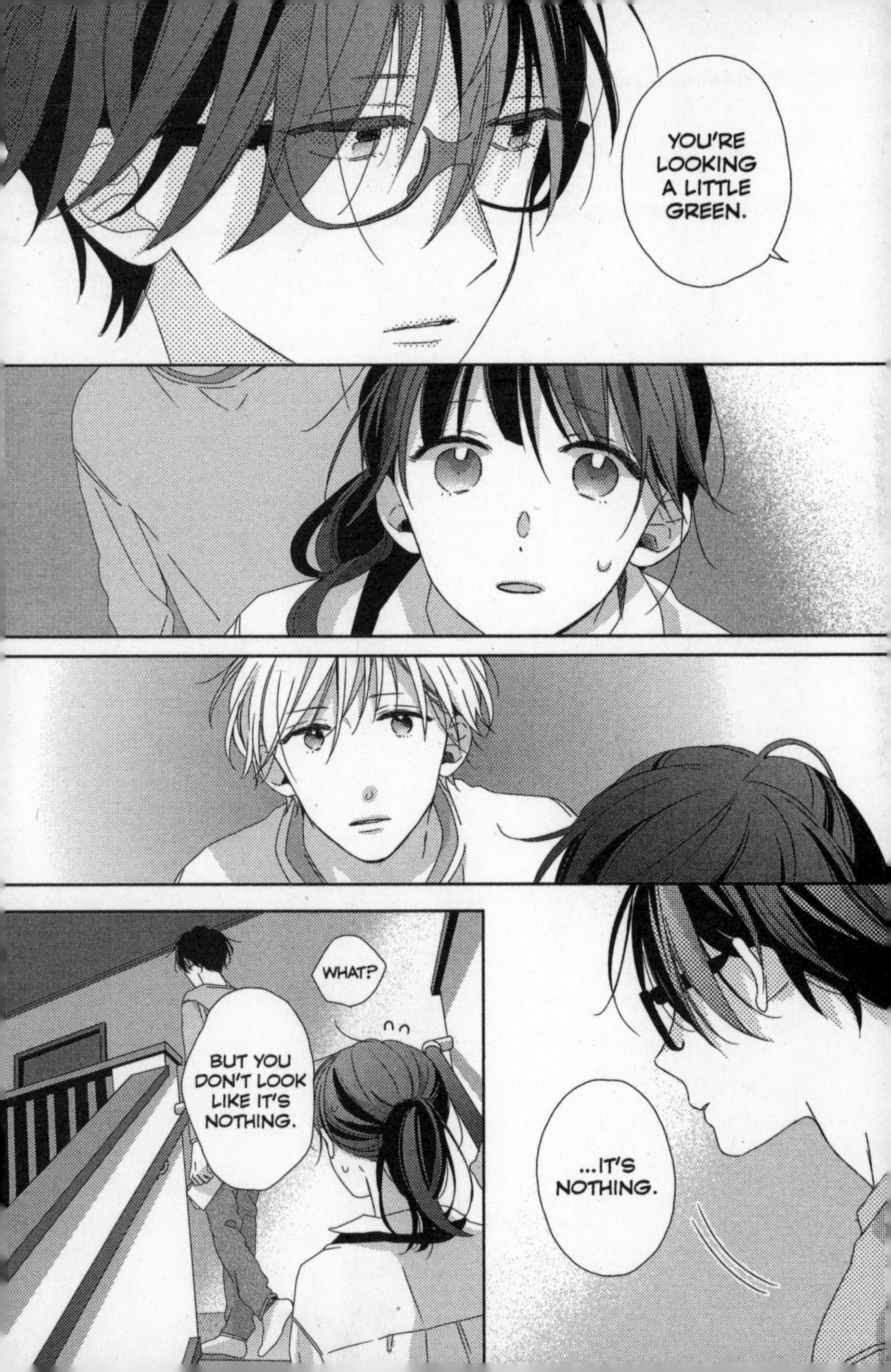
YOU'RE LOOKING A LITTLE GREEN.
...IT'S NOTHING.
WHAT?
BUT YOU DON'T LOOK LIKE IT'S NOTHING.

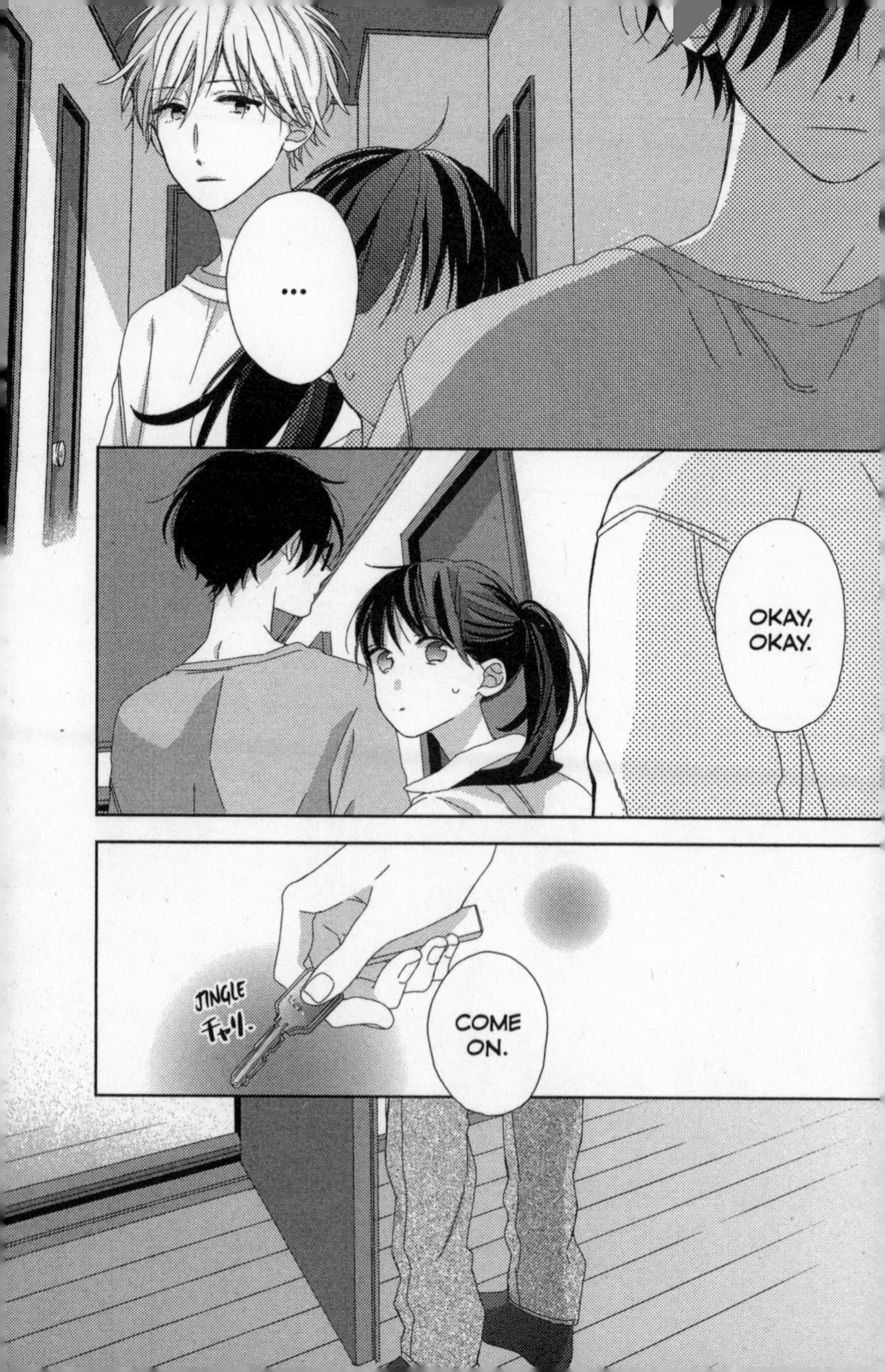
...
OKAY, OKAY.
JINGLE
チャリ
COME ON.

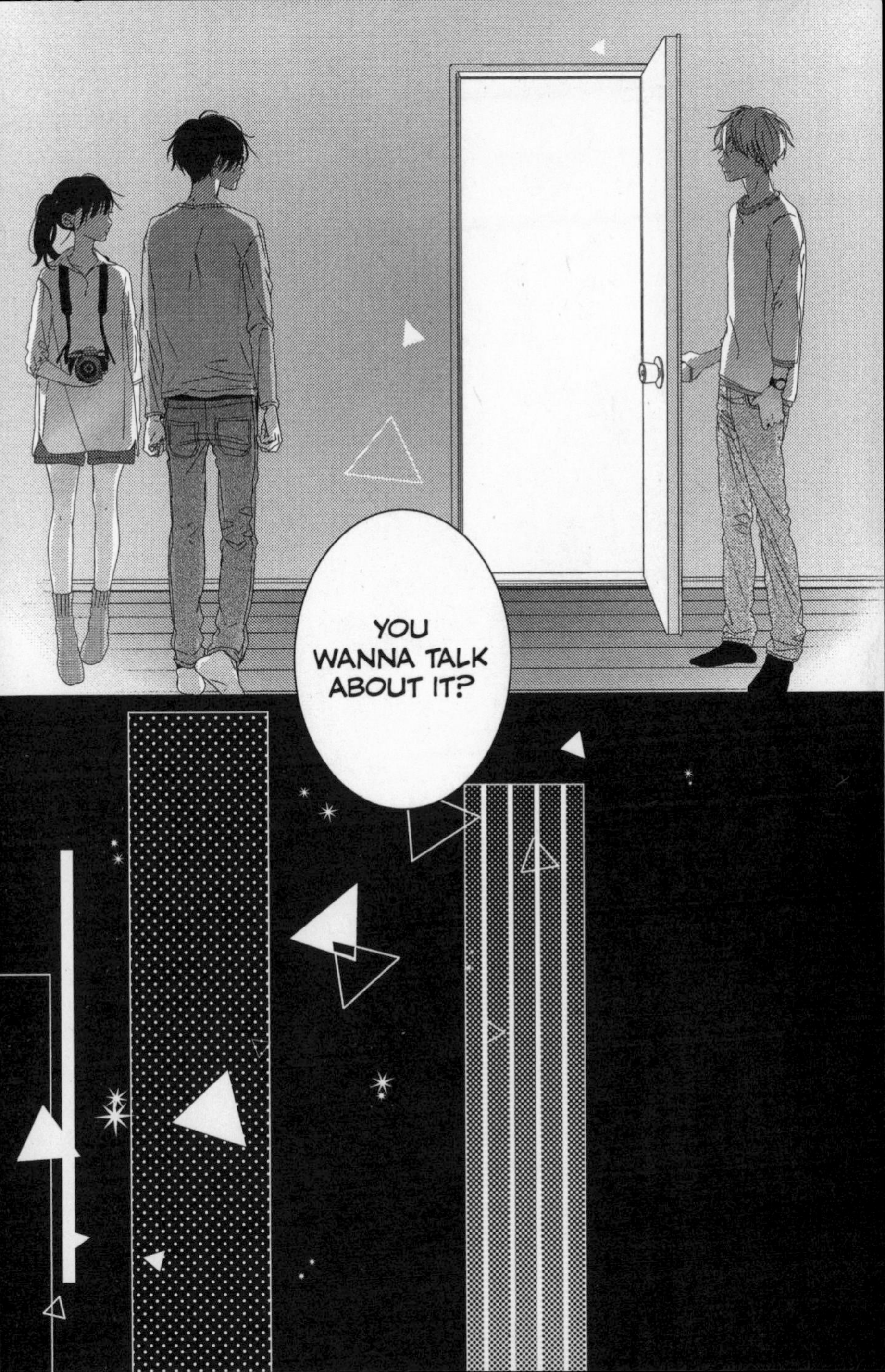
YOU WANNA TALK ABOUT IT?

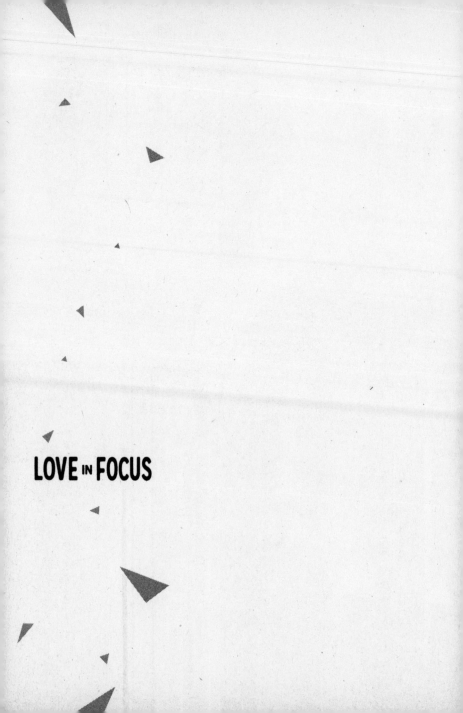

LOVE IN FOCUS

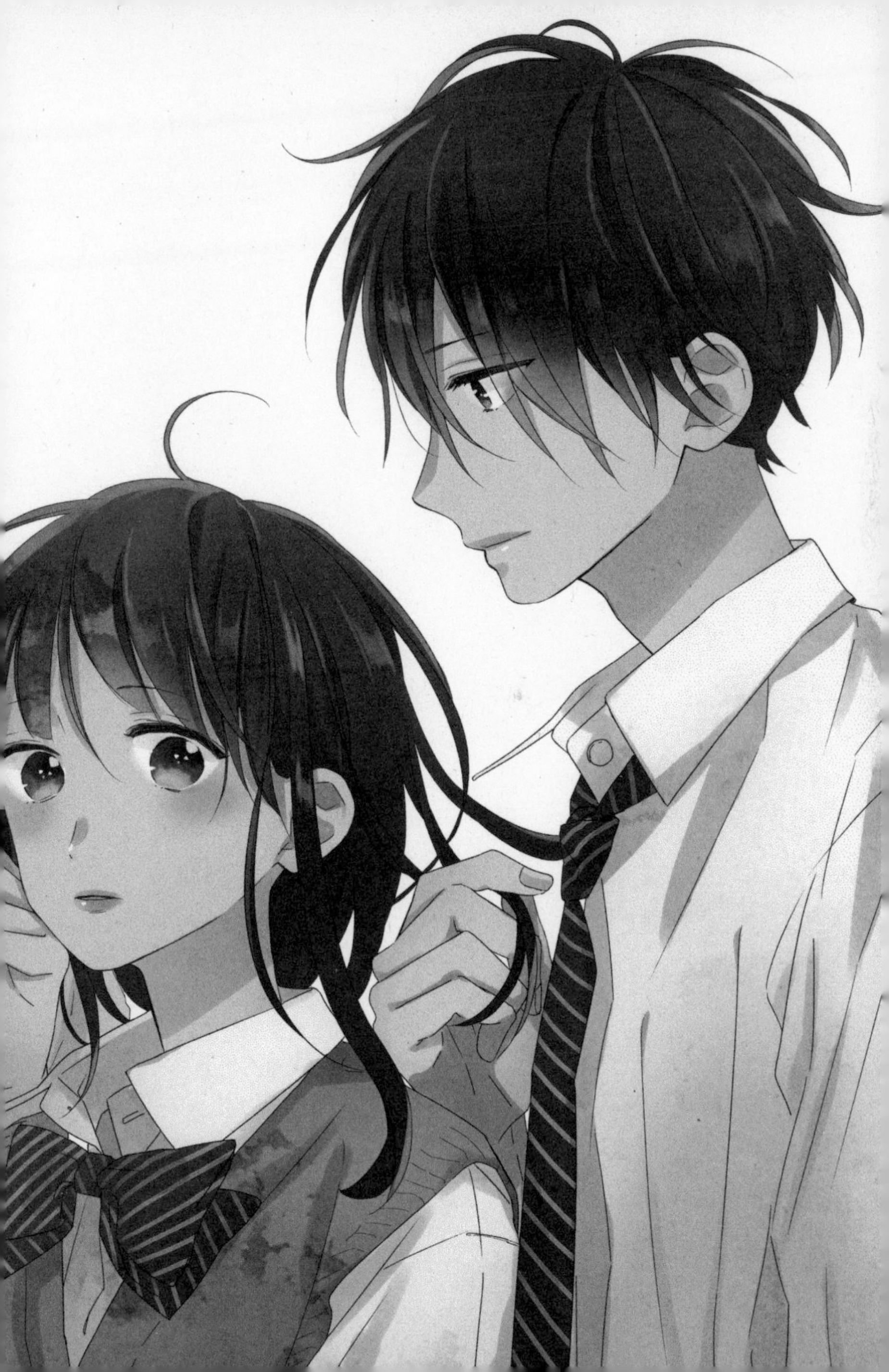

FILM 12

A Made-up Mind and a Smile

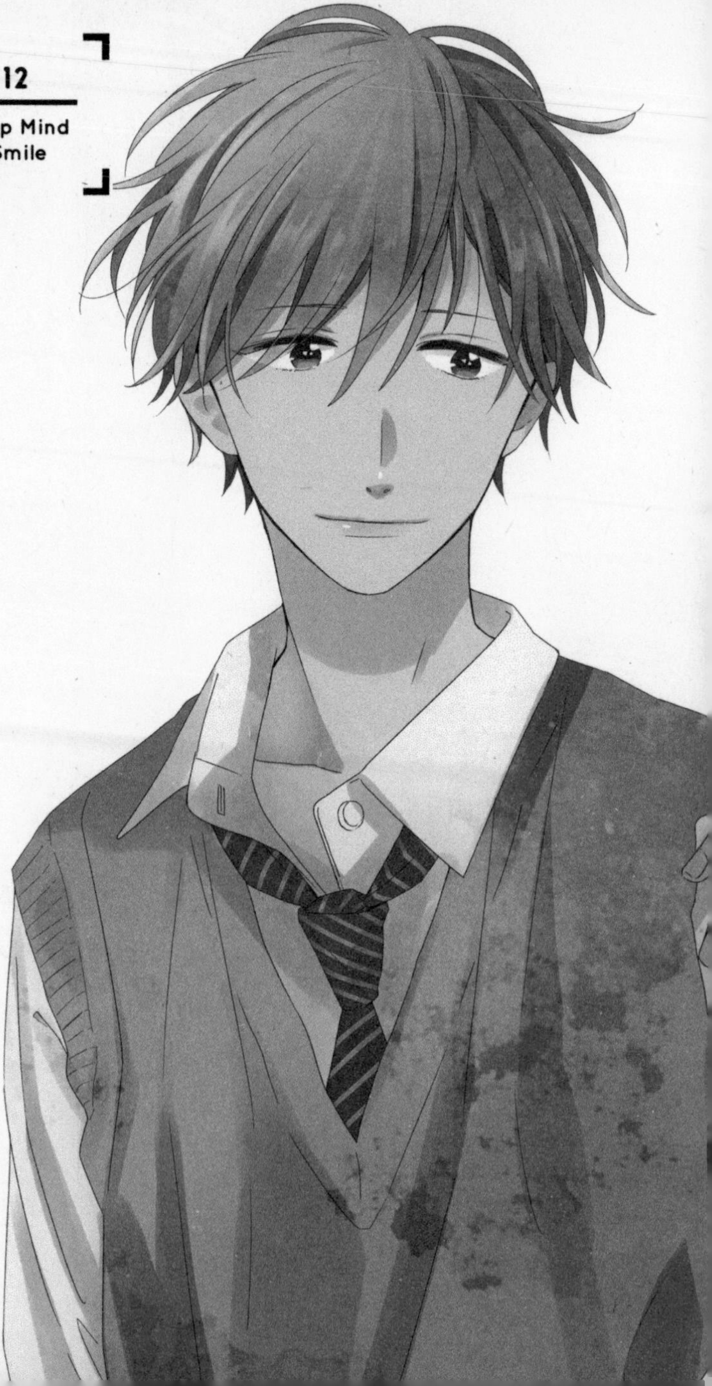

LOVE IN FOCUS

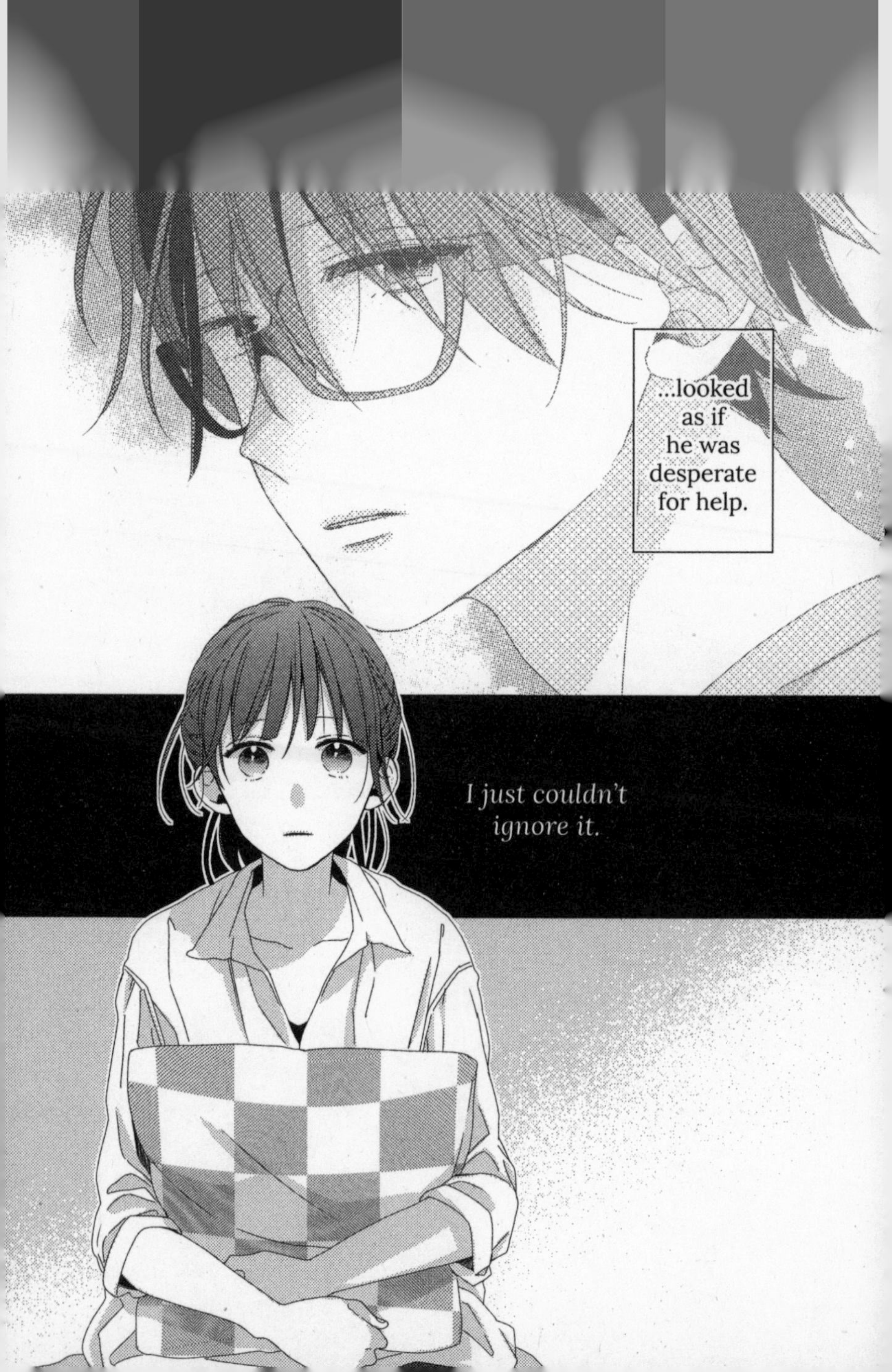
...looked as if he was desperate for help.
I just couldn't ignore it.

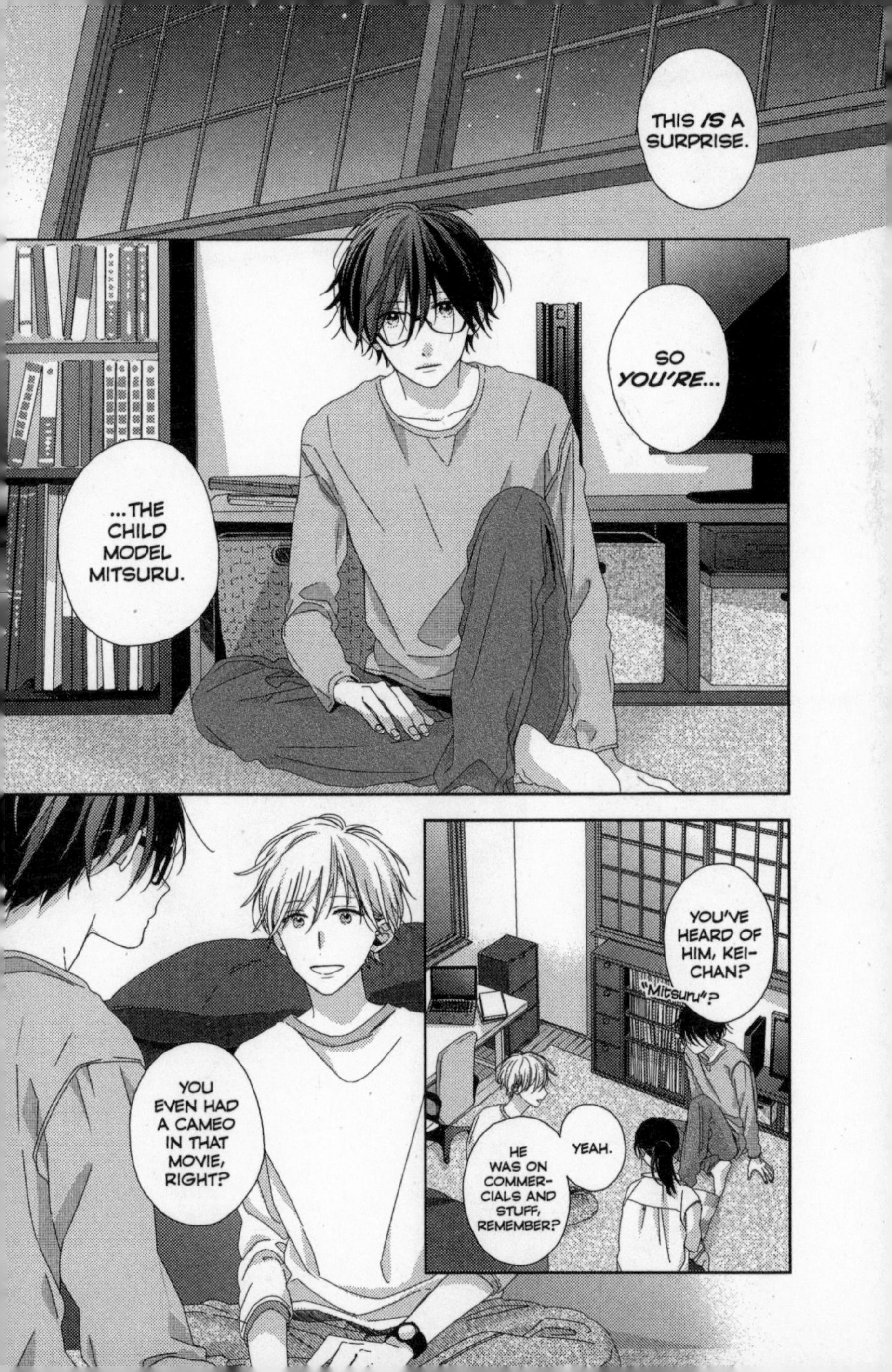
THIS *IS* A SURPRISE.
SO *YOU'RE*...
...THE CHILD MODEL MITSURU.
YOU'VE HEARD OF HIM, KEI-CHAN?
"Mitsuru"?
YEAH.
HE WAS ON COMMERCIALS AND STUFF, REMEMBER?
YOU EVEN HAD A CAMEO IN THAT MOVIE, RIGHT?

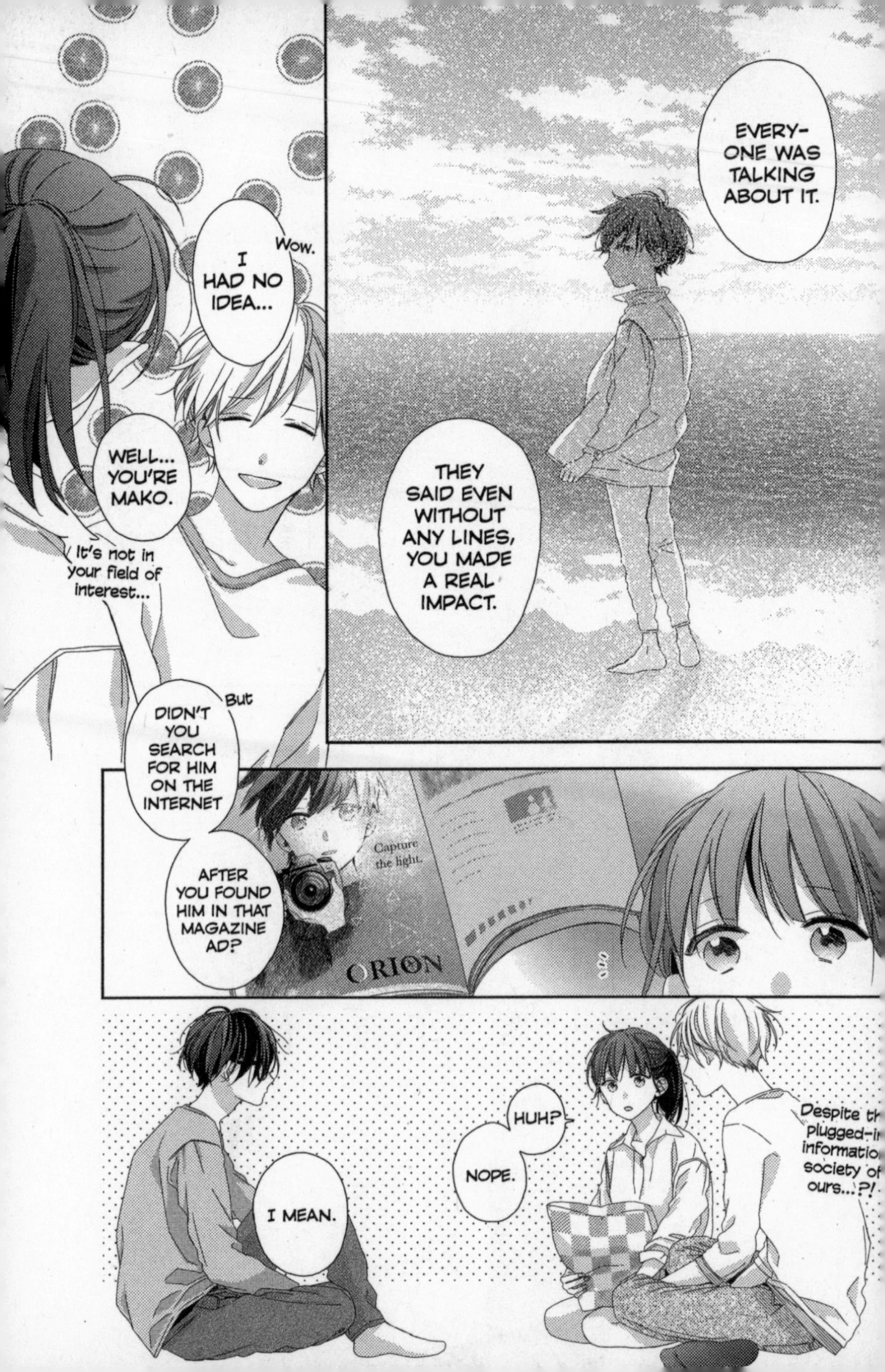
EVERY-ONE WAS TALKING ABOUT IT.
THEY SAID EVEN WITHOUT ANY LINES, YOU MADE A REAL IMPACT.
Wow.
I HAD NO IDEA...
WELL... YOU'RE MAKO.
It's not in your field of interest...
But
DIDN'T YOU SEARCH FOR HIM ON THE INTERNET
AFTER YOU FOUND HIM IN THAT MAGAZINE AD?
Capture the light.
ORION
Despite th plugged-i informatio society of ours...?!
HUH?
NOPE.
I MEAN.

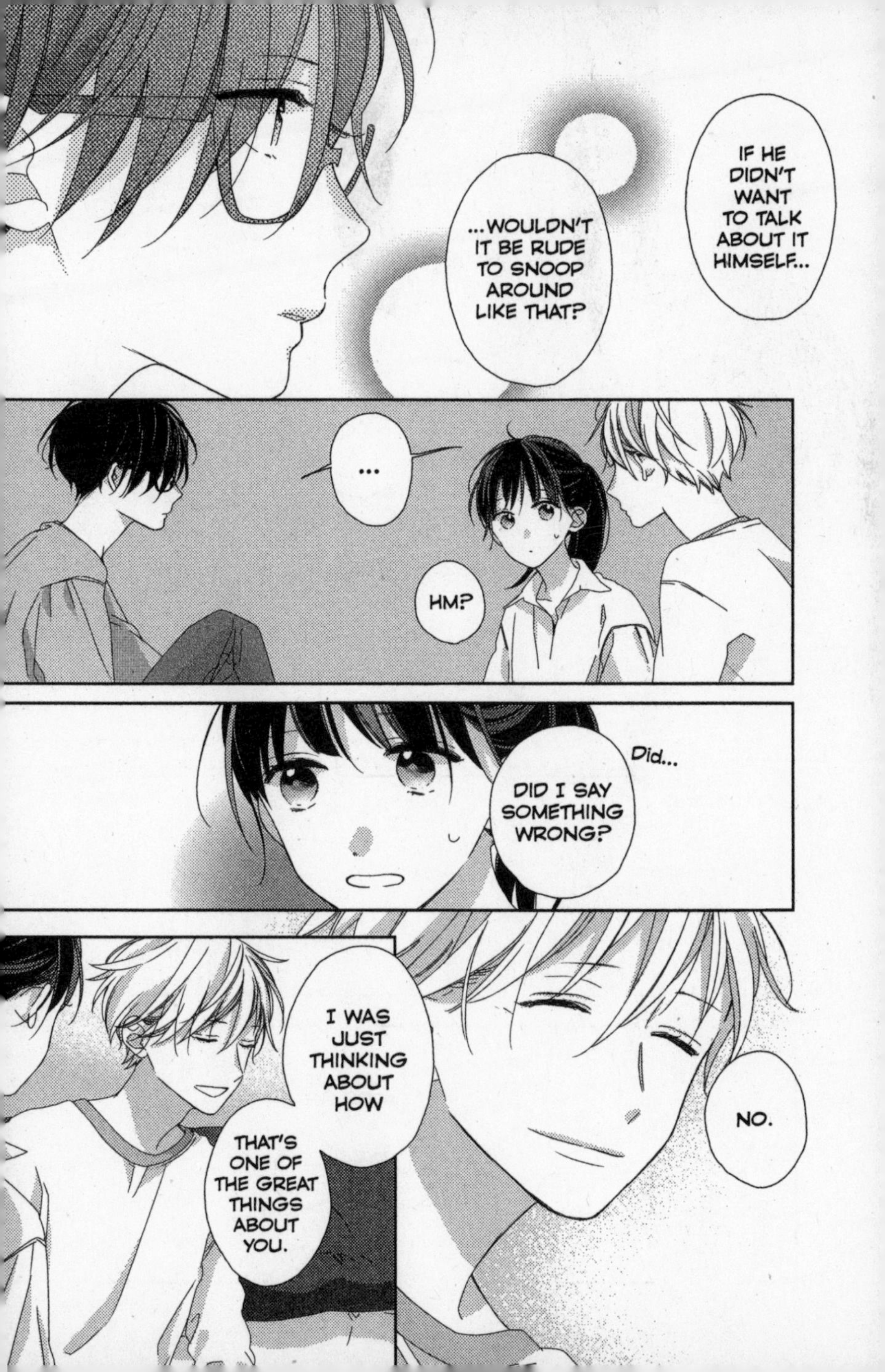
IF HE DIDN'T WANT TO TALK ABOUT IT HIMSELF...
...WOULDN'T IT BE RUDE TO SNOOP AROUND LIKE THAT?
...
HM?
Did...
DID I SAY SOMETHING WRONG?
NO.
I WAS JUST THINKING ABOUT HOW
THAT'S ONE OF THE GREAT THINGS ABOUT YOU.

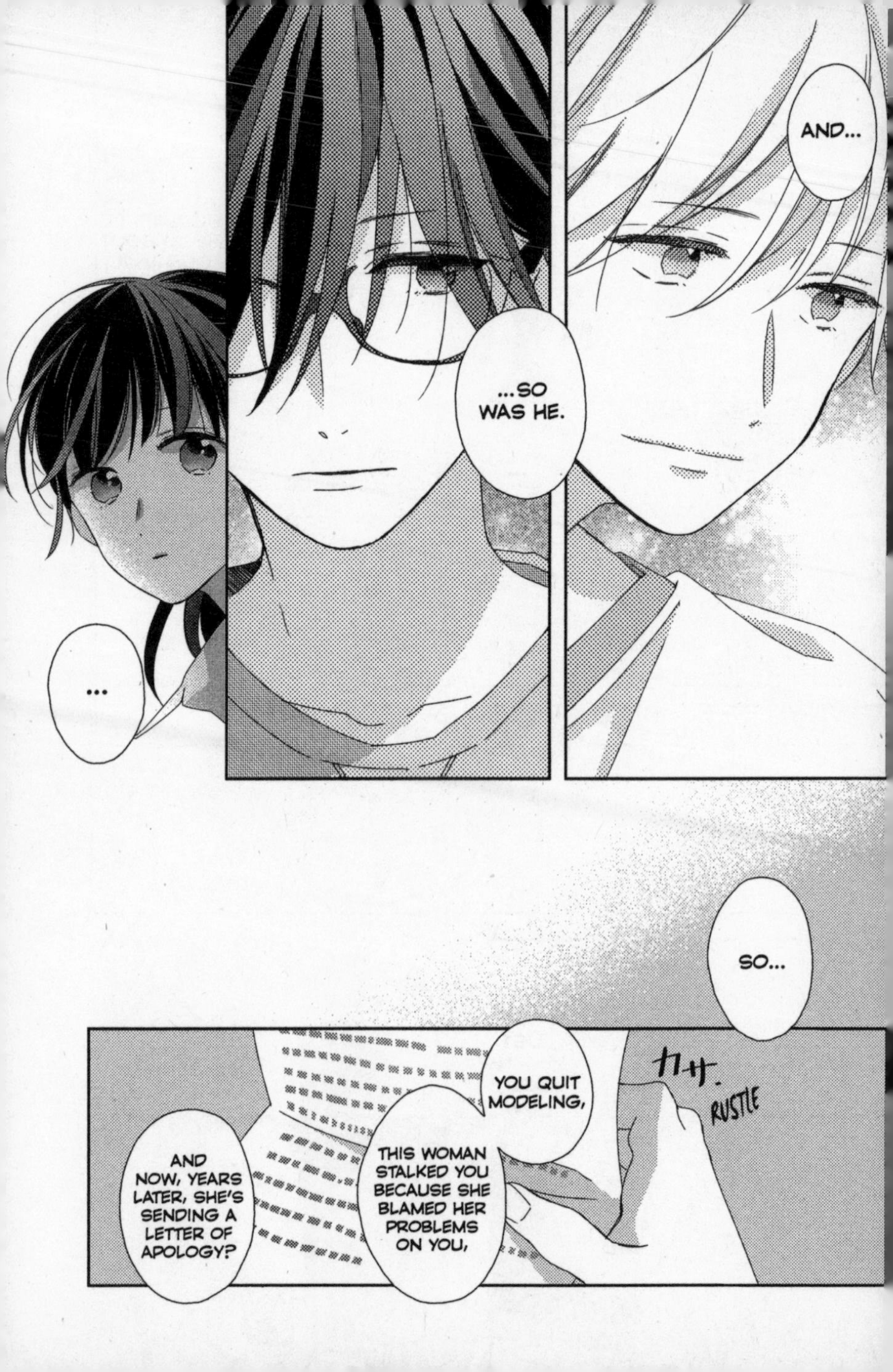
AND...
...SO WAS HE.
...
SO...
カサ
RUSTLE
YOU QUIT MODELING,
THIS WOMAN STALKED YOU BECAUSE SHE BLAMED HER PROBLEMS ON YOU,
AND NOW, YEARS LATER, SHE'S SENDING A LETTER OF APOLOGY?

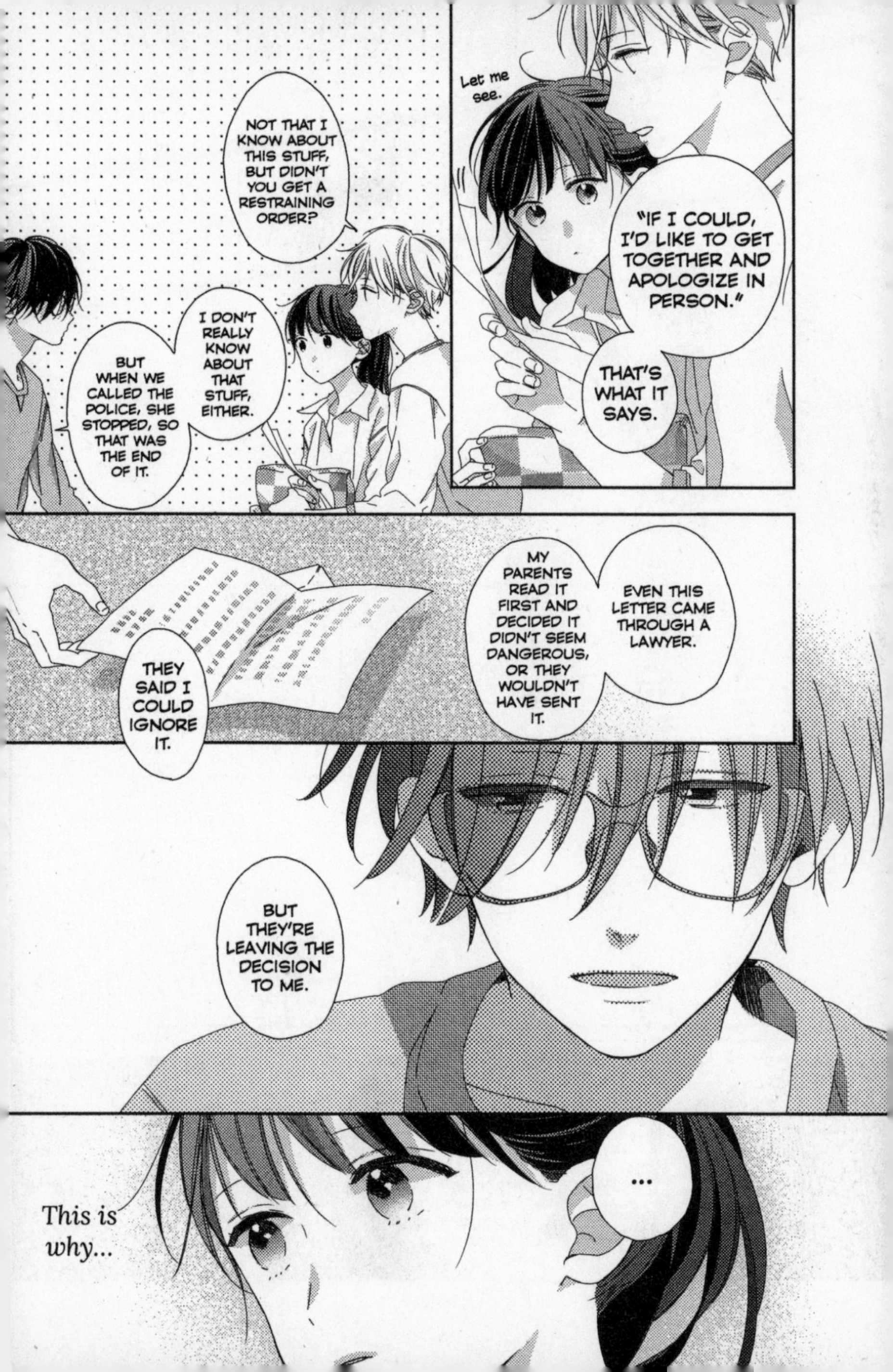
Let me see.
"IF I COULD, I'D LIKE TO GET TOGETHER AND APOLOGIZE IN PERSON."
THAT'S WHAT IT SAYS.
NOT THAT I KNOW ABOUT THIS STUFF, BUT DIDN'T YOU GET A RESTRAINING ORDER?
I DON'T REALLY KNOW ABOUT THAT STUFF, EITHER.
BUT WHEN WE CALLED THE POLICE, SHE STOPPED, SO THAT WAS THE END OF IT.
EVEN THIS LETTER CAME THROUGH A LAWYER.
MY PARENTS READ IT FIRST AND DECIDED IT DIDN'T SEEM DANGEROUS, OR THEY WOULDN'T HAVE SENT IT.
THEY SAID I COULD IGNORE IT.
BUT THEY'RE LEAVING THE DECISION TO ME.
...
This is why...

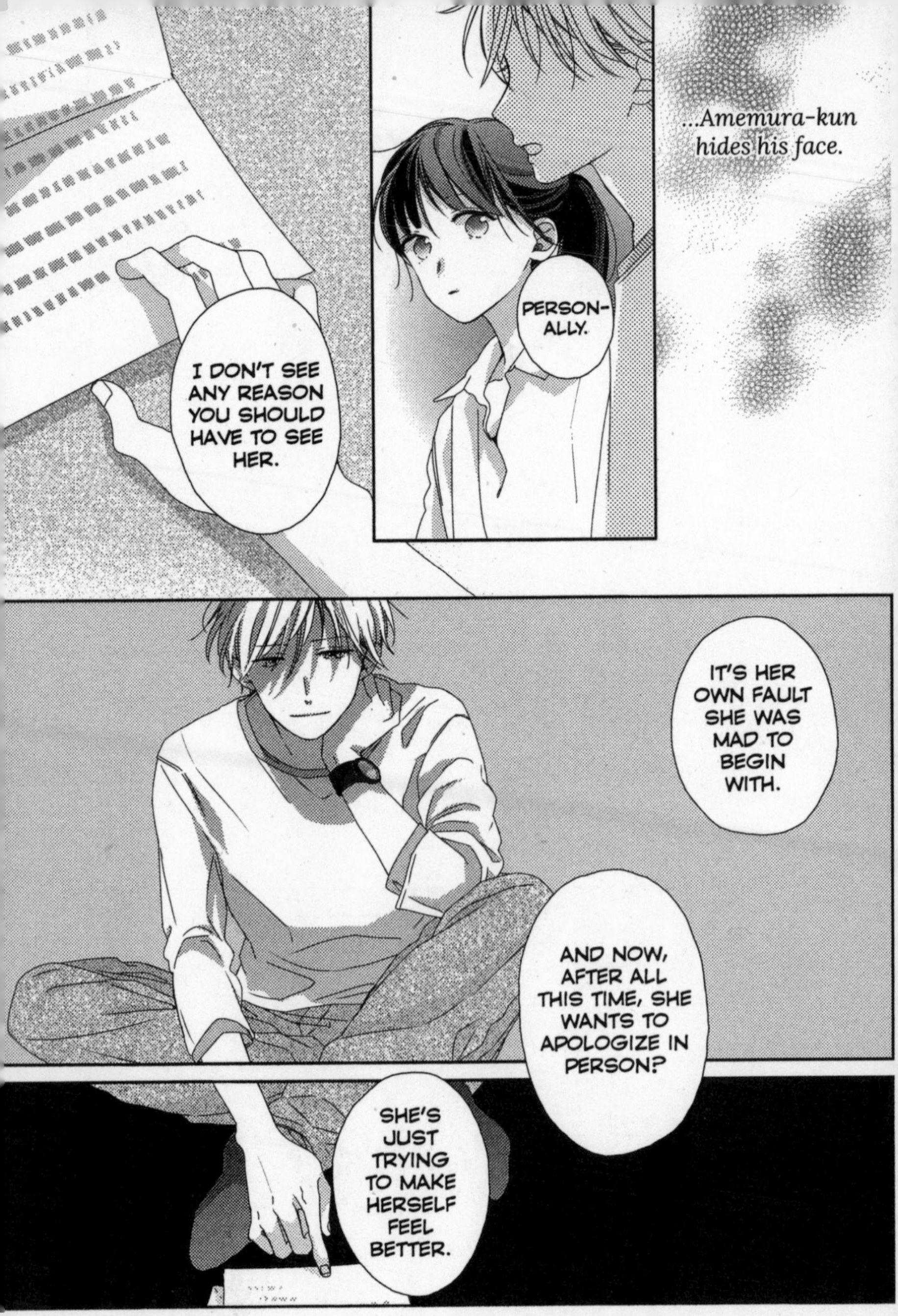
...Amemura-kun hides his face.
PERSON-ALLY.
I DON'T SEE ANY REASON YOU SHOULD HAVE TO SEE HER.
IT'S HER OWN FAULT SHE WAS MAD TO BEGIN WITH.
AND NOW, AFTER ALL THIS TIME, SHE WANTS TO APOLOGIZE IN PERSON?
SHE'S JUST TRYING TO MAKE HERSELF FEEL BETTER.

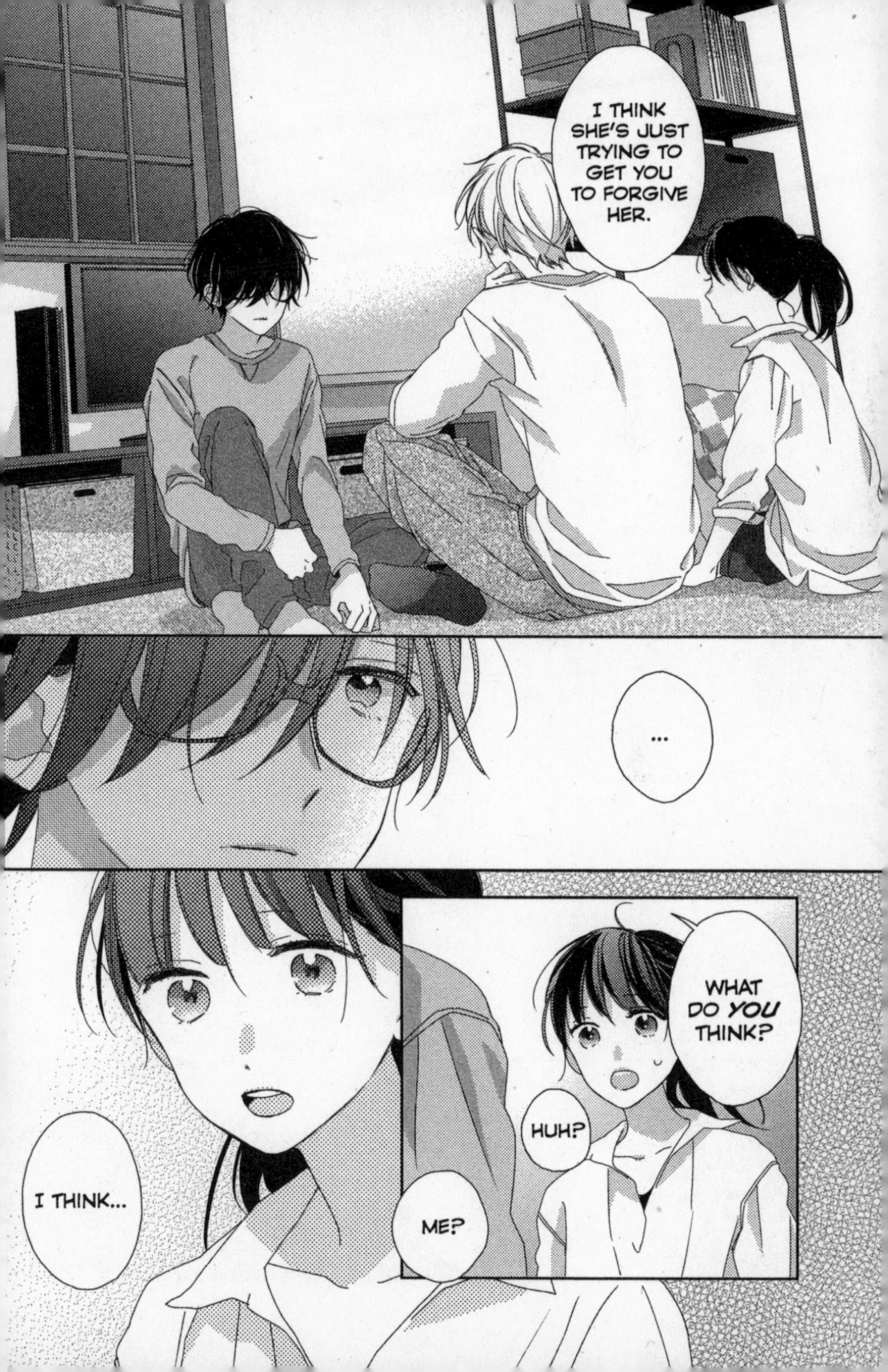
I THINK SHE'S JUST TRYING TO GET YOU TO FORGIVE HER.
...
WHAT DO *YOU* THINK?
HUH?
ME?
I THINK...

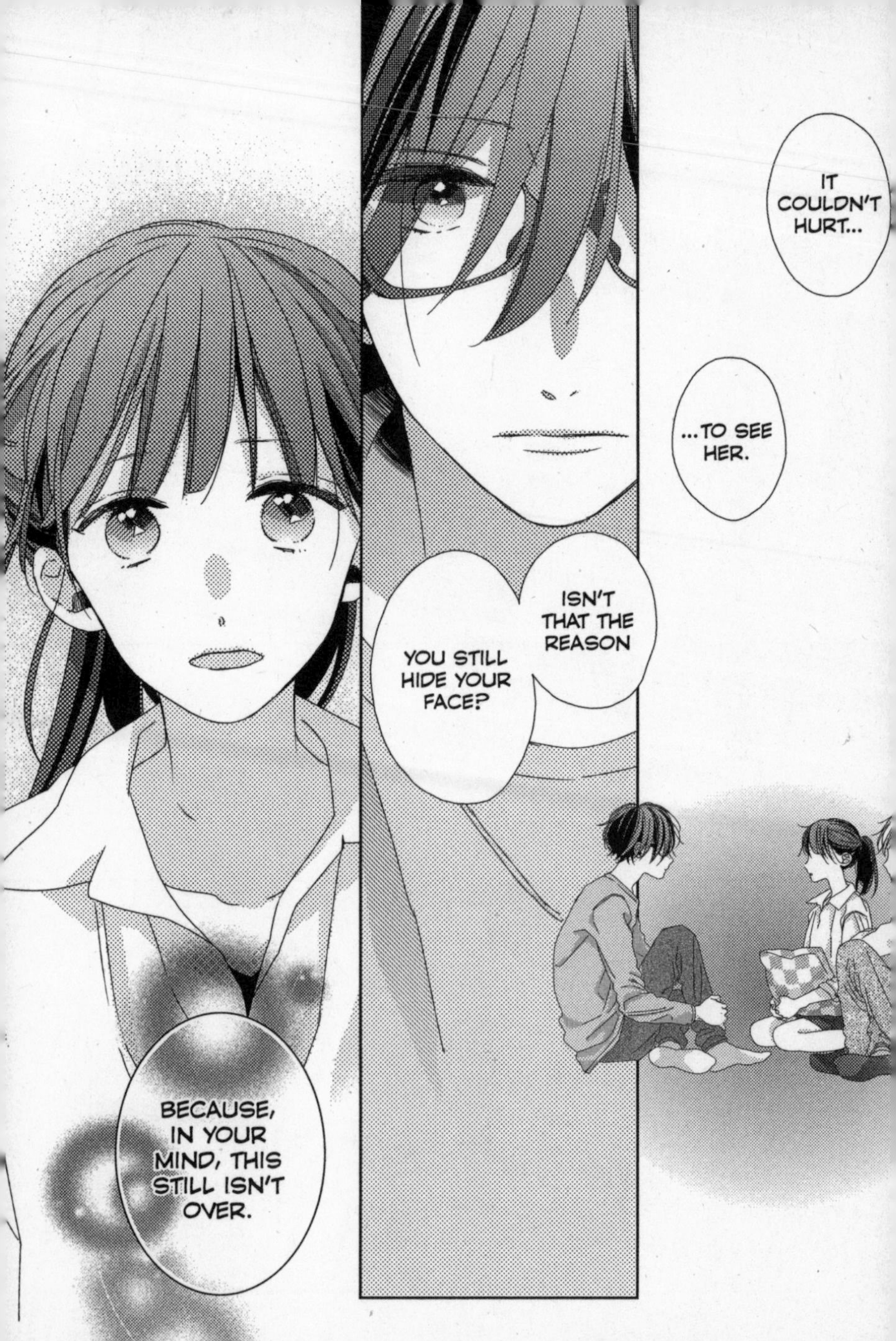
IT COULDN'T HURT...
...TO SEE HER.
ISN'T THAT THE REASON
YOU STILL HIDE YOUR FACE?
BECAUSE, IN YOUR MIND, THIS STILL ISN'T OVER.

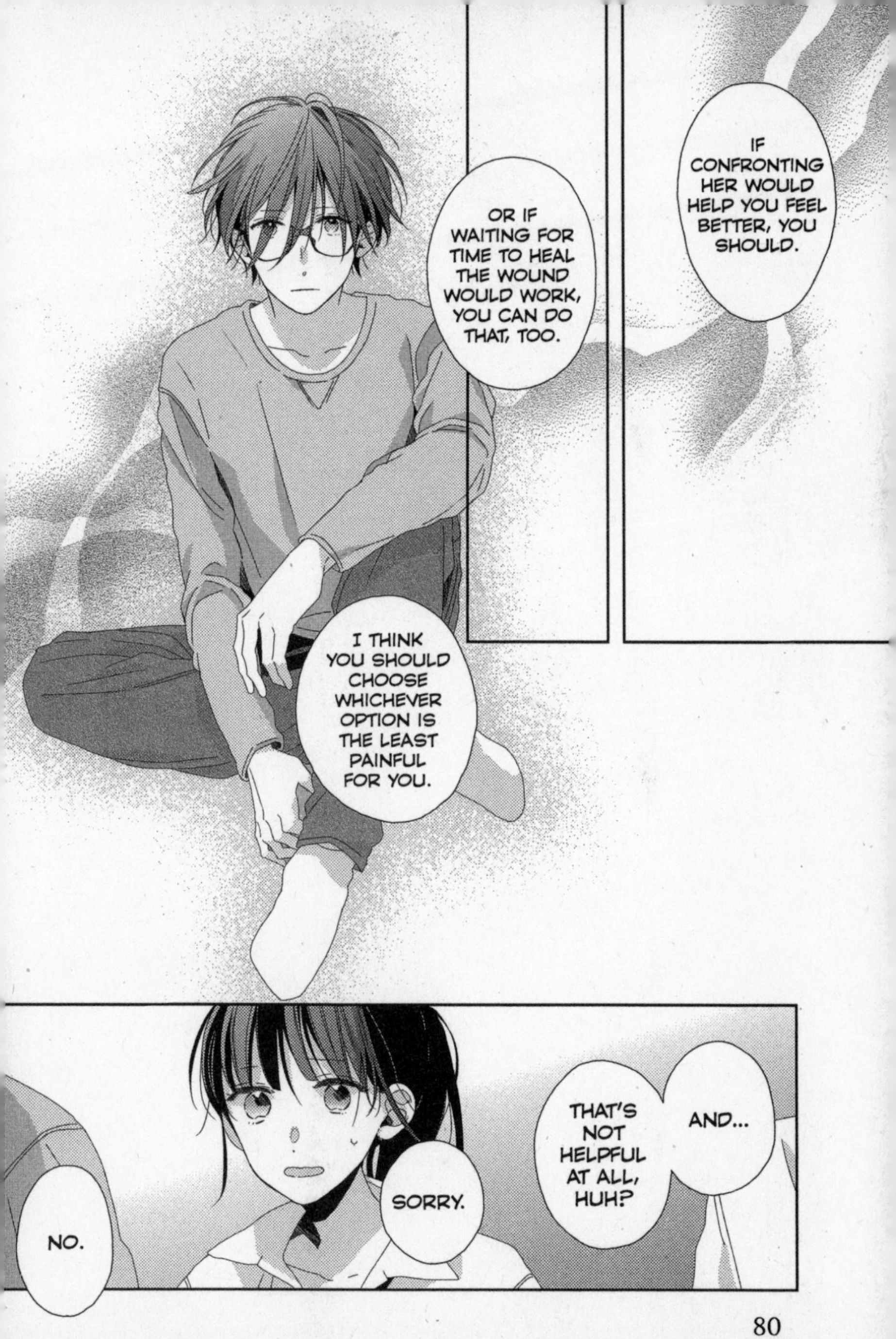
IF CONFRONTING HER WOULD HELP YOU FEEL BETTER, YOU SHOULD.
OR IF WAITING FOR TIME TO HEAL THE WOUND WOULD WORK, YOU CAN DO THAT, TOO.
I THINK YOU SHOULD CHOOSE WHICHEVER OPTION IS THE LEAST PAINFUL FOR YOU.
AND...
THAT'S NOT HELPFUL AT ALL, HUH?
SORRY.
NO.

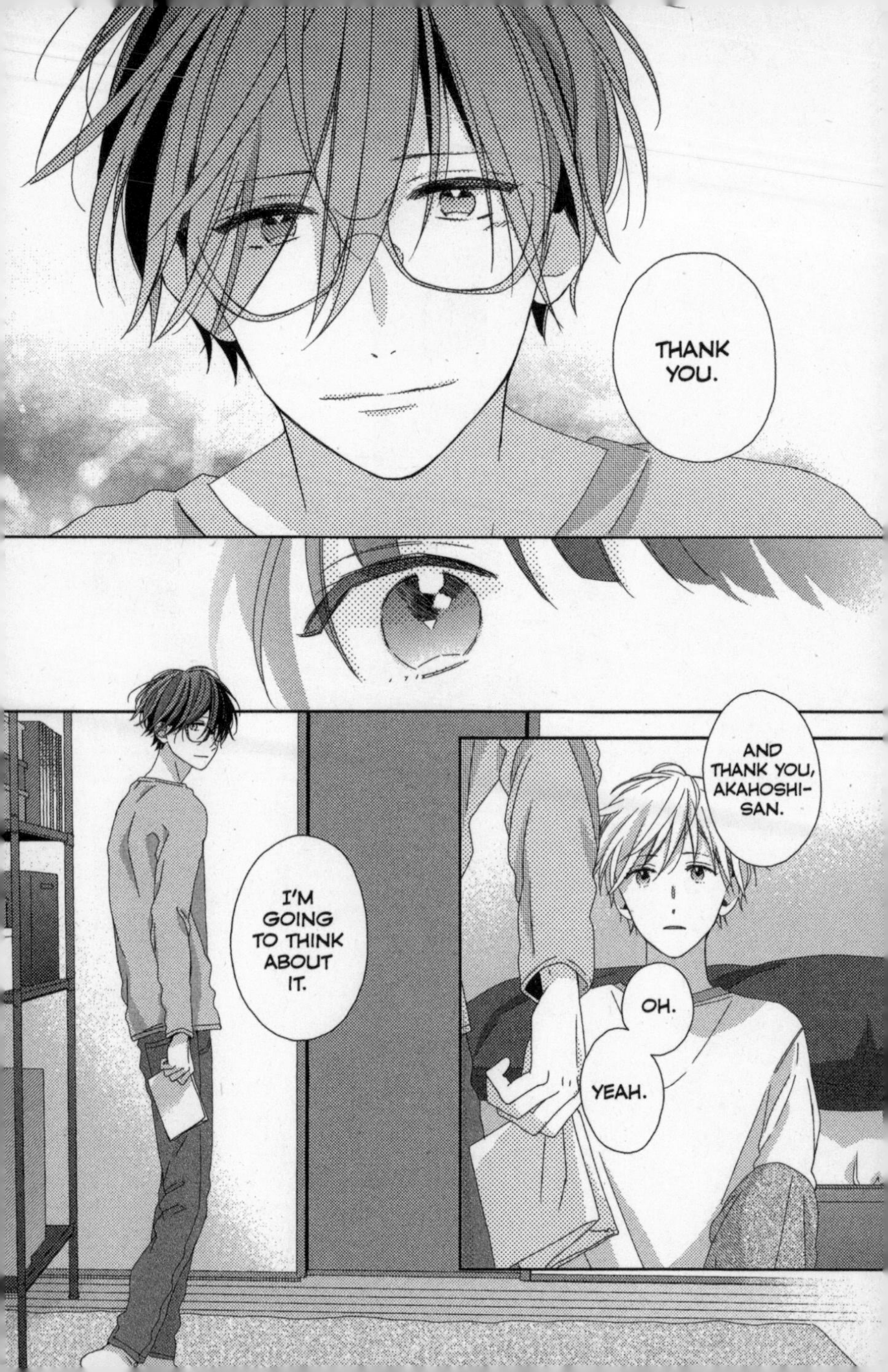
THANK YOU.
AND THANK YOU, AKAHOSHI-SAN.
OH.
YEAH.
I'M GOING TO THINK ABOUT IT.

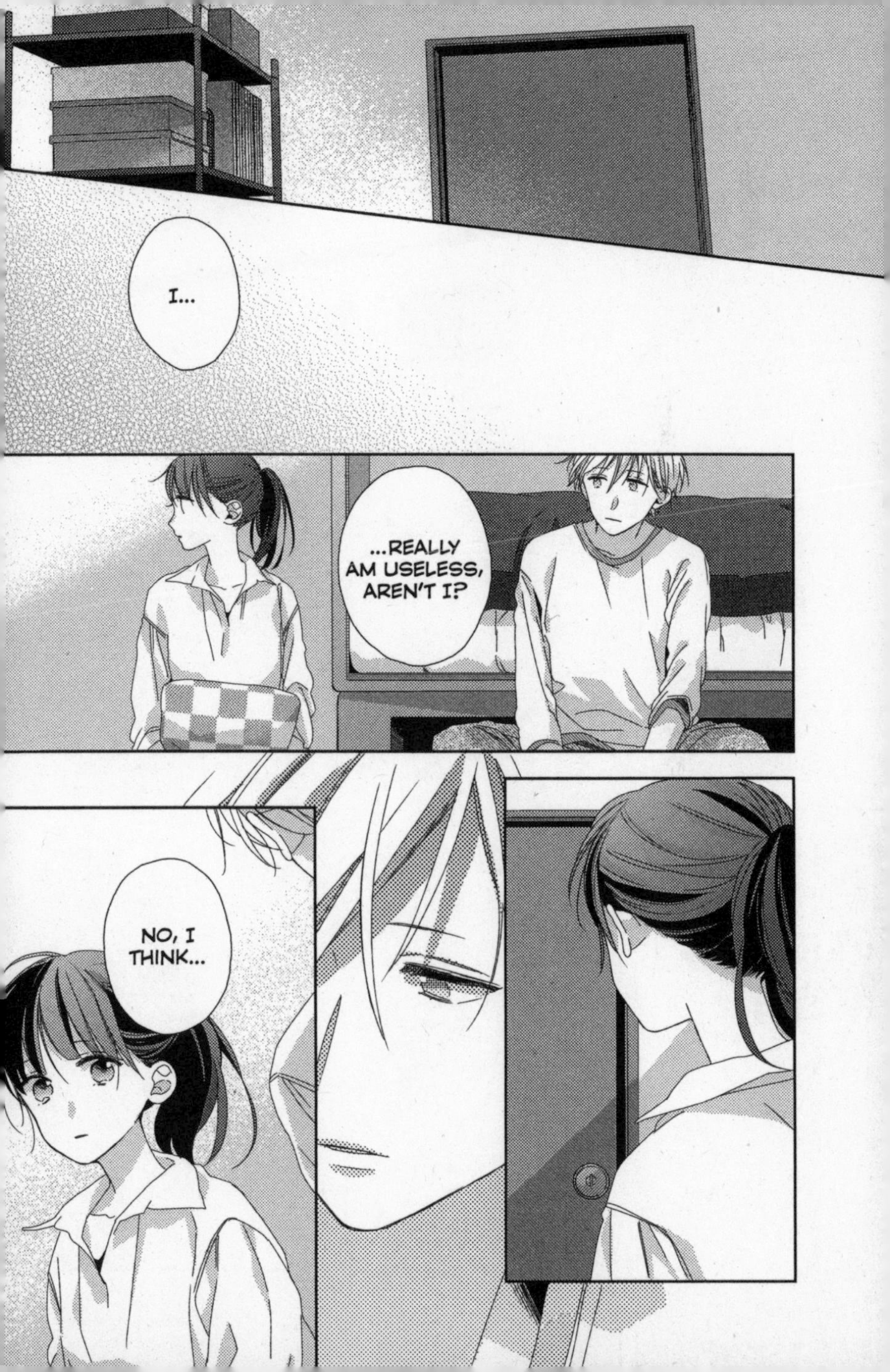
I...
...REALLY AM USELESS, AREN'T I?
NO, I THINK...

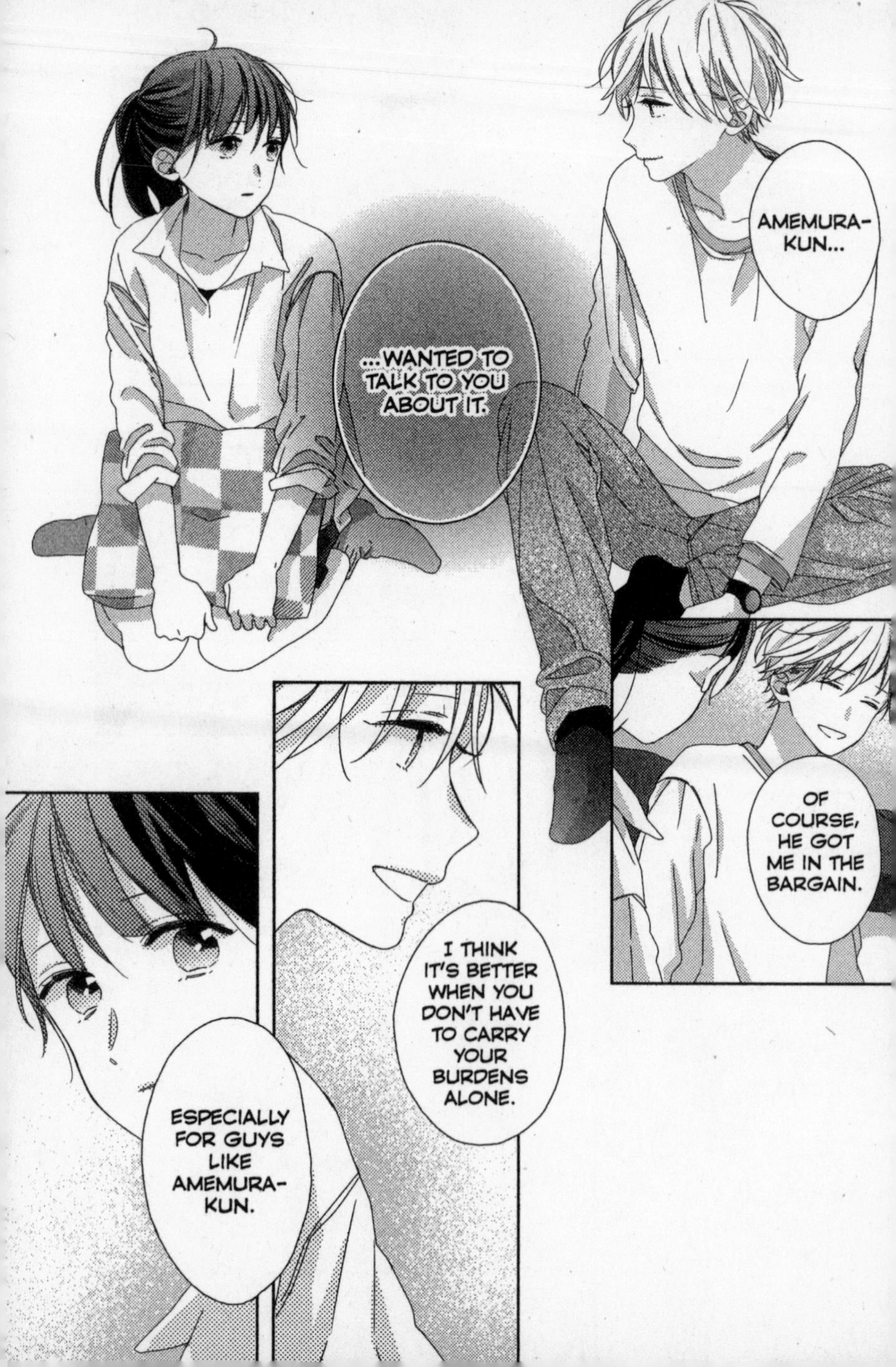
AMEMURA-KUN...
...WANTED TO TALK TO YOU ABOUT IT.
OF COURSE, HE GOT ME IN THE BARGAIN.
I THINK IT'S BETTER WHEN YOU DON'T HAVE TO CARRY YOUR BURDENS ALONE.
ESPECIALLY FOR GUYS LIKE AMEMURA-KUN.

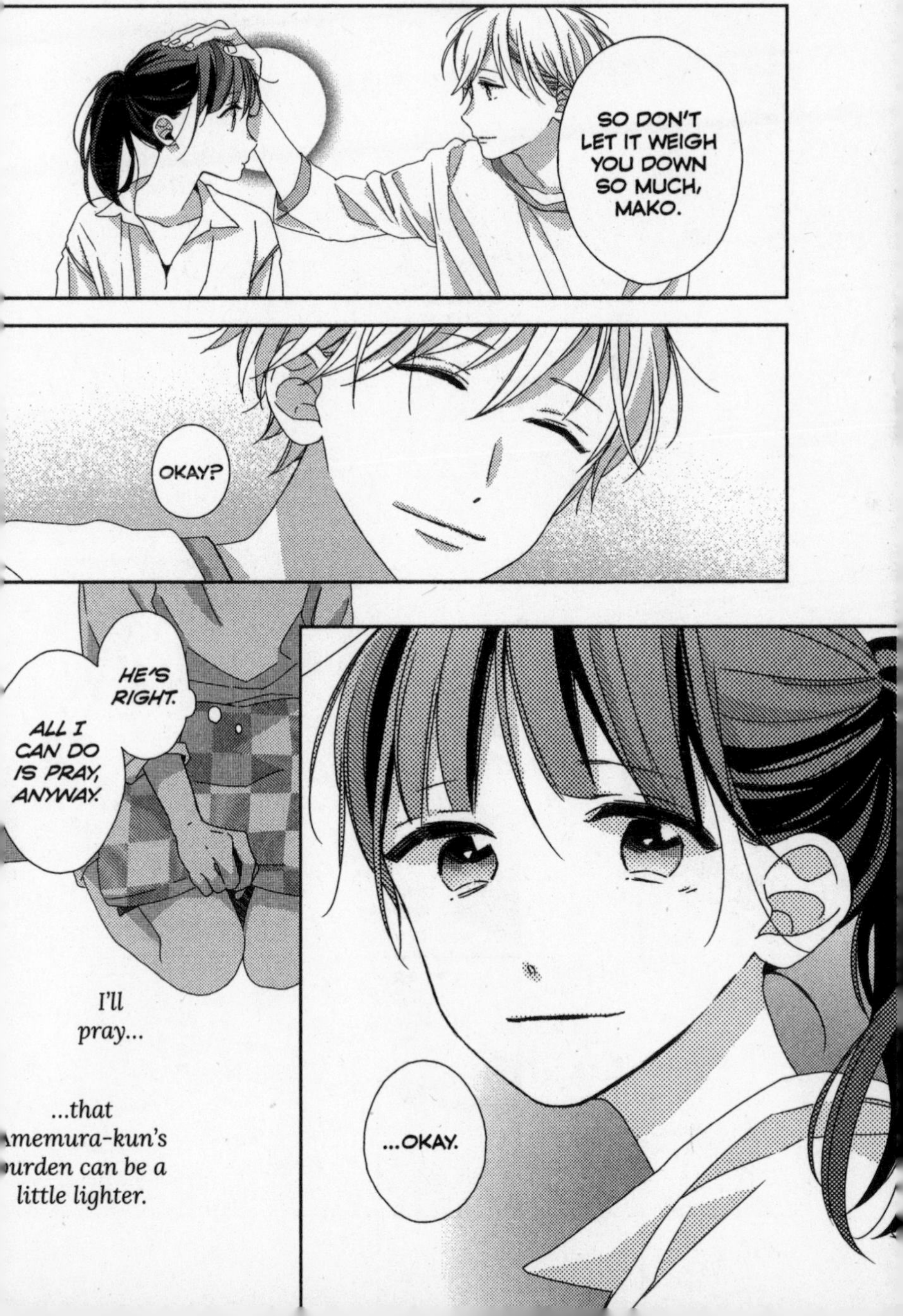
SO DON'T LET IT WEIGH YOU DOWN SO MUCH, MAKO.
OKAY?
...OKAY.
HE'S RIGHT.
ALL I CAN DO IS PRAY, ANYWAY.
I'll pray...
...that memura-kun's urden can be a little lighter.

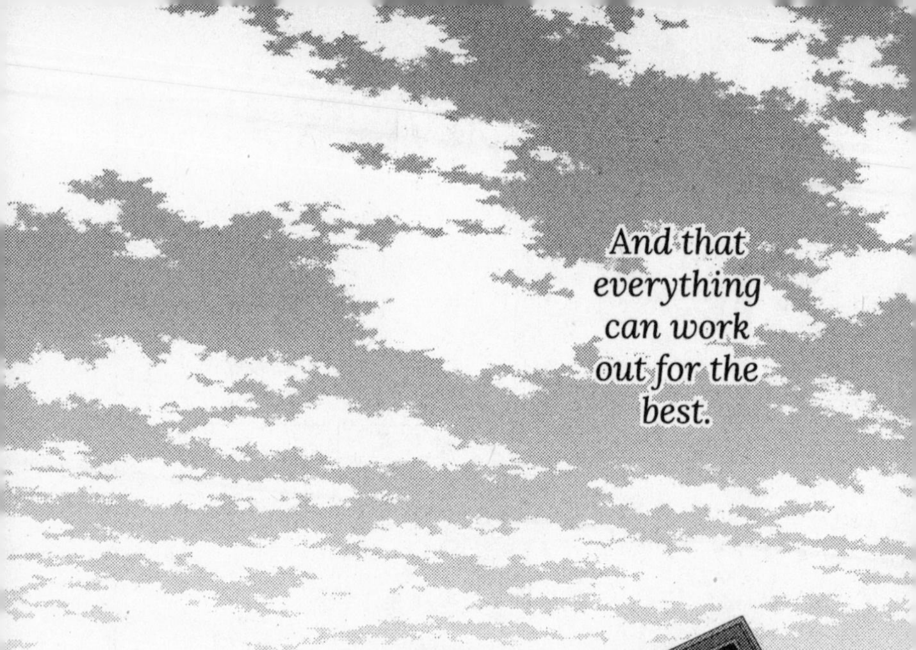
And that everything can work out for the best.
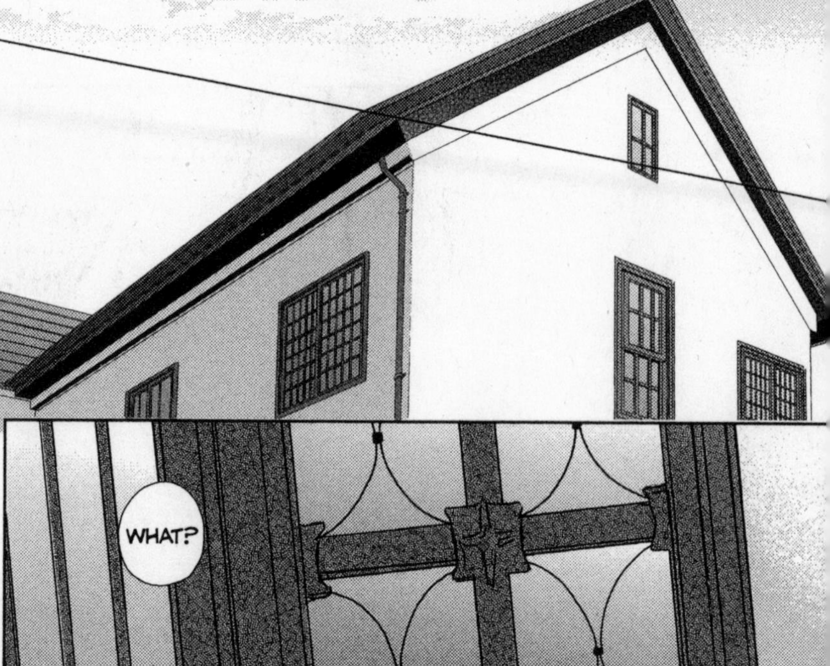
WHAT?

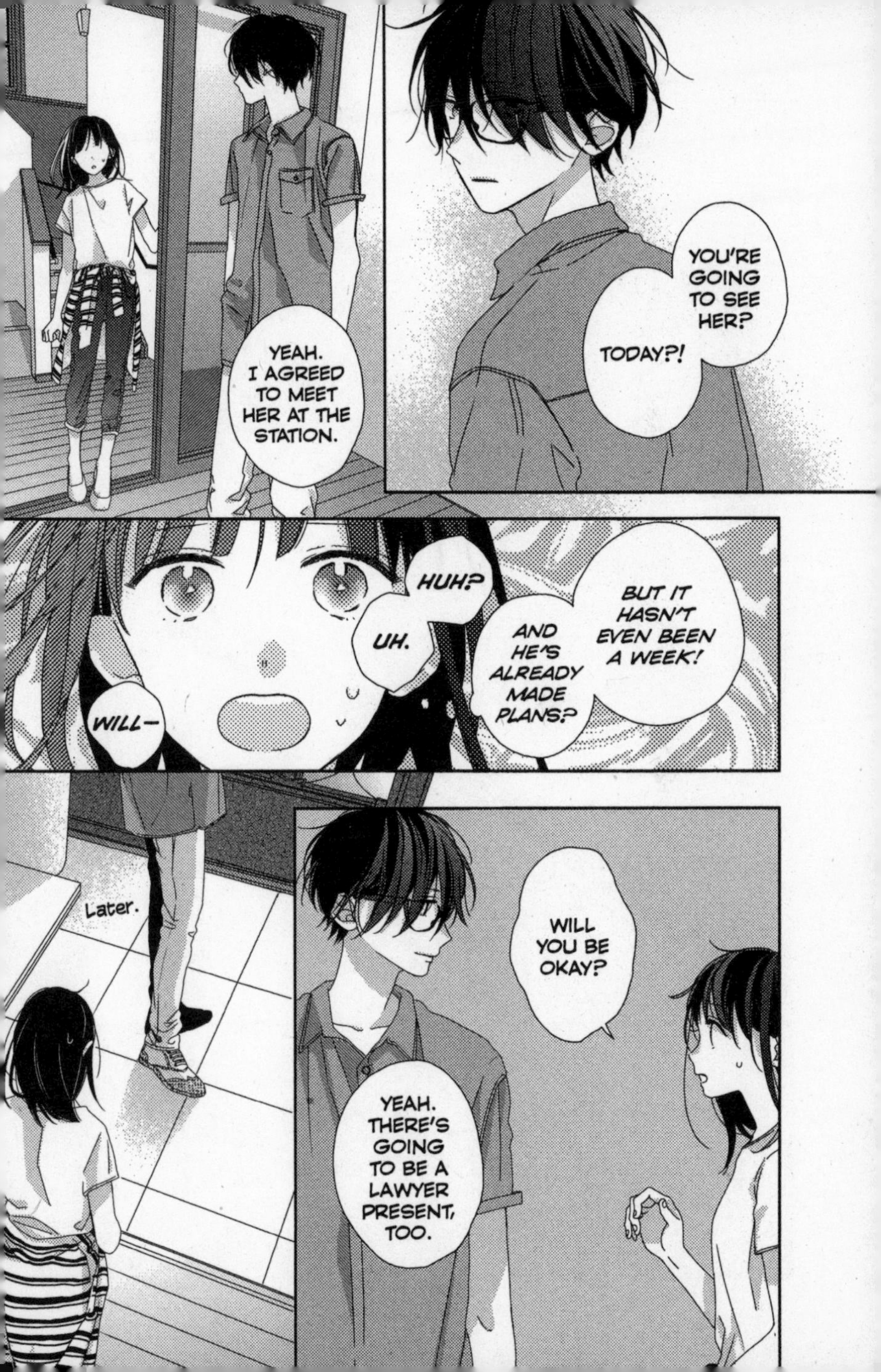
YOU'RE GOING TO SEE HER?
TODAY?!
YEAH. I AGREED TO MEET HER AT THE STATION.
BUT IT HASN'T EVEN BEEN A WEEK!
AND HE'S ALREADY MADE PLANS?
HUH?
UH.
WILL–
WILL YOU BE OKAY?
YEAH. THERE'S GOING TO BE A LAWYER PRESENT, TOO.
Later.

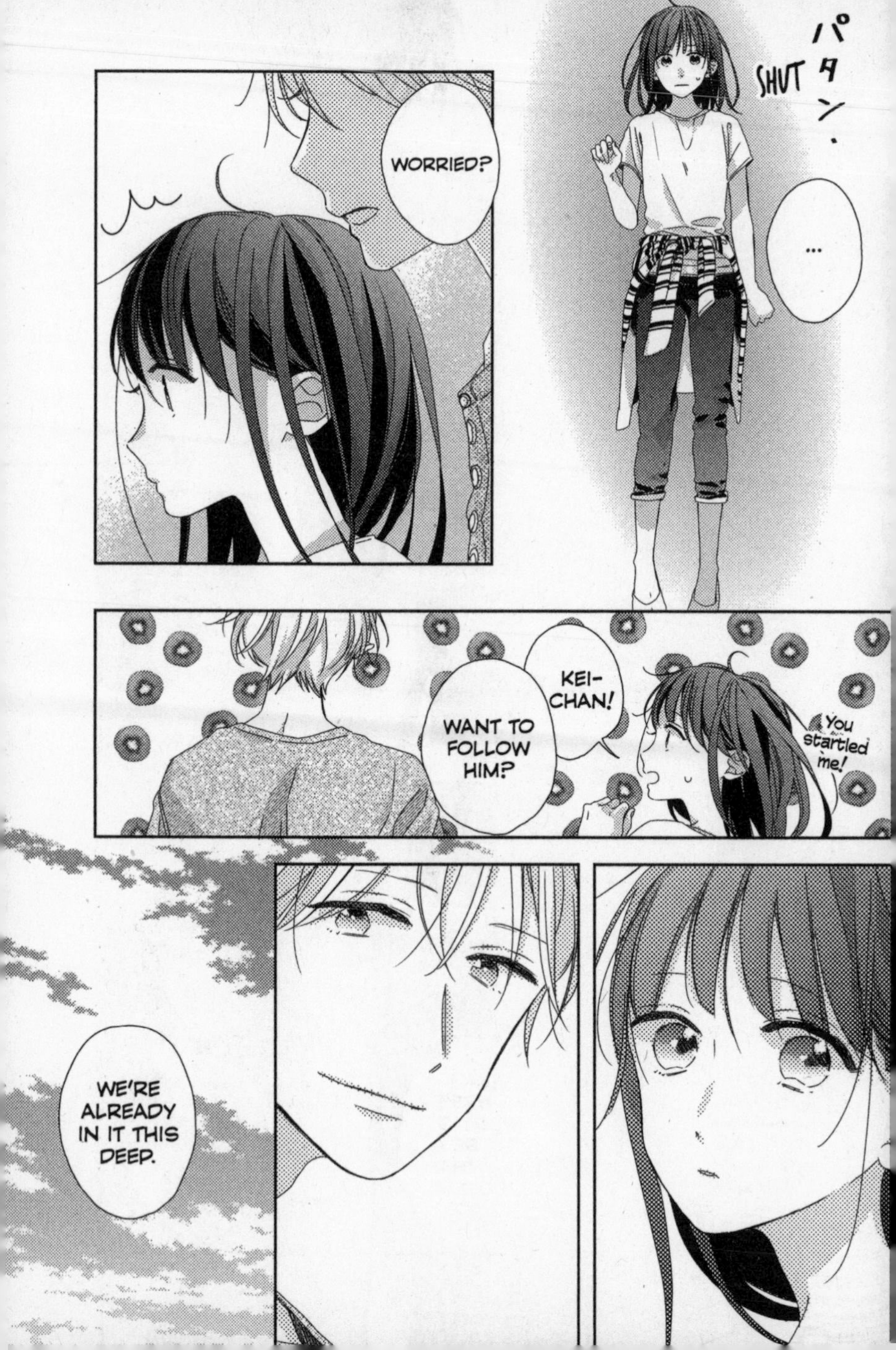
パタン
SHUT
...
WORRIED?
KEI-CHAN!
You startled me!
WANT TO FOLLOW HIM?
WE'RE ALREADY IN IT THIS DEEP.

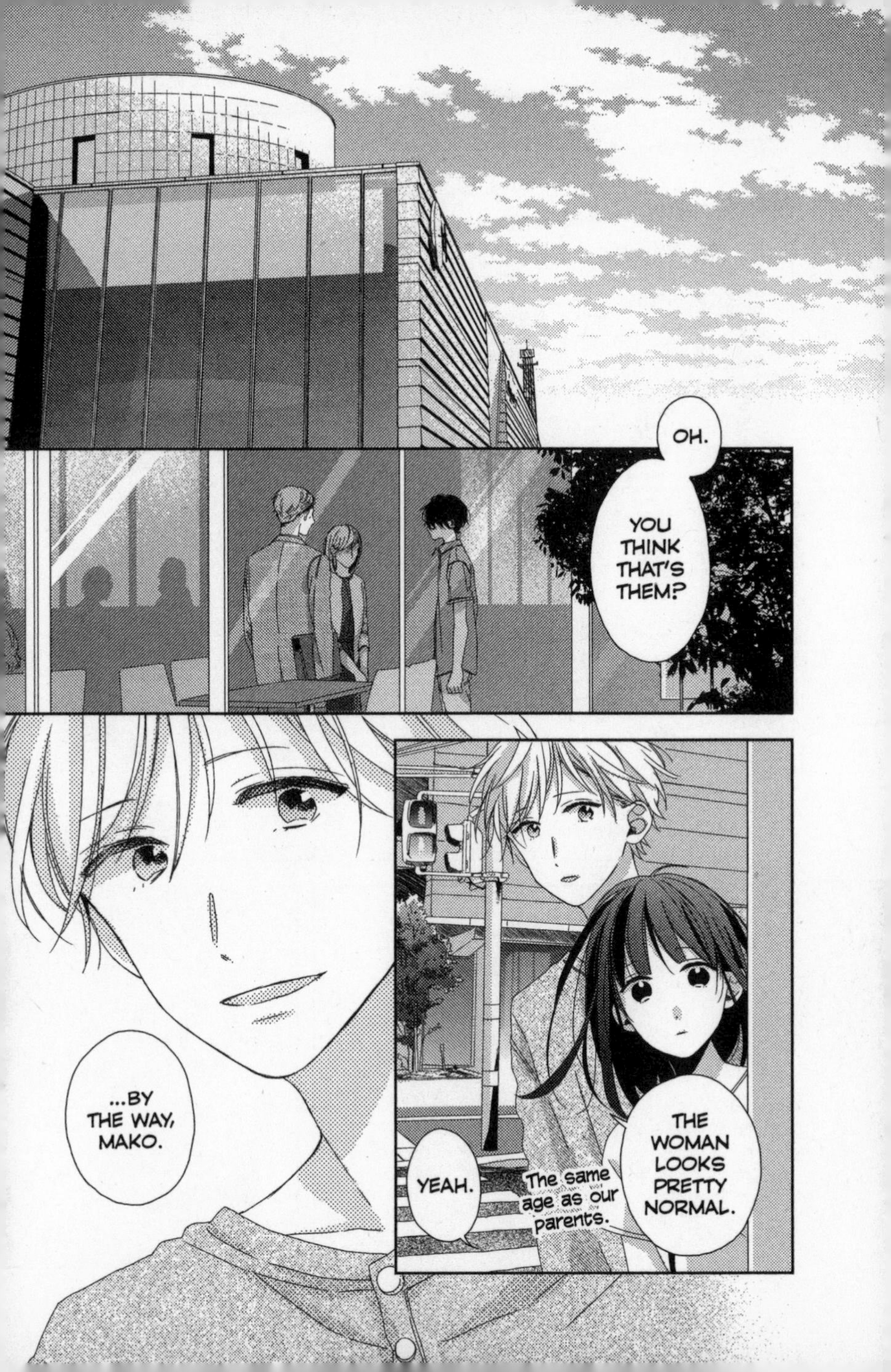
OH.
YOU THINK THAT'S THEM?
THE WOMAN LOOKS PRETTY NORMAL.
The same age as our parents.
YEAH.
...BY THE WAY, MAKO.

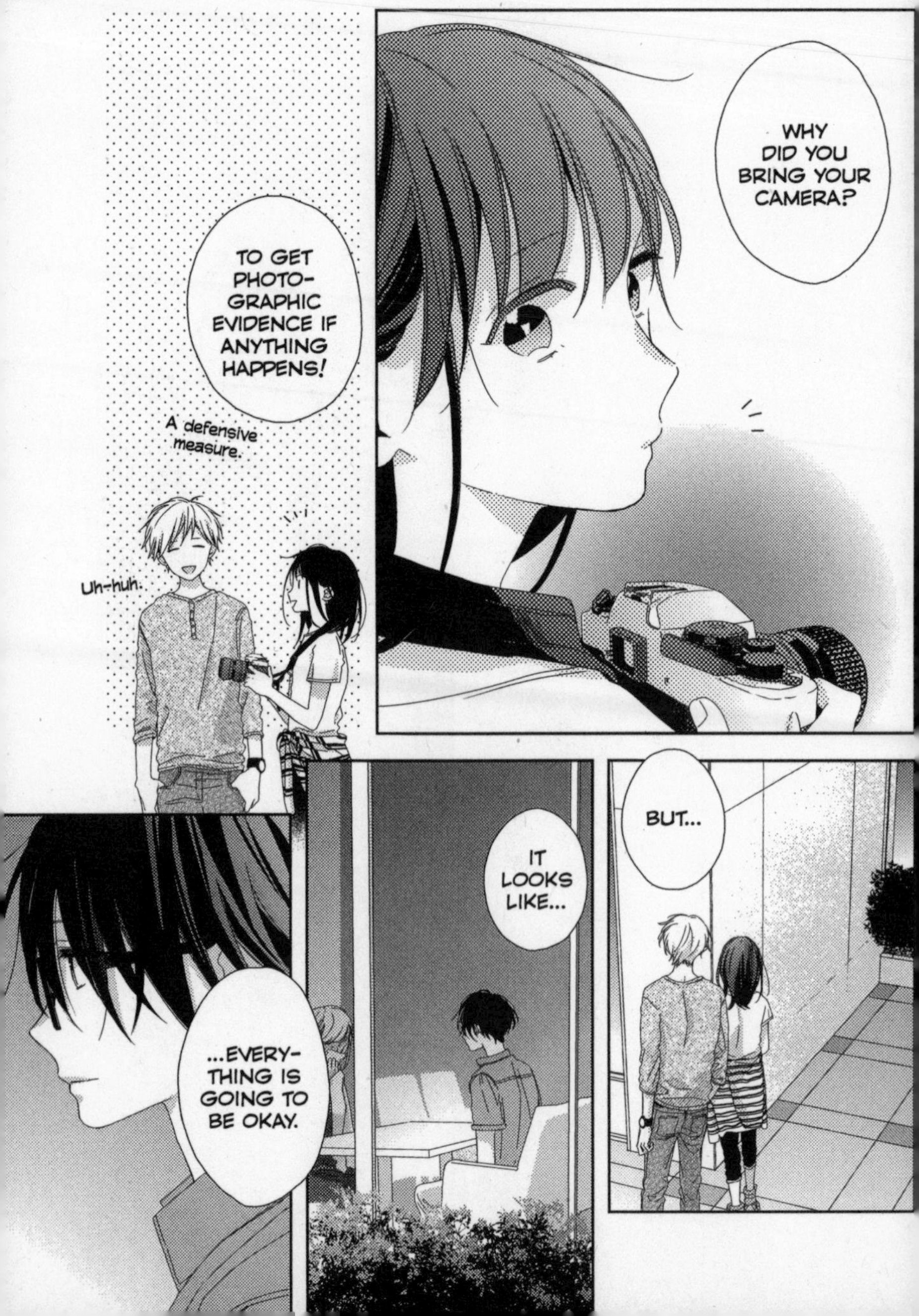
WHY DID YOU BRING YOUR CAMERA?
TO GET PHOTO-GRAPHIC EVIDENCE IF ANYTHING HAPPENS!
A defensive measure.
Uh-huh.
BUT...
IT LOOKS LIKE...
...EVERY-THING IS GOING TO BE OKAY.

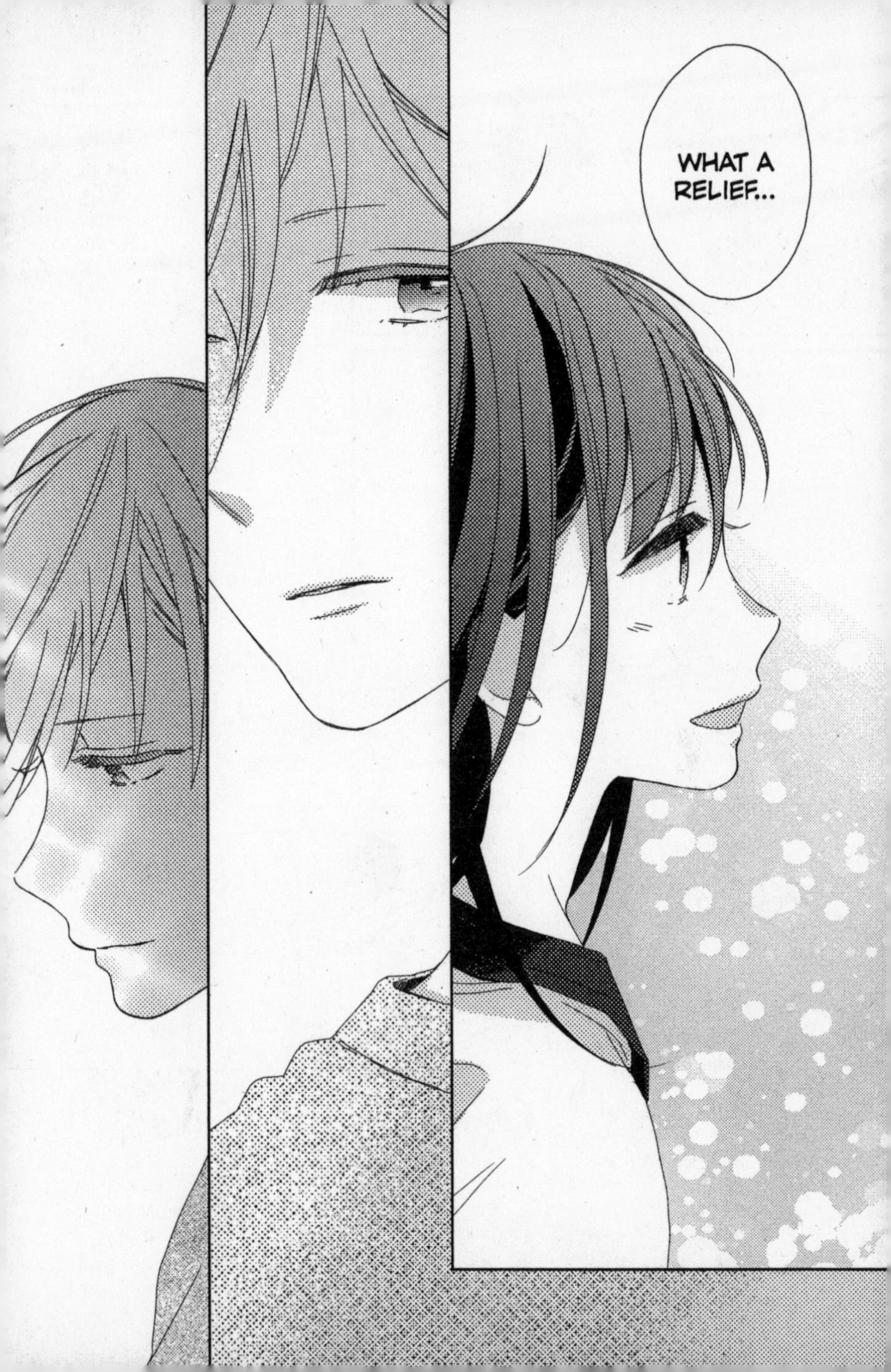
WHAT A RELIEF...

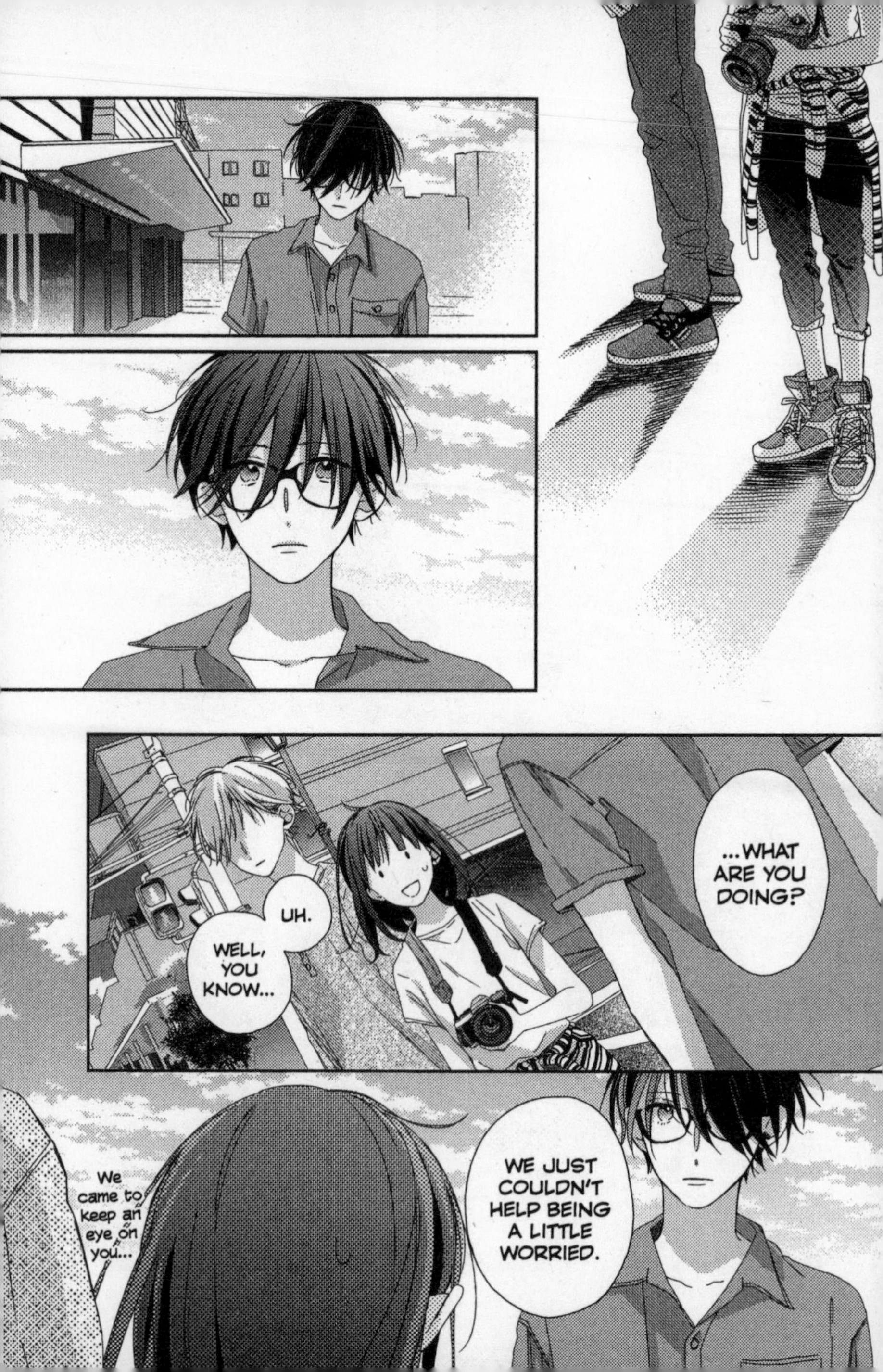
...WHAT ARE YOU DOING?
UH.
WELL, YOU KNOW...
WE JUST COULDN'T HELP BEING A LITTLE WORRIED.
We came to keep an eye on you...

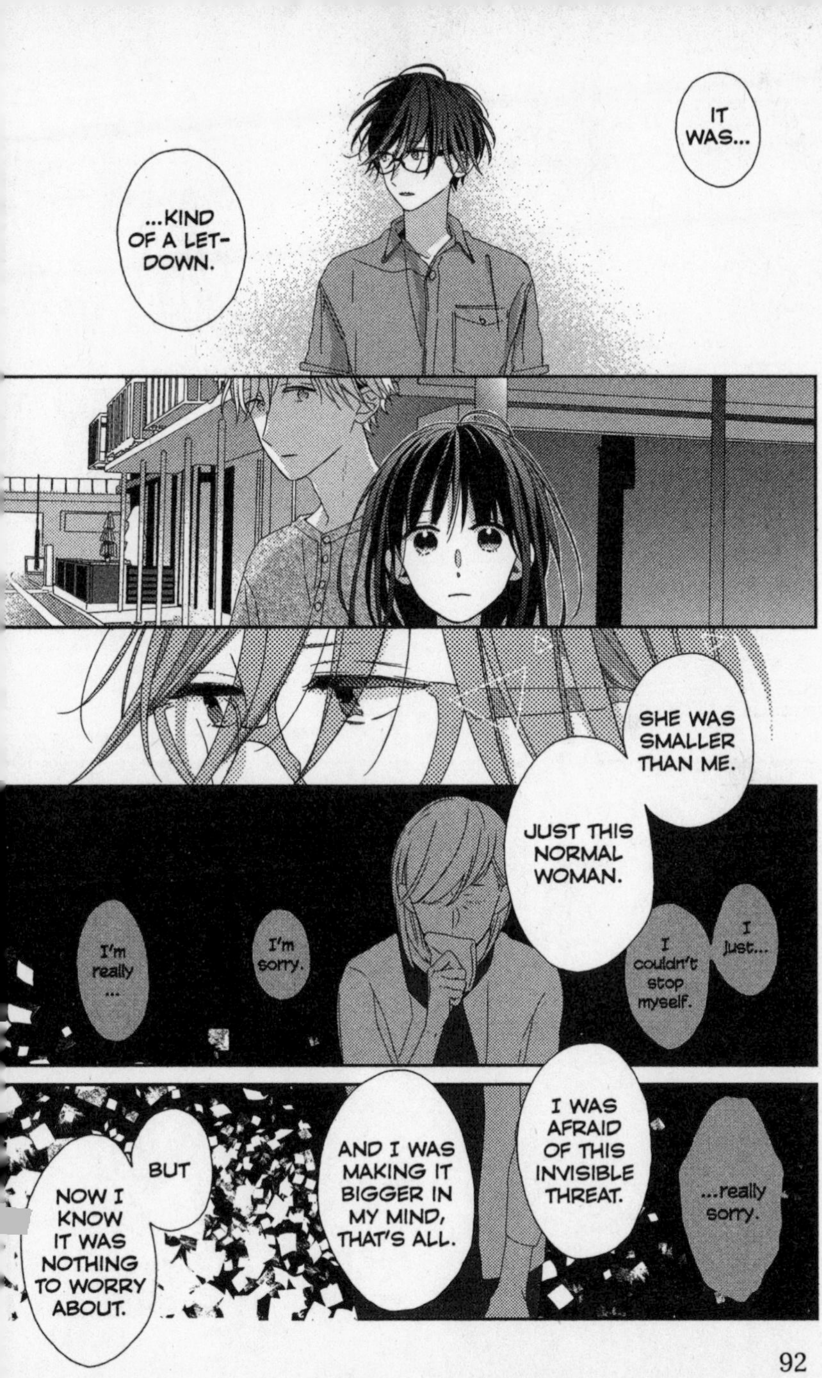
IT WAS...
...KIND OF A LET-DOWN.
SHE WAS SMALLER THAN ME.
JUST THIS NORMAL WOMAN.
I just...
I couldn't stop myself.
I'm sorry.
I'm really ...
...really sorry.
I WAS AFRAID OF THIS INVISIBLE THREAT.
AND I WAS MAKING IT BIGGER IN MY MIND, THAT'S ALL.
BUT
NOW I KNOW IT WAS NOTHING TO WORRY ABOUT.

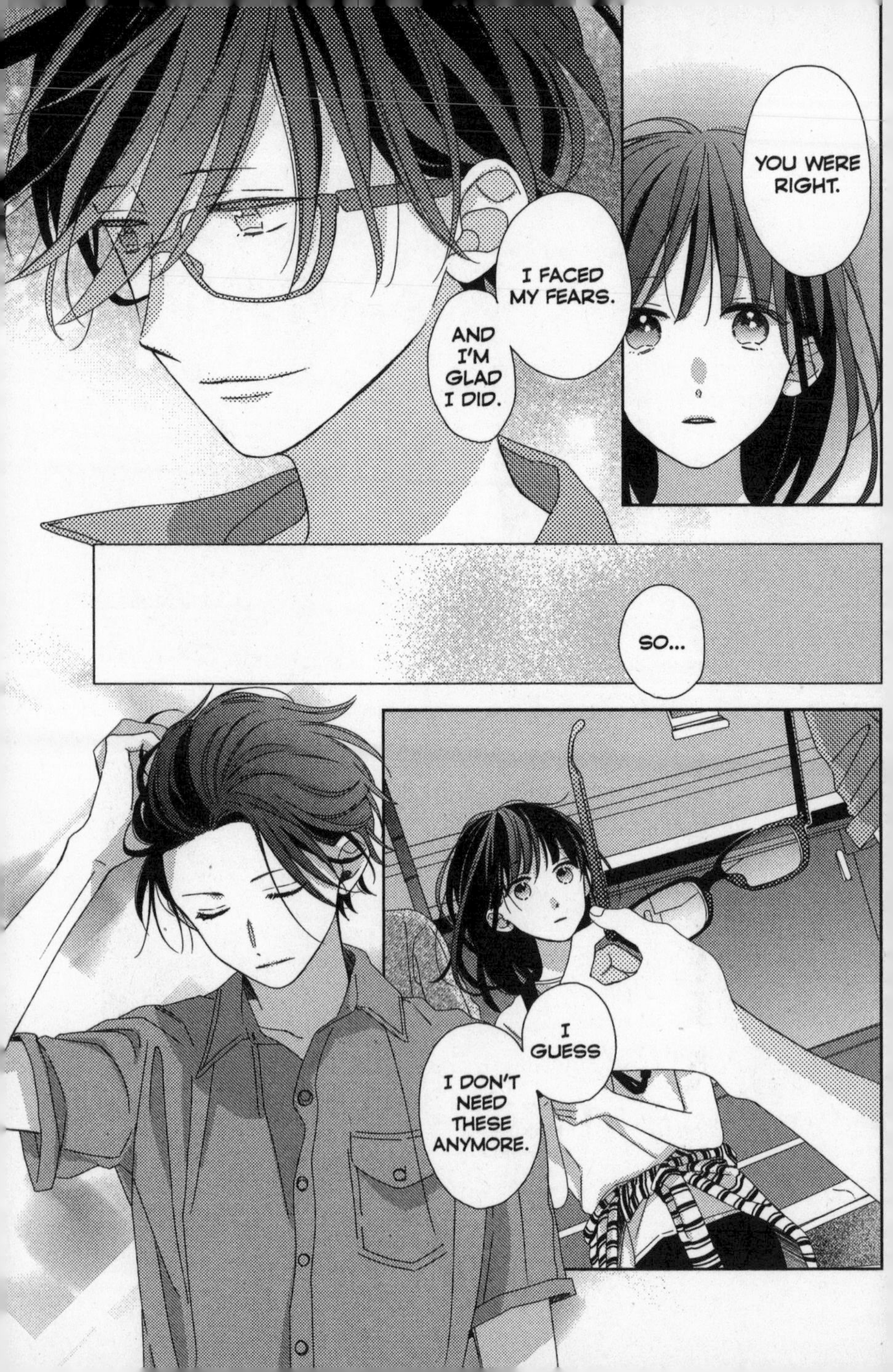
YOU WERE RIGHT.
I FACED MY FEARS.
AND I'M GLAD I DID.
SO...
I GUESS I DON'T NEED THESE ANYMORE.

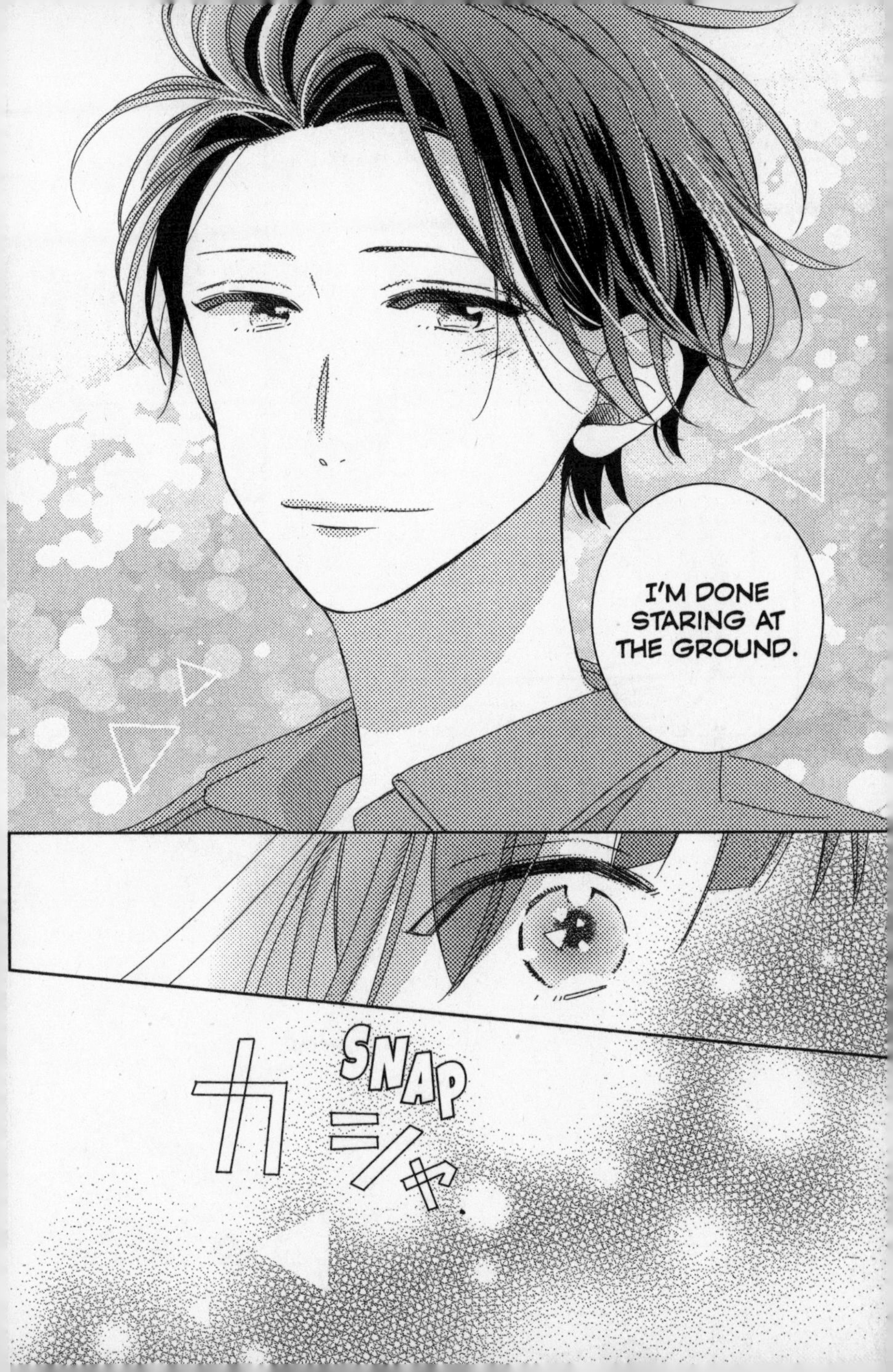
I'M DONE STARING AT THE GROUND.
SNAP
カシャ

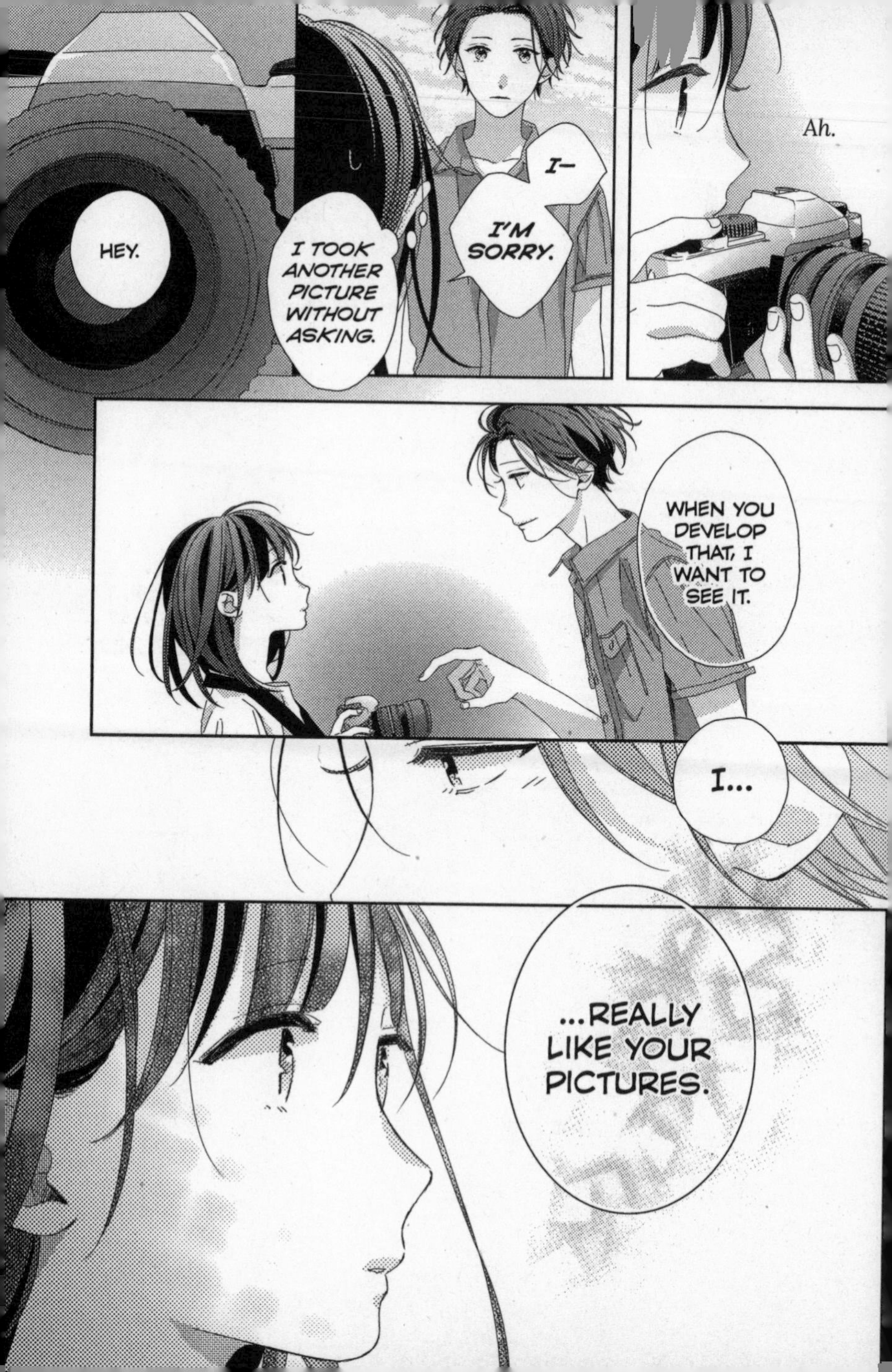
Ah.
I—
I'M SORRY.
I TOOK ANOTHER PICTURE WITHOUT ASKING.
HEY.
WHEN YOU DEVELOP THAT, I WANT TO SEE IT.
I...
...REALLY LIKE YOUR PICTURES.

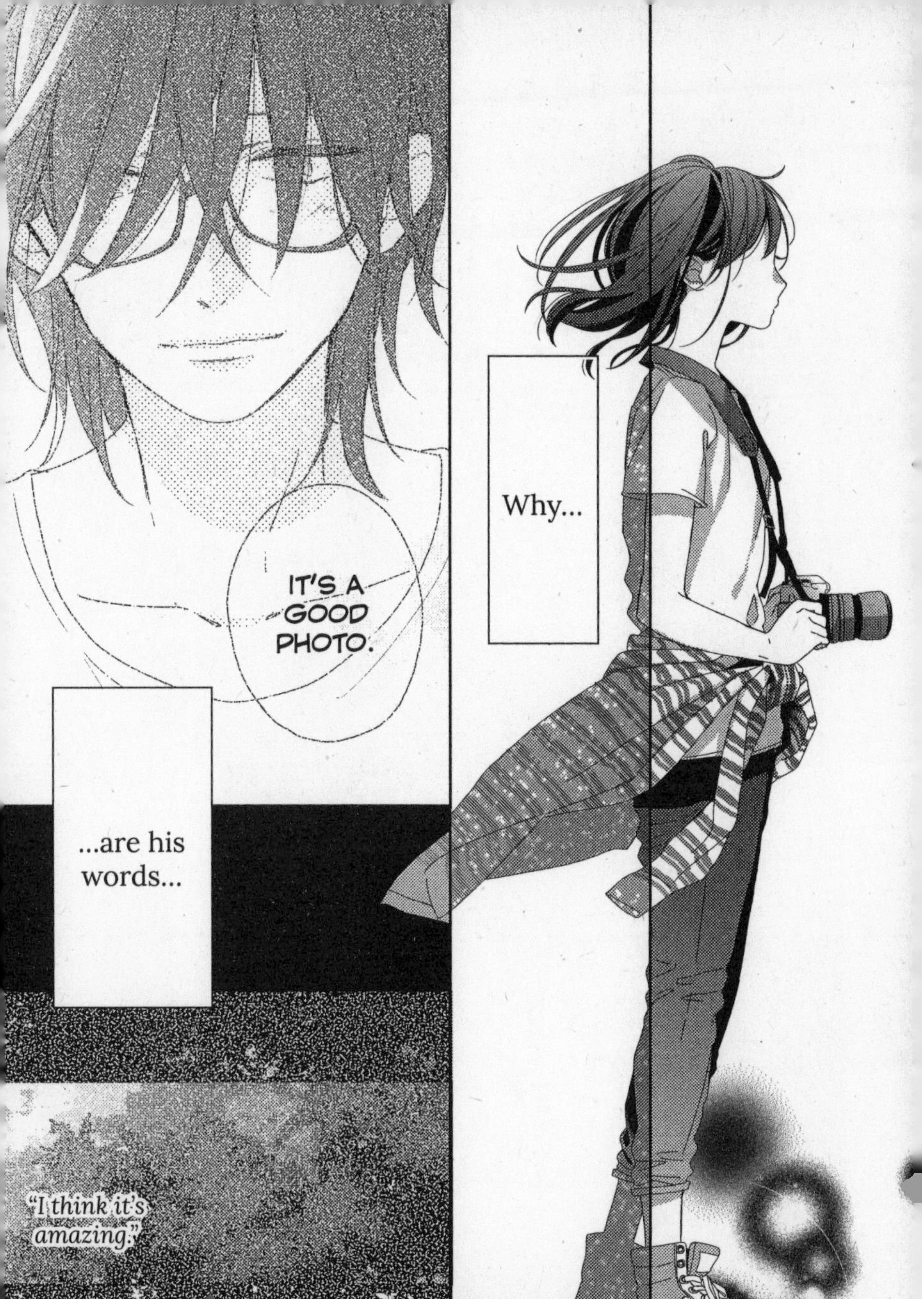
Why...
IT'S A GOOD PHOTO.
...are his words...
"I think it's amazing."

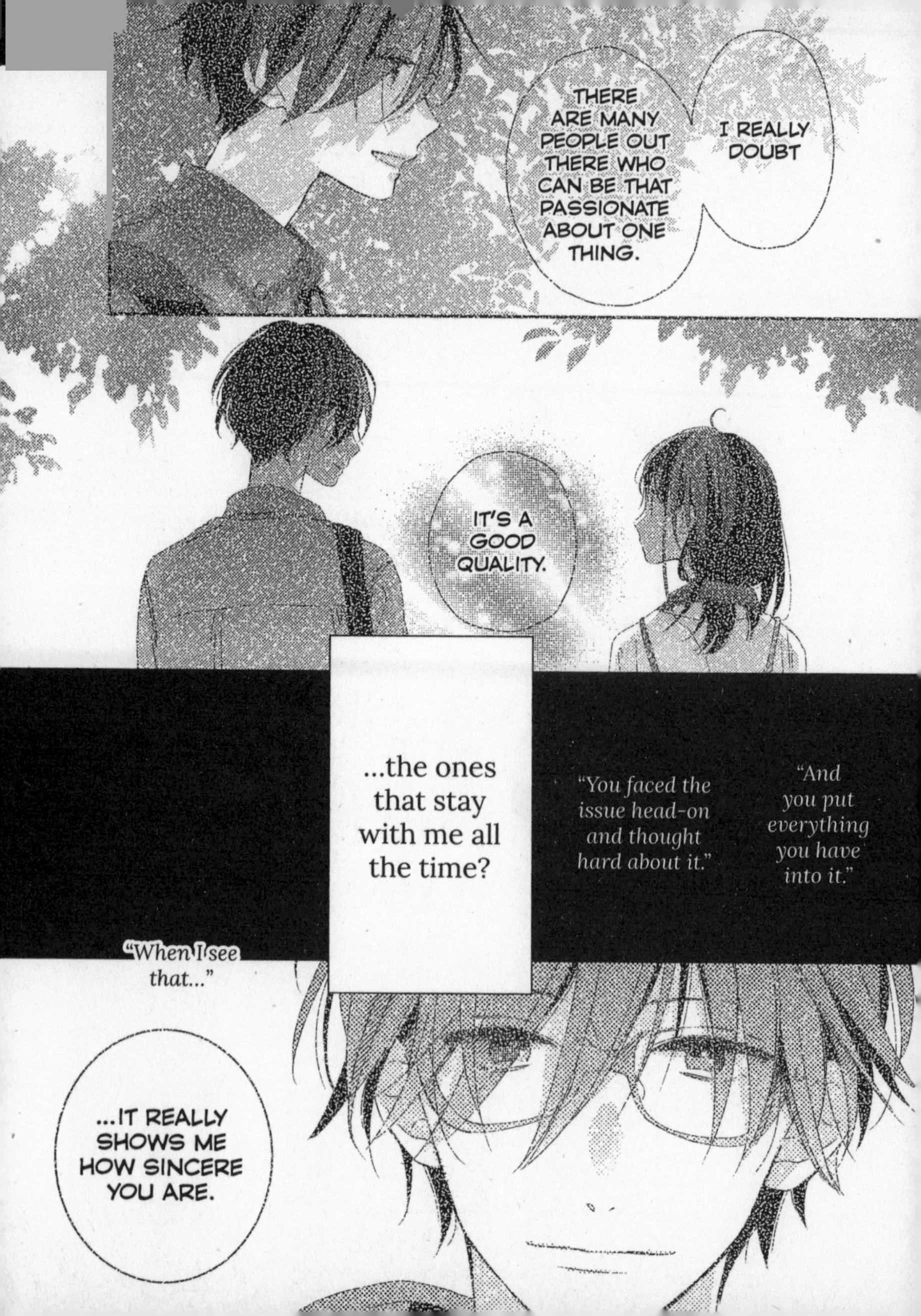
I REALLY DOUBT
THERE ARE MANY PEOPLE OUT THERE WHO CAN BE THAT PASSIONATE ABOUT ONE THING.
IT'S A GOOD QUALITY.
"And you put everything you have into it."
"You faced the issue head-on and thought hard about it."
...the ones that stay with me all the time?
"When I see that..."
...IT REALLY SHOWS ME HOW SINCERE YOU ARE.

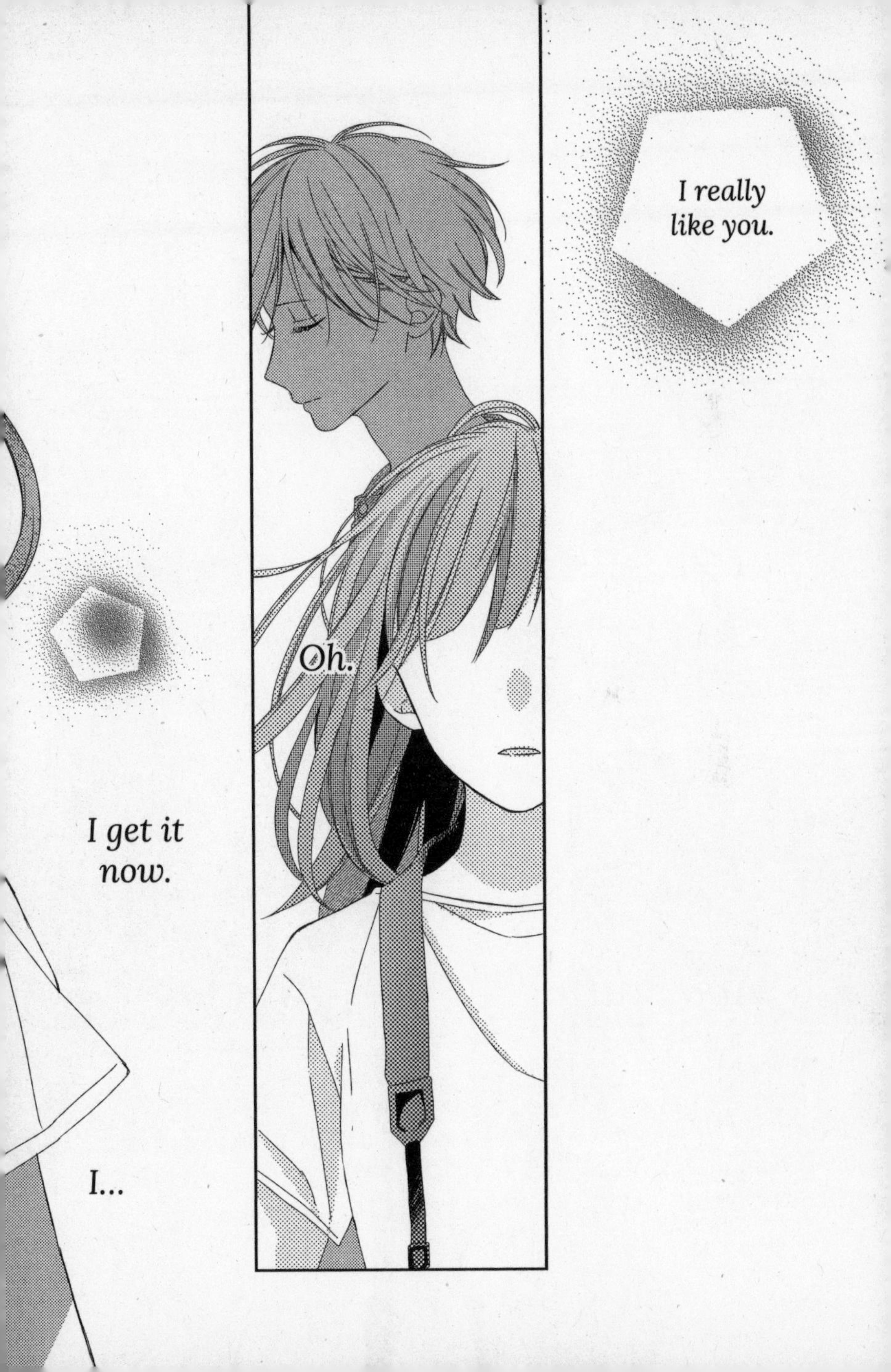
I really like you.
Oh.
I get it now.
I...

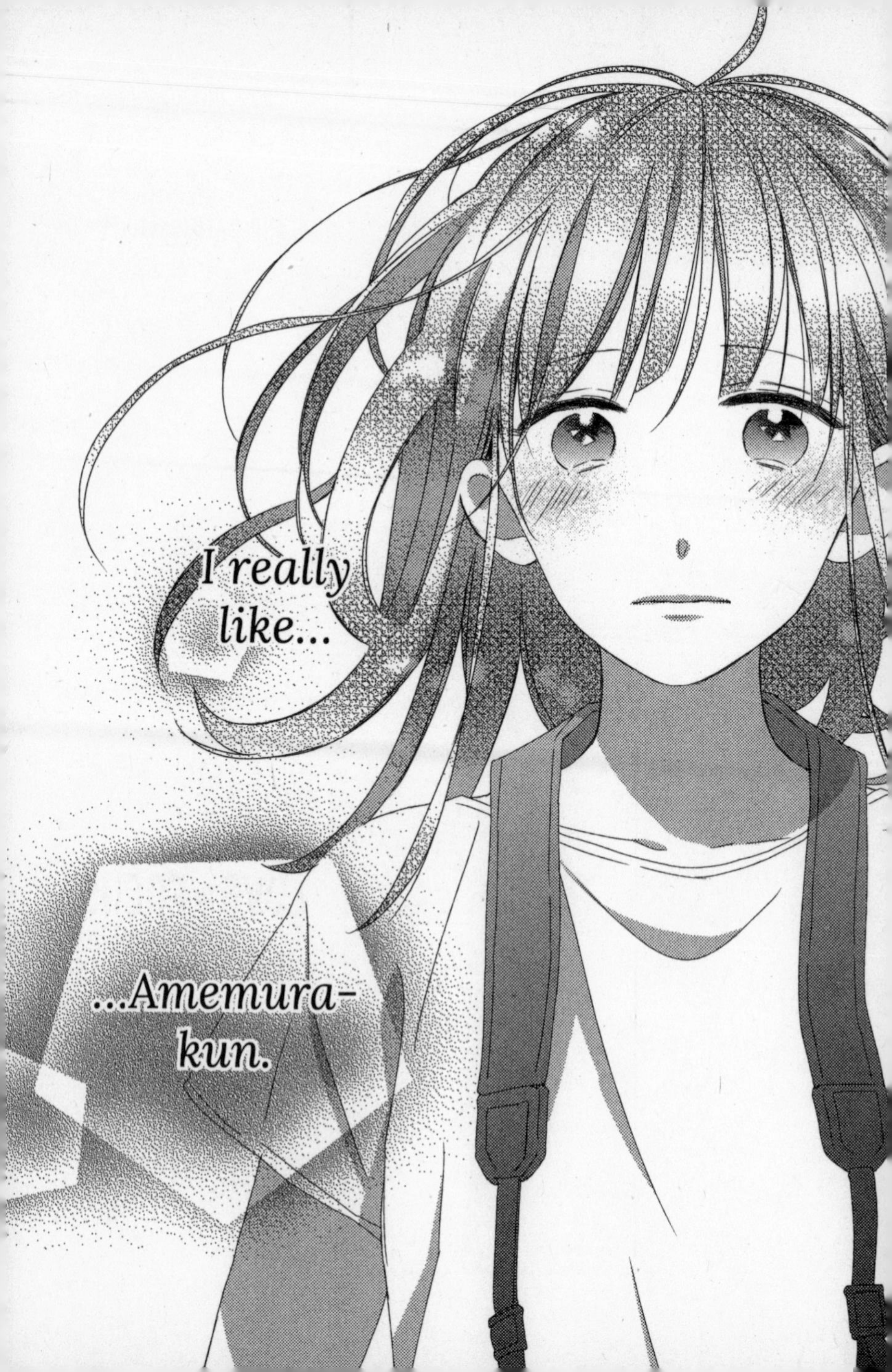
I really like...
...Amemura-kun.

LOVE IN FOCUS

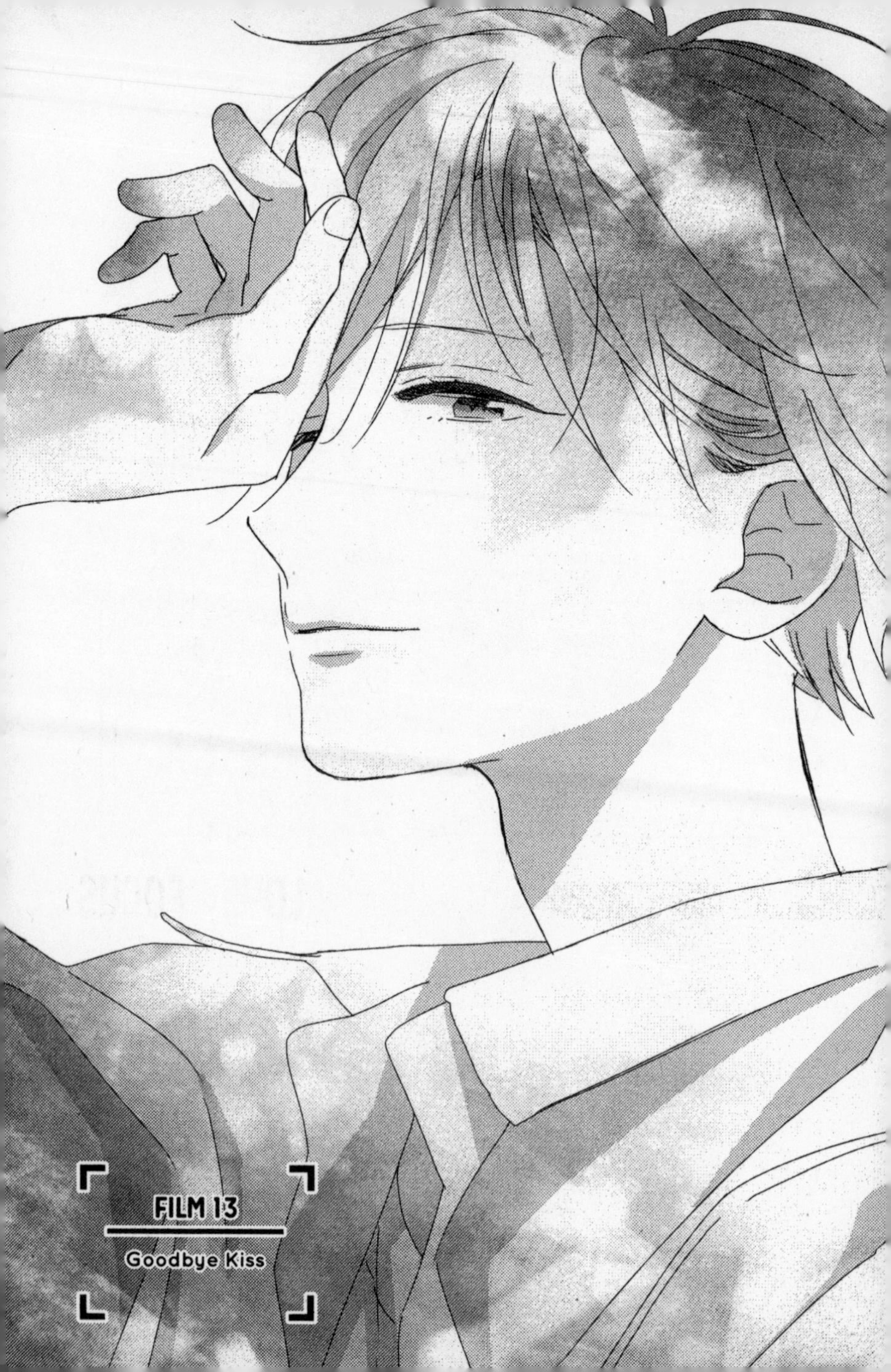
FILM 13
Goodbye Kiss

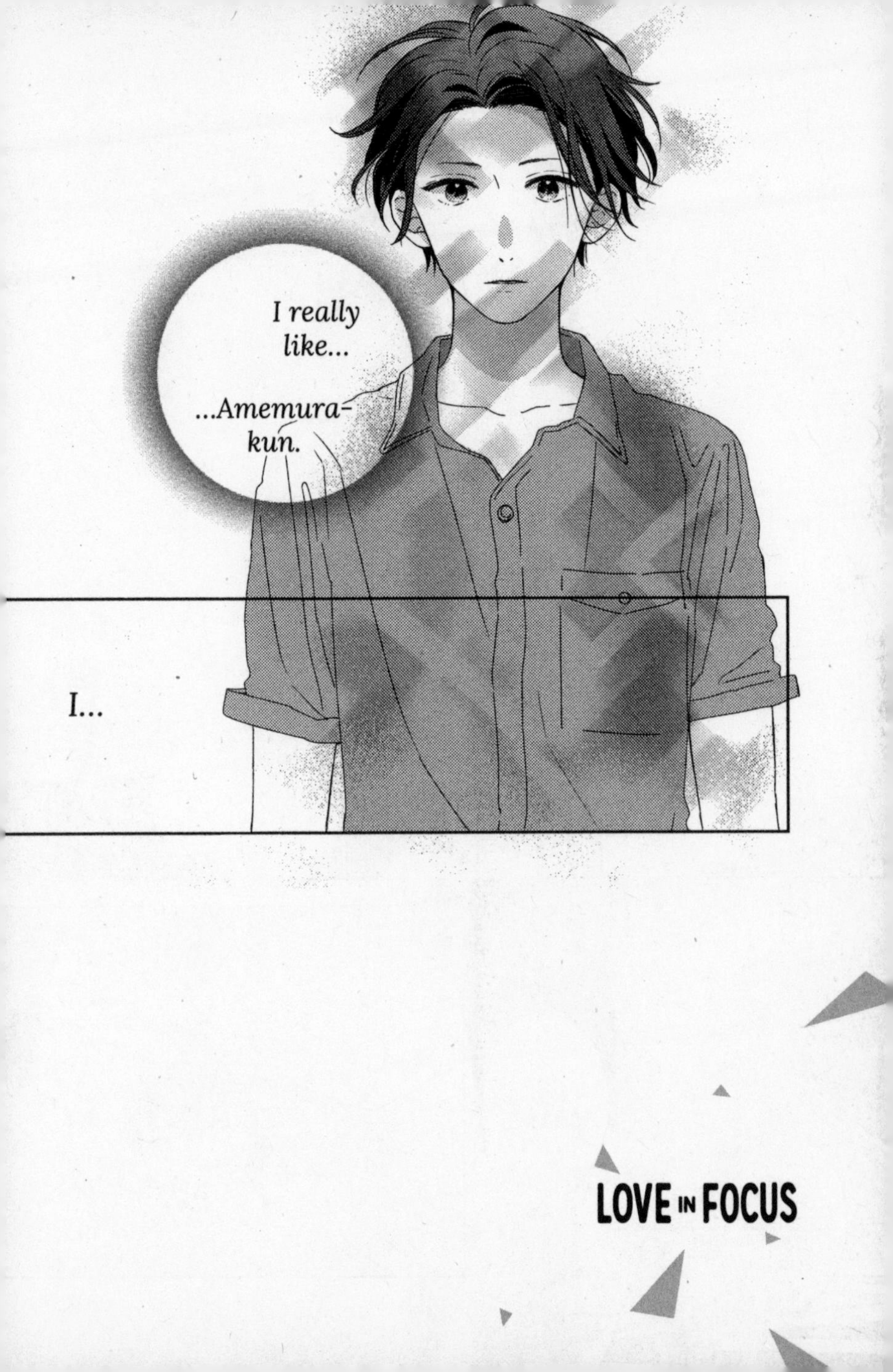
I really like... ...Amemura-kun.
I...
LOVE IN FOCUS

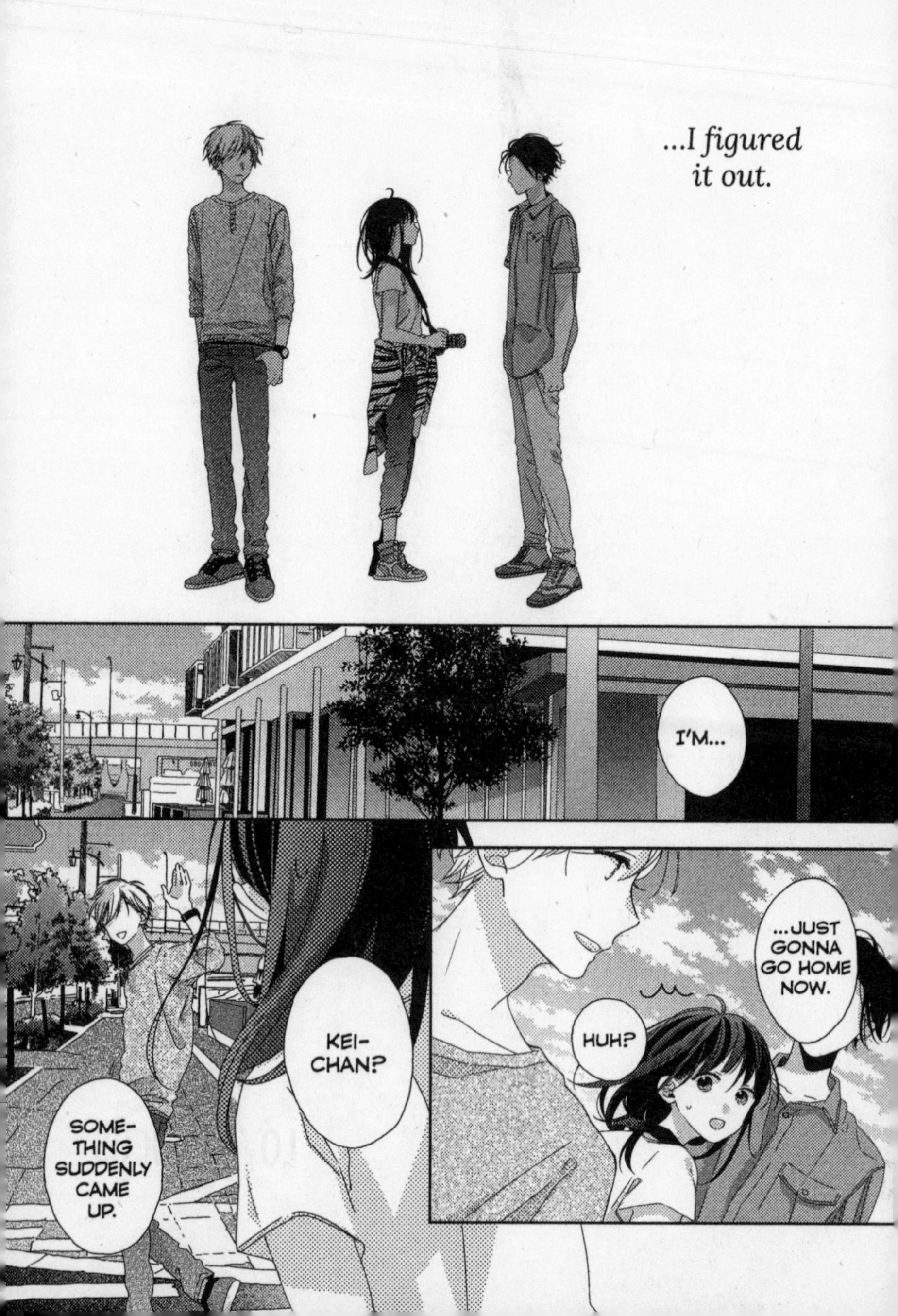
...I figured it out.
I'M...
...JUST GONNA GO HOME NOW.
HUH?
KEI-CHAN?
SOME-THING SUDDENLY CAME UP.

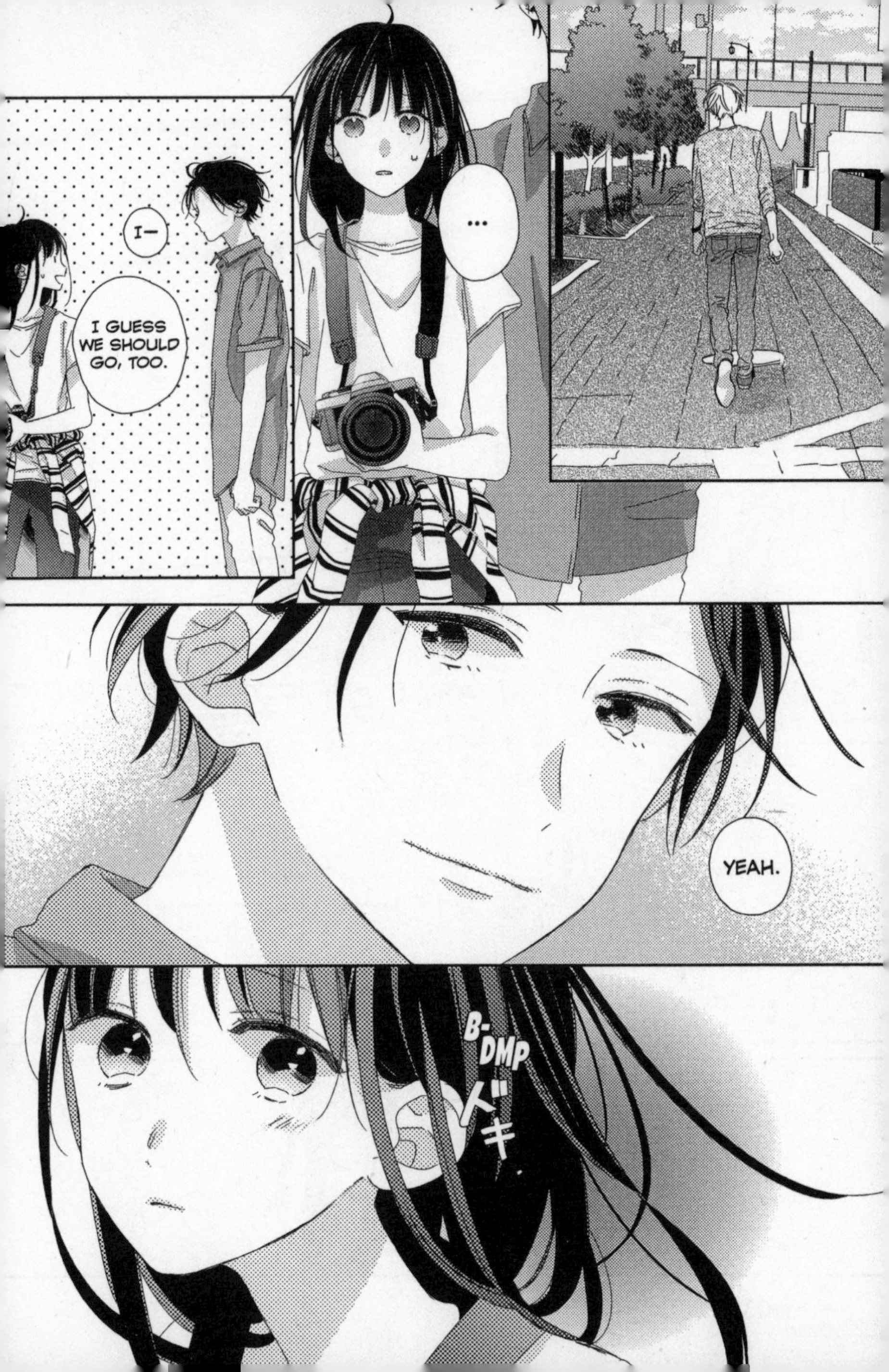
...
I—
I GUESS WE SHOULD GO, TOO.
YEAH.
B-DMP
ドキ

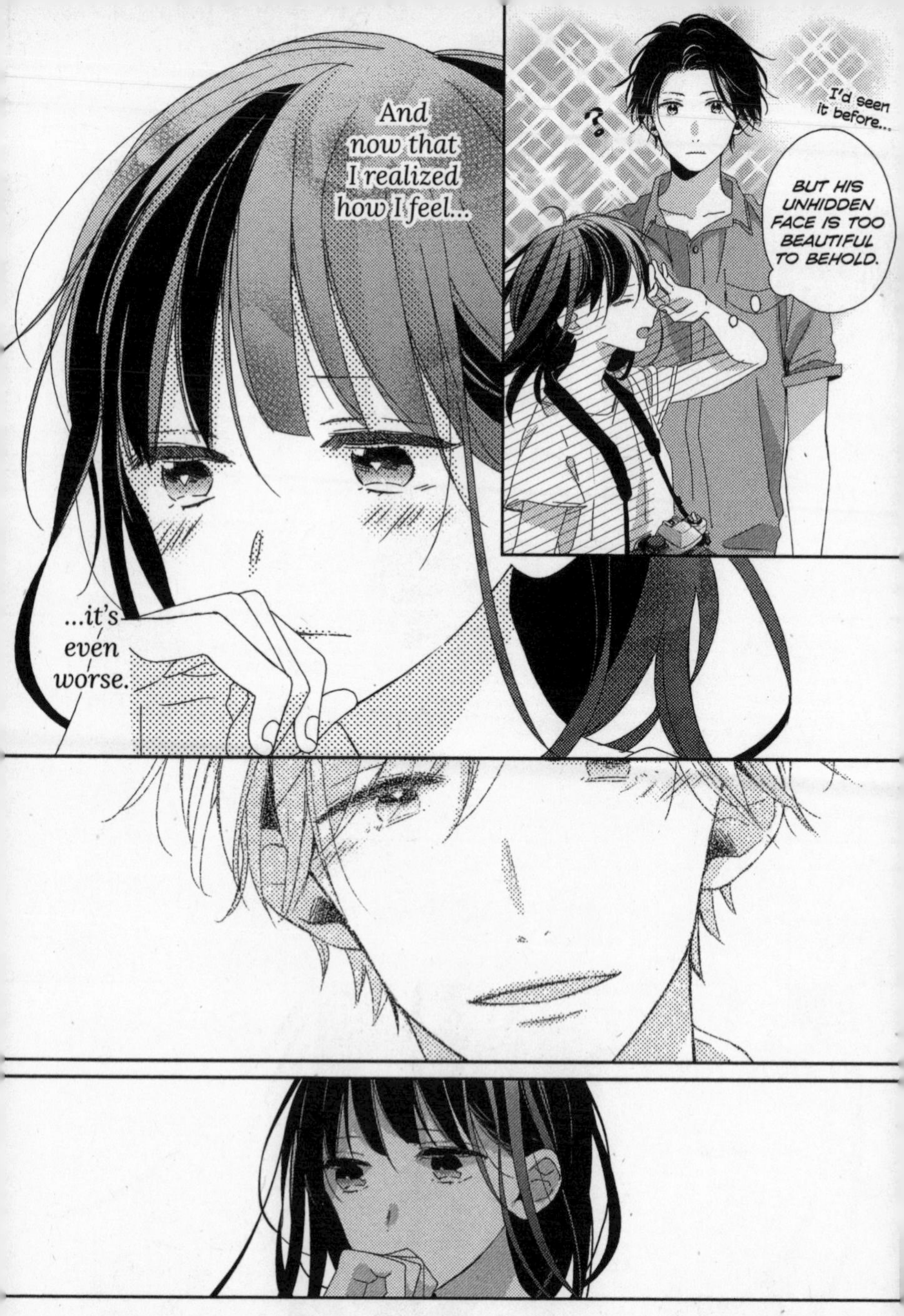
I'd seen it before...
?
BUT HIS UNHIDDEN FACE IS TOO BEAUTIFUL TO BEHOLD.
And now that I realized how I feel...
...it's even worse.

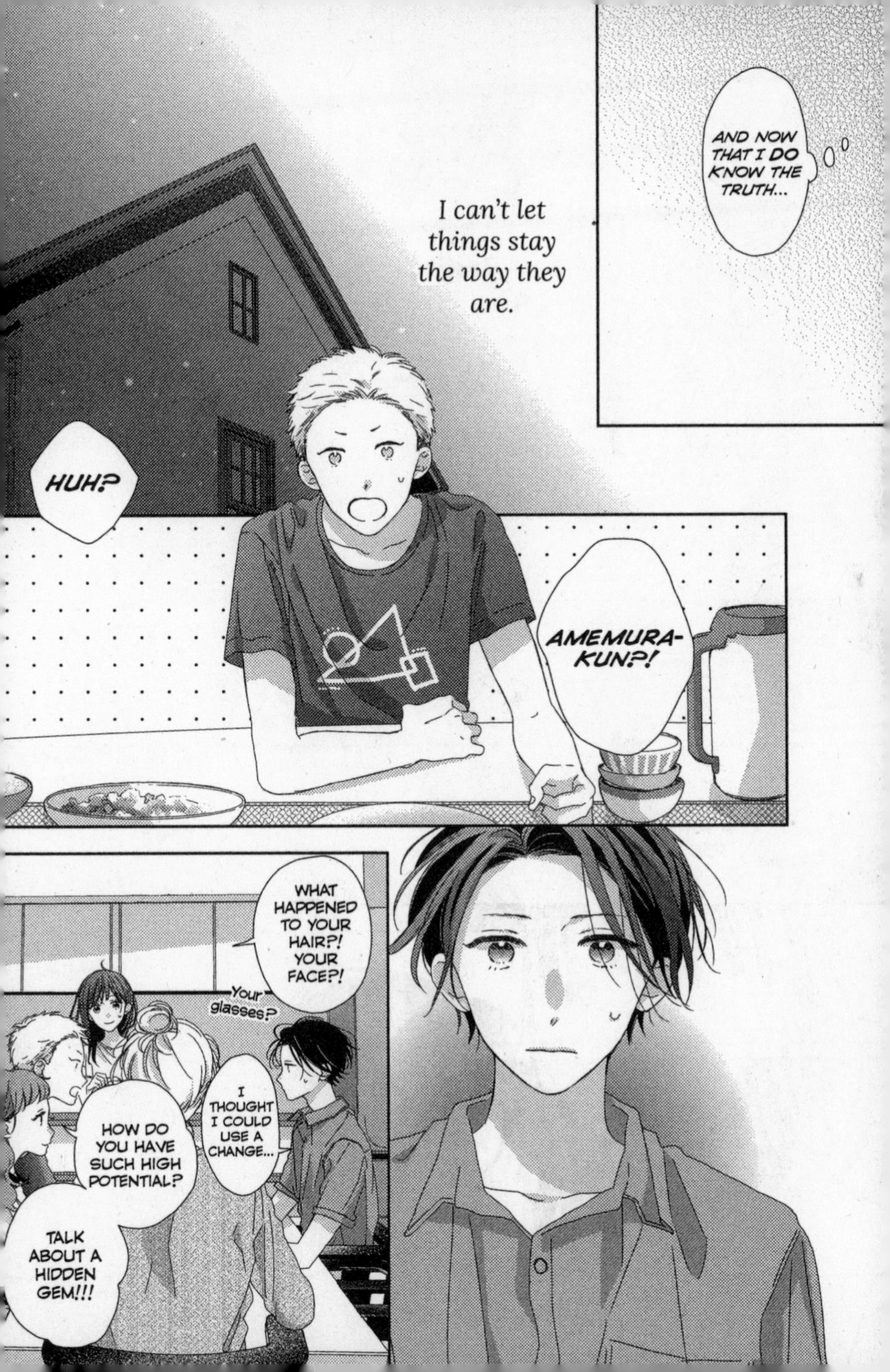
AND NOW THAT I DO KNOW THE TRUTH...
I can't let things stay the way they are.
HUH?
AMEMURA-KUN?!
WHAT HAPPENED TO YOUR HAIR?! YOUR FACE?!
Your glasses?
I THOUGHT I COULD USE A CHANGE...
HOW DO YOU HAVE SUCH HIGH POTENTIAL?
TALK ABOUT A HIDDEN GEM!!!

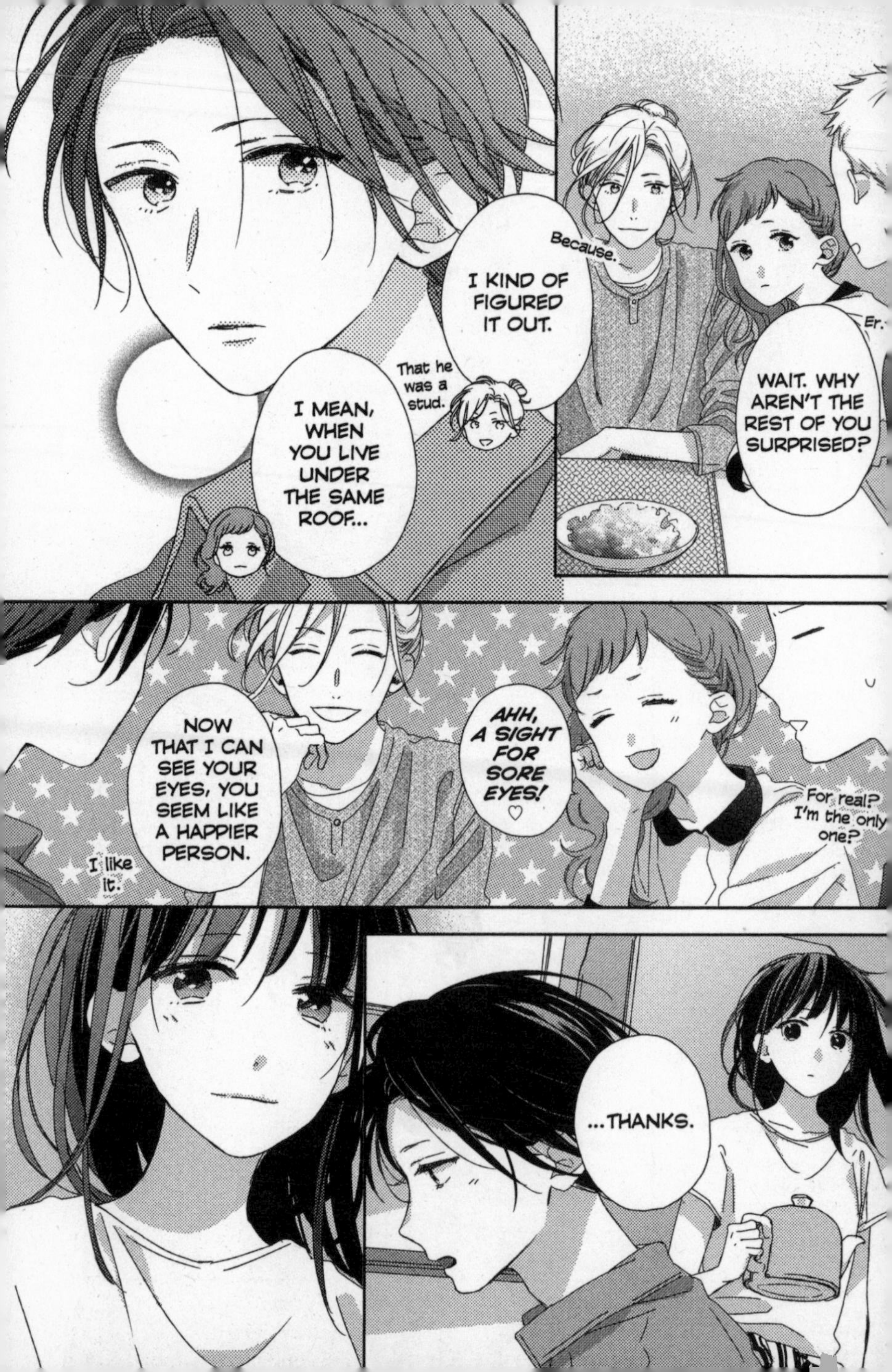
Er.
WAIT. WHY AREN'T THE REST OF YOU SURPRISED?
Because.
I KIND OF FIGURED IT OUT.
That he was a stud.
I MEAN, WHEN YOU LIVE UNDER THE SAME ROOF...
For real? I'm the only one?
AHH, A SIGHT FOR SORE EYES! ♡
NOW THAT I CAN SEE YOUR EYES, YOU SEEM LIKE A HAPPIER PERSON.
I like it.
...THANKS.

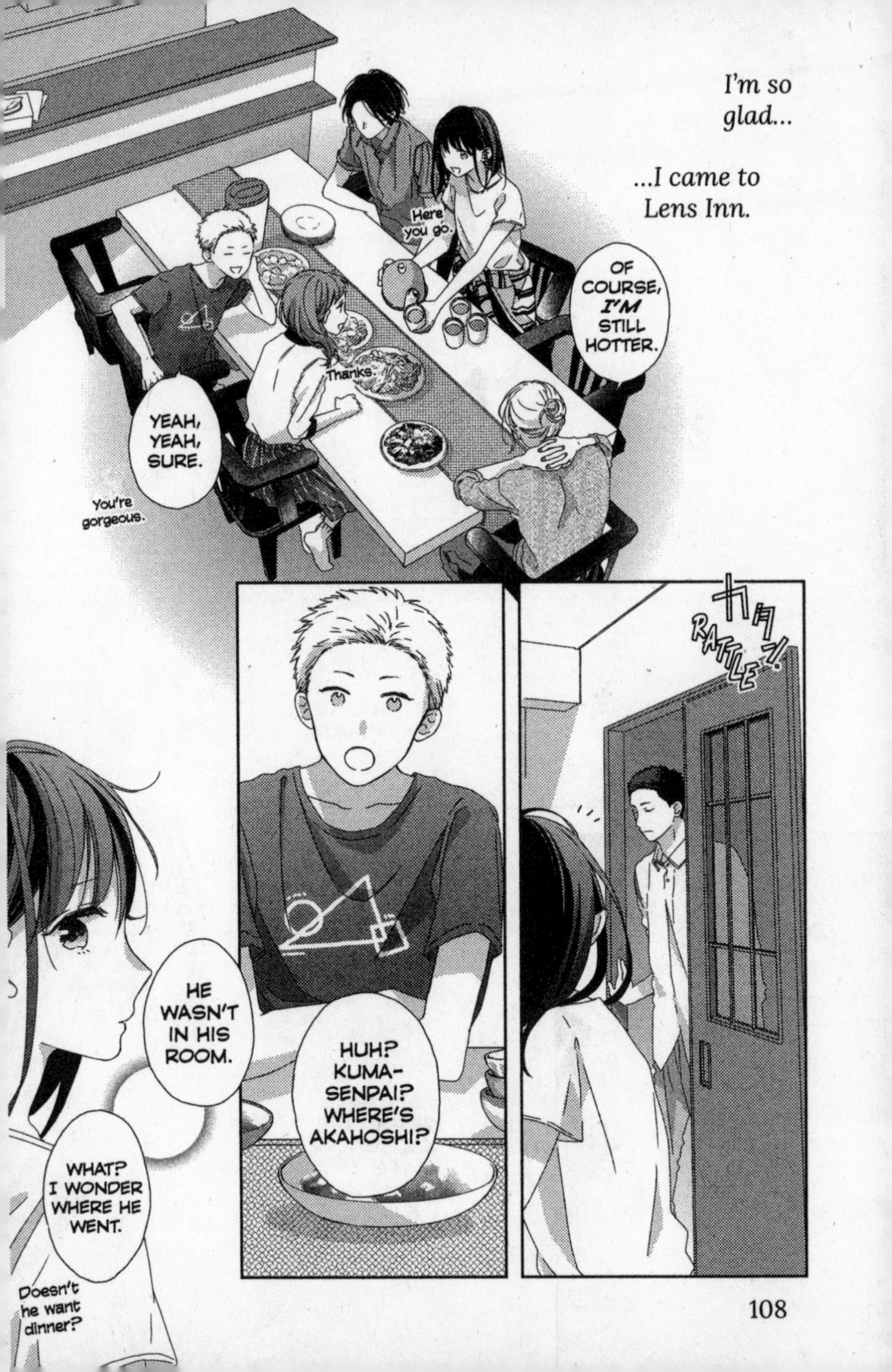
I'm so glad...
...I came to Lens Inn.
Here you go.
OF COURSE, *I'M* STILL HOTTER.
Thanks.
YEAH, YEAH, SURE.
You're gorgeous.
RATTLE!
HUH? KUMA-SENPAI? WHERE'S AKAHOSHI?
HE WASN'T IN HIS ROOM.
WHAT? I WONDER WHERE HE WENT.
Doesn't he want dinner?

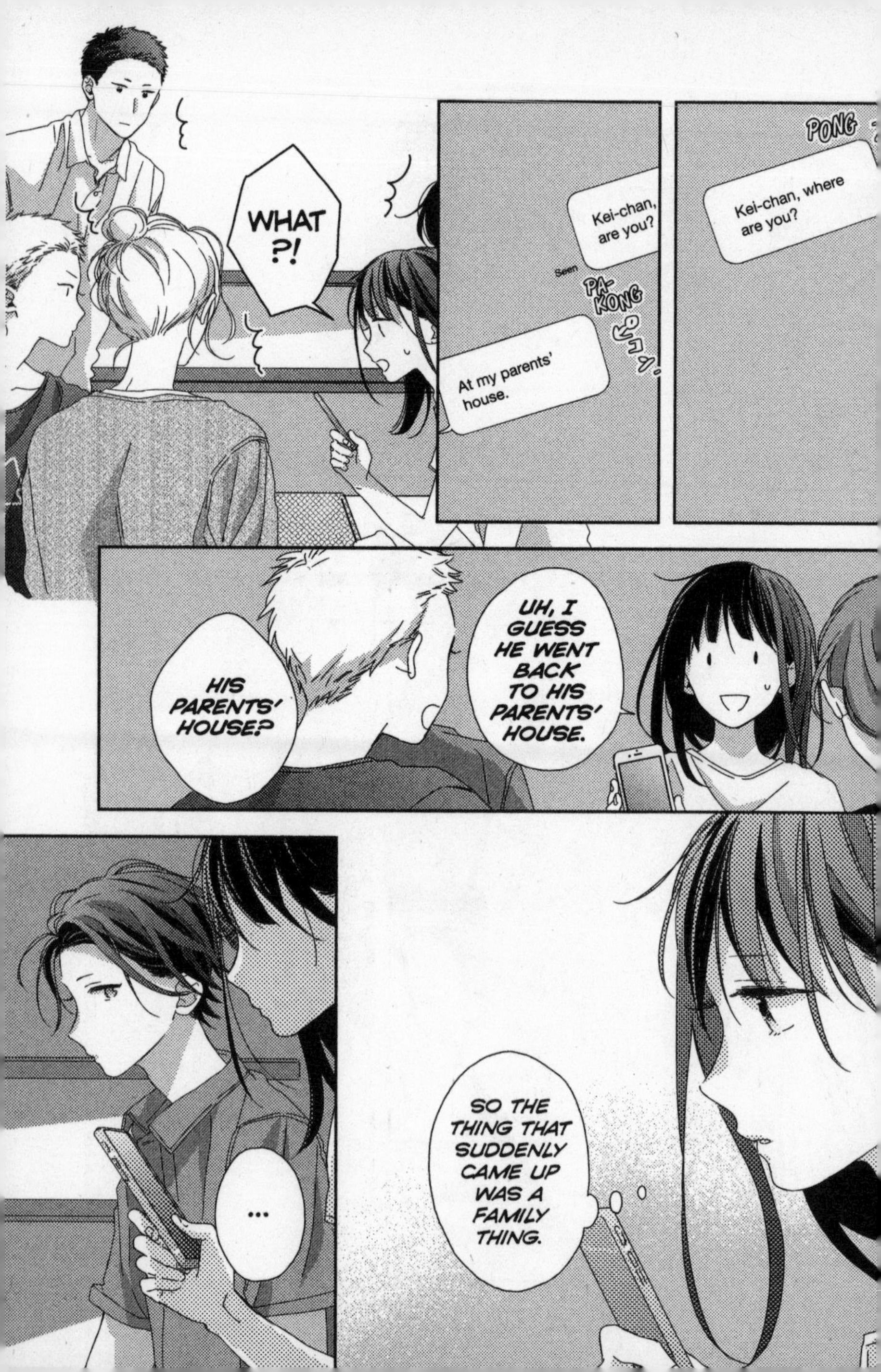
PONG
Kei-chan, where are you?
Kei-chan, are you?
Seen
PA-KONG
At my parents' house.
WHAT ?!
UH, I GUESS HE WENT BACK TO HIS PARENTS' HOUSE.
HIS PARENTS' HOUSE?
SO THE THING THAT SUDDENLY CAME UP WAS A FAMILY THING.
...

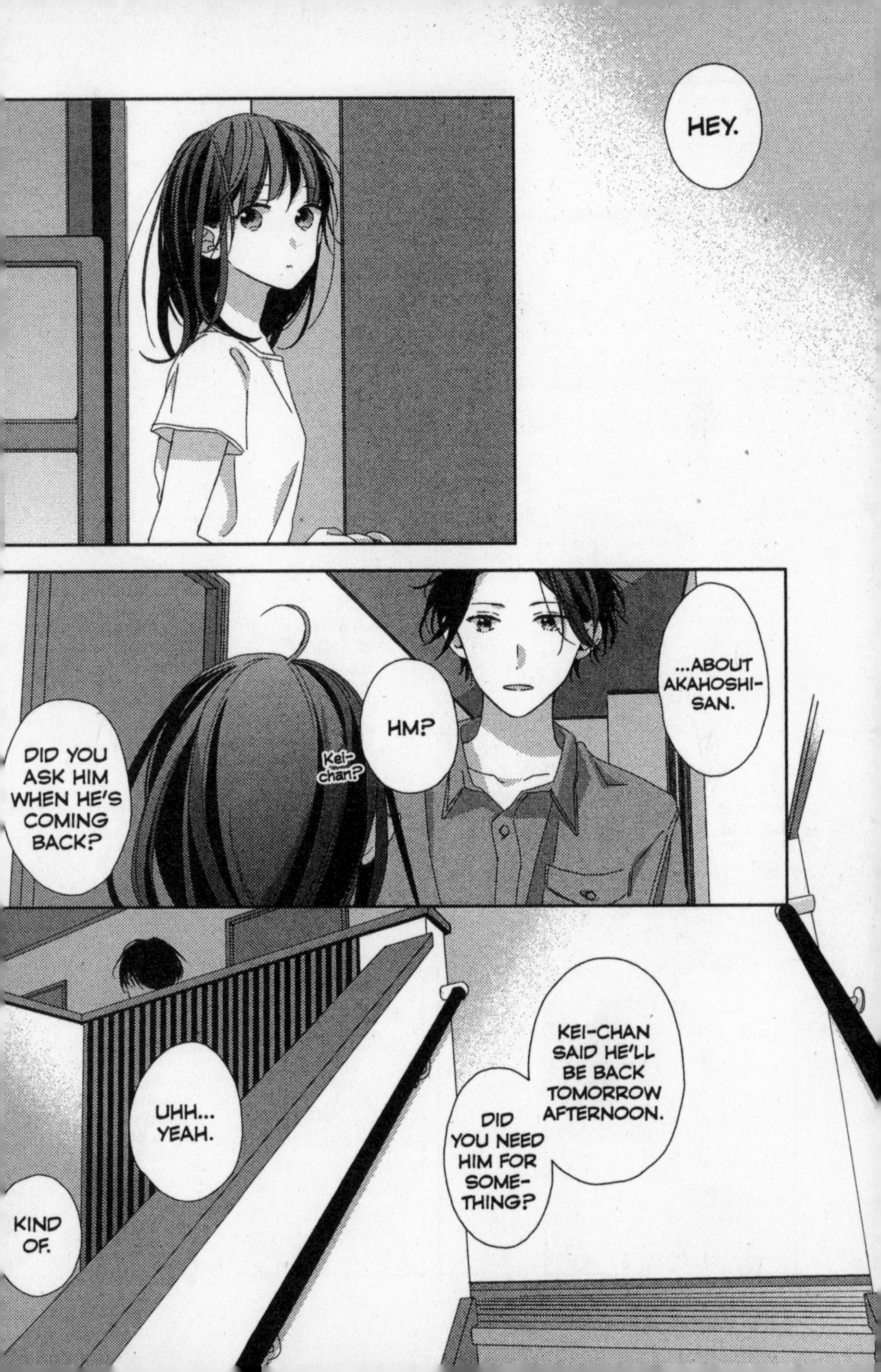
HEY.
...ABOUT AKAHOSHI-SAN.
HM?
Kei-chan?
DID YOU ASK HIM WHEN HE'S COMING BACK?
KEI-CHAN SAID HE'LL BE BACK TOMORROW AFTERNOON.
DID YOU NEED HIM FOR SOME-THING?
UHH... YEAH.
KIND OF.

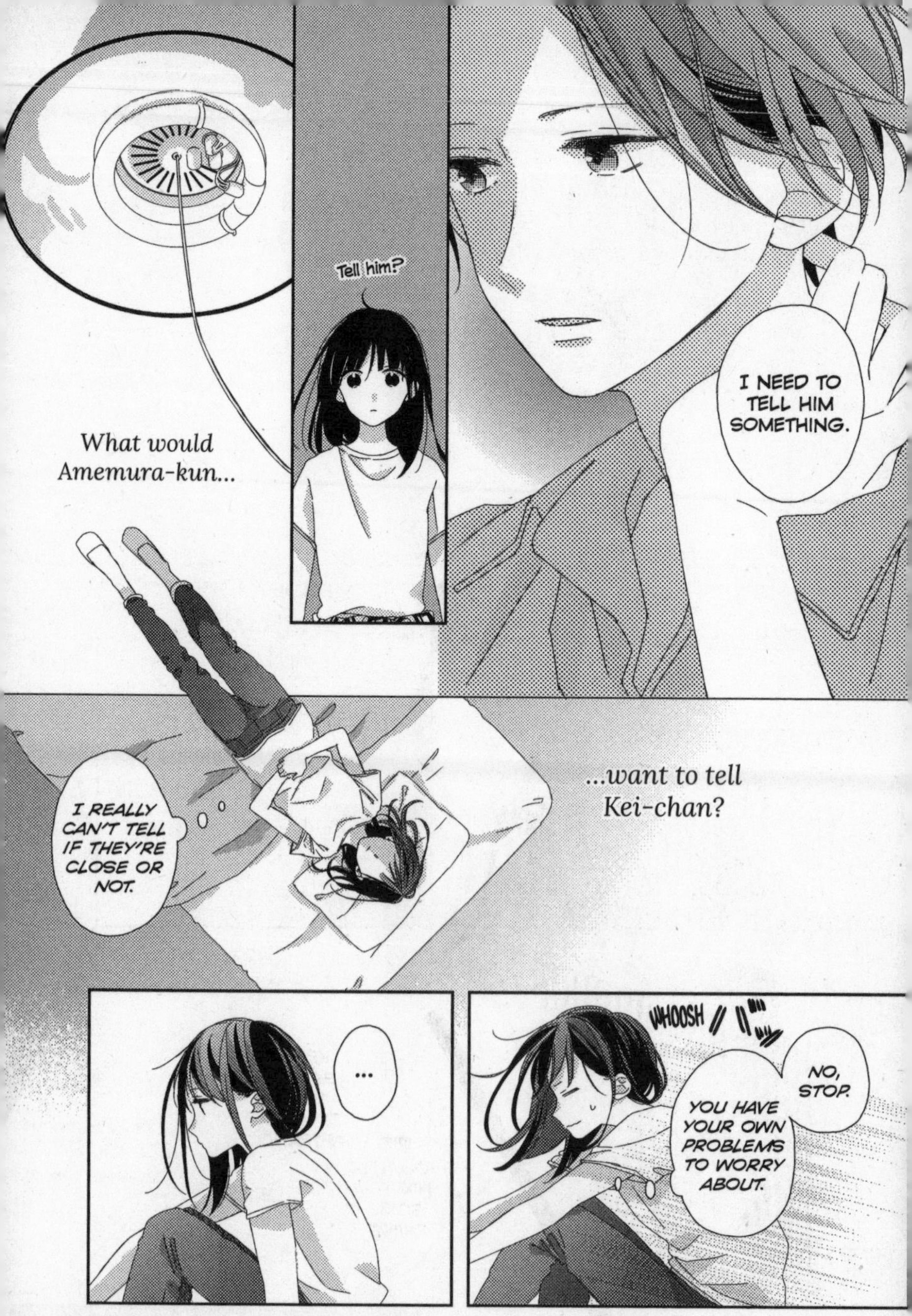
I NEED TO TELL HIM SOMETHING.
Tell him?
What would Amemura-kun...
...want to tell Kei-chan?
I REALLY CAN'T TELL IF THEY'RE CLOSE OR NOT.
WHOOSH
NO, STOP.
YOU HAVE YOUR OWN PROBLEMS TO WORRY ABOUT.
...

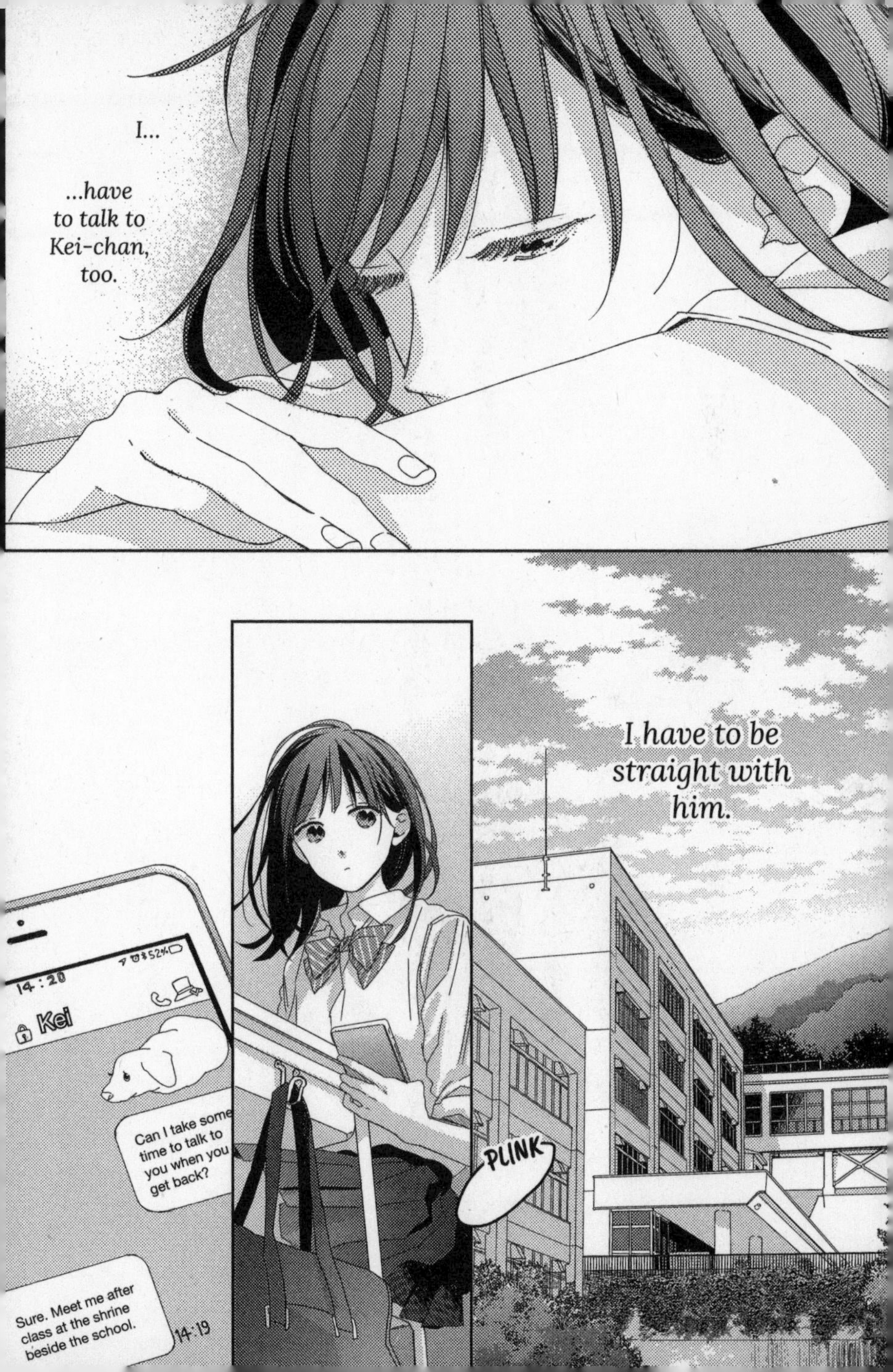

I...
...have to talk to Kei-chan, too.
I have to be straight with him.
PLINK
14:20
Kei
Can I take some time to talk to you when you get back?
Sure. Meet me after class at the shrine beside the school.
14:19

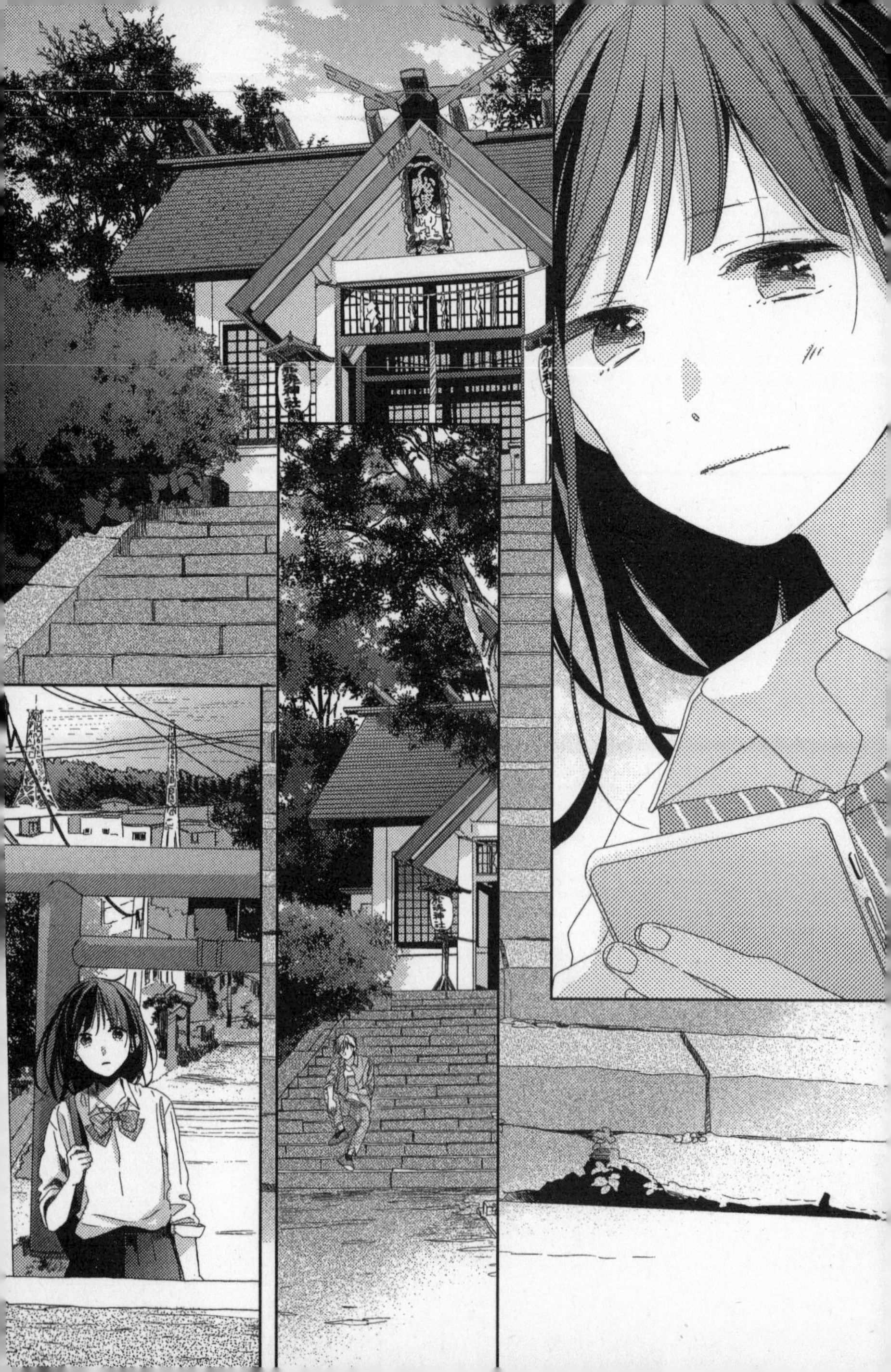

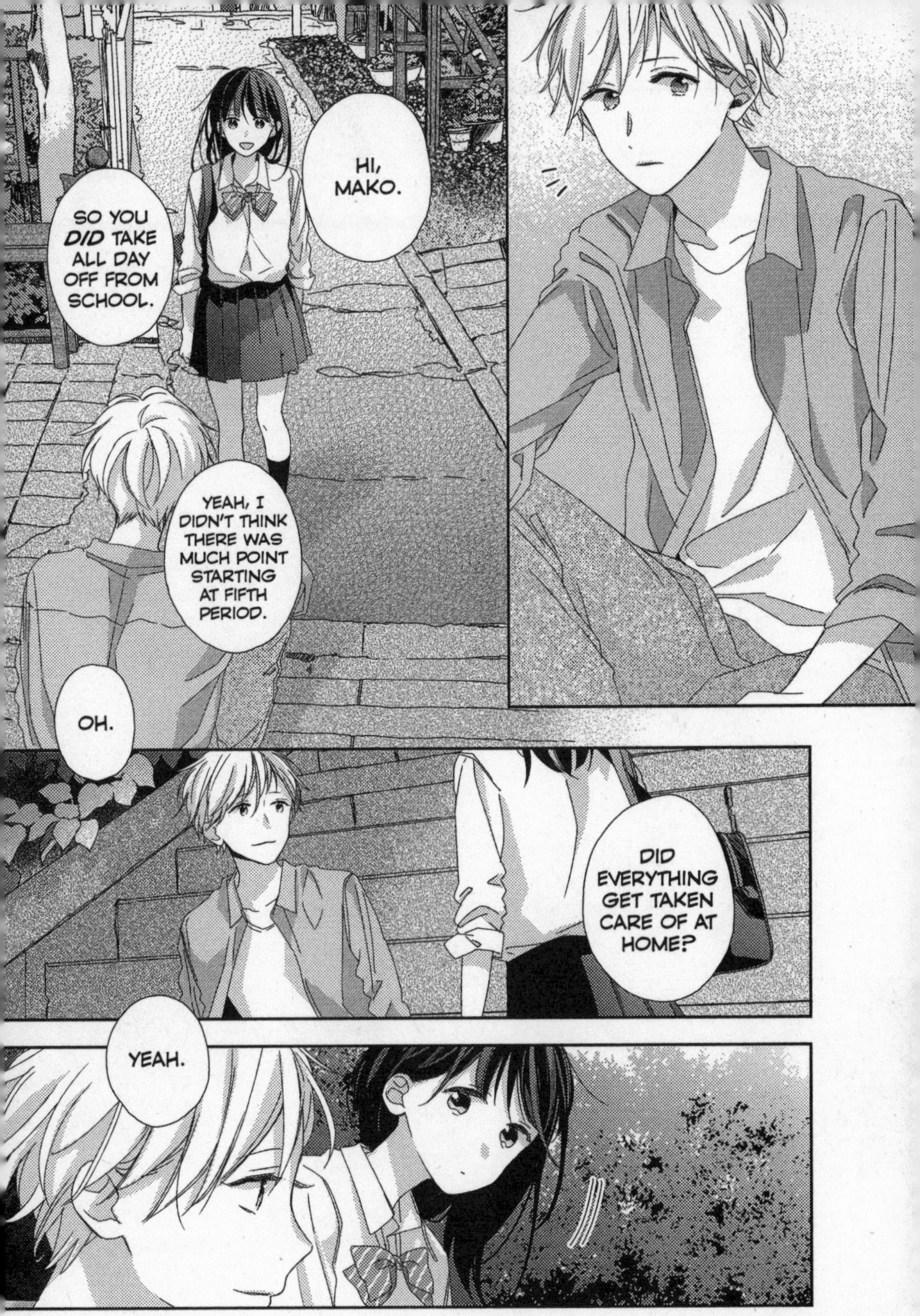
HI, MAKO.
SO YOU *DID* TAKE ALL DAY OFF FROM SCHOOL.
YEAH, I DIDN'T THINK THERE WAS MUCH POINT STARTING AT FIFTH PERIOD.
OH.
DID EVERYTHING GET TAKEN CARE OF AT HOME?
YEAH.

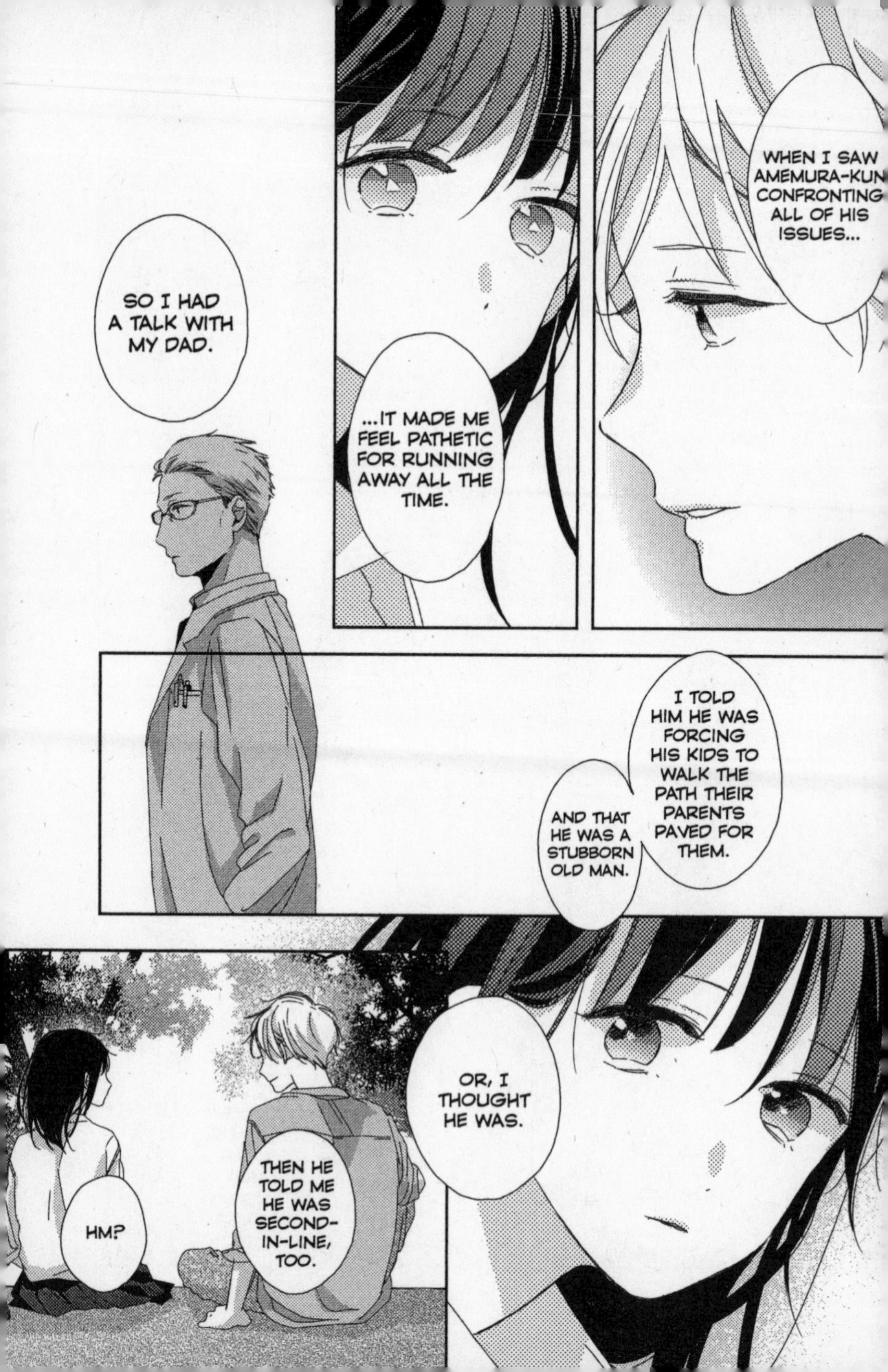
WHEN I SAW AMEMURA-KUN CONFRONTING ALL OF HIS ISSUES...
...IT MADE ME FEEL PATHETIC FOR RUNNING AWAY ALL THE TIME.
SO I HAD A TALK WITH MY DAD.
I TOLD HIM HE WAS FORCING HIS KIDS TO WALK THE PATH THEIR PARENTS PAVED FOR THEM.
AND THAT HE WAS A STUBBORN OLD MAN.
OR, I THOUGHT HE WAS.
THEN HE TOLD ME HE WAS SECOND-IN-LINE, TOO.
HM?

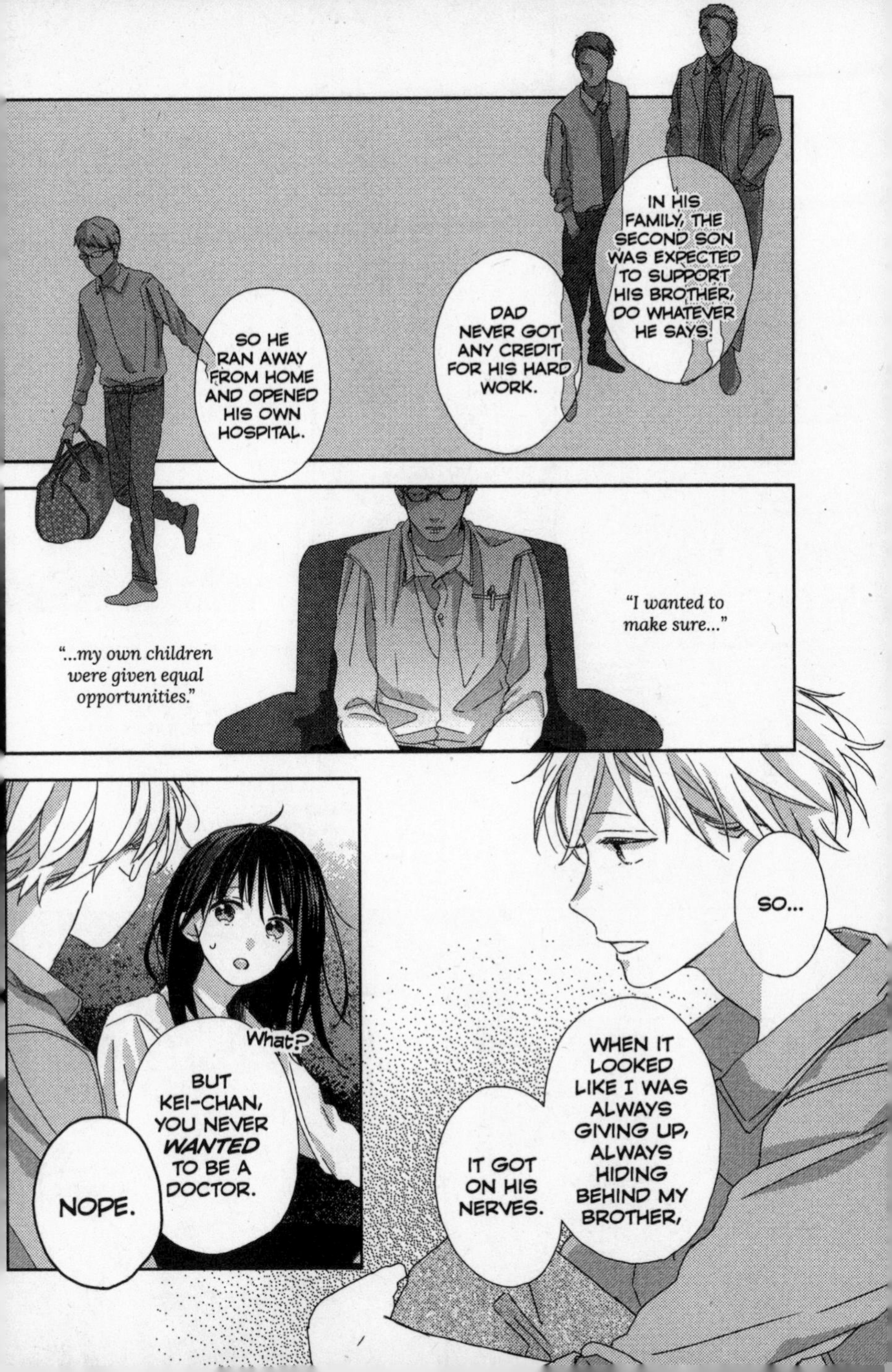
IN HIS FAMILY, THE SECOND SON WAS EXPECTED TO SUPPORT HIS BROTHER, DO WHATEVER HE SAYS.
DAD NEVER GOT ANY CREDIT FOR HIS HARD WORK.
SO HE RAN AWAY FROM HOME AND OPENED HIS OWN HOSPITAL.
"I wanted to make sure..."
"...my own children were given equal opportunities."
SO...
WHEN IT LOOKED LIKE I WAS ALWAYS GIVING UP, ALWAYS HIDING BEHIND MY BROTHER,
IT GOT ON HIS NERVES.
What?
BUT KEI-CHAN, YOU NEVER *WANTED* TO BE A DOCTOR.
NOPE.

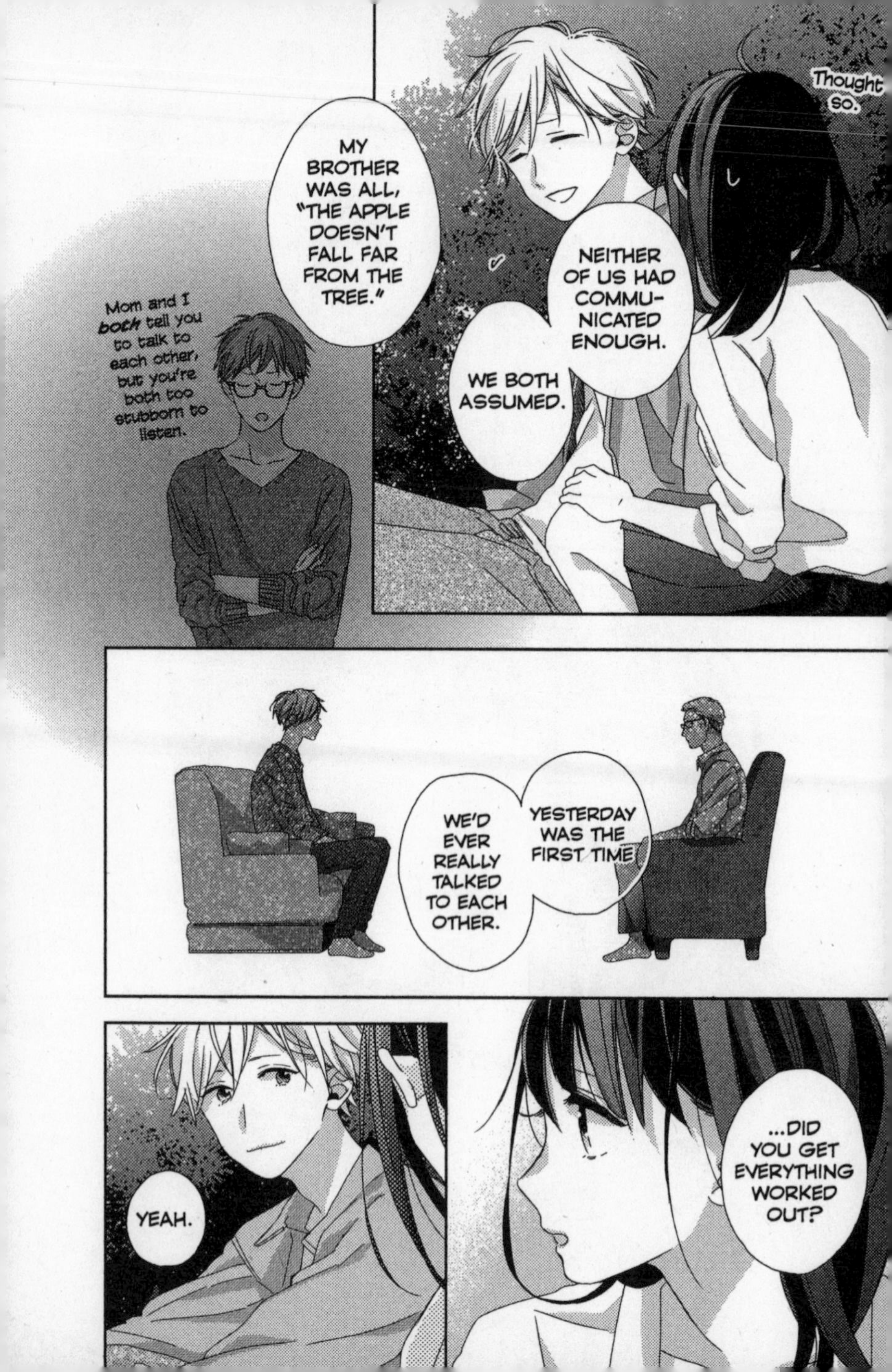
Thought so.
NEITHER OF US HAD COMMUNICATED ENOUGH.
WE BOTH ASSUMED.
MY BROTHER WAS ALL, "THE APPLE DOESN'T FALL FAR FROM THE TREE."
Mom and I *both* tell you to talk to each other, but you're both too stubborn to listen.
YESTERDAY WAS THE FIRST TIME
WE'D EVER REALLY TALKED TO EACH OTHER.
...DID YOU GET EVERYTHING WORKED OUT?
YEAH.

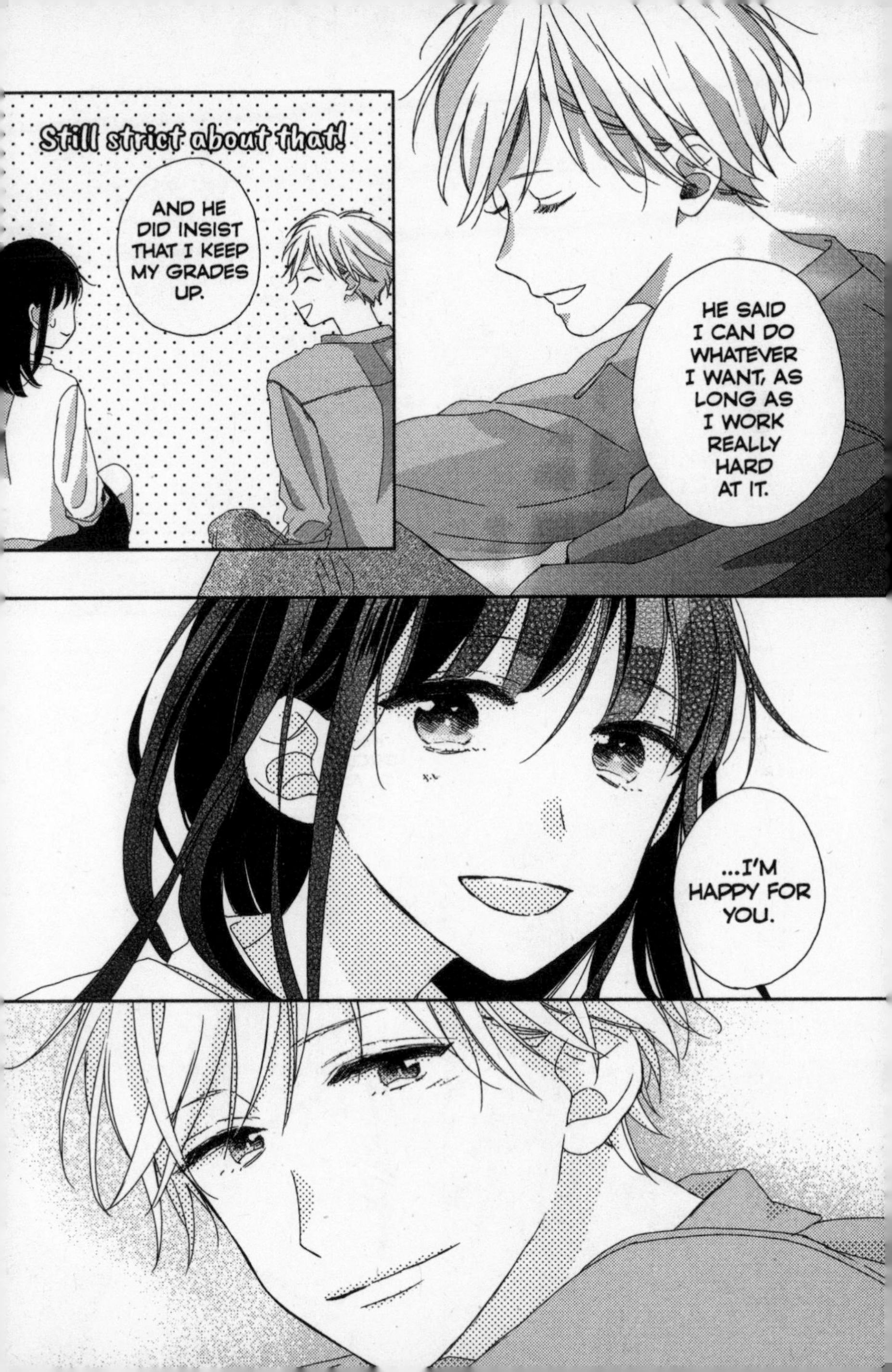
HE SAID I CAN DO WHATEVER I WANT, AS LONG AS I WORK REALLY HARD AT IT.
Still strict about that!
AND HE DID INSIST THAT I KEEP MY GRADES UP.
...I'M HAPPY FOR YOU.

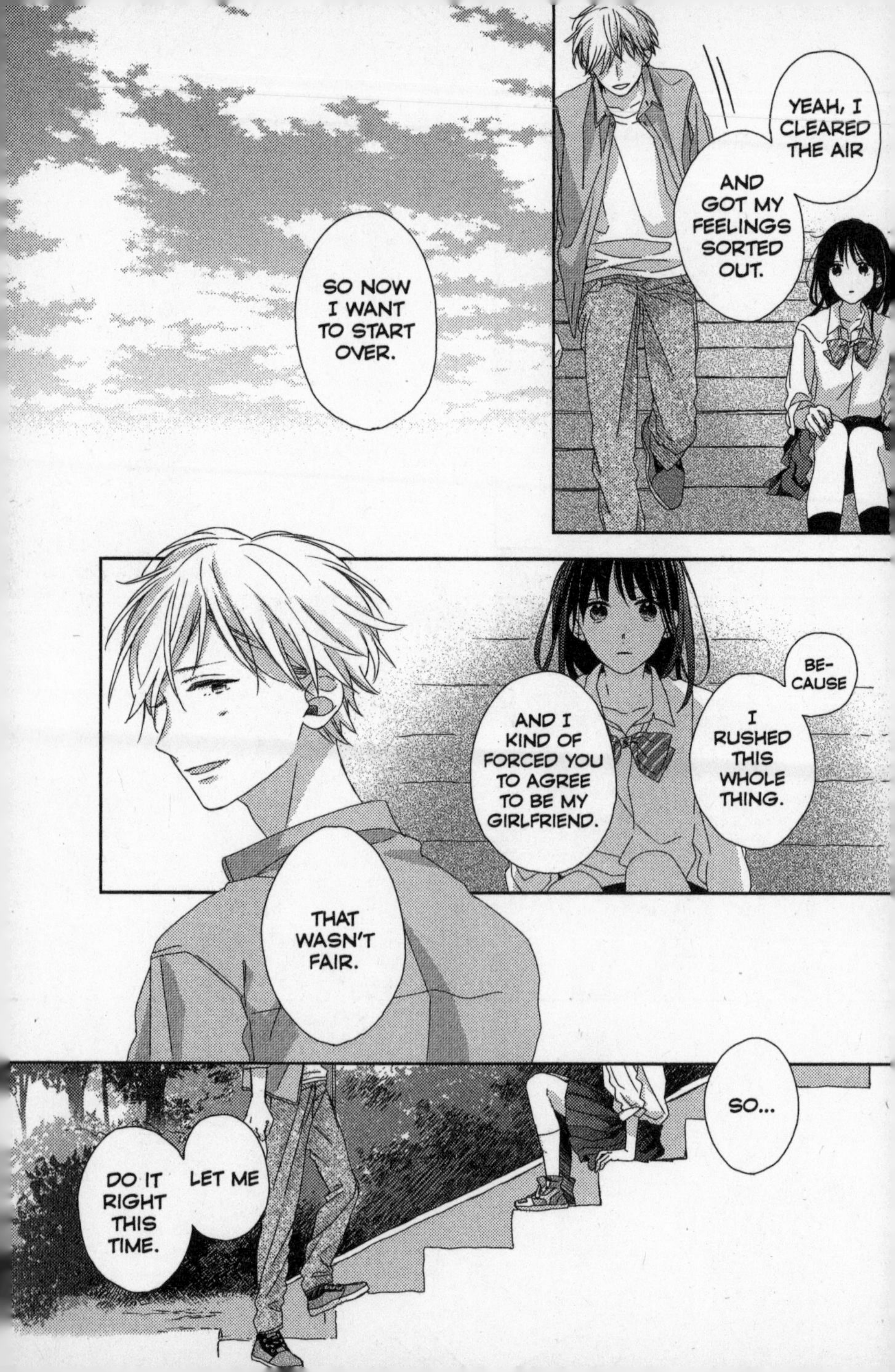
YEAH, I CLEARED THE AIR
AND GOT MY FEELINGS SORTED OUT.
SO NOW I WANT TO START OVER.
BE-CAUSE I RUSHED THIS WHOLE THING.
AND I KIND OF FORCED YOU TO AGREE TO BE MY GIRLFRIEND.
THAT WASN'T FAIR.
SO...
LET ME DO IT RIGHT THIS TIME.

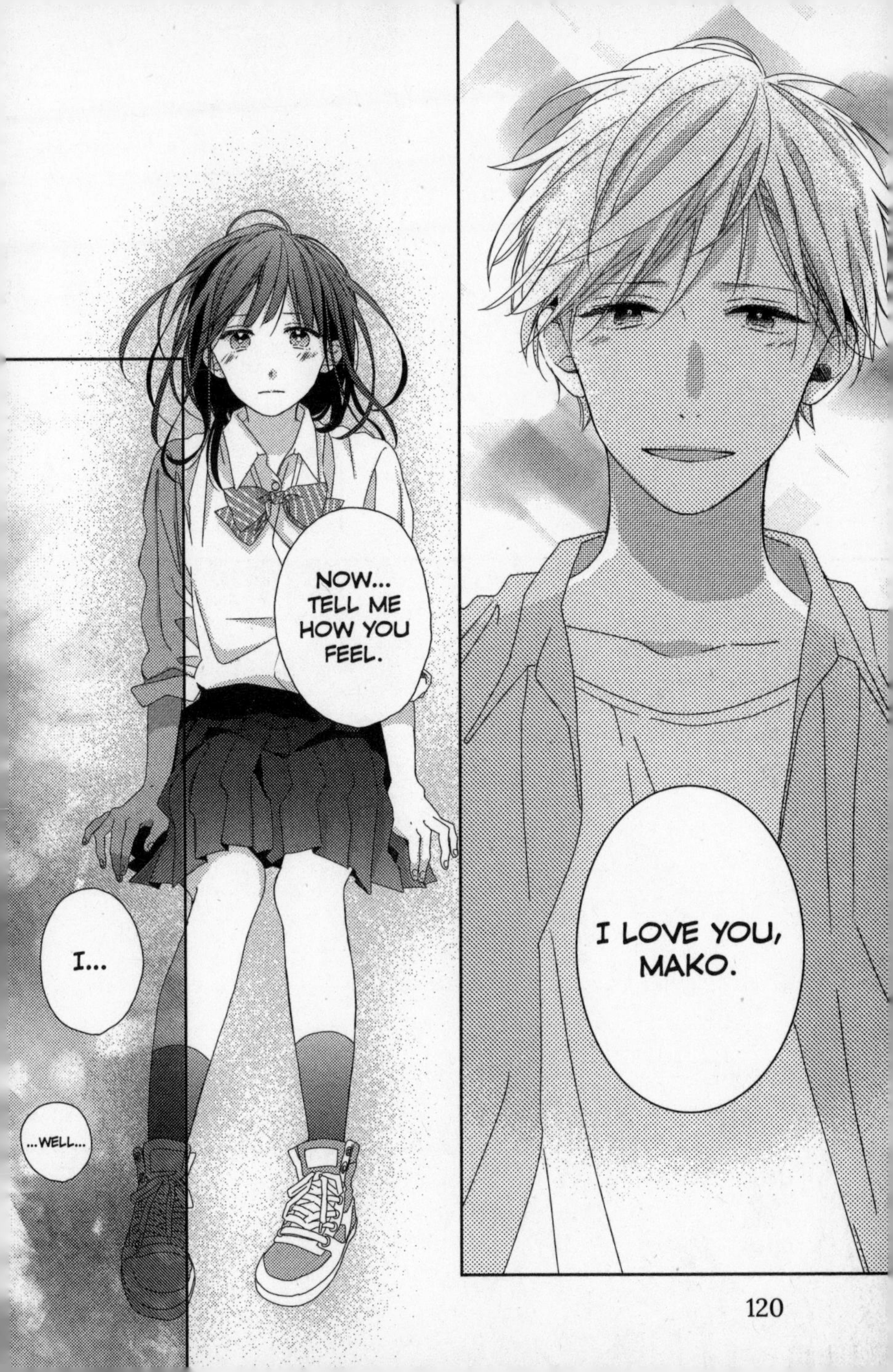
I LOVE YOU, MAKO.
NOW... TELL ME HOW YOU FEEL.
I...
...WELL...

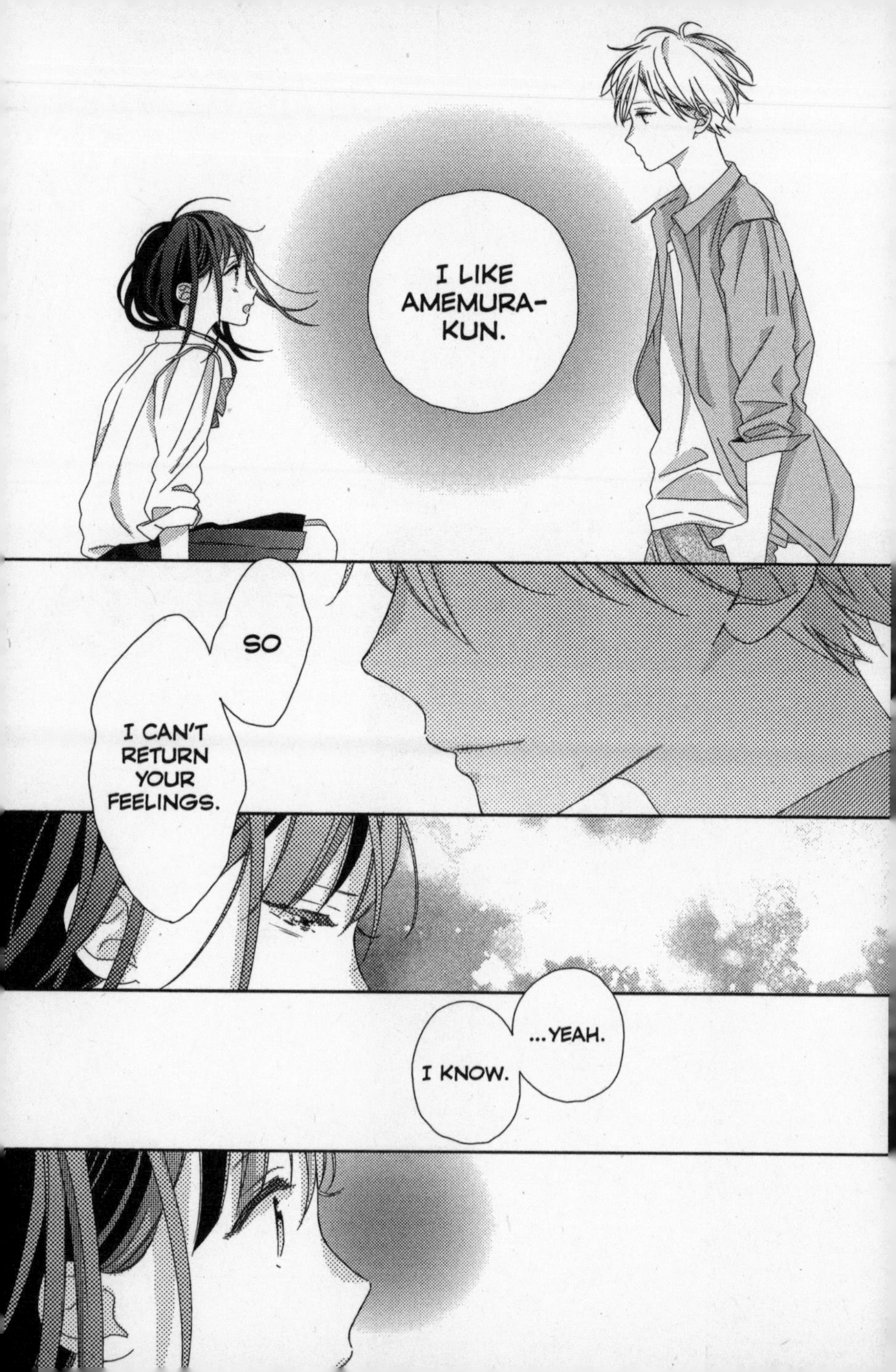
I LIKE AMEMURA-KUN.
SO
I CAN'T RETURN YOUR FEELINGS.
...YEAH.
I KNOW.

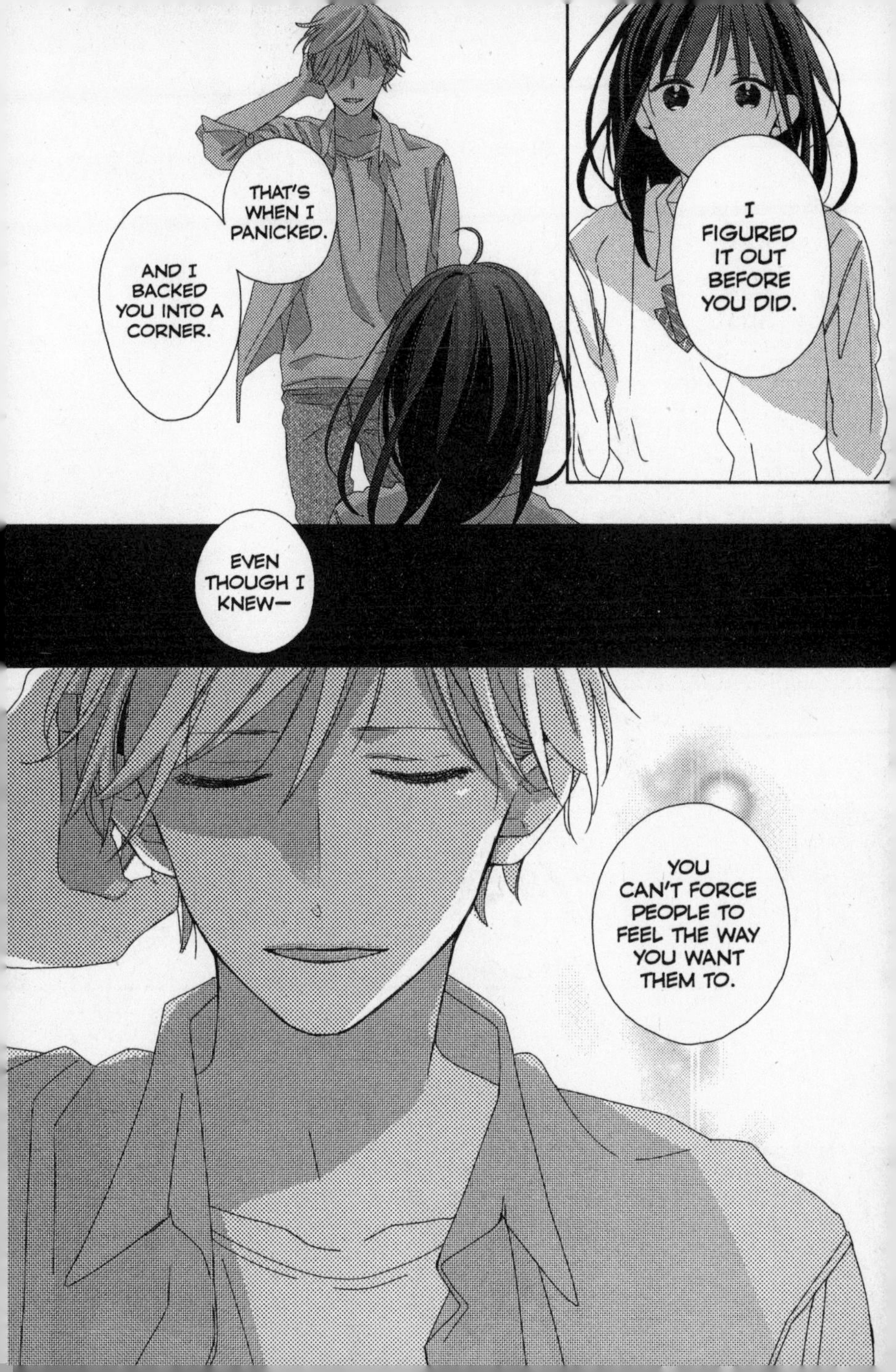
I FIGURED IT OUT BEFORE YOU DID.
THAT'S WHEN I PANICKED.
AND I BACKED YOU INTO A CORNER.
EVEN THOUGH I KNEW—
YOU CAN'T FORCE PEOPLE TO FEEL THE WAY YOU WANT THEM TO.

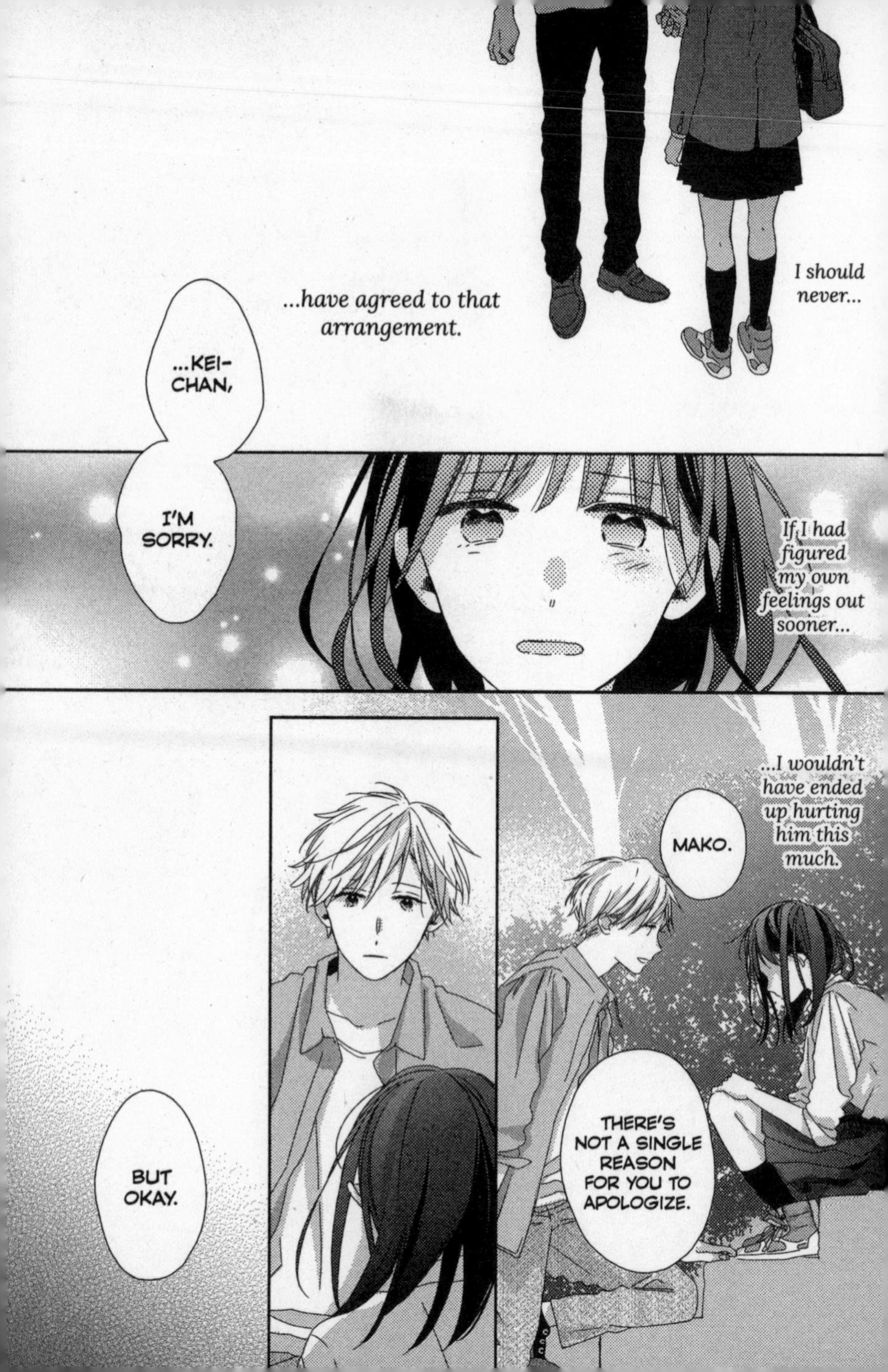
I should never...
...have agreed to that arrangement.
...KEI-CHAN,
I'M SORRY.
If I had figured my own feelings out sooner...
...I wouldn't have ended up hurting him this much.
MAKO.
THERE'S NOT A SINGLE REASON FOR YOU TO APOLOGIZE.
BUT OKAY.

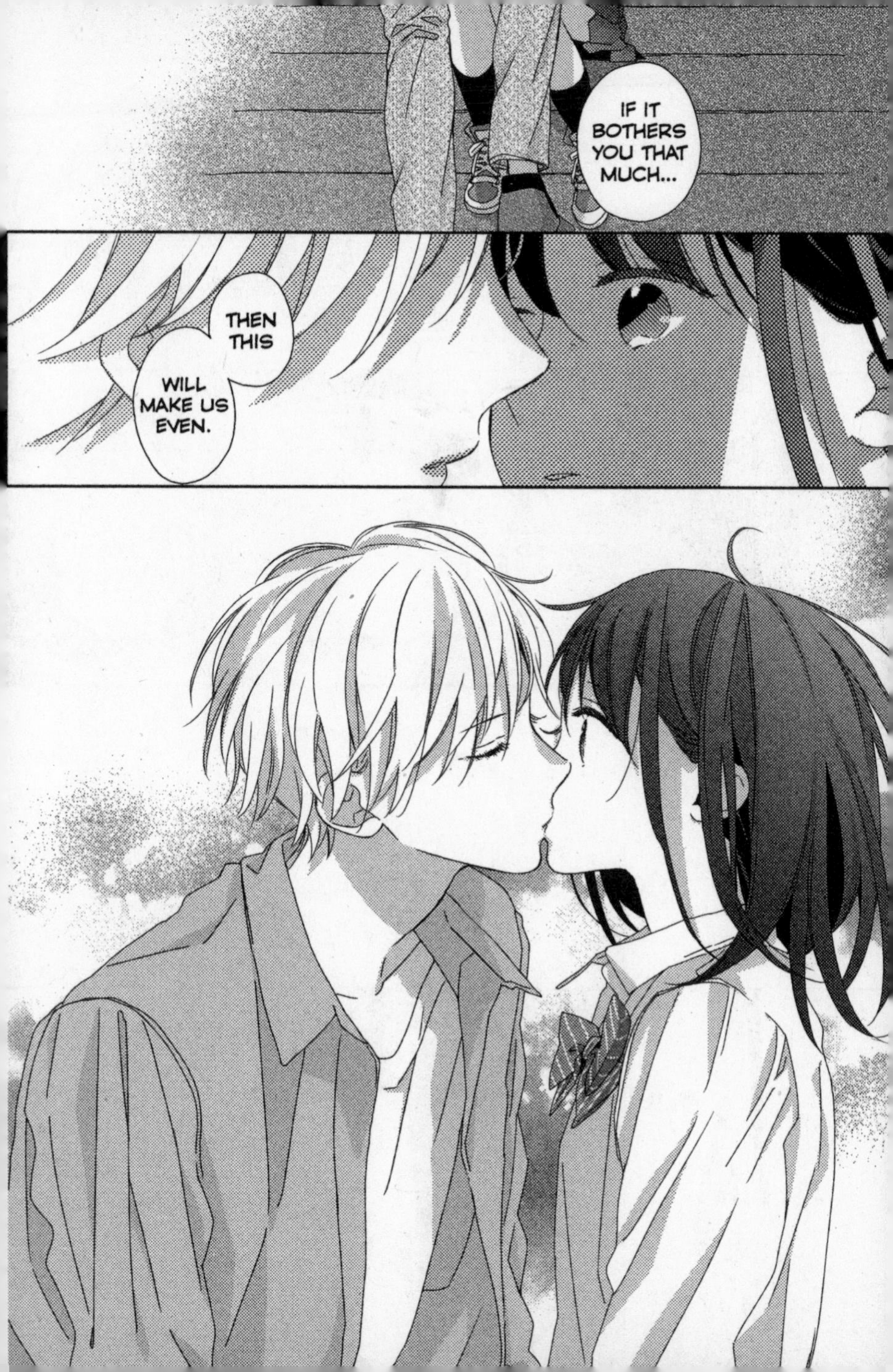
IF IT BOTHERS YOU THAT MUCH...
THEN THIS
WILL MAKE US EVEN.

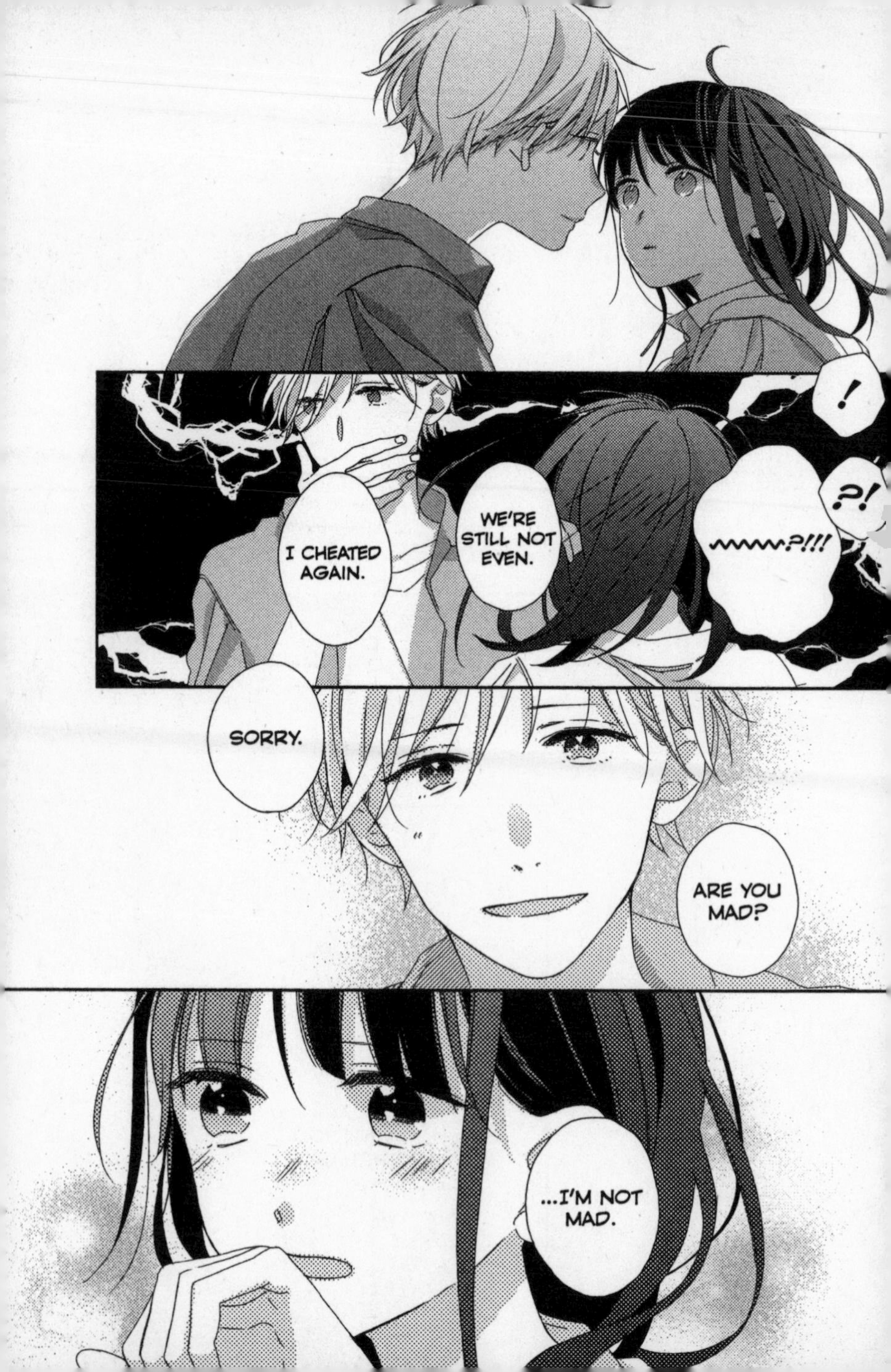
!
?!
~~~~?!!!
WE'RE STILL NOT EVEN.
I CHEATED AGAIN.
SORRY.
ARE YOU MAD?
...I'M NOT MAD.
~~~~

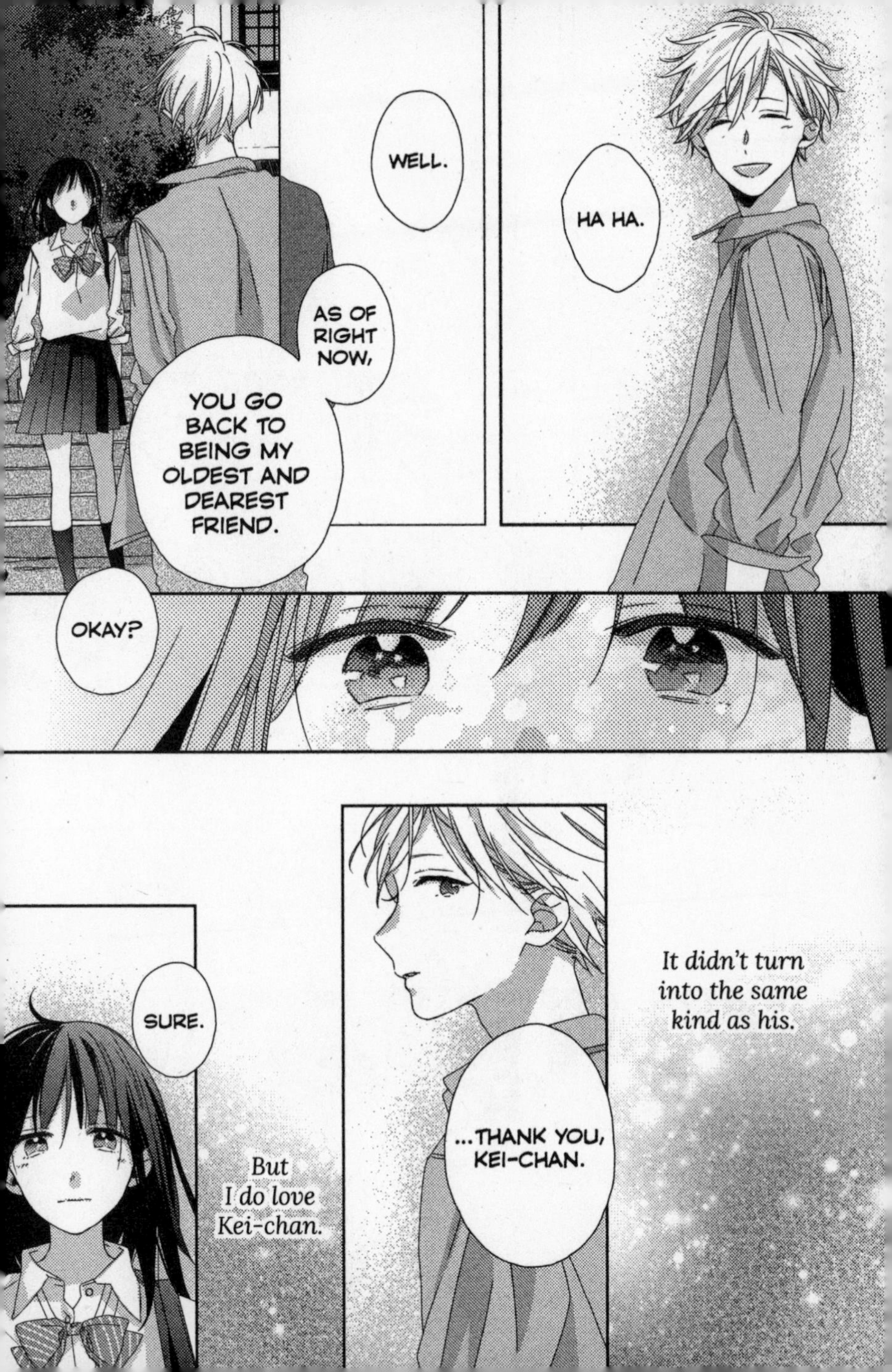
HA HA.
WELL.
AS OF RIGHT NOW,
YOU GO BACK TO BEING MY OLDEST AND DEAREST FRIEND.
OKAY?
It didn't turn into the same kind as his.
...THANK YOU, KEI-CHAN.
SURE.
But I do love Kei-chan.

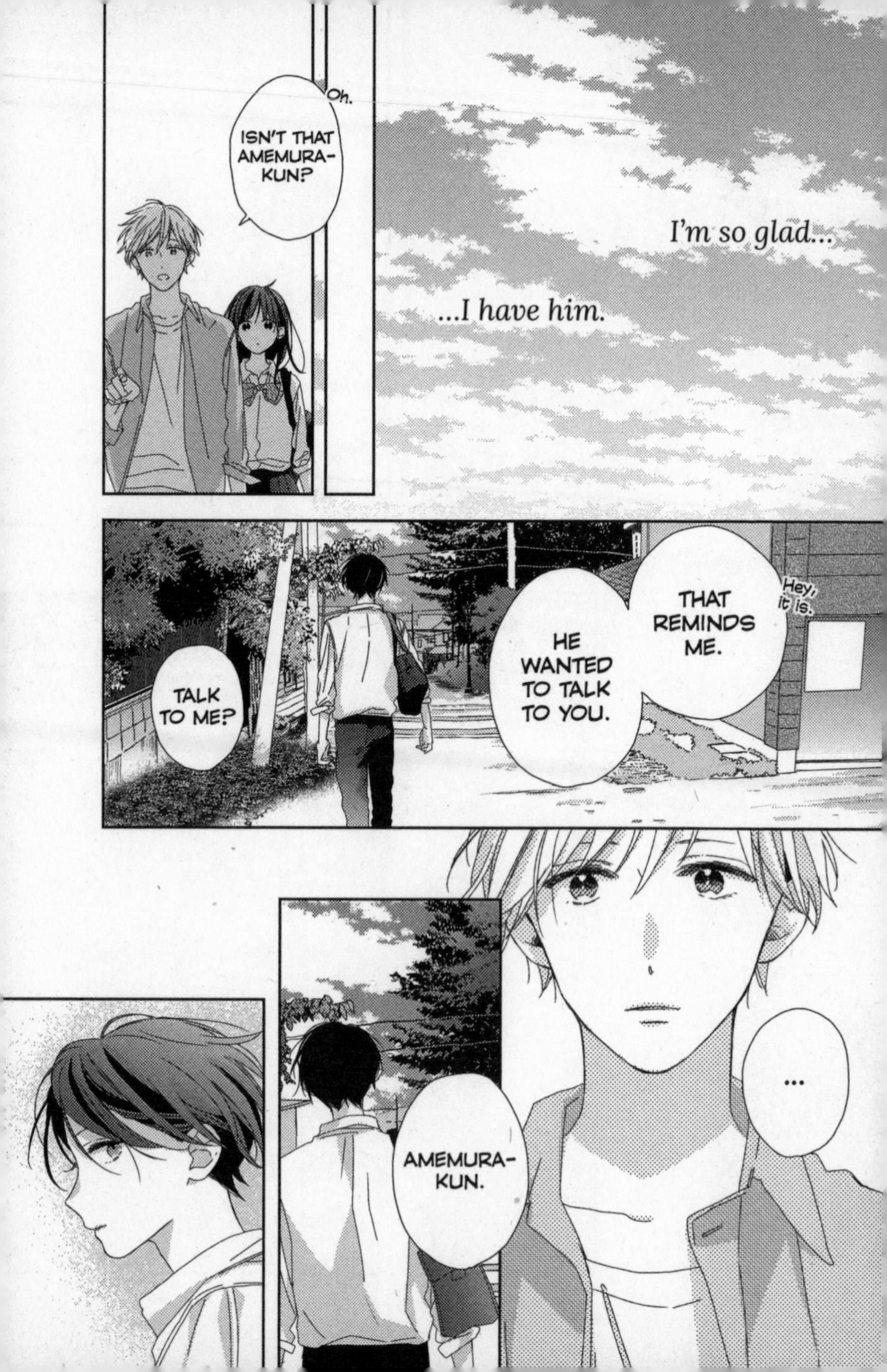
I'm so glad...
...I have him.
Oh.
ISN'T THAT AMEMURA-KUN?
Hey, it is.
THAT REMINDS ME.
HE WANTED TO TALK TO YOU.
TALK TO ME?
...
AMEMURA-KUN.

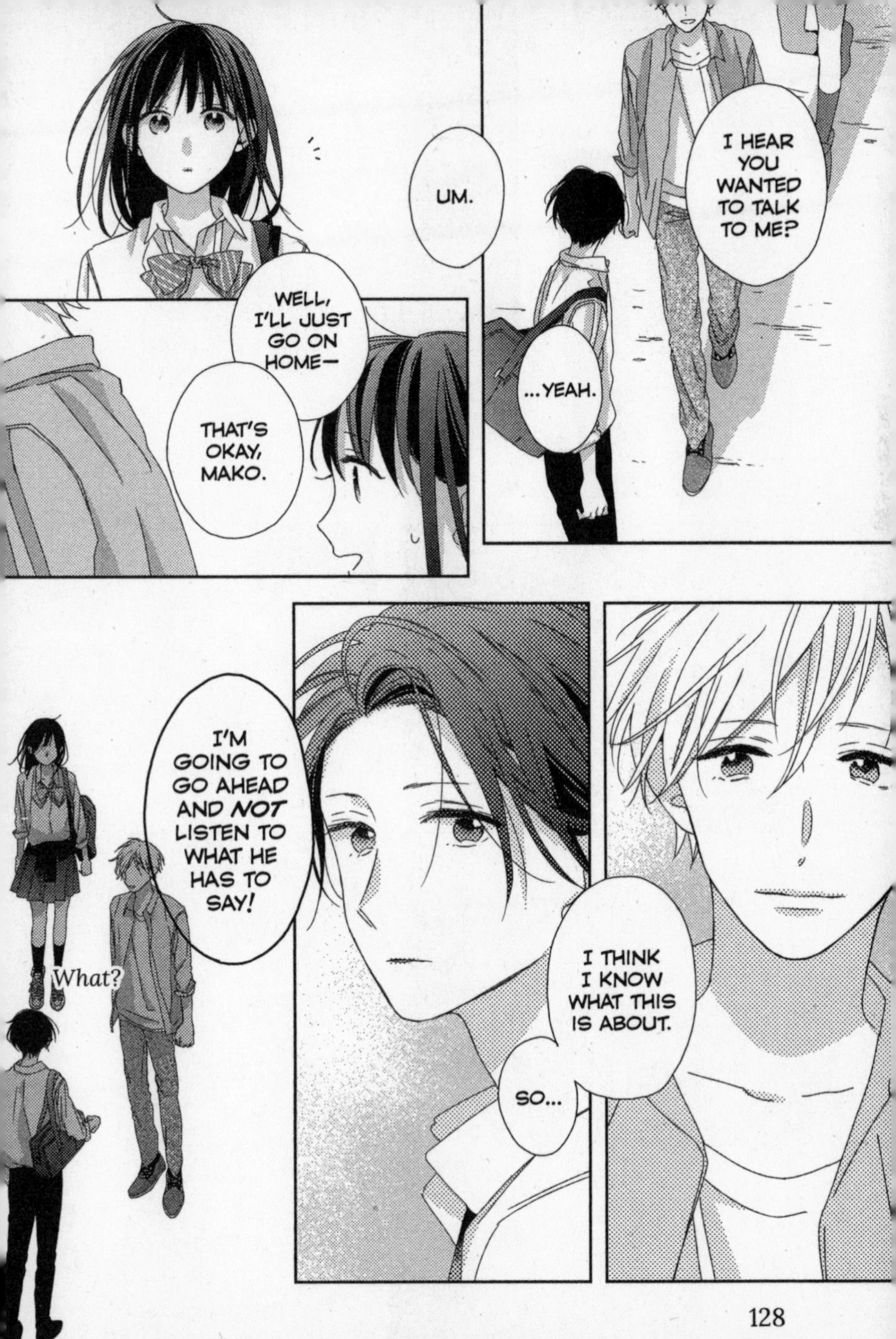
I HEAR YOU WANTED TO TALK TO ME?
...YEAH.
UM.
WELL, I'LL JUST GO ON HOME—
THAT'S OKAY, MAKO.
I THINK I KNOW WHAT THIS IS ABOUT.
SO...
I'M GOING TO GO AHEAD AND NOT LISTEN TO WHAT HE HAS TO SAY!
What?

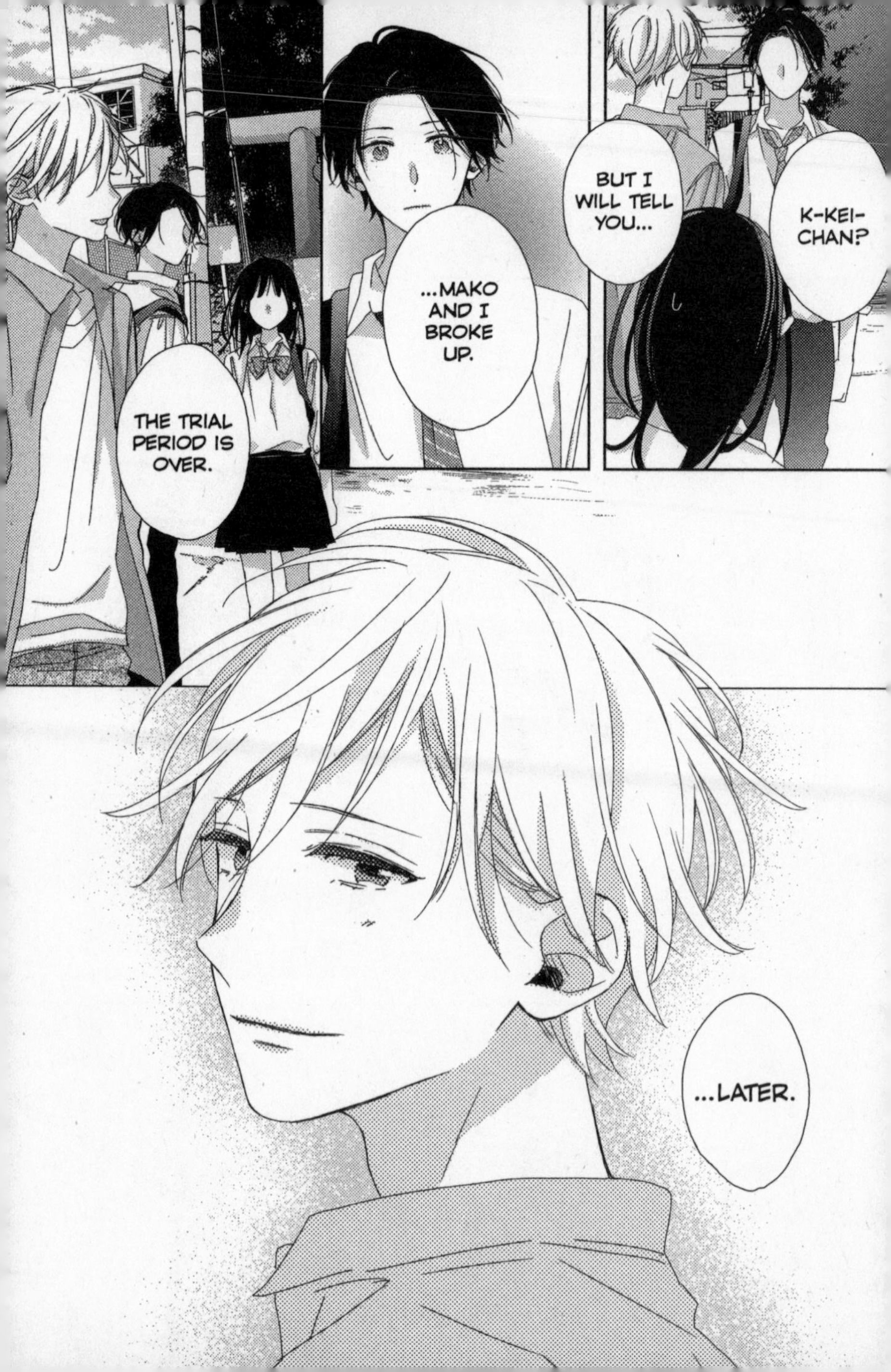
K-KEI-CHAN?
BUT I WILL TELL YOU...
...MAKO AND I BROKE UP.
THE TRIAL PERIOD IS OVER.
...LATER.

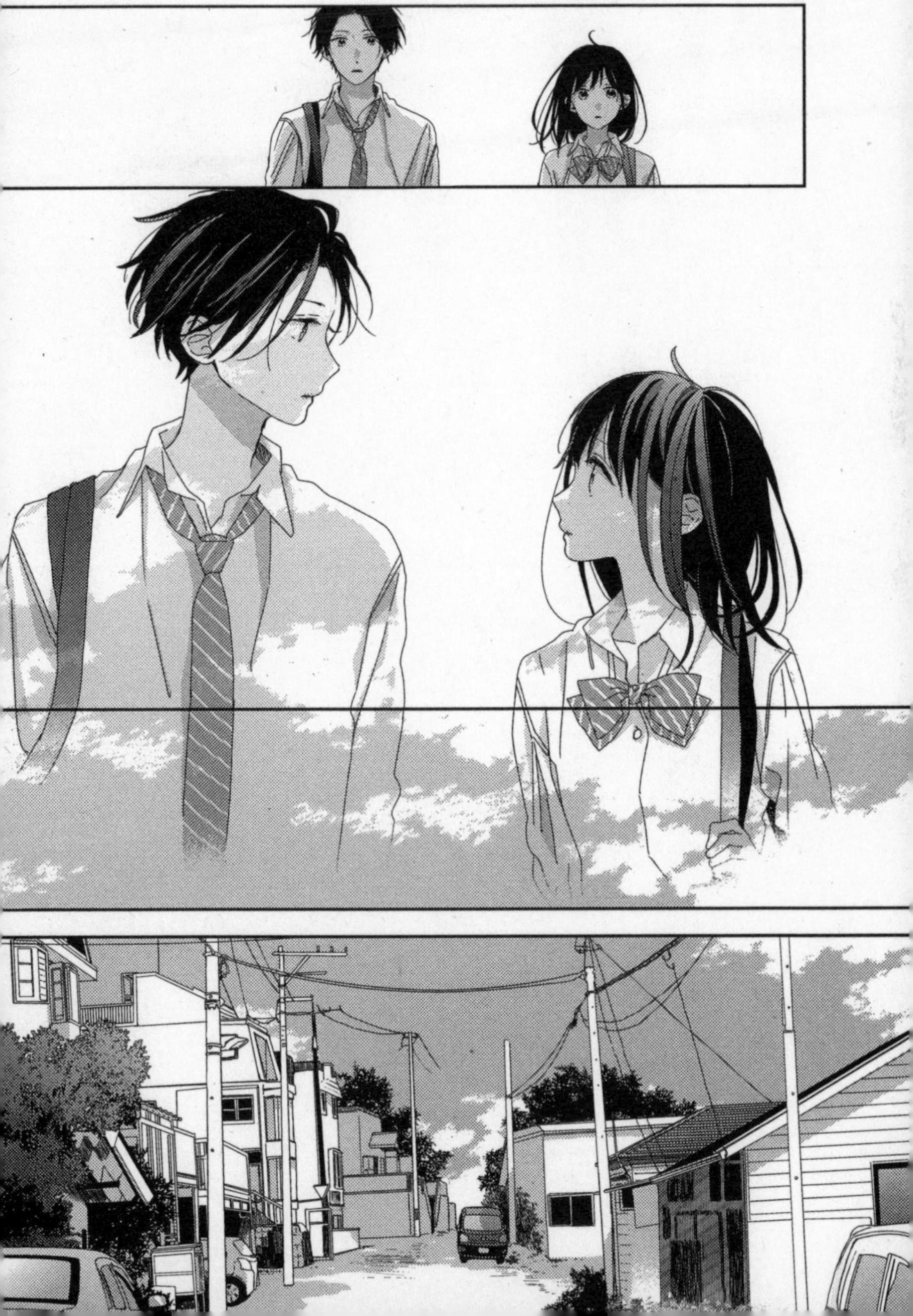

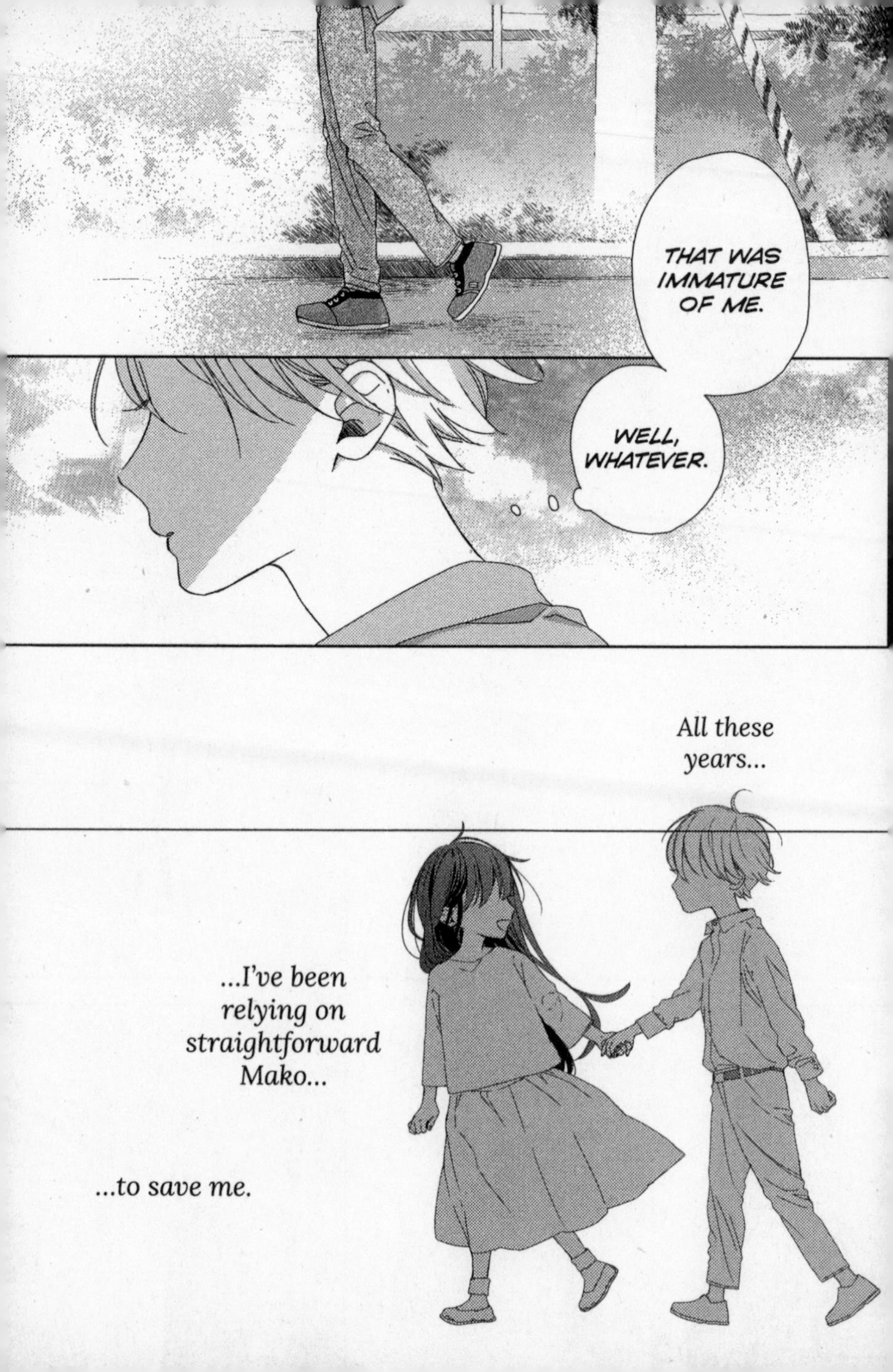
THAT WAS IMMATURE OF ME.
WELL, WHATEVER.
All these years...
...I've been relying on straightforward Mako...
...to save me.

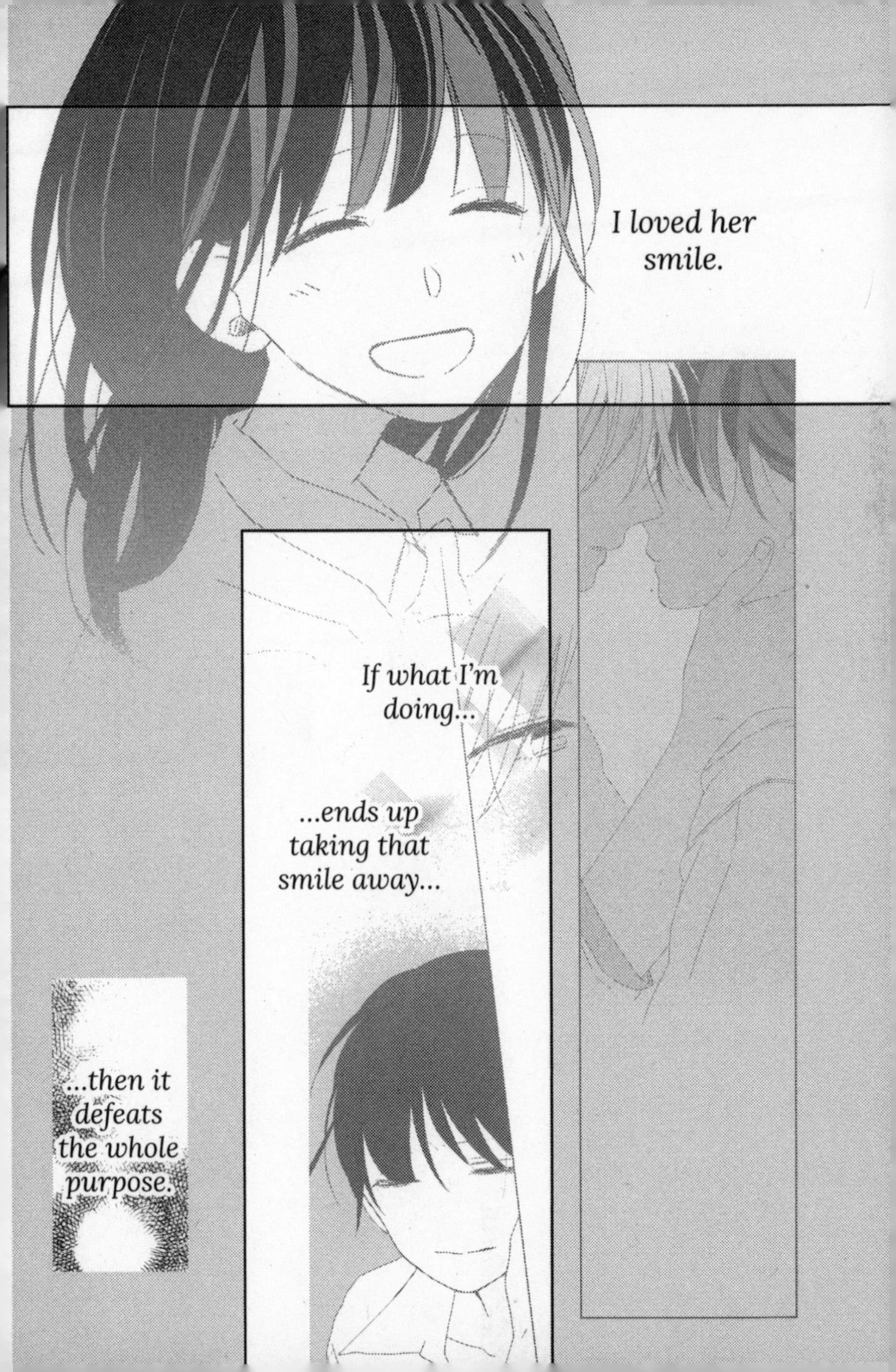
I loved her smile.
If what I'm doing...
...ends up taking that smile away...
...then it defeats the whole purpose.

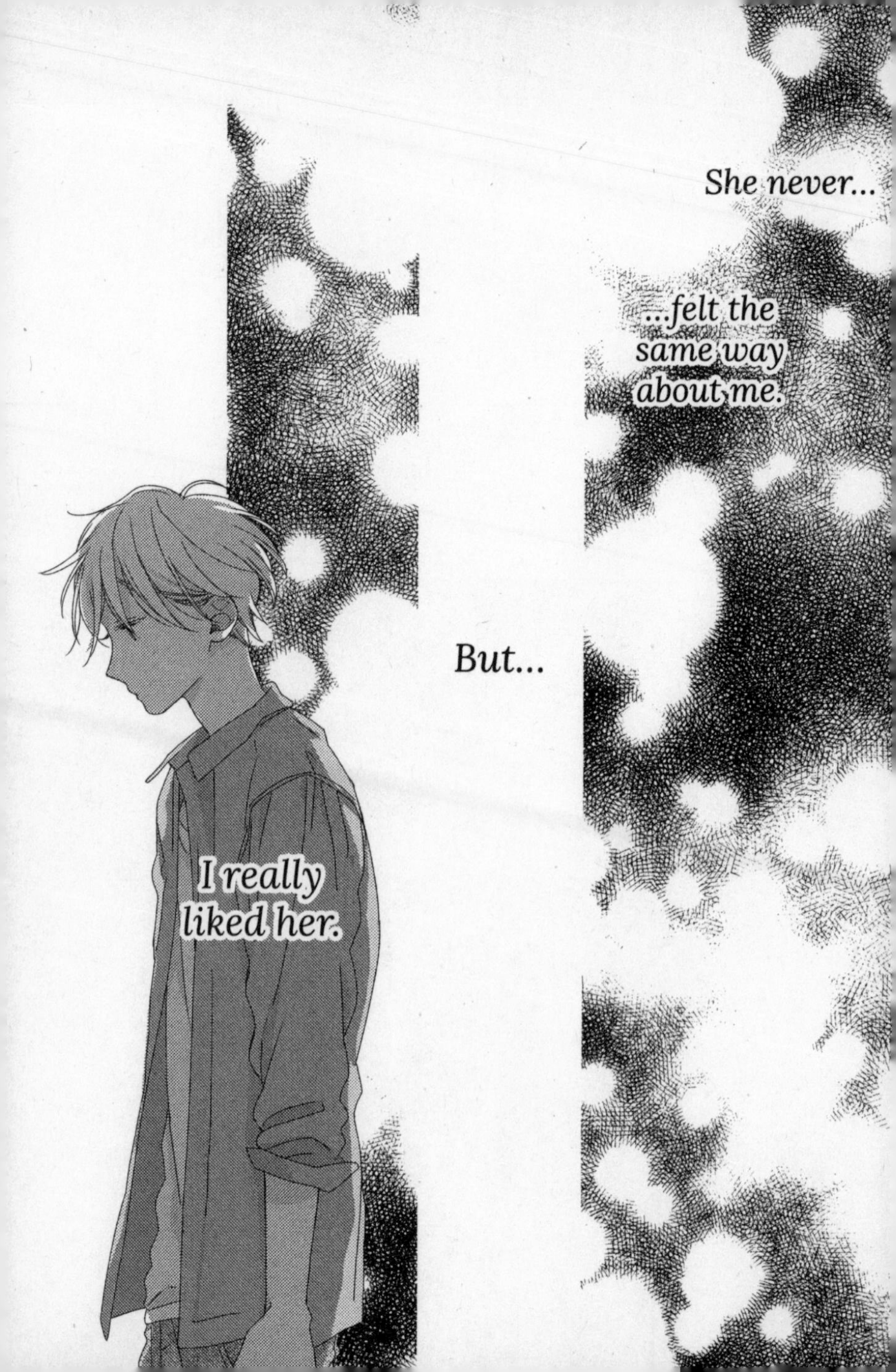
She never...
...felt the same way about me.
But...
I really liked her.

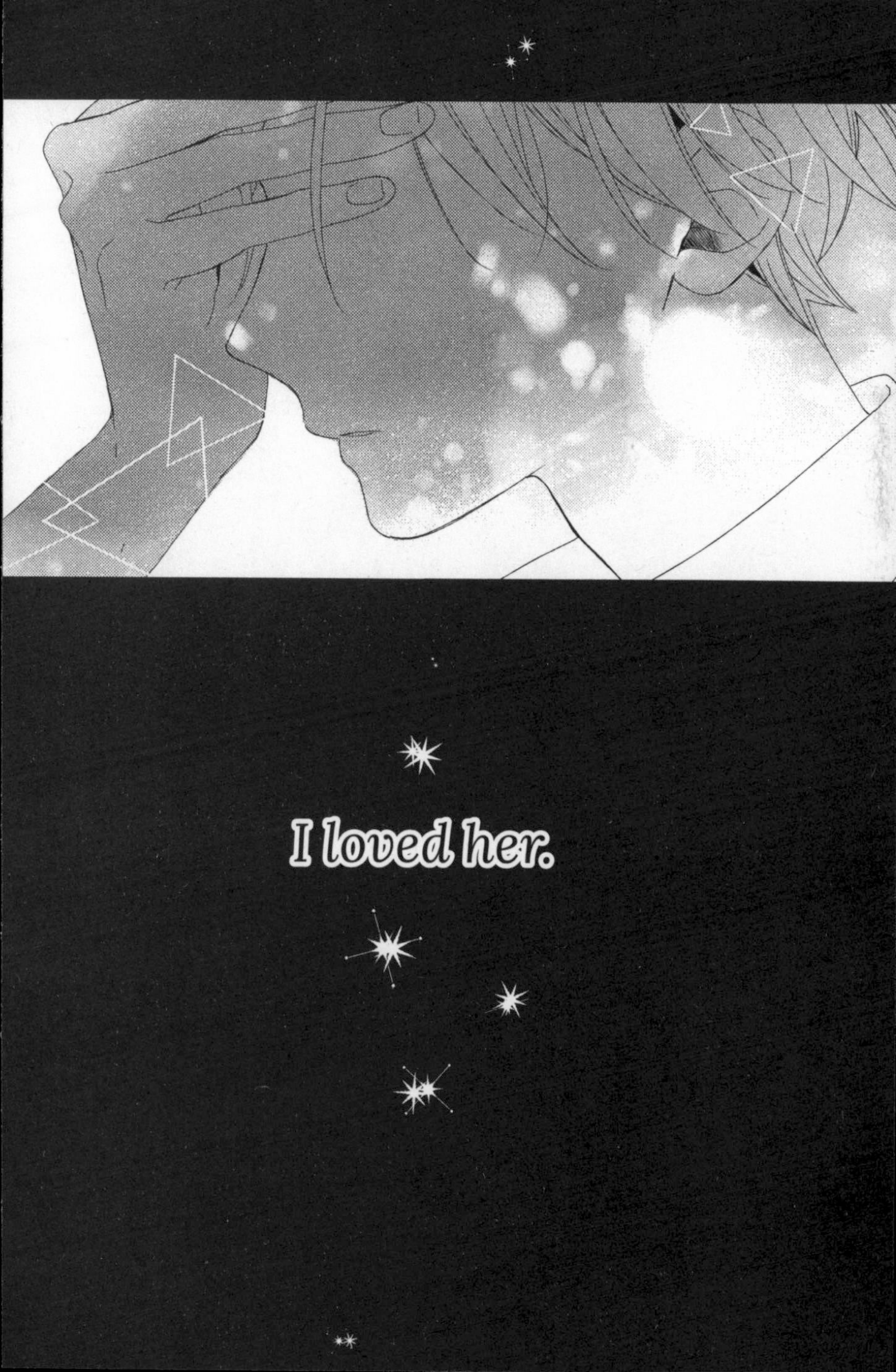
I loved her.

FILM 14

I Love You the Way You Are

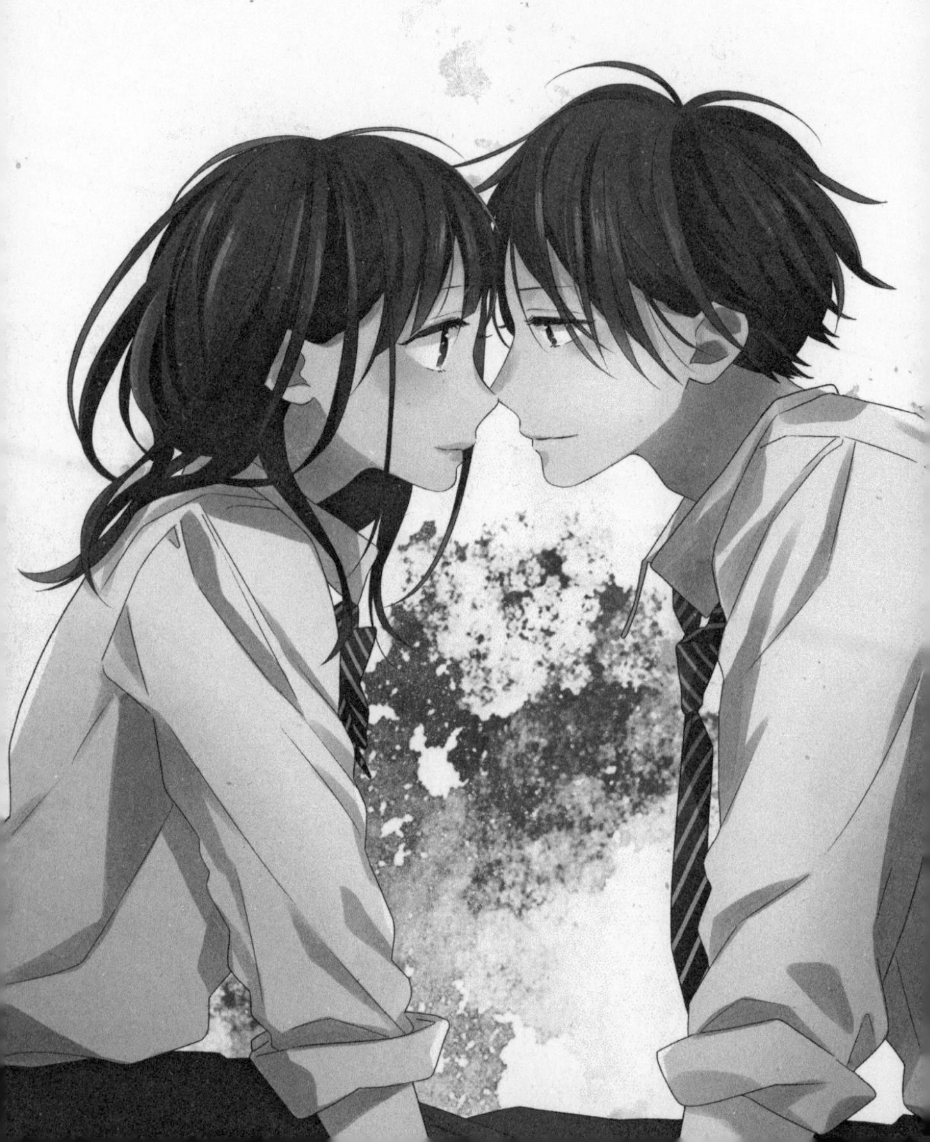

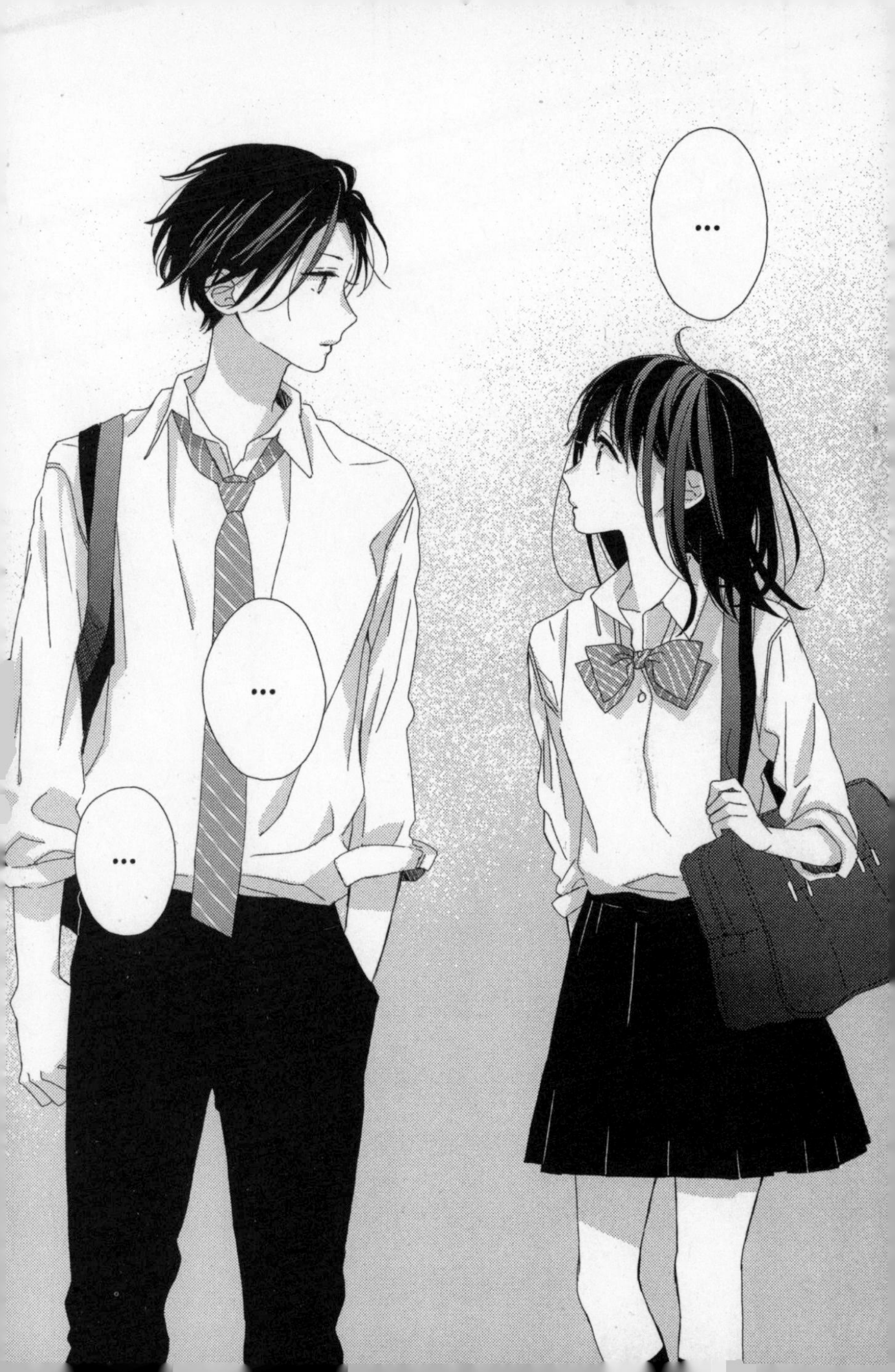
…
…
…

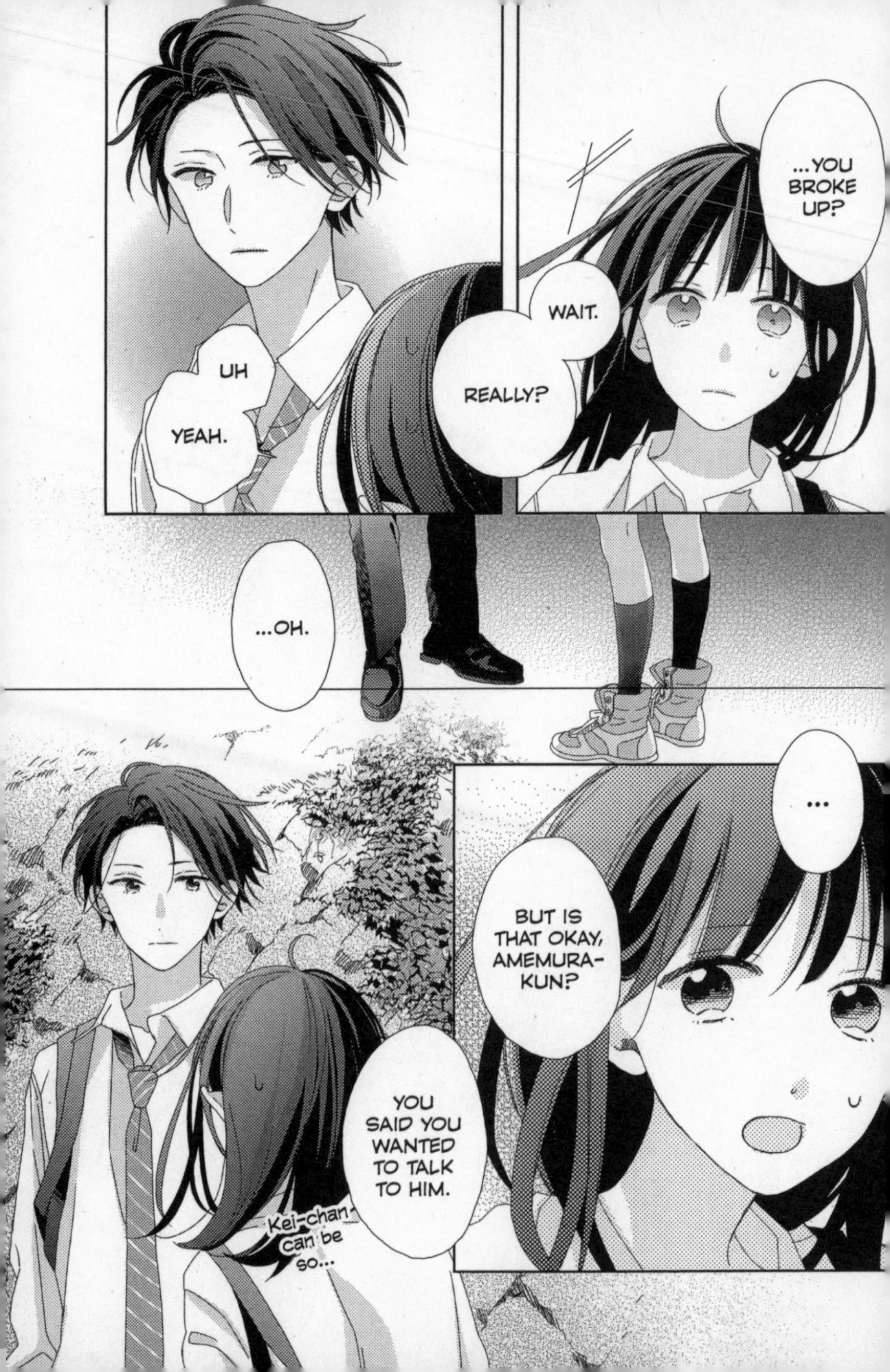

...YOU BROKE UP?
WAIT.
REALLY?
UH
YEAH.
...OH.
...
BUT IS THAT OKAY, AMEMURA-KUN?
YOU SAID YOU WANTED TO TALK TO HIM.
Kei-chan can be so...

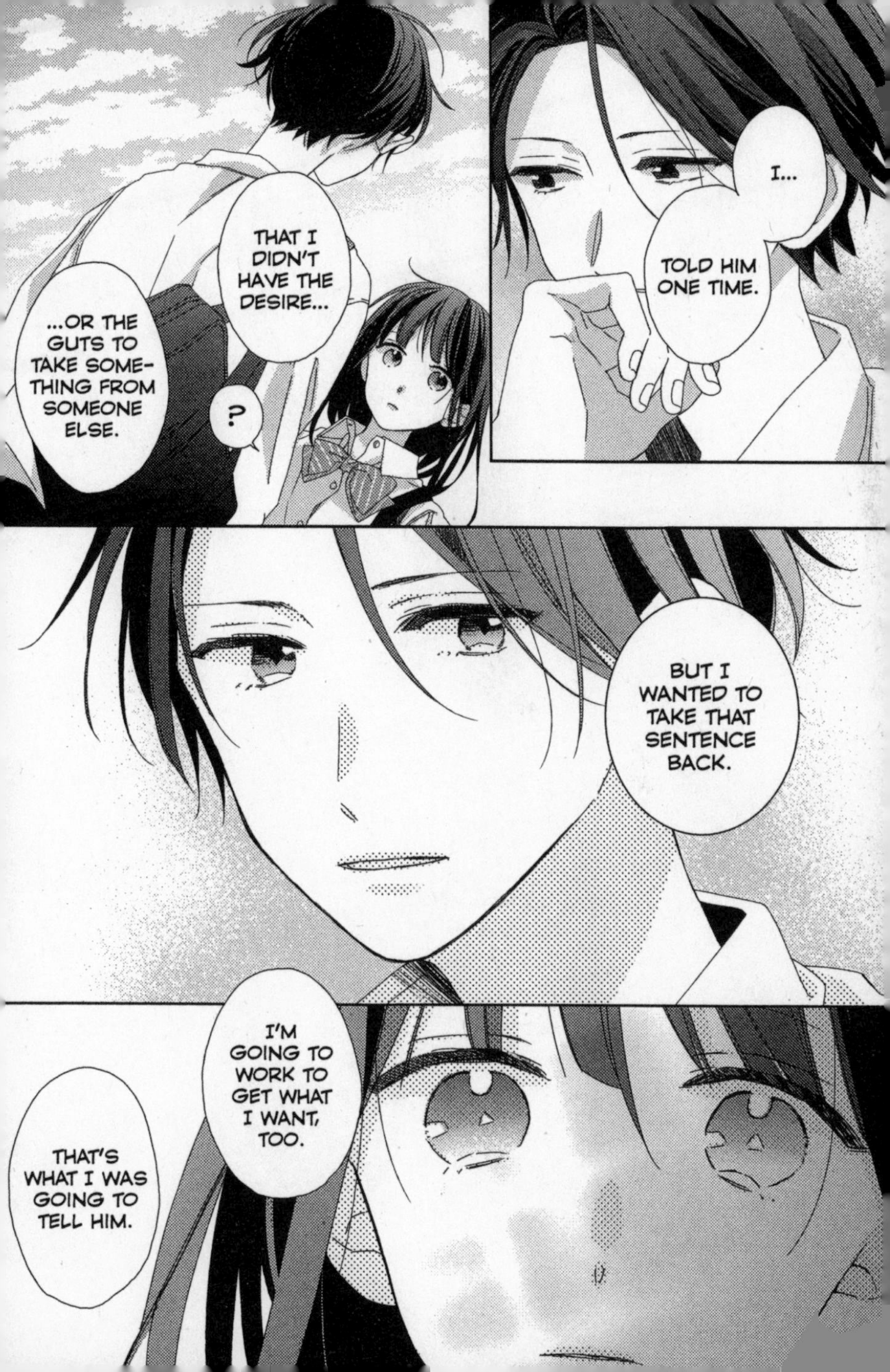
I...
TOLD HIM ONE TIME.
THAT I DIDN'T HAVE THE DESIRE...
...OR THE GUTS TO TAKE SOMETHING FROM SOMEONE ELSE.
?
BUT I WANTED TO TAKE THAT SENTENCE BACK.
I'M GOING TO WORK TO GET WHAT I WANT, TOO.
THAT'S WHAT I WAS GOING TO TELL HIM.

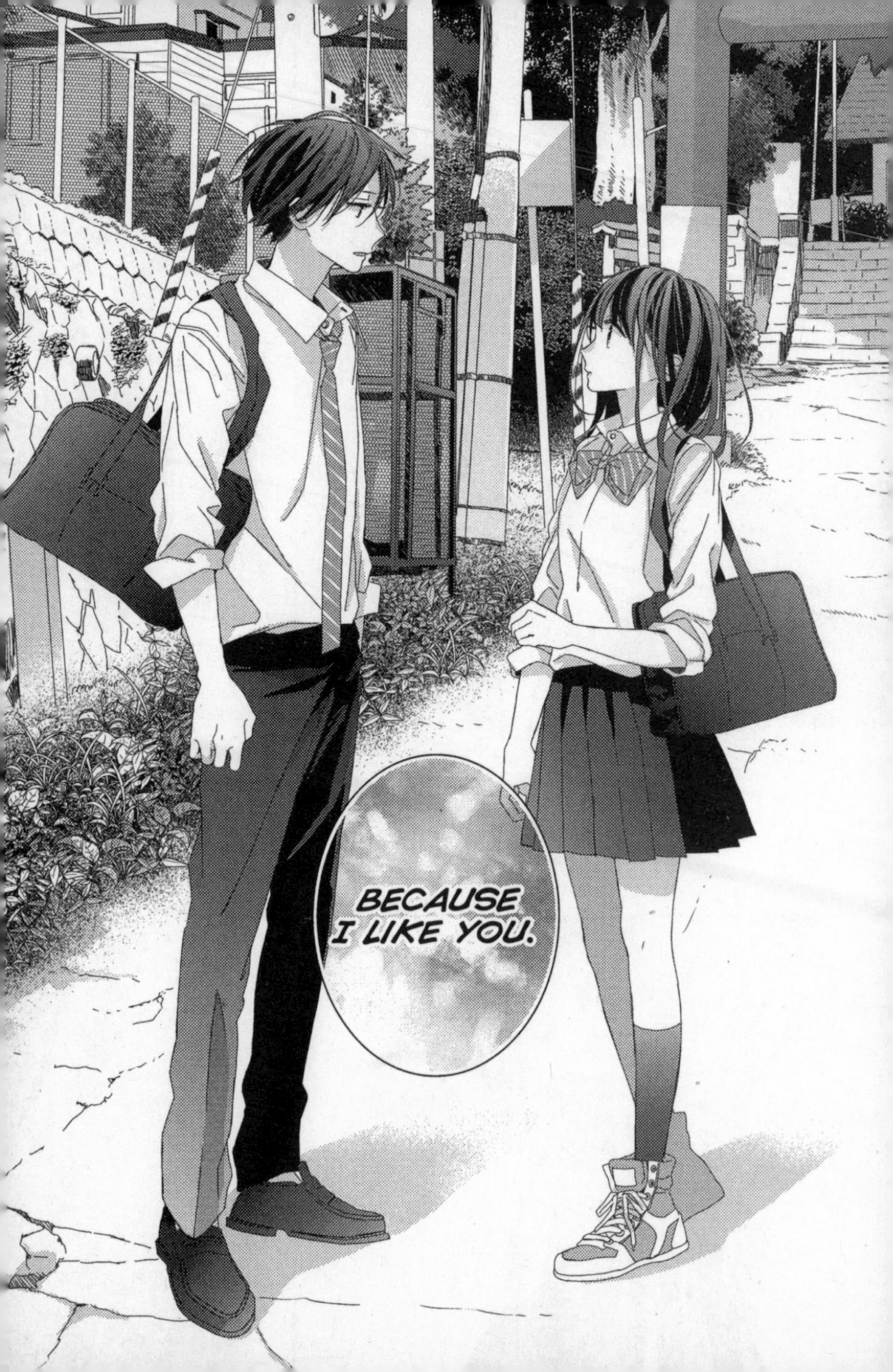
BECAUSE I LIKE YOU.

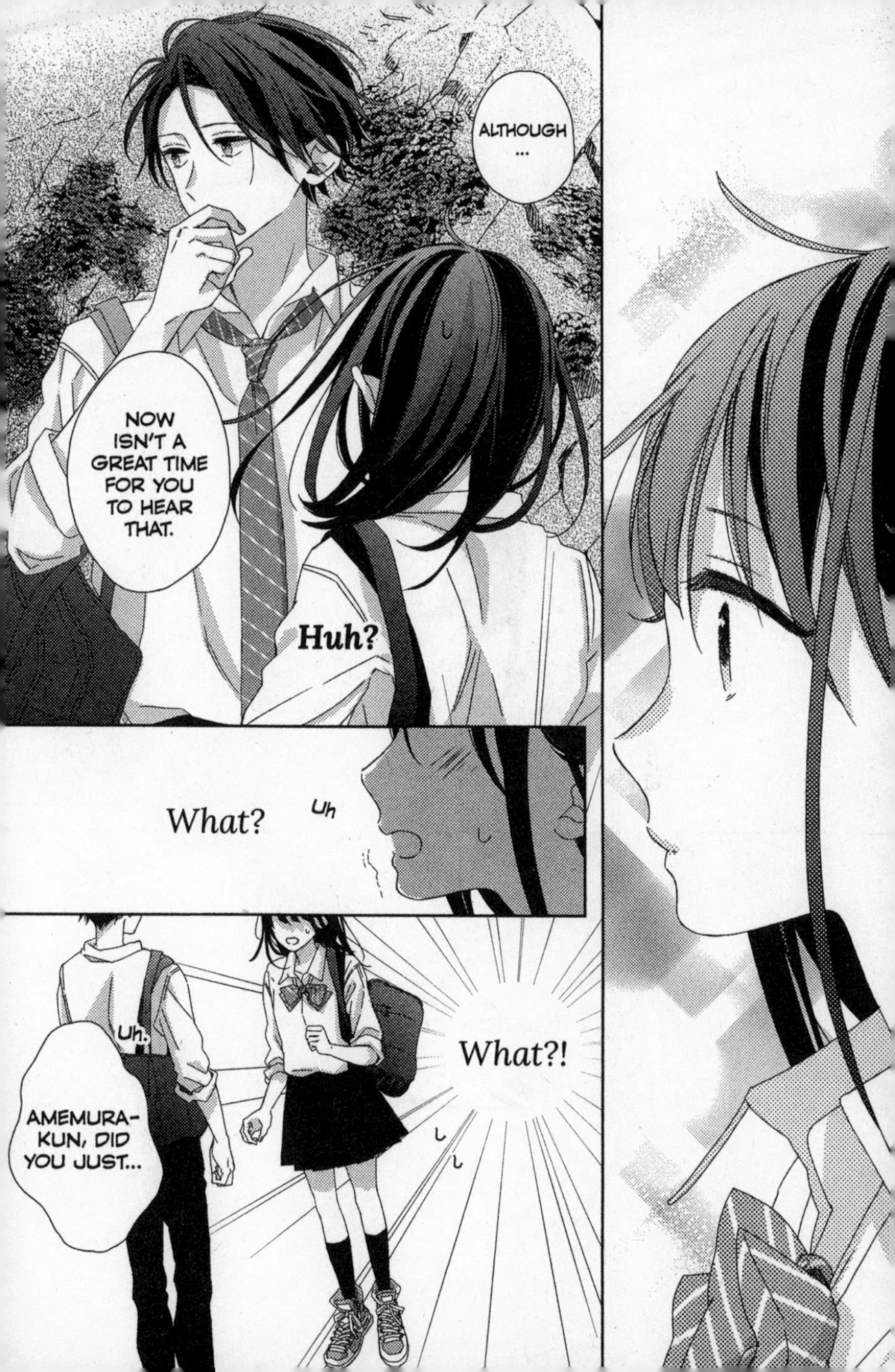
ALTHOUGH ...
NOW ISN'T A GREAT TIME FOR YOU TO HEAR THAT.
Huh?
Uh
What?
What?!
Uh.
AMEMURA-KUN, DID YOU JUST...

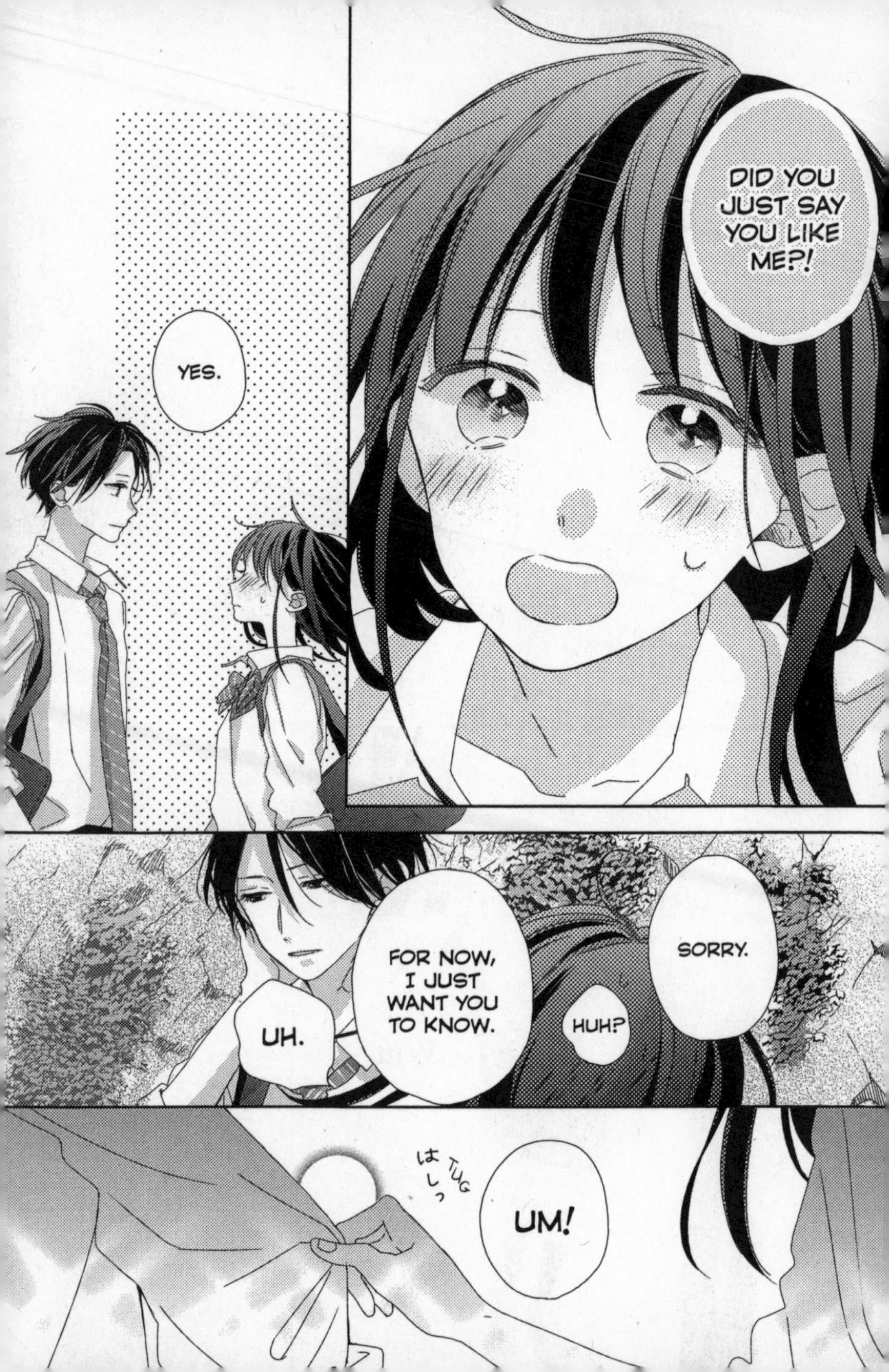
DID YOU JUST SAY YOU LIKE ME?!
YES.
SORRY.
HUH?
FOR NOW, I JUST WANT YOU TO KNOW.
UH.
UM!
はしっ TUG

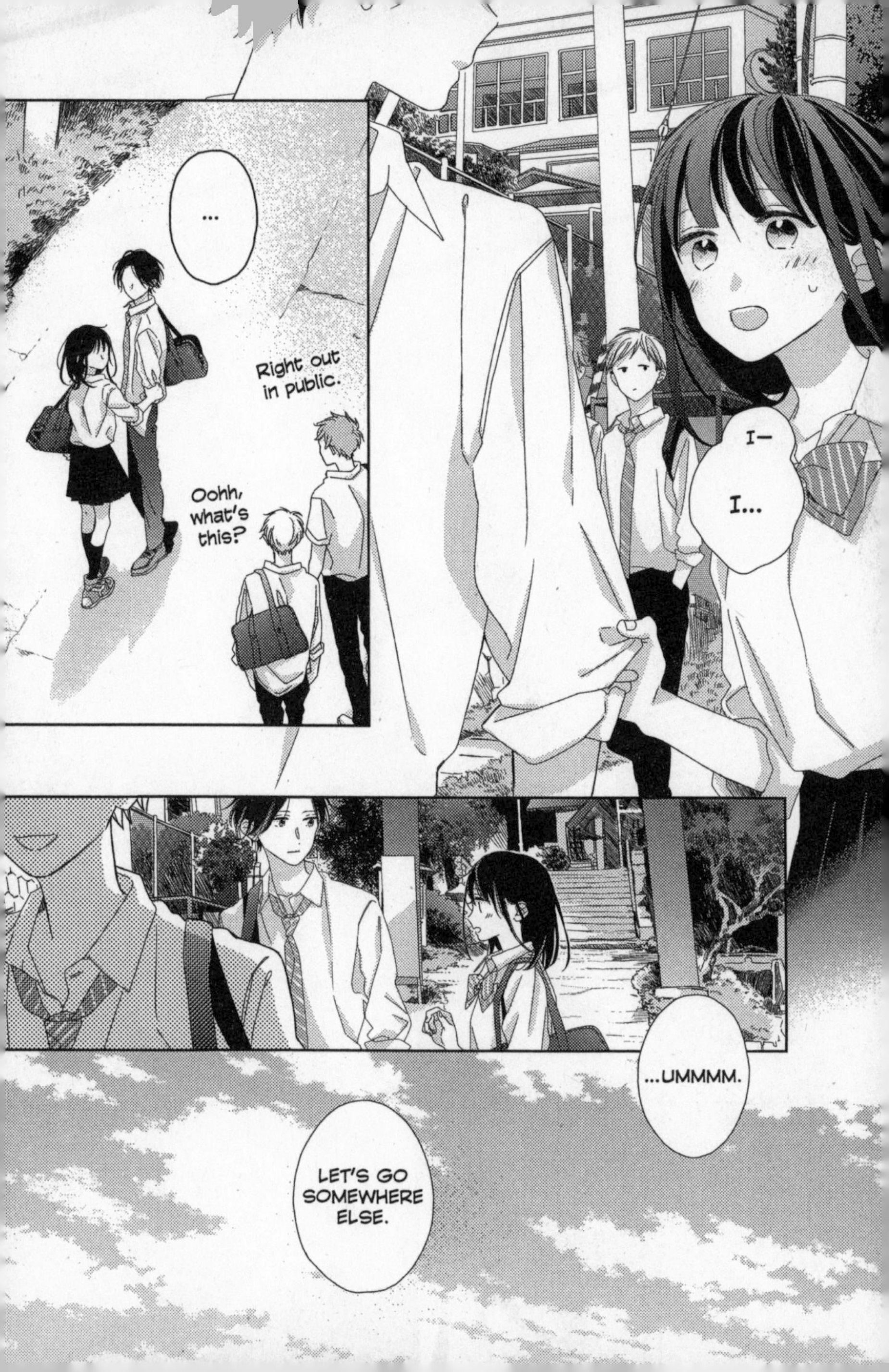
I— I...
...
Right out in public.
Oohh, what's this?
...UMMMM.
LET'S GO SOMEWHERE ELSE.

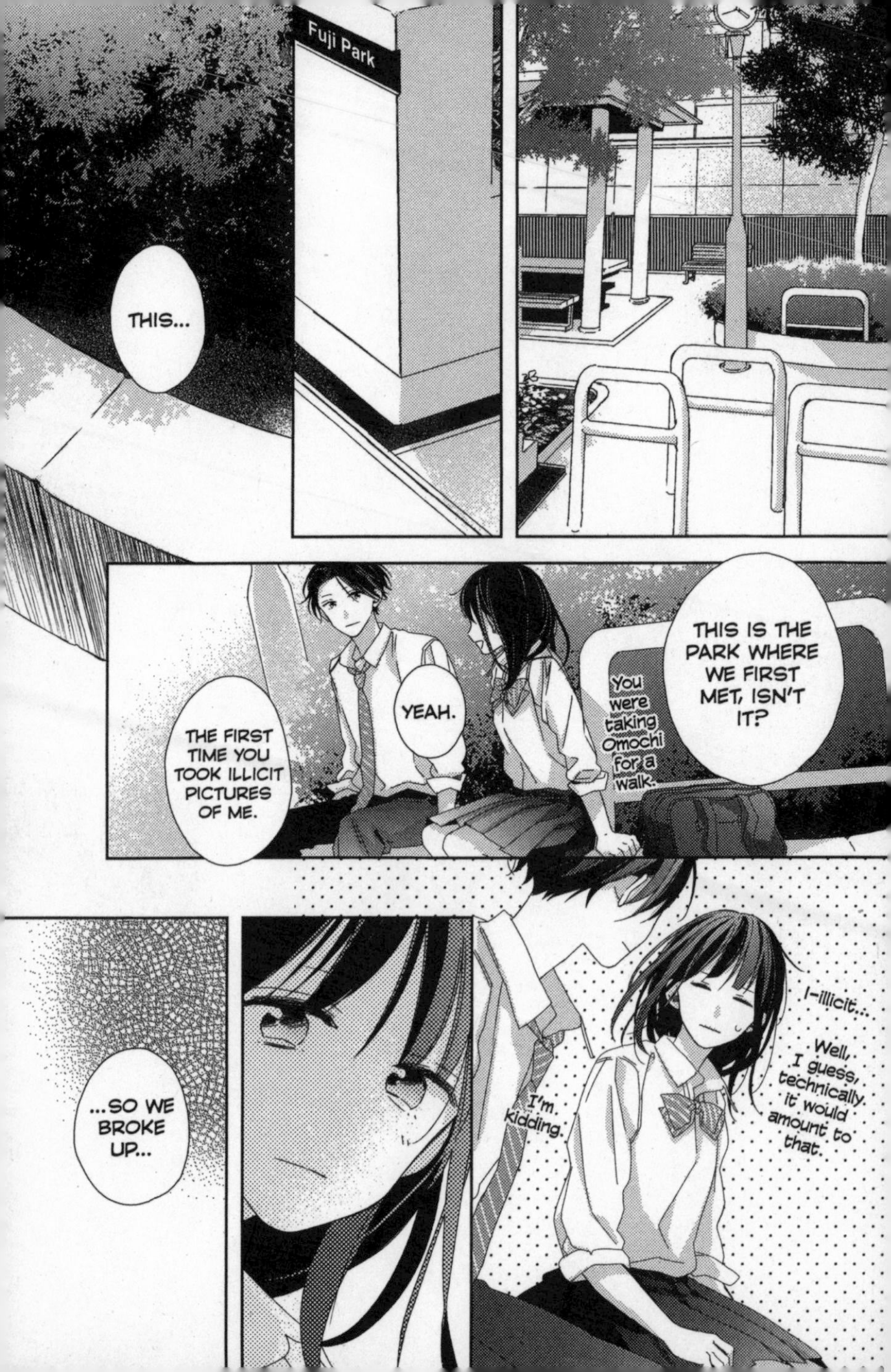
Fuji Park
THIS...
THIS IS THE PARK WHERE WE FIRST MET, ISN'T IT?
You were taking Omochi for a walk.
YEAH.
THE FIRST TIME YOU TOOK ILLICIT PICTURES OF ME.
I-illicit...
Well, I guess, technically it would amount to that.
I'm kidding.
...SO WE BROKE UP...

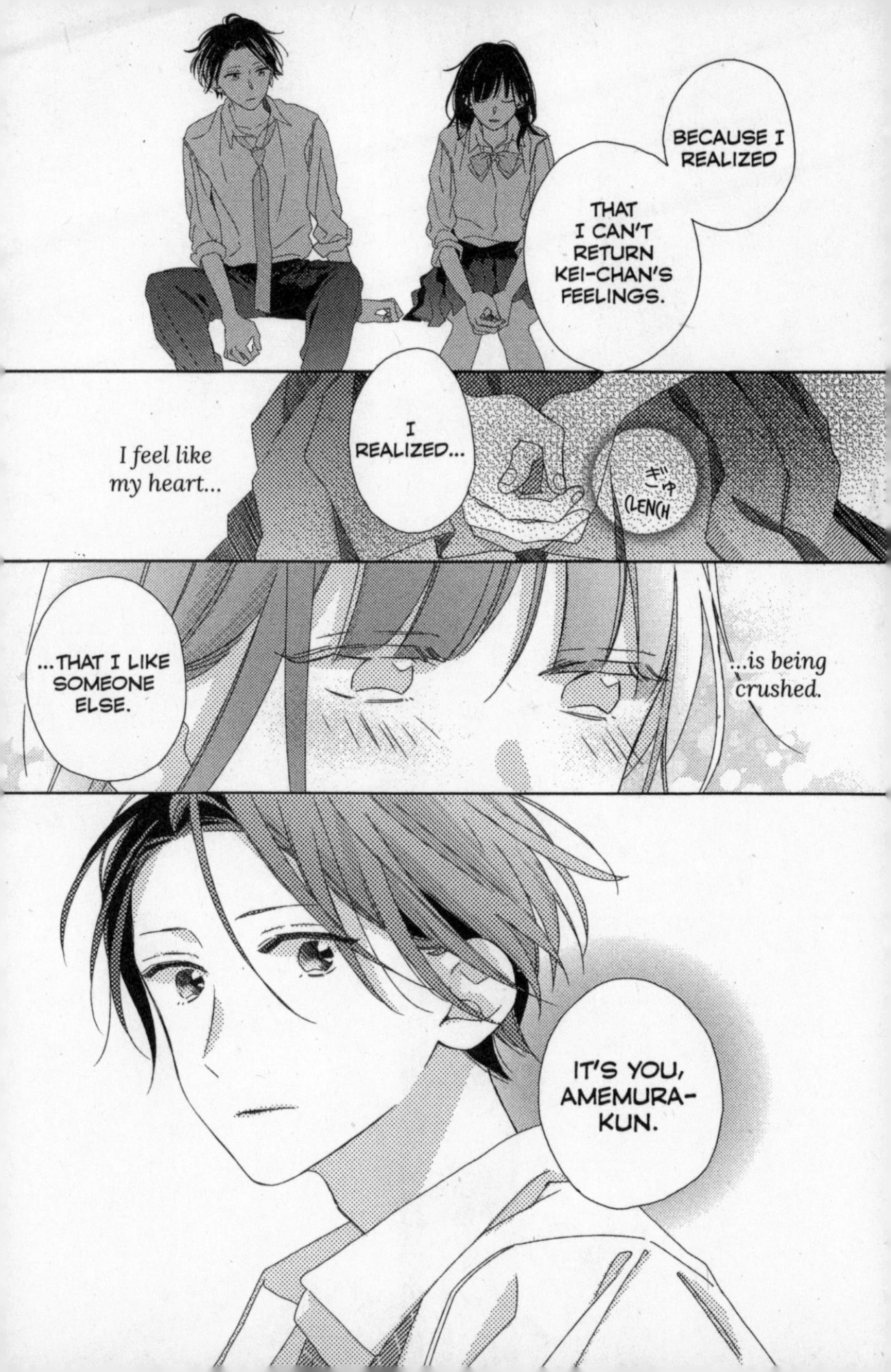
BECAUSE I REALIZED
THAT I CAN'T RETURN KEI-CHAN'S FEELINGS.
ぎゅ CLENCH
I REALIZED...
I feel like my heart...
...is being crushed.
...THAT I LIKE SOMEONE ELSE.
IT'S YOU, AMEMURA-KUN.

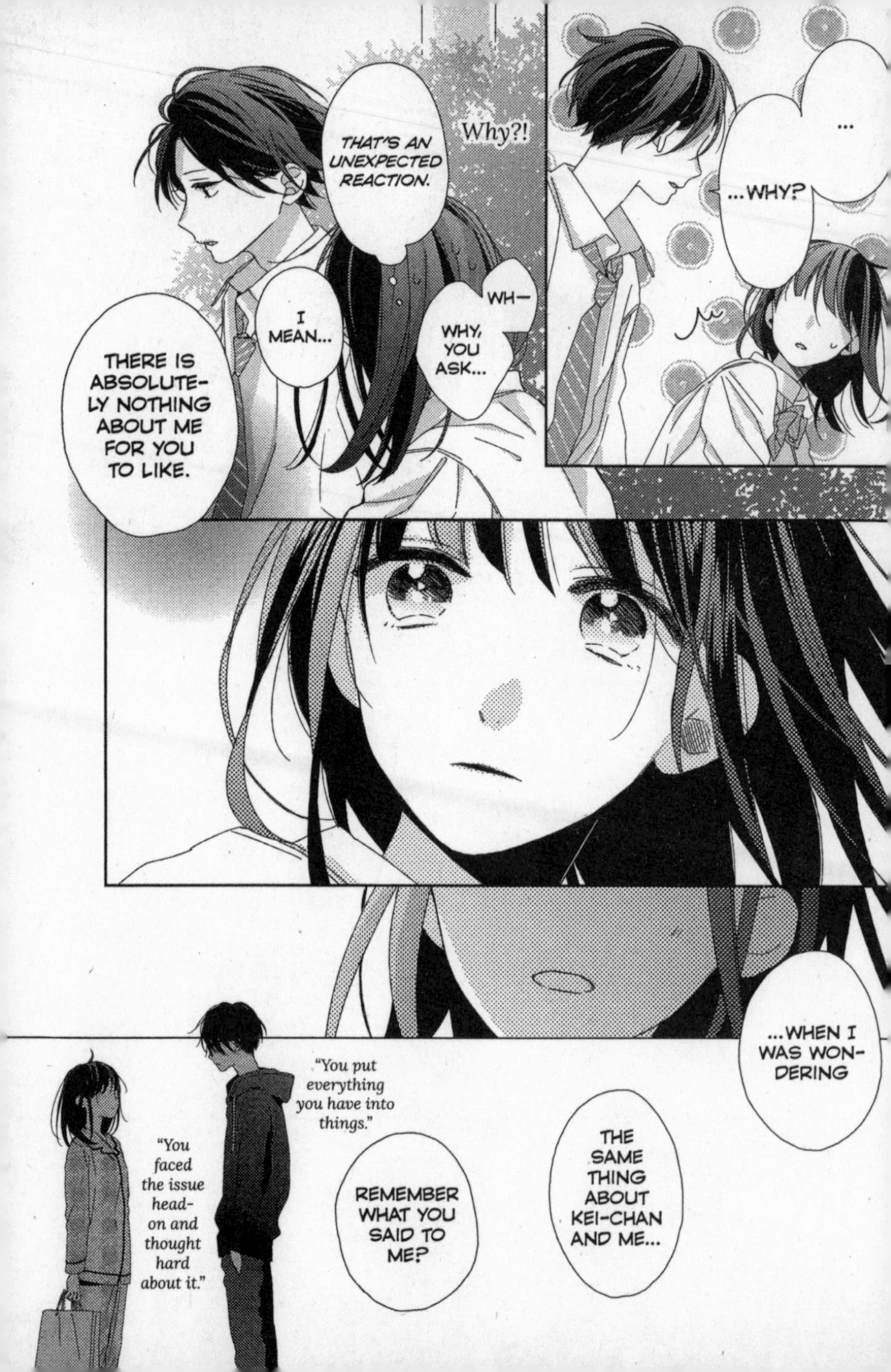
...
...WHY?
Why?!
THAT'S AN UNEXPECTED REACTION.
WH— WHY, YOU ASK...
I MEAN...
THERE IS ABSOLUTE-LY NOTHING ABOUT ME FOR YOU TO LIKE.
...WHEN I WAS WON-DERING
THE SAME THING ABOUT KEI-CHAN AND ME...
REMEMBER WHAT YOU SAID TO ME?
"You put everything you have into things."
"You faced the issue head-on and thought hard about it."

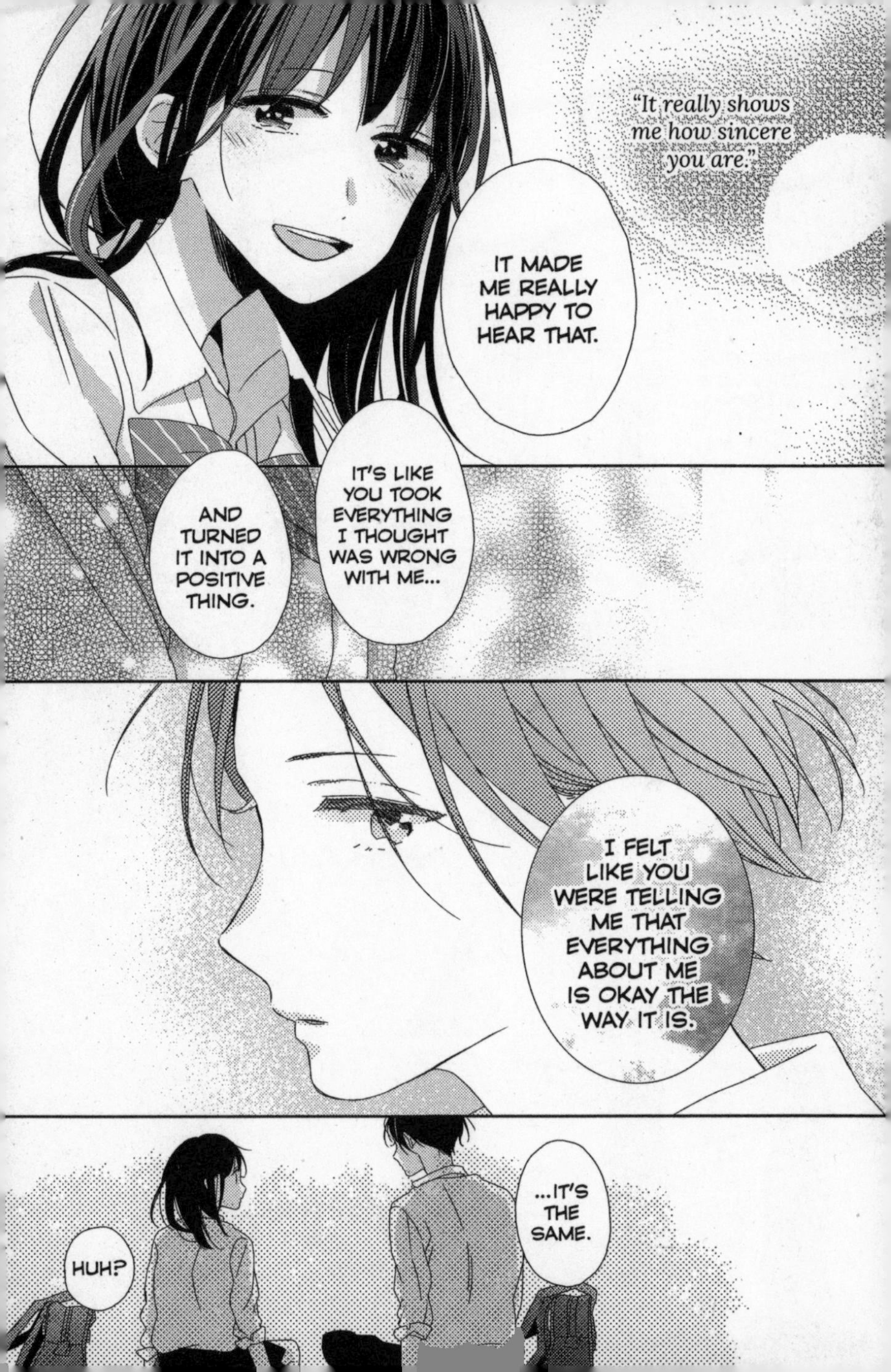
"It really shows me how sincere you are."
IT MADE ME REALLY HAPPY TO HEAR THAT.
IT'S LIKE YOU TOOK EVERYTHING I THOUGHT WAS WRONG WITH ME...
AND TURNED IT INTO A POSITIVE THING.
I FELT LIKE YOU WERE TELLING ME THAT EVERYTHING ABOUT ME IS OKAY THE WAY IT IS.
...IT'S THE SAME.
HUH?

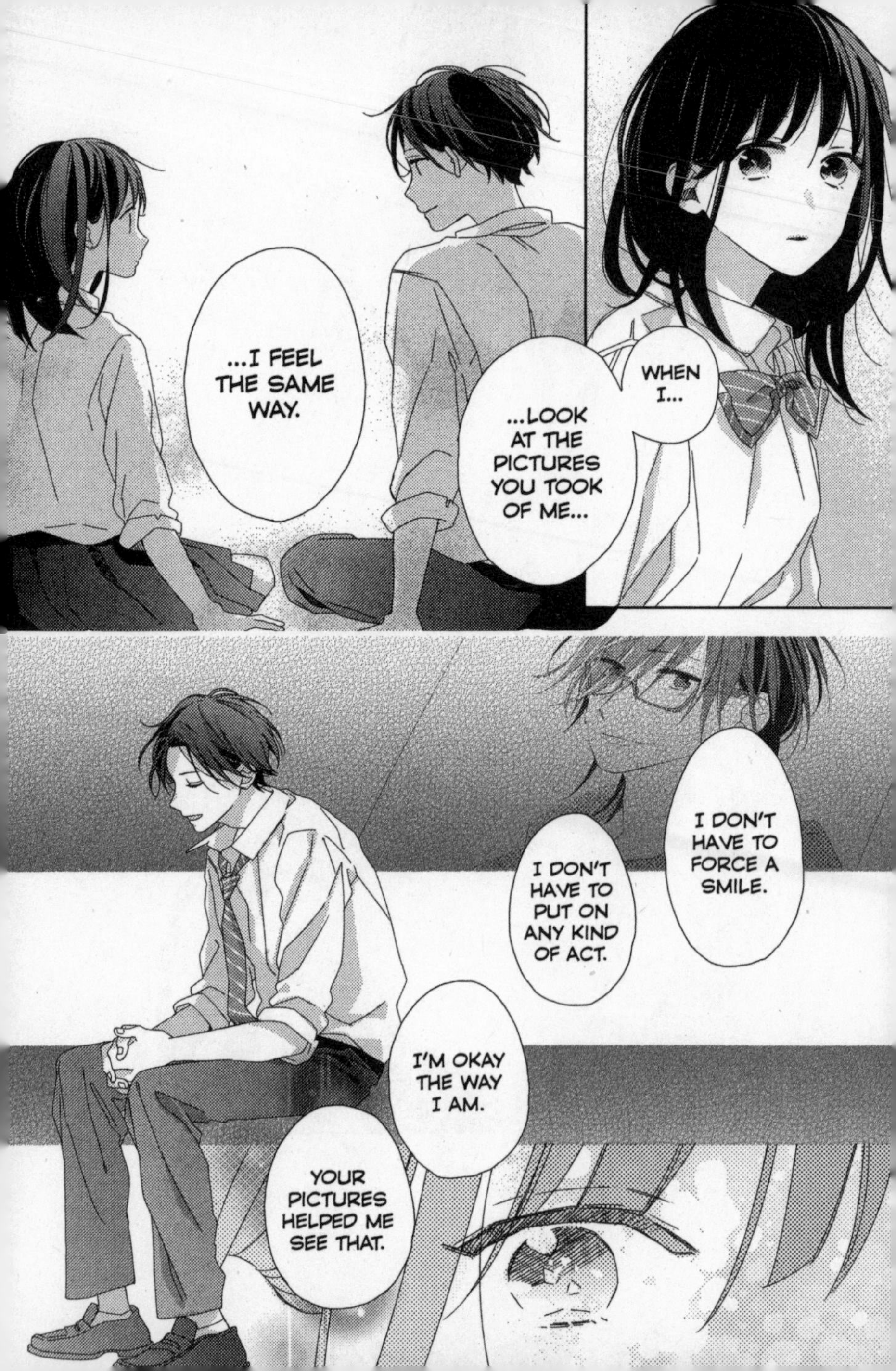
WHEN I...
...LOOK AT THE PICTURES YOU TOOK OF ME...
...I FEEL THE SAME WAY.
I DON'T HAVE TO FORCE A SMILE.
I DON'T HAVE TO PUT ON ANY KIND OF ACT.
I'M OKAY THE WAY I AM.
YOUR PICTURES HELPED ME SEE THAT.

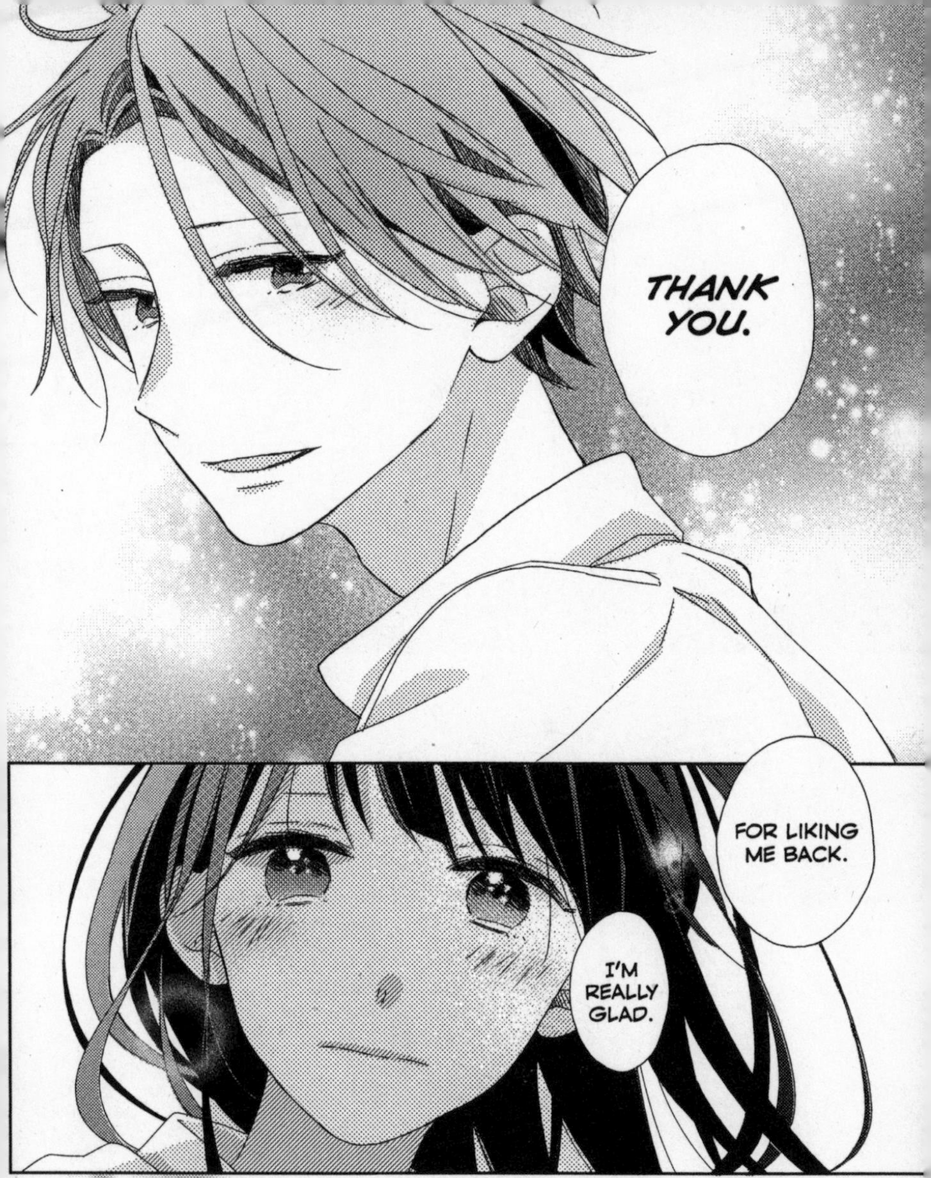
THANK YOU.
FOR LIKING ME BACK.
I'M REALLY GLAD.

I don't know...

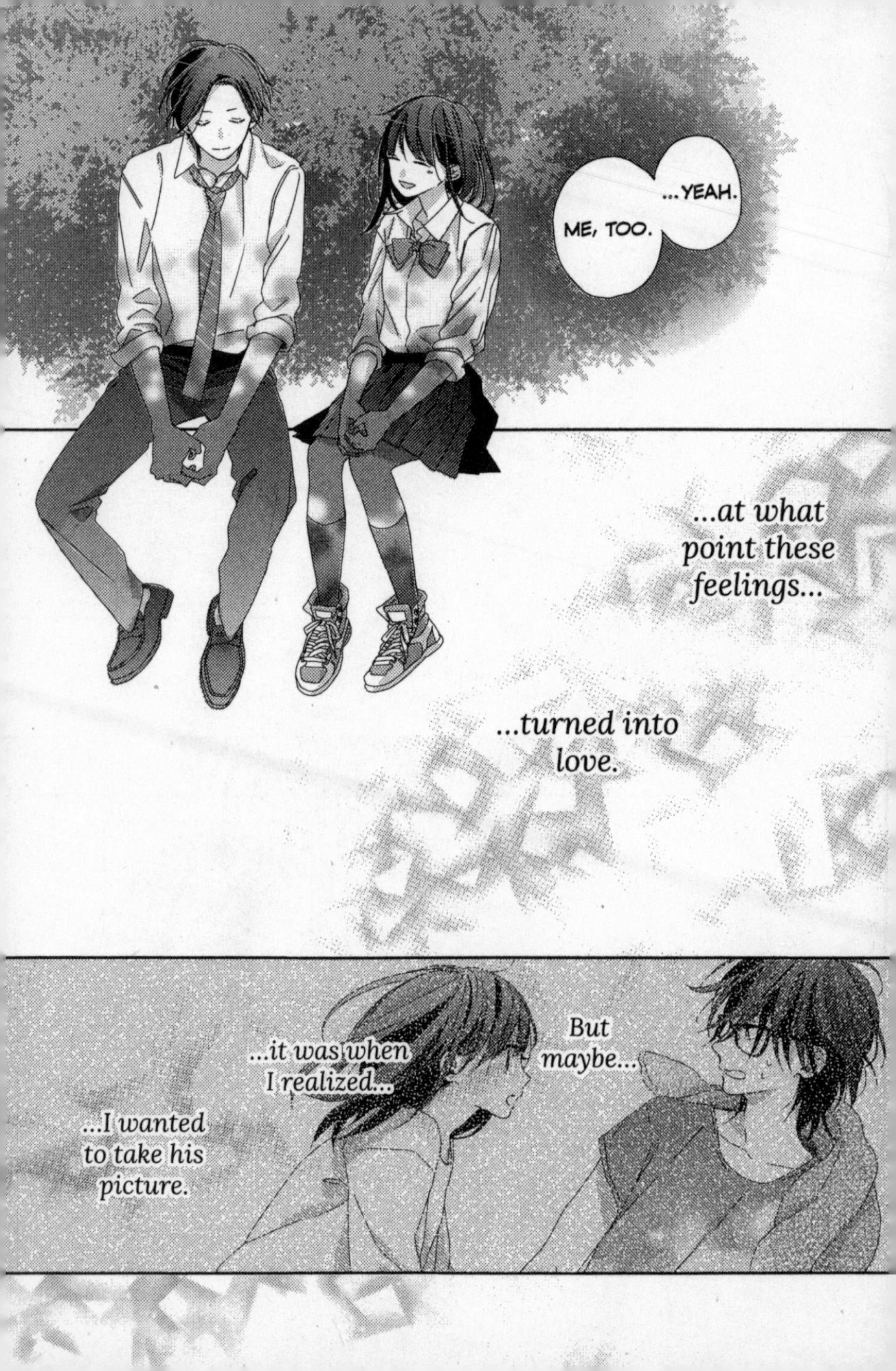
...YEAH.
ME, TOO.
...at what point these feelings...
...turned into love.
But maybe...
...it was when I realized...
...I wanted to take his picture.

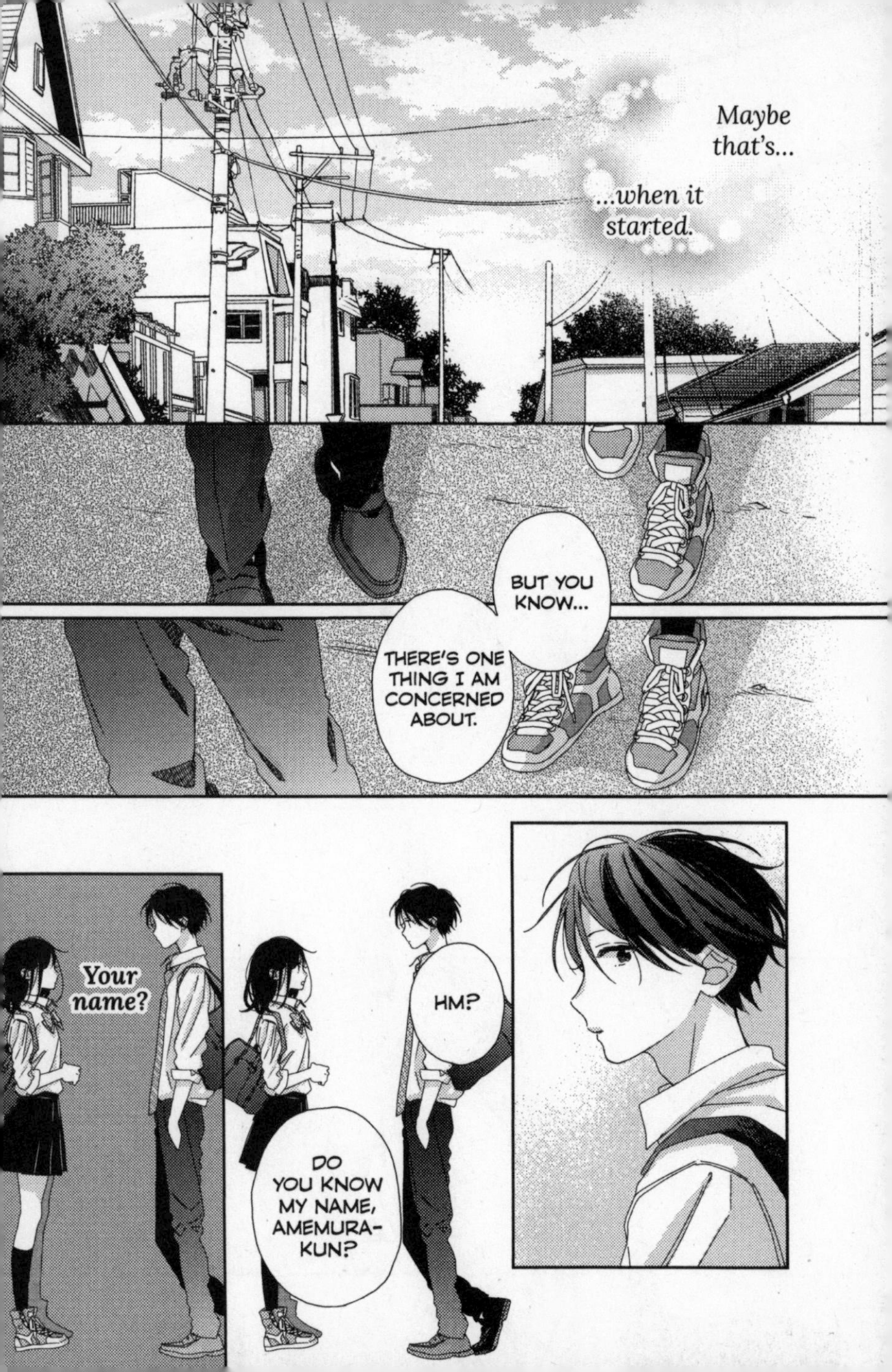
Maybe that's...
...when it started.
BUT YOU KNOW...
THERE'S ONE THING I AM CONCERNED ABOUT.
HM?
DO YOU KNOW MY NAME, AMEMURA-KUN?
Your name?

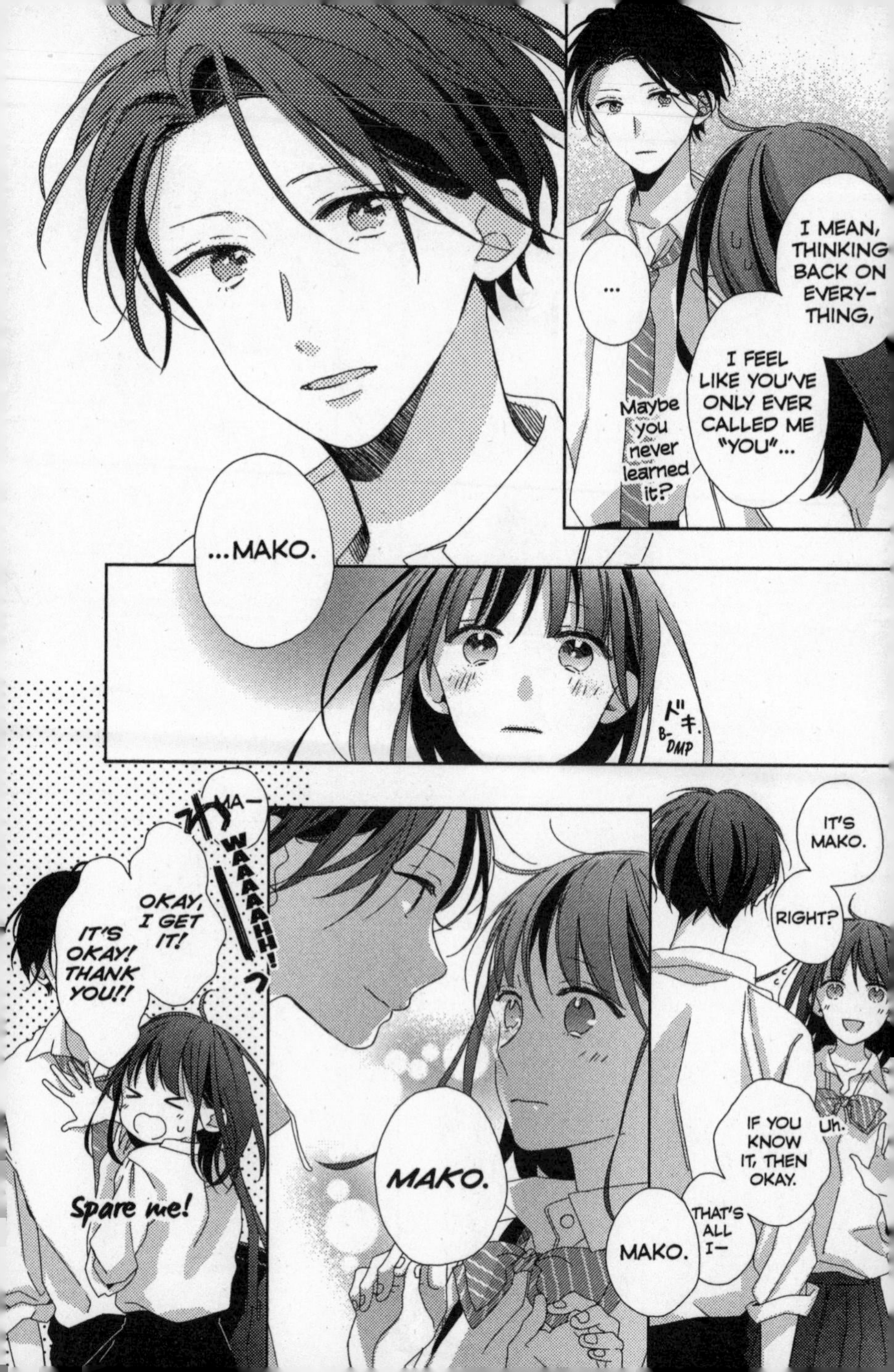
I MEAN, THINKING BACK ON EVERY-THING,
I FEEL LIKE YOU'VE ONLY EVER CALLED ME "YOU"...
Maybe you never learned it?
...
...MAKO.
ドキ
B-DMP
IT'S MAKO.
RIGHT?
Uh.
IF YOU KNOW IT, THEN OKAY.
THAT'S ALL I—
MAKO.
MAKO.
MA—
WAAAAAAH!
OKAY, I GET IT!
IT'S OKAY! THANK YOU!!
Spare me!

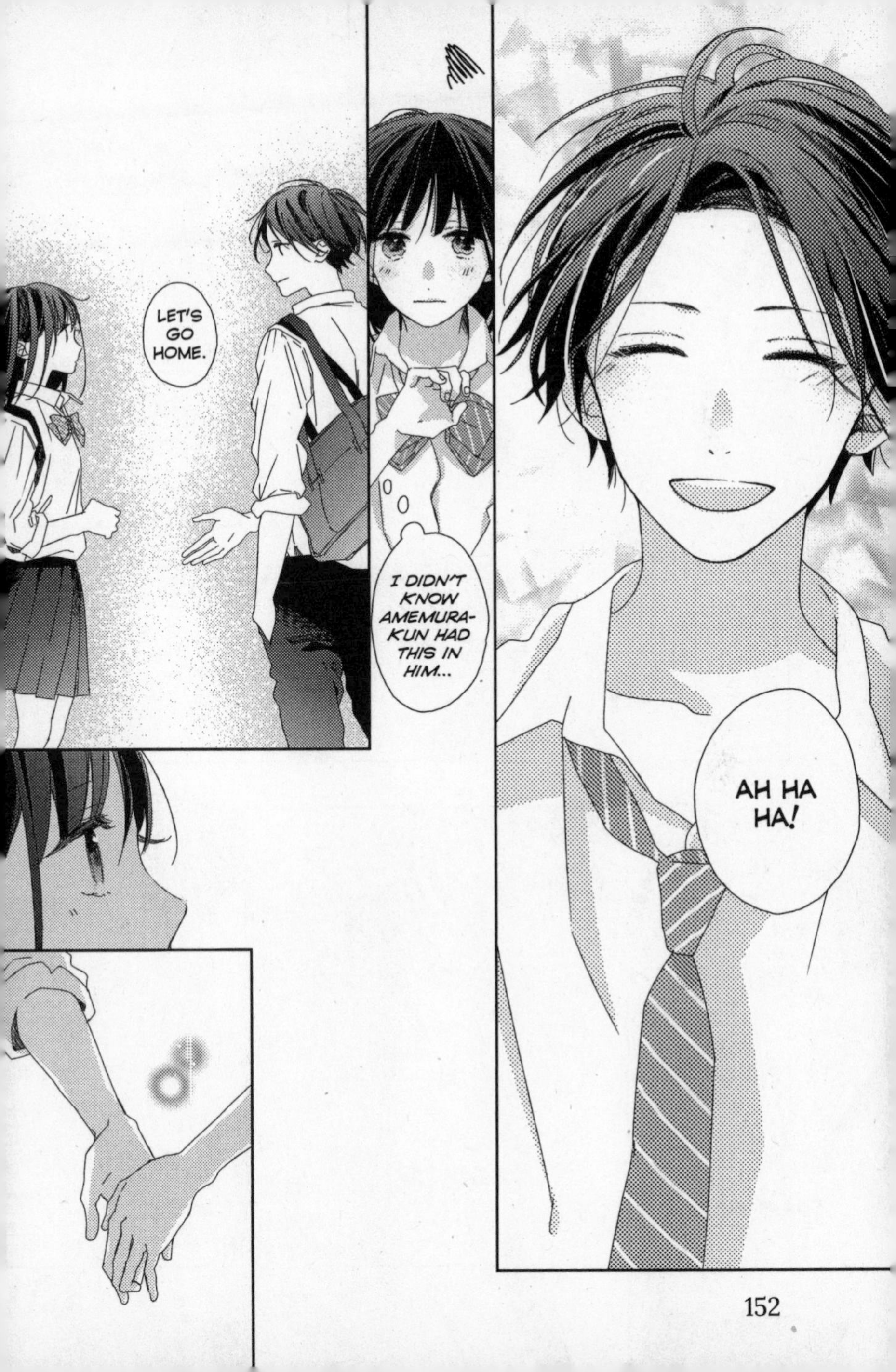
AH HA HA!
I DIDN'T KNOW AMEMURA-KUN HAD THIS IN HIM...
LET'S GO HOME.

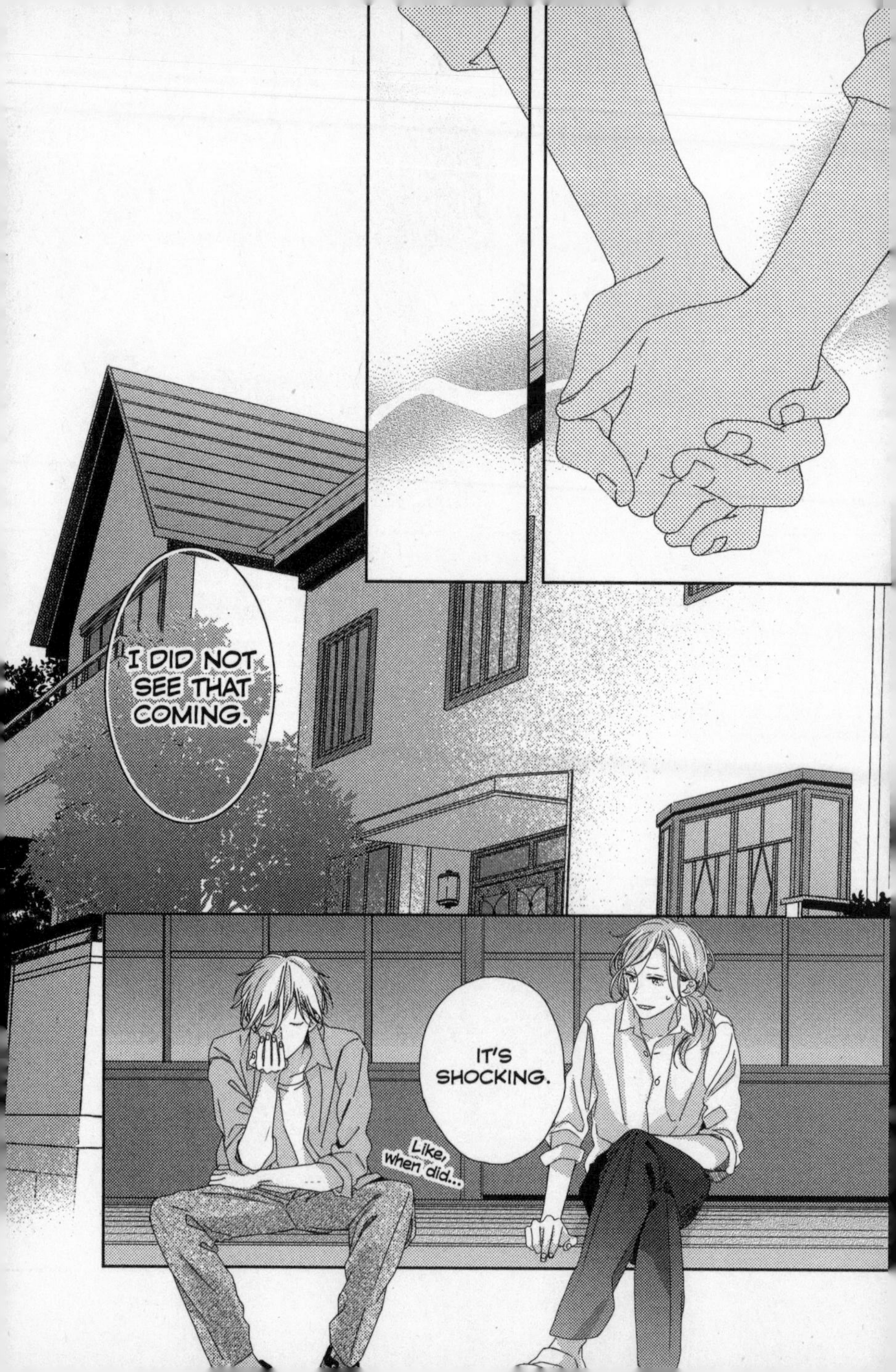
I DID NOT SEE THAT COMING.
IT'S SHOCKING.
Like, when did...

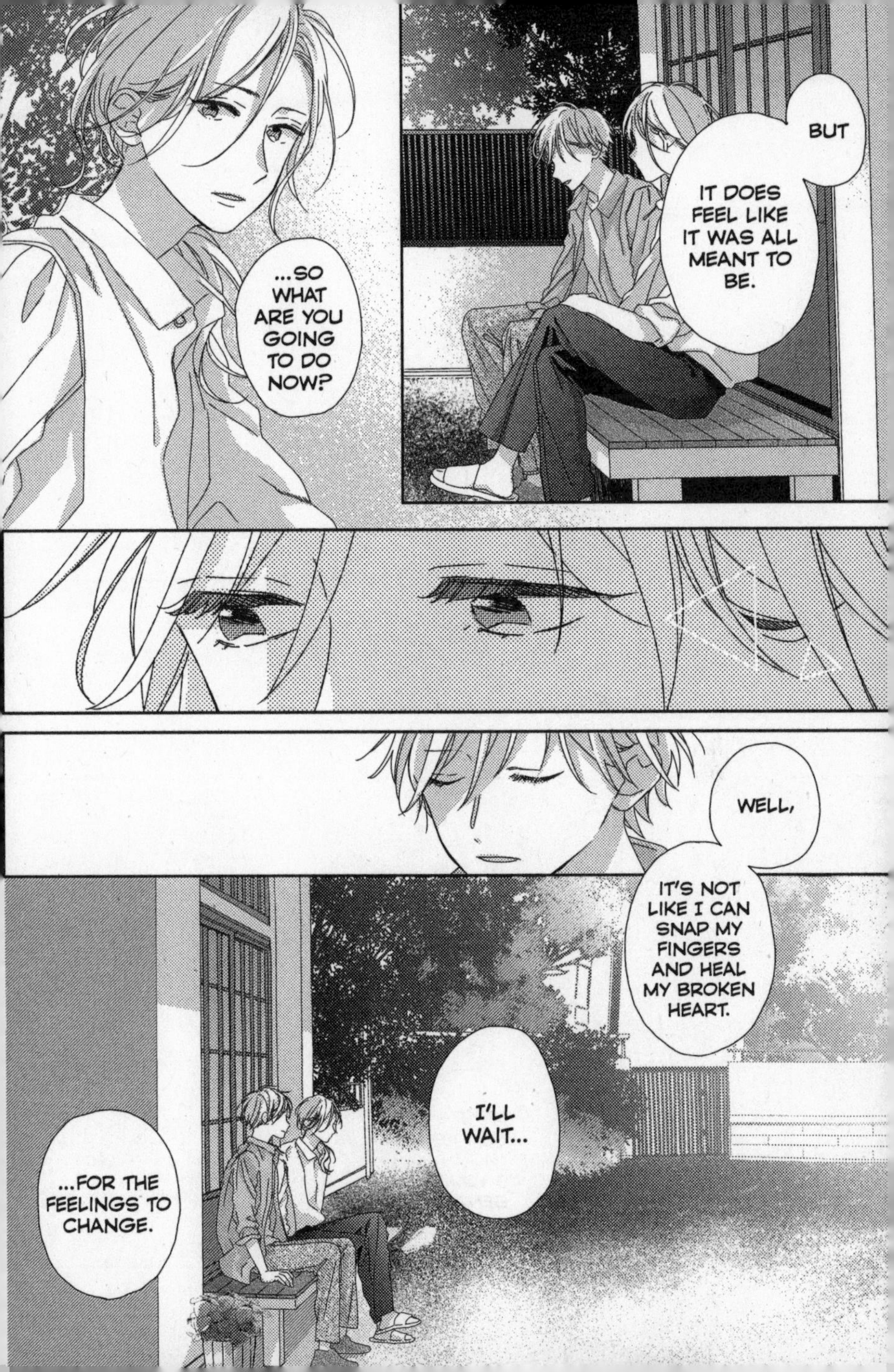
BUT
IT DOES FEEL LIKE IT WAS ALL MEANT TO BE.
...SO WHAT ARE YOU GOING TO DO NOW?
WELL,
IT'S NOT LIKE I CAN SNAP MY FINGERS AND HEAL MY BROKEN HEART.
I'LL WAIT...
...FOR THE FEELINGS TO CHANGE.

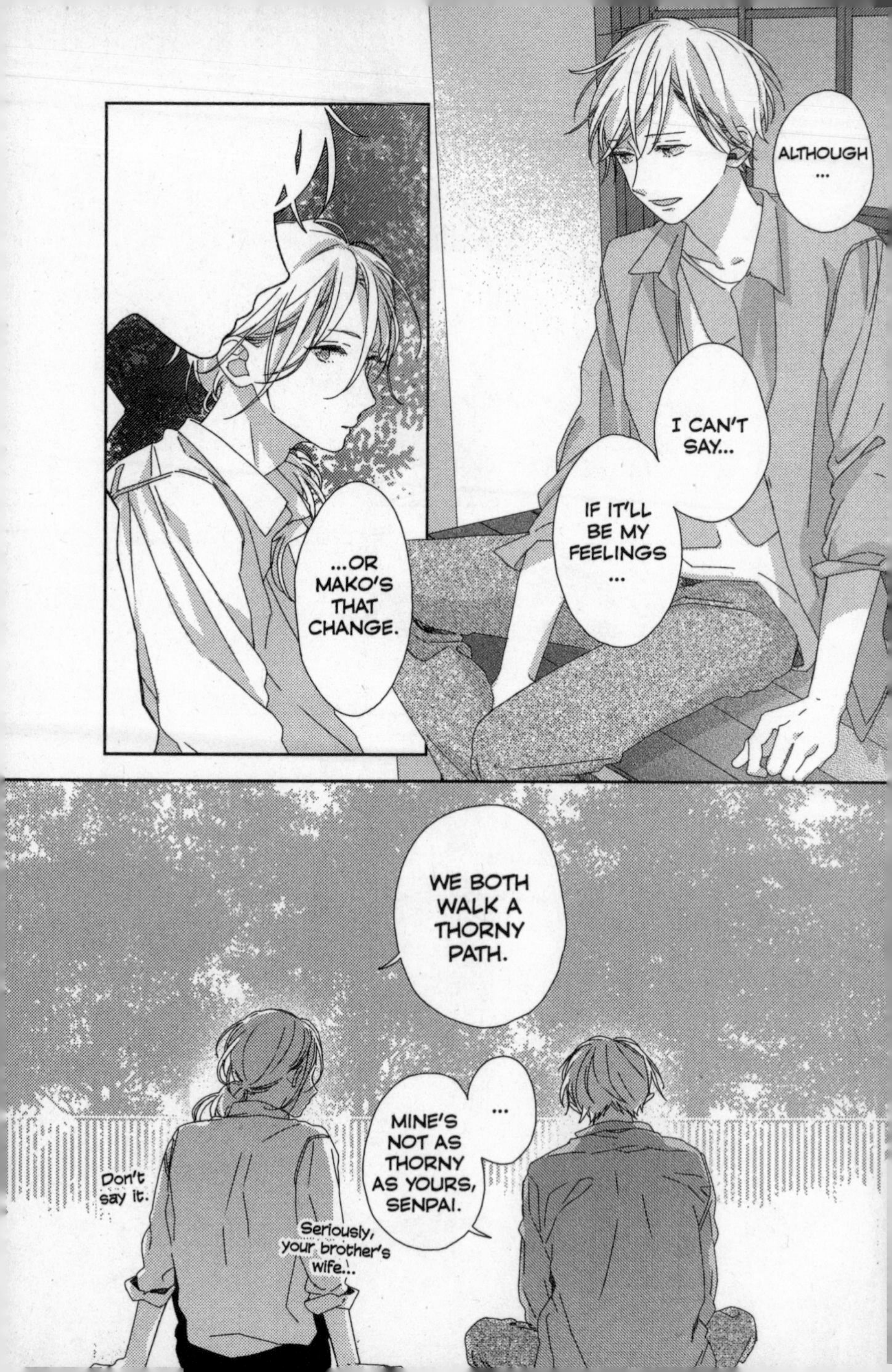
ALTHOUGH ...
I CAN'T SAY...
IF IT'LL BE MY FEELINGS ...
...OR MAKO'S THAT CHANGE.
WE BOTH WALK A THORNY PATH.
...
MINE'S NOT AS THORNY AS YOURS, SENPAI.
Seriously, your brother's wife...
Don't say it.

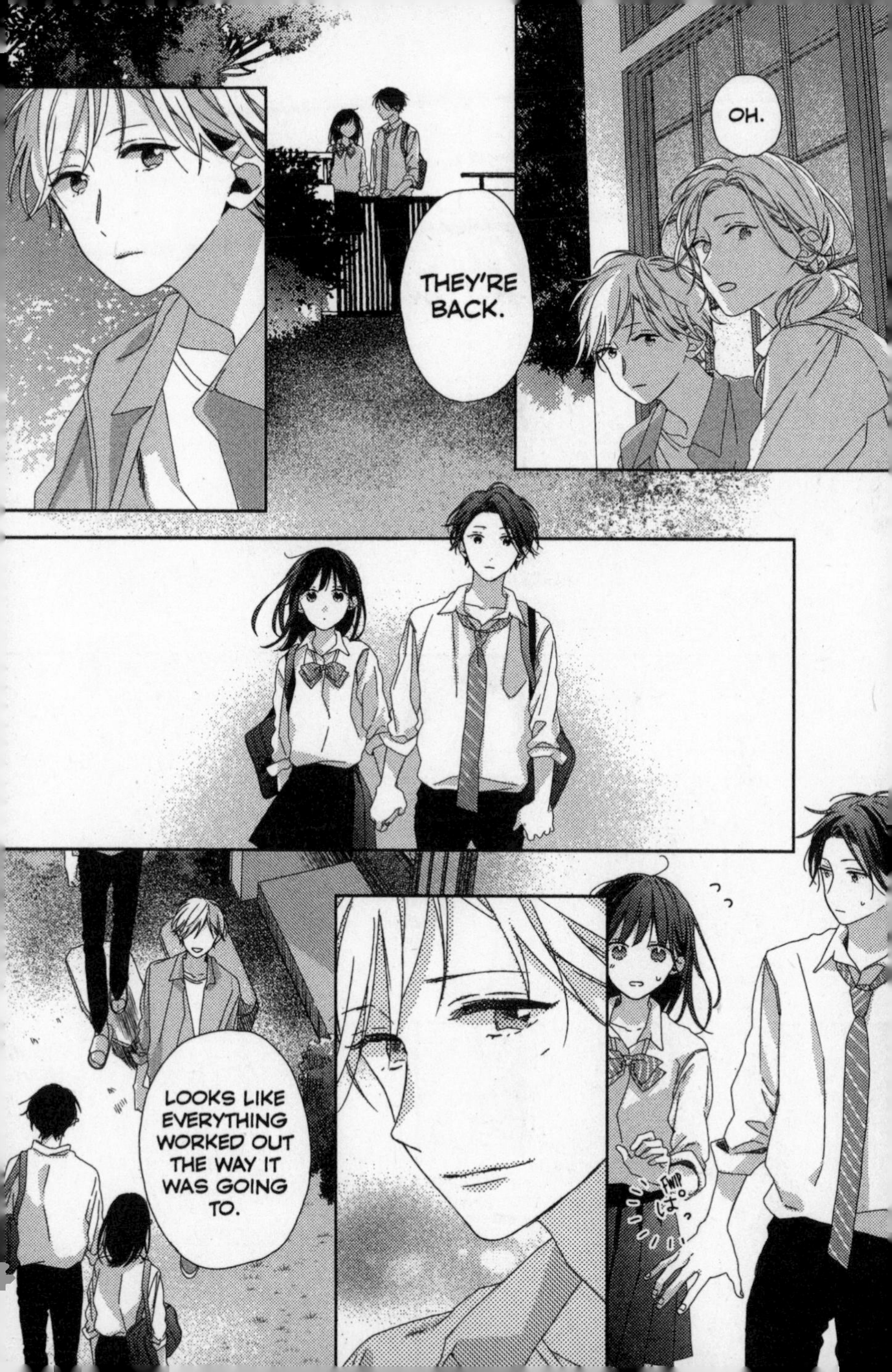
OH.
THEY'RE BACK.
FWIP
ぱっ
LOOKS LIKE EVERYTHING WORKED OUT THE WAY IT WAS GOING TO.

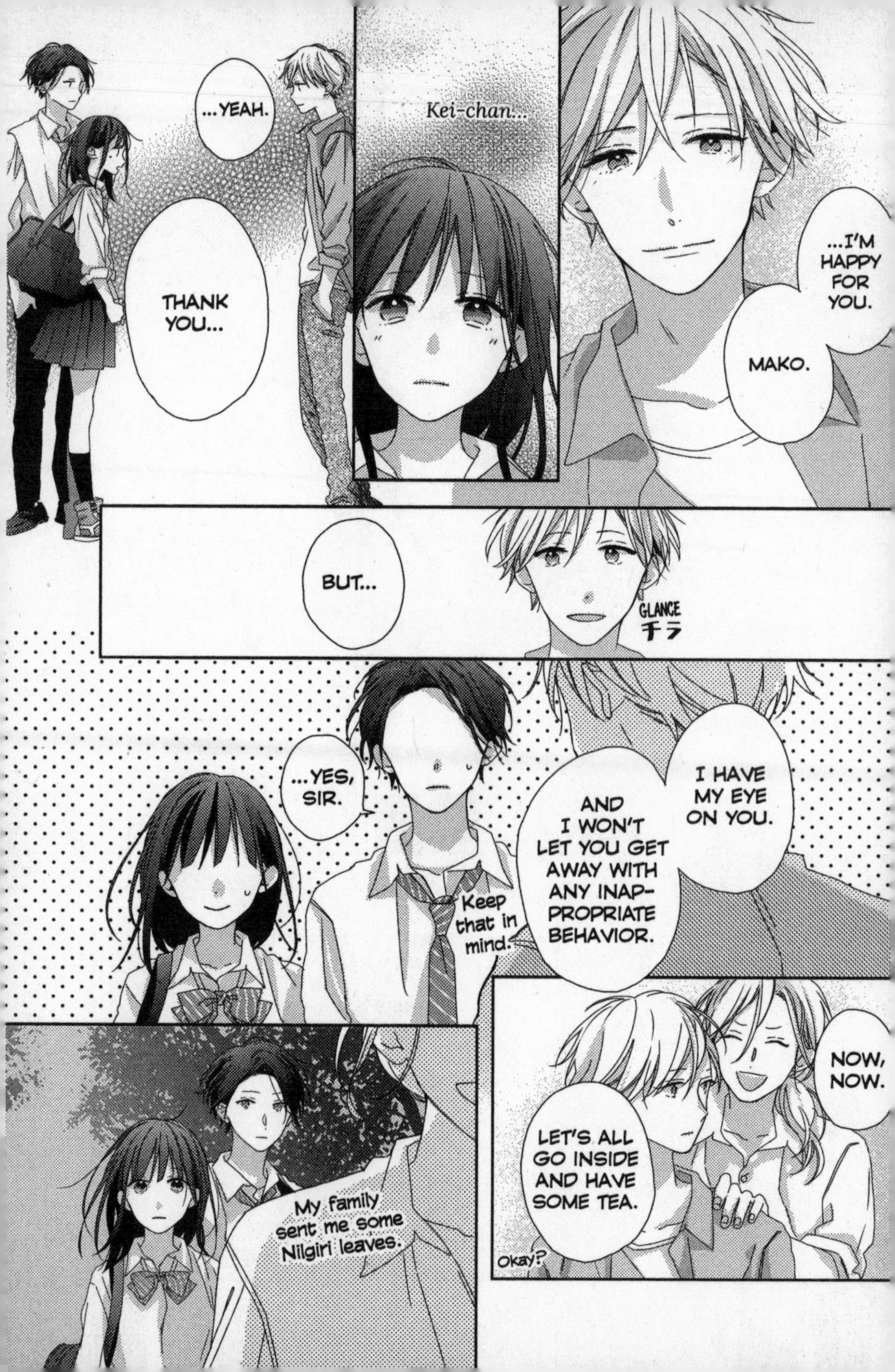
...I'M HAPPY FOR YOU.
MAKO.
Kei-chan...
...YEAH.
THANK YOU...
BUT...
GLANCE チラ
I HAVE MY EYE ON YOU.
AND I WON'T LET YOU GET AWAY WITH ANY INAP-PROPRIATE BEHAVIOR.
Keep that in mind.
...YES, SIR.
NOW, NOW.
LET'S ALL GO INSIDE AND HAVE SOME TEA.
Okay?
My family sent me some Nilgiri leaves.

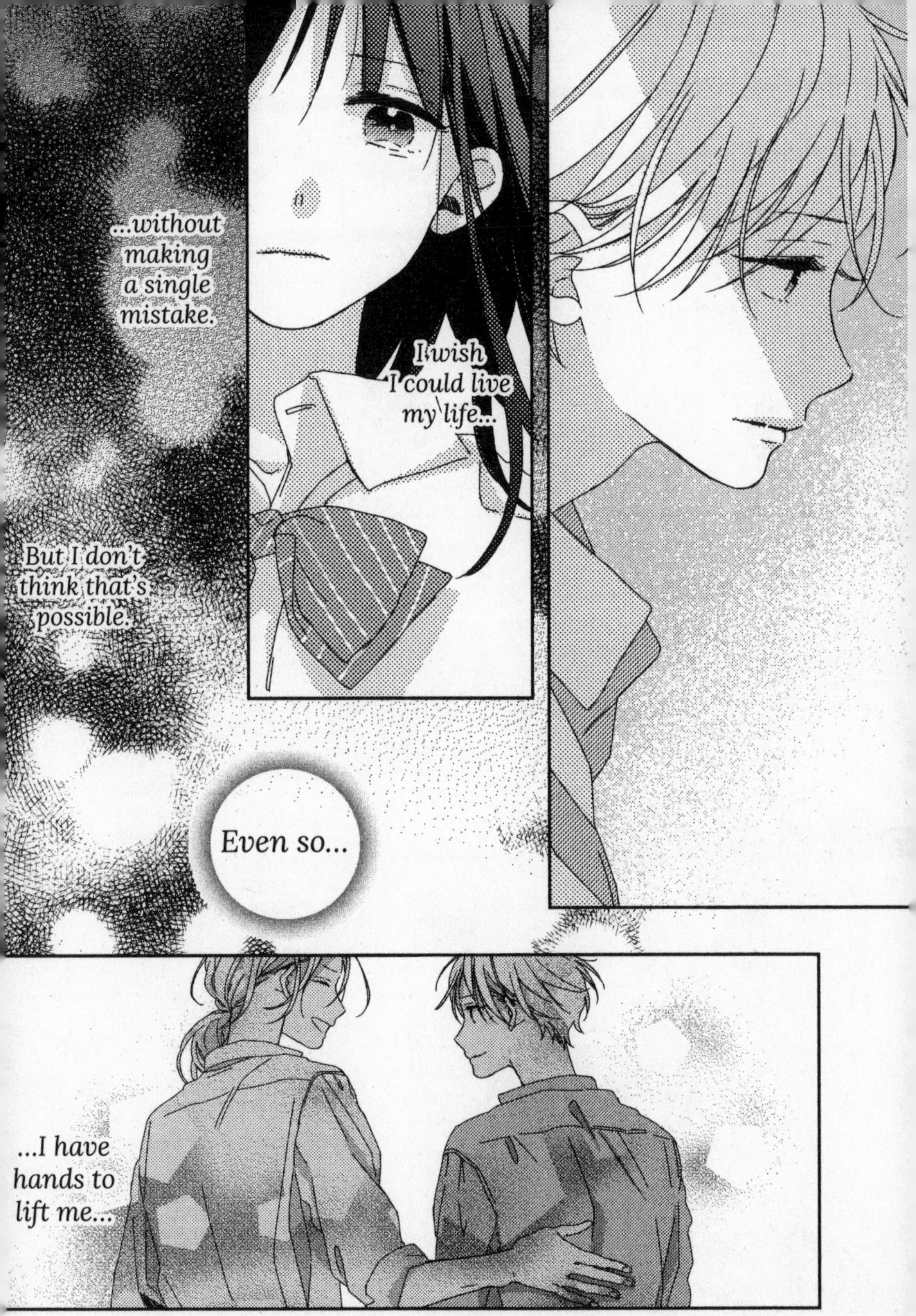
I wish I could live my life...
...without making a single mistake.
But I don't think that's possible.
Even so...
...I have hands to lift me...

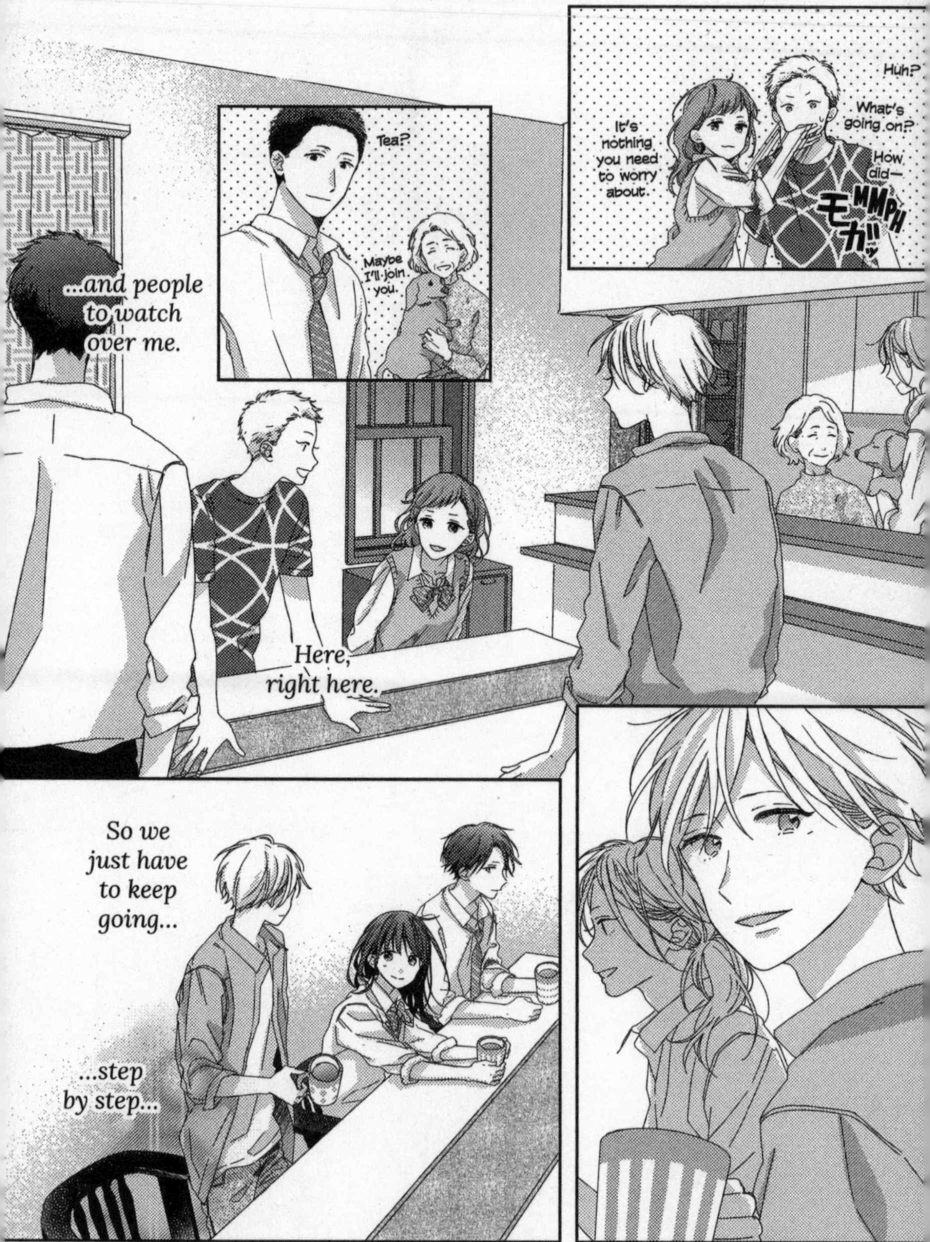
Huh?
What's going on?
How did—
MMPH
モガッ
It's nothing you need to worry about.
Tea?
Maybe I'll join you.
...and people to watch over me.
Here, right here.
So we just have to keep going...
...step by step...

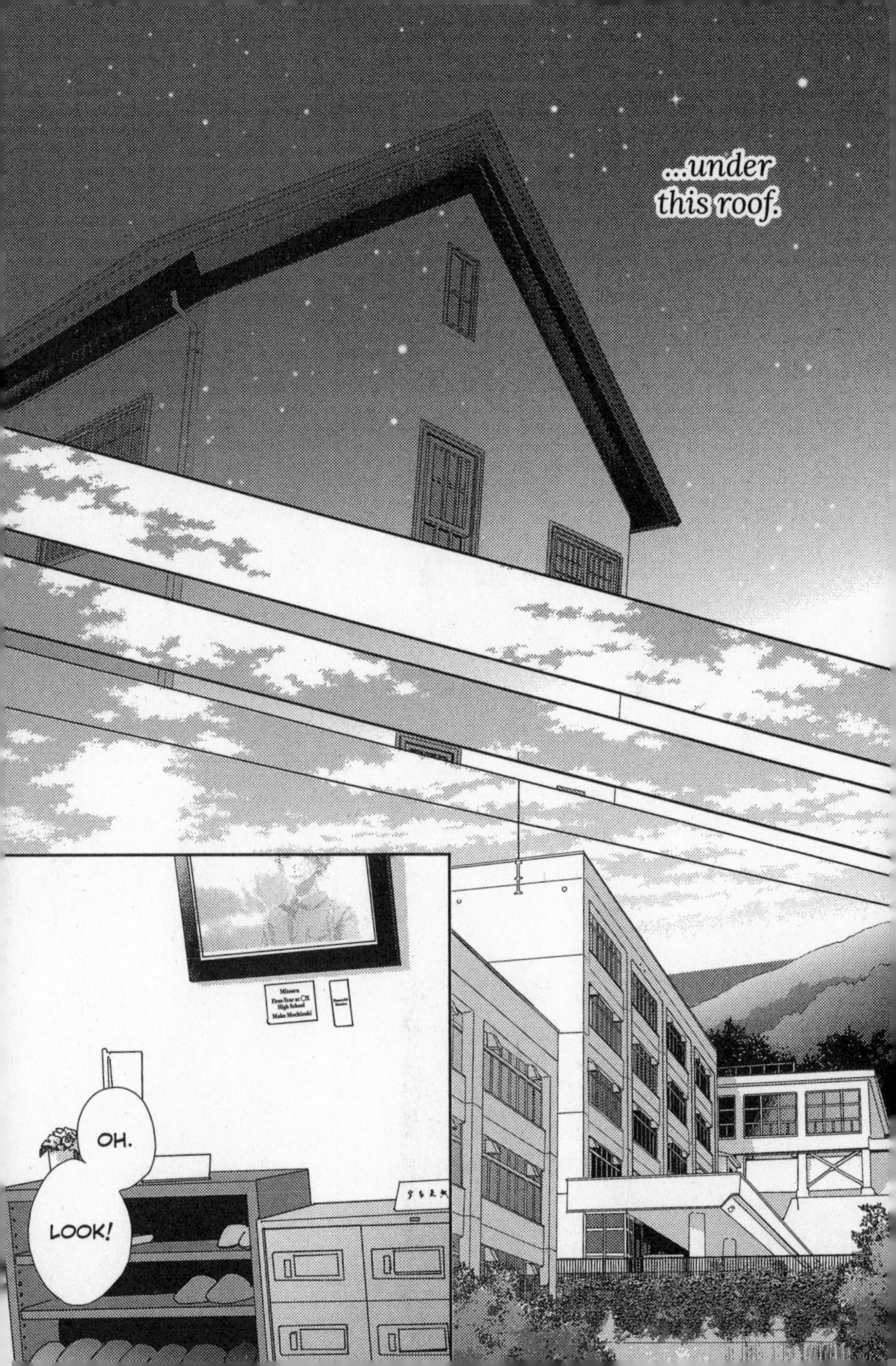
...under this roof.
Mitsuru
First-Year at ○X High School
Mako Mochizuki
OH.
LOOK!

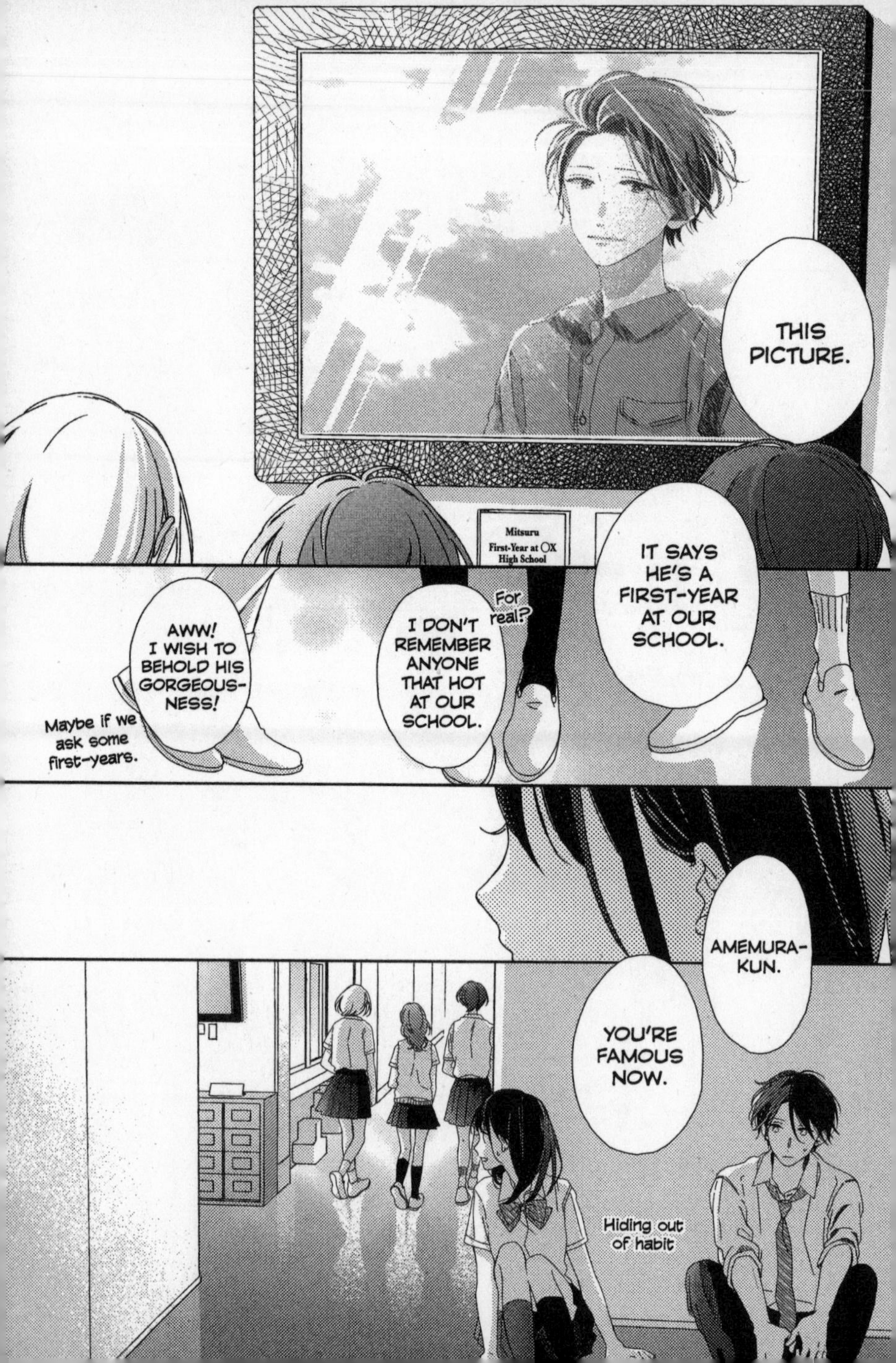
THIS PICTURE.
Mitsuru
First-Year at ○X High School
IT SAYS HE'S A FIRST-YEAR AT OUR SCHOOL.
For real?
I DON'T REMEMBER ANYONE THAT HOT AT OUR SCHOOL.
AWW! I WISH TO BEHOLD HIS GORGEOUS-NESS!
Maybe if we ask some first-years.
AMEMURA-KUN.
YOU'RE FAMOUS NOW.
Hiding out of habit

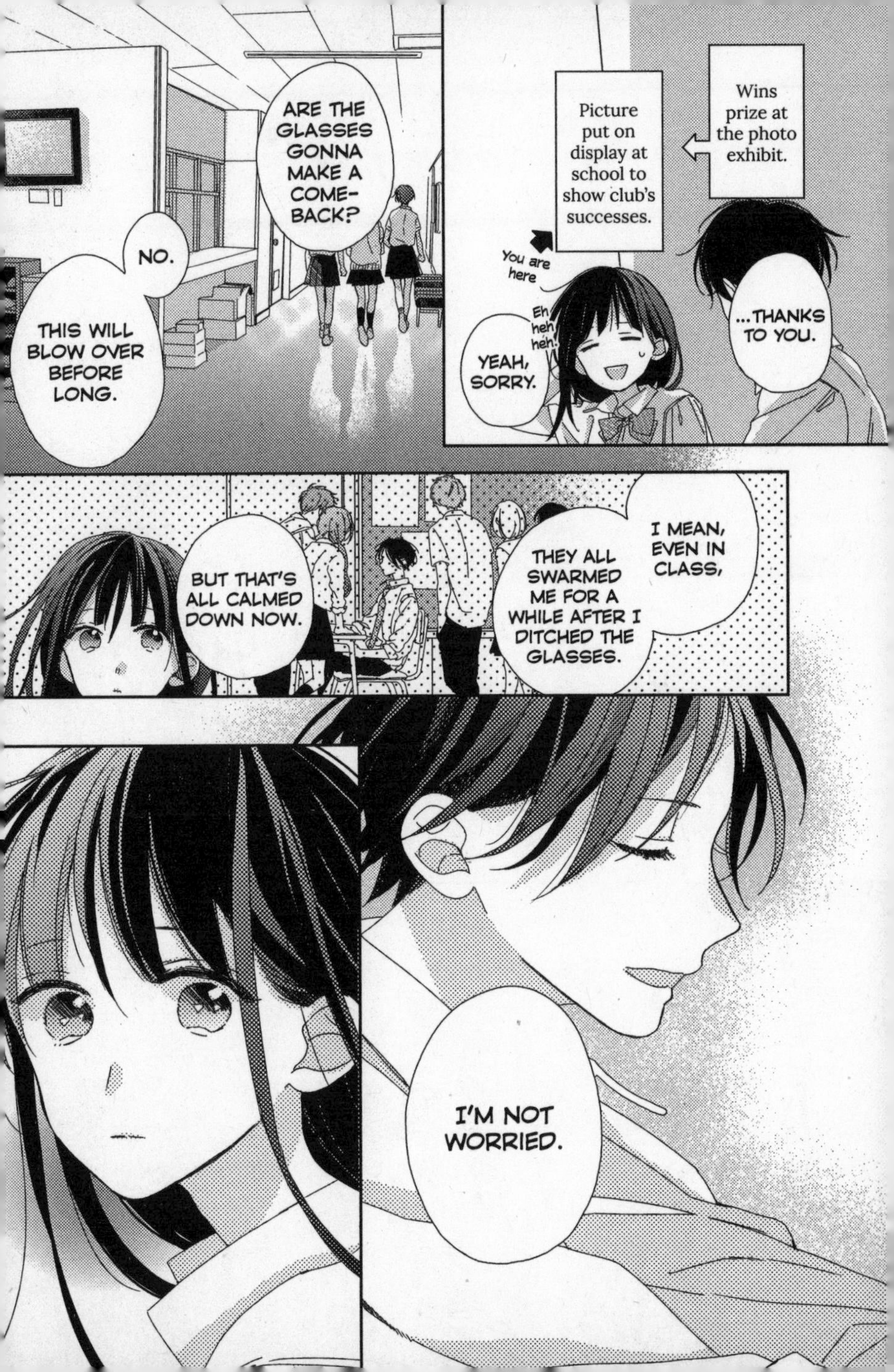

Wins prize at the photo exhibit.
Picture put on display at school to show club's successes.
You are here
...THANKS TO YOU.
Eh heh heh
YEAH, SORRY.
ARE THE GLASSES GONNA MAKE A COME-BACK?
NO.
THIS WILL BLOW OVER BEFORE LONG.
I MEAN, EVEN IN CLASS,
THEY ALL SWARMED ME FOR A WHILE AFTER I DITCHED THE GLASSES.
BUT THAT'S ALL CALMED DOWN NOW.
I'M NOT WORRIED.

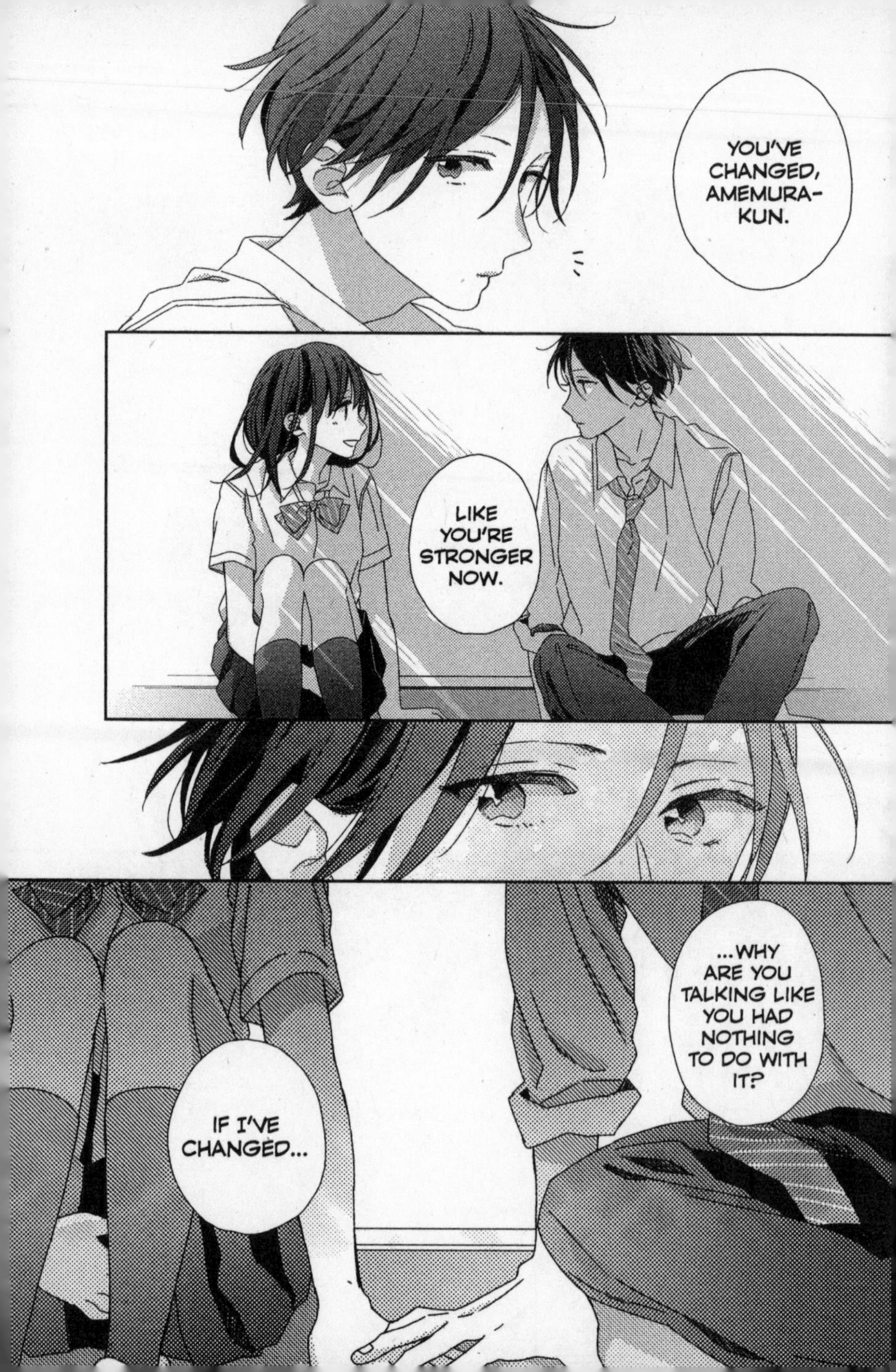
YOU'VE CHANGED, AMEMURA-KUN.
LIKE YOU'RE STRONGER NOW.
...WHY ARE YOU TALKING LIKE YOU HAD NOTHING TO DO WITH IT?
IF I'VE CHANGED...

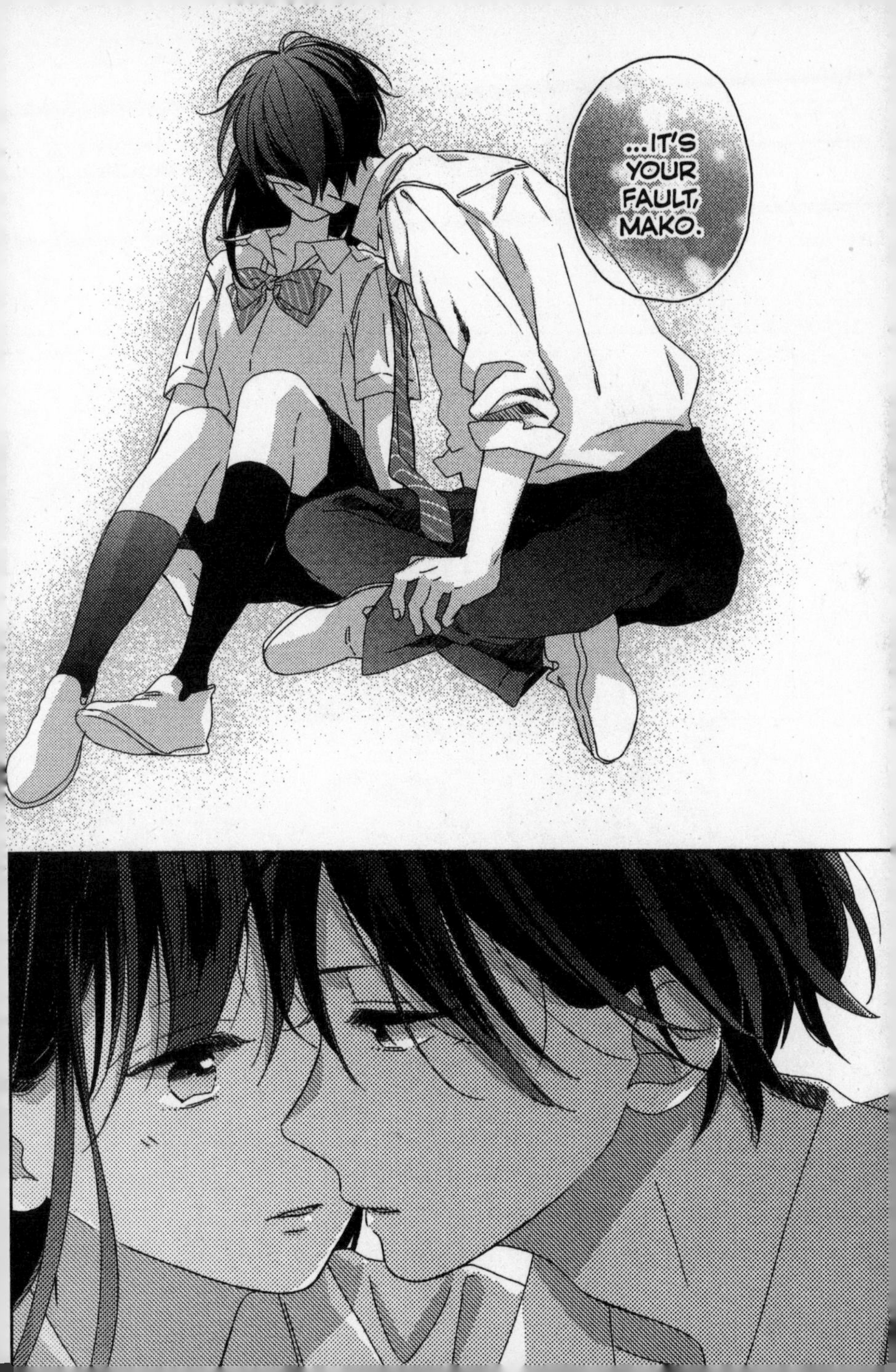
...IT'S YOUR FAULT, MAKO.

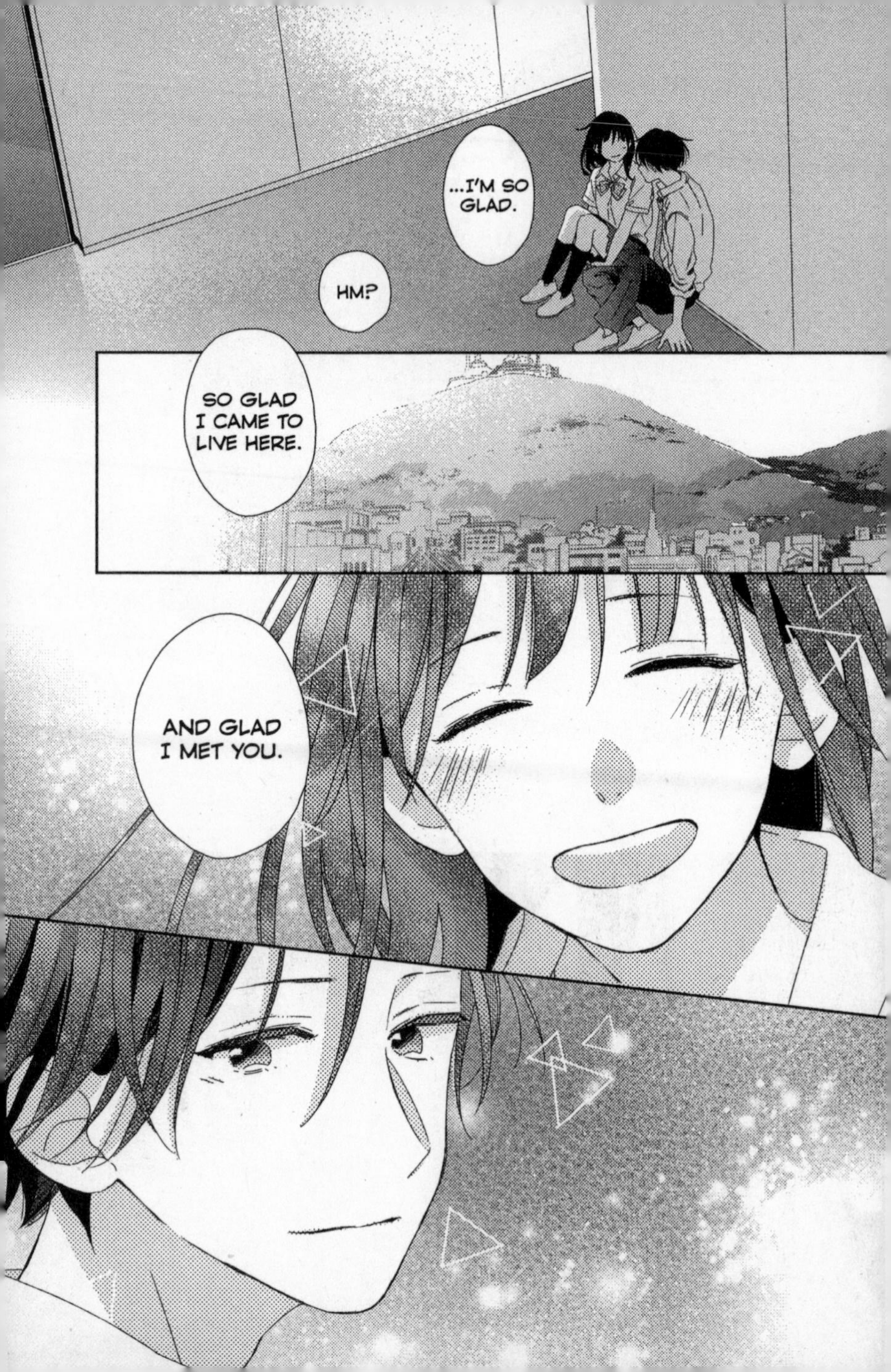
...I'M SO GLAD.
HM?
SO GLAD I CAME TO LIVE HERE.
AND GLAD I MET YOU.

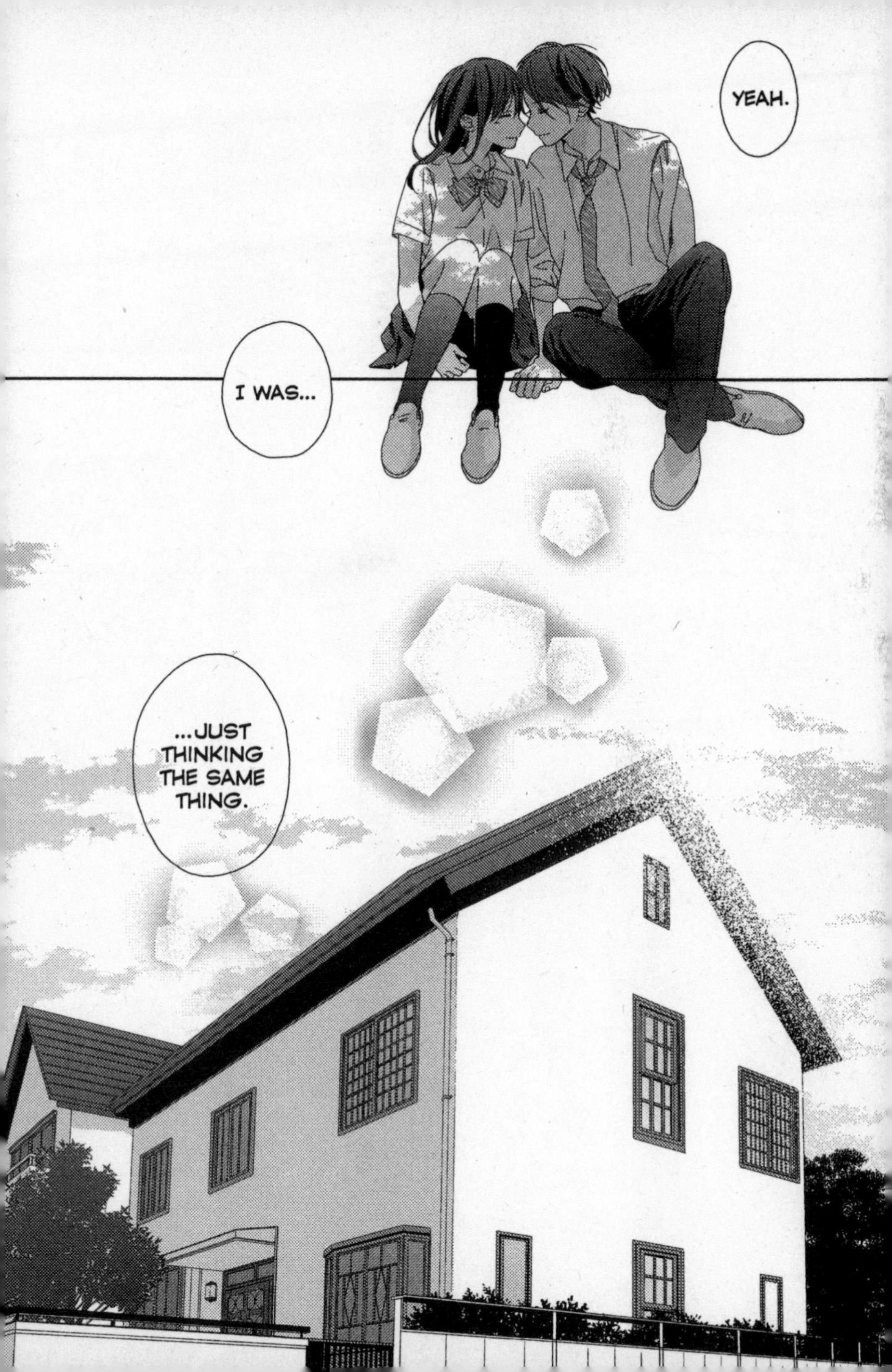
YEAH.
I WAS...
...JUST THINKING THE SAME THING.

fin

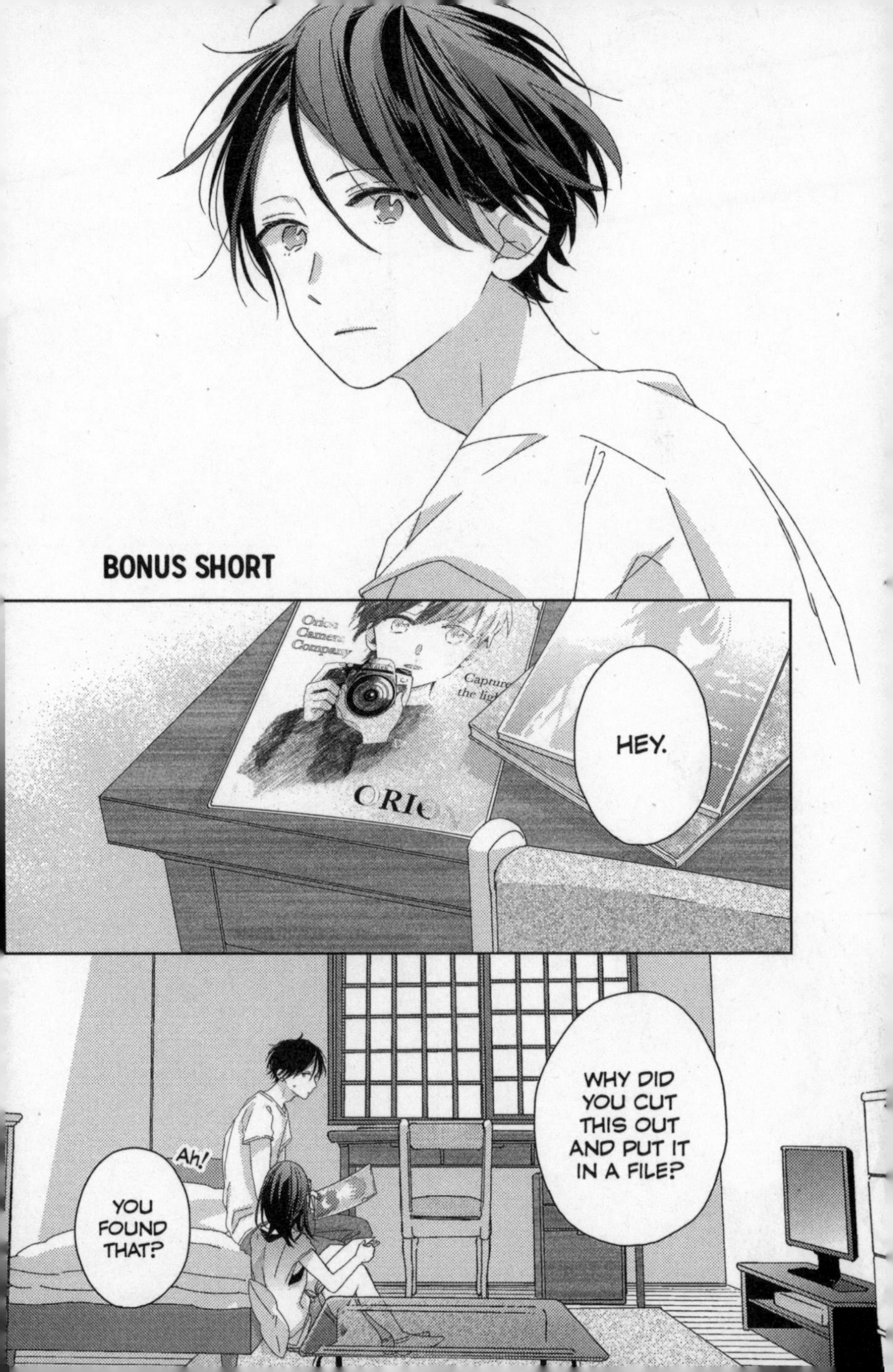
BONUS SHORT
HEY.
WHY DID YOU CUT THIS OUT AND PUT IT IN A FILE?
Ah!
YOU FOUND THAT?

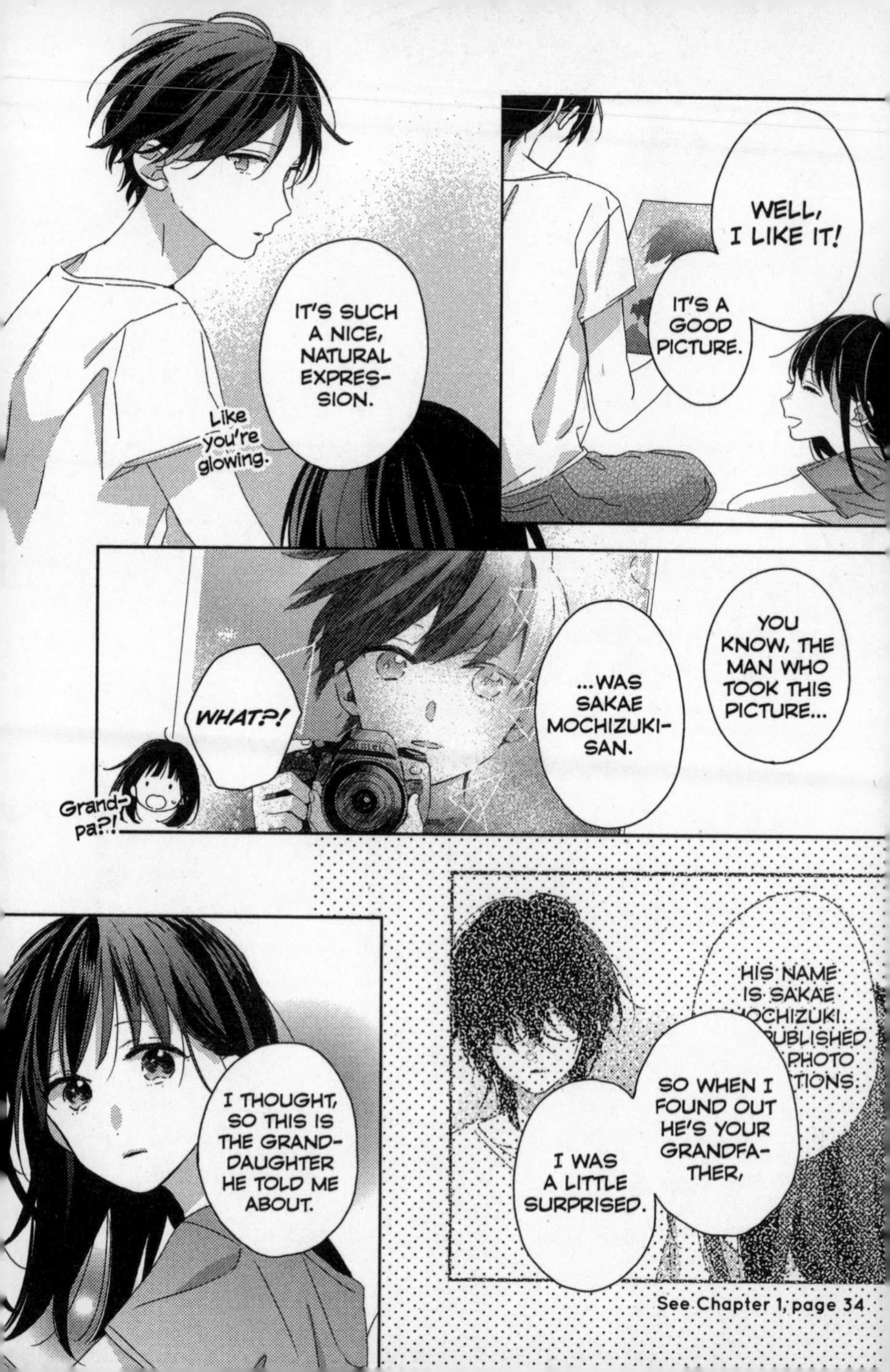
WELL, I LIKE IT!
IT'S A GOOD PICTURE.
IT'S SUCH A NICE, NATURAL EXPRESSION.
Like you're glowing.
YOU KNOW, THE MAN WHO TOOK THIS PICTURE...
...WAS SAKAE MOCHIZUKI-SAN.
WHAT?!
Grandpa?!
HIS NAME IS SAKAE OCHIZUKI. UBLISHED PHOTO TIONS.
SO WHEN I FOUND OUT HE'S YOUR GRANDFATHER,
I WAS A LITTLE SURPRISED.
I THOUGHT, SO THIS IS THE GRANDDAUGHTER HE TOLD ME ABOUT.

See Chapter 1, page 34.

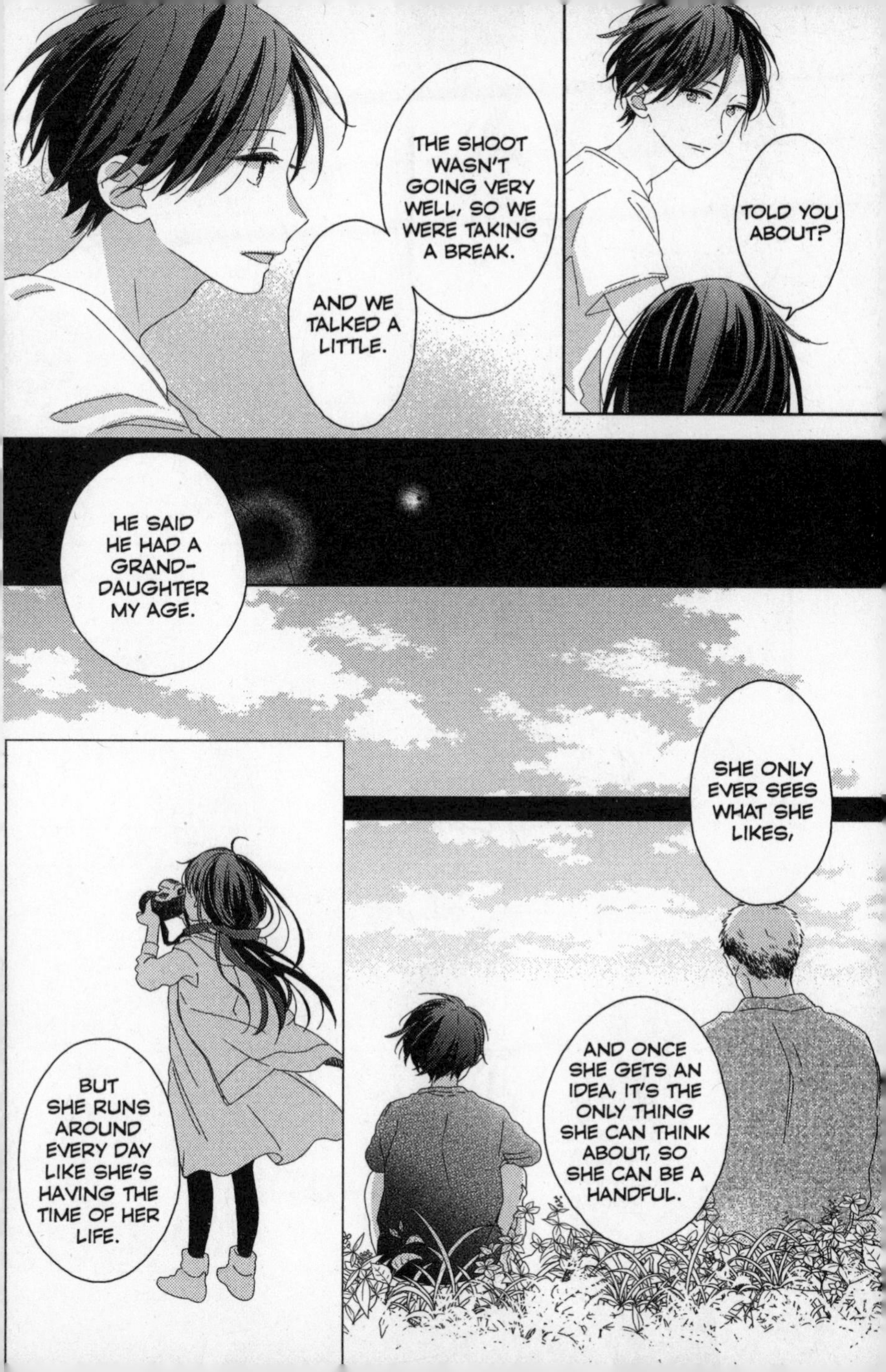
TOLD YOU ABOUT?
THE SHOOT WASN'T GOING VERY WELL, SO WE WERE TAKING A BREAK.
AND WE TALKED A LITTLE.
HE SAID HE HAD A GRAND-DAUGHTER MY AGE.
SHE ONLY EVER SEES WHAT SHE LIKES,
AND ONCE SHE GETS AN IDEA, IT'S THE ONLY THING SHE CAN THINK ABOUT, SO SHE CAN BE A HANDFUL.
BUT SHE RUNS AROUND EVERY DAY LIKE SHE'S HAVING THE TIME OF HER LIFE.

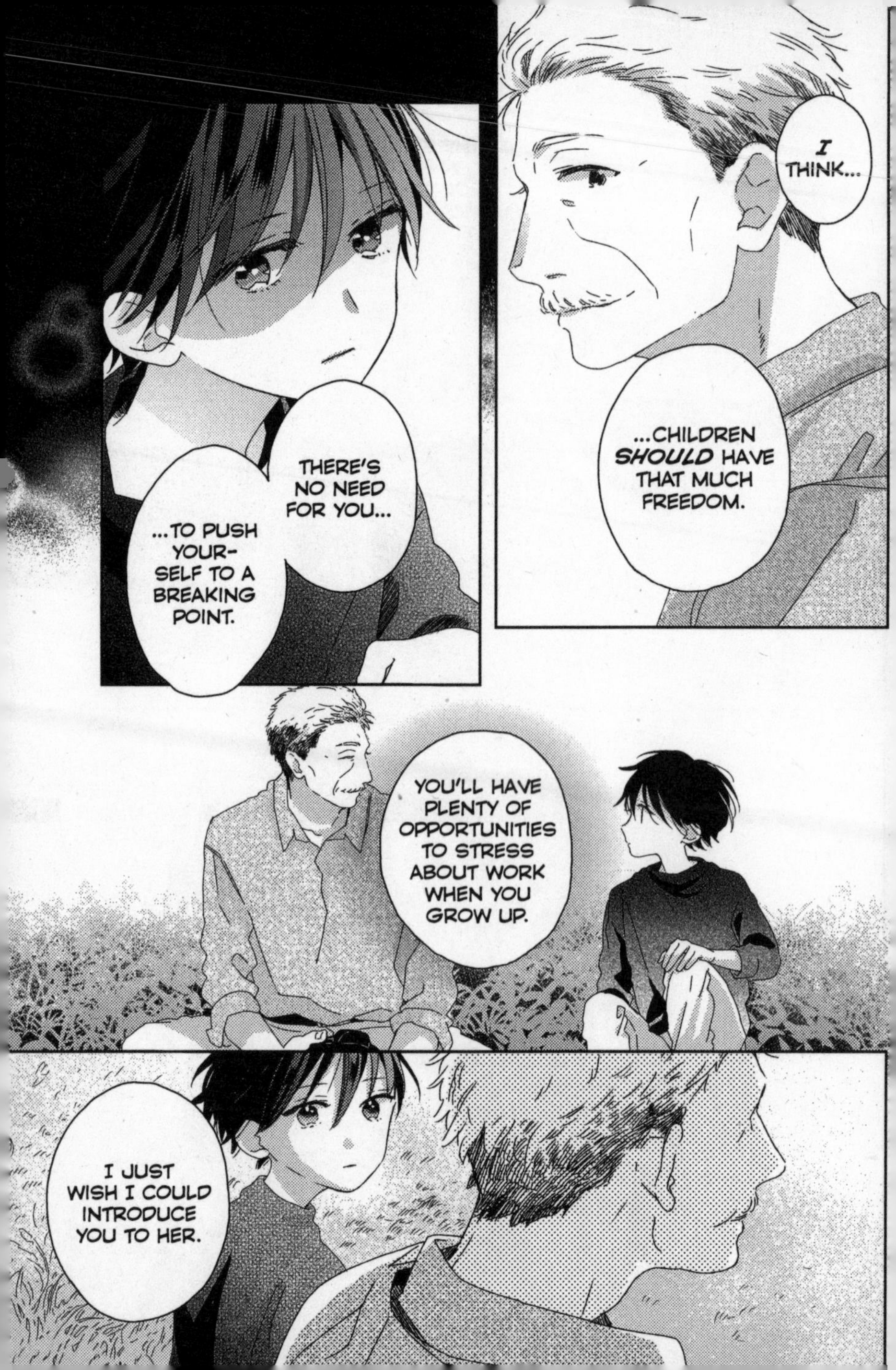
I THINK...
...CHILDREN SHOULD HAVE THAT MUCH FREEDOM.
THERE'S NO NEED FOR YOU...
...TO PUSH YOUR-SELF TO A BREAKING POINT.
YOU'LL HAVE PLENTY OF OPPORTUNITIES TO STRESS ABOUT WORK WHEN YOU GROW UP.
I JUST WISH I COULD INTRODUCE YOU TO HER.

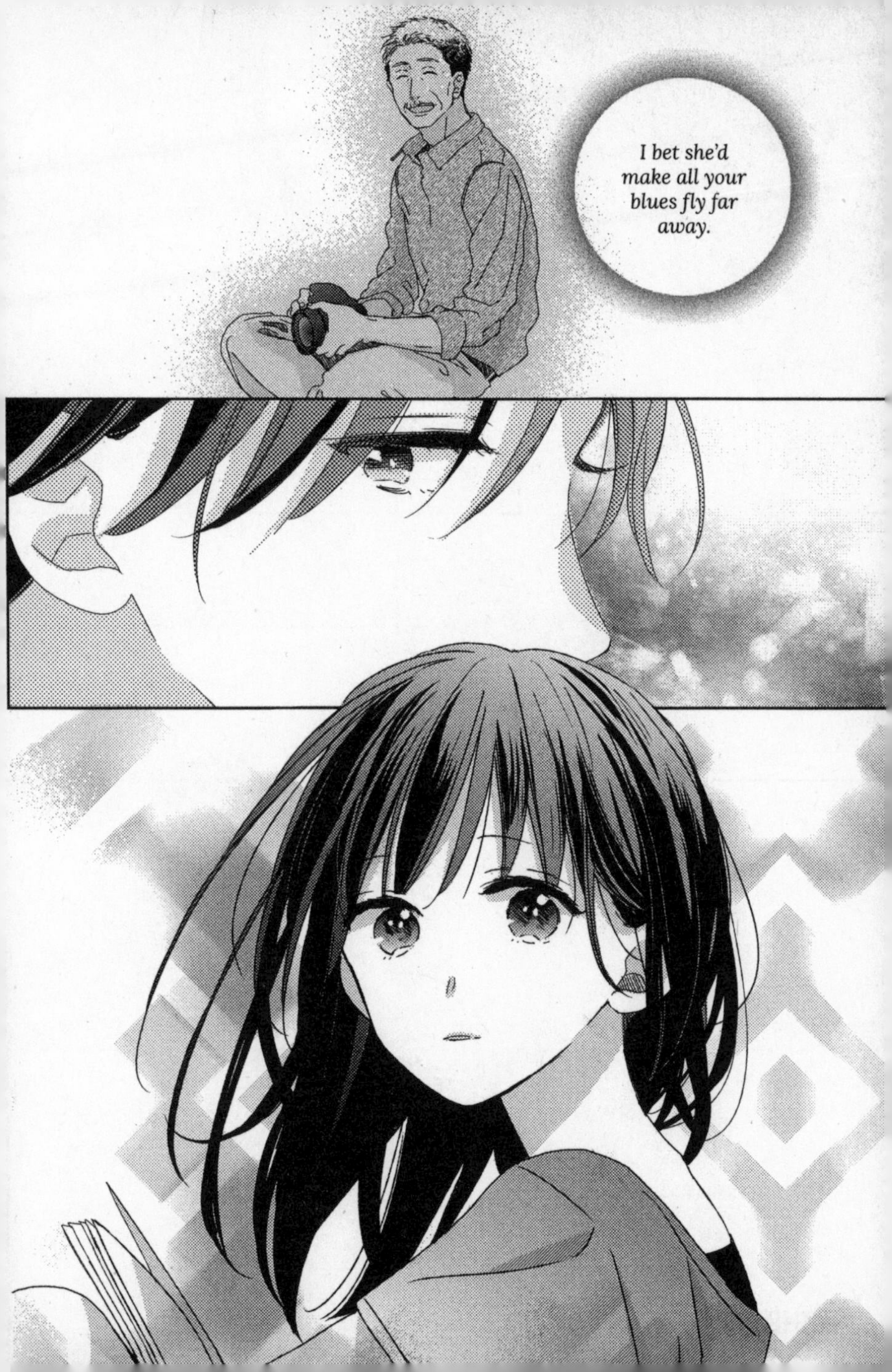
I bet she'd make all your blues fly far away.

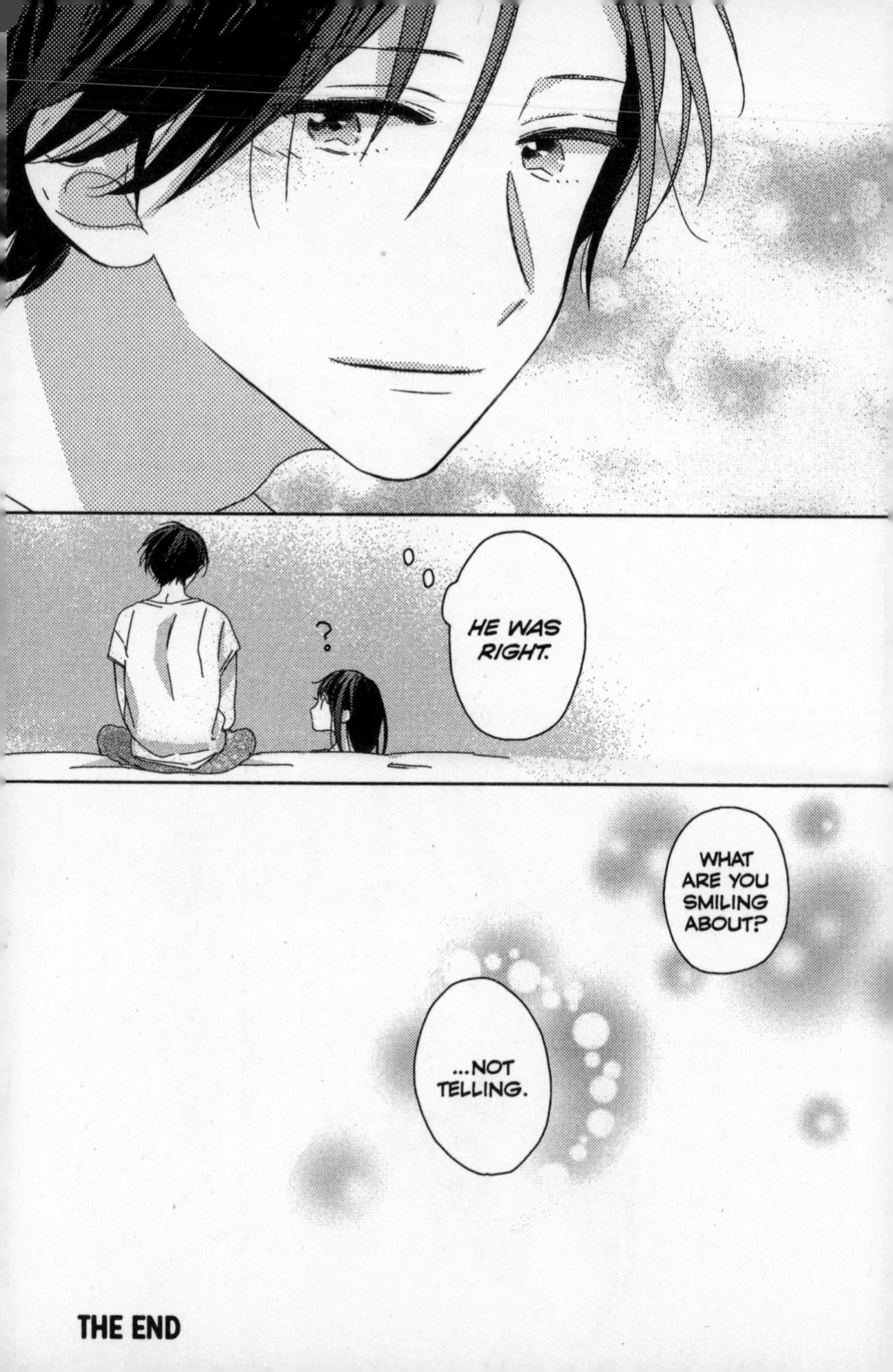
HE WAS RIGHT.
WHAT ARE YOU SMILING ABOUT?
...NOT TELLING.
THE END

Afterword

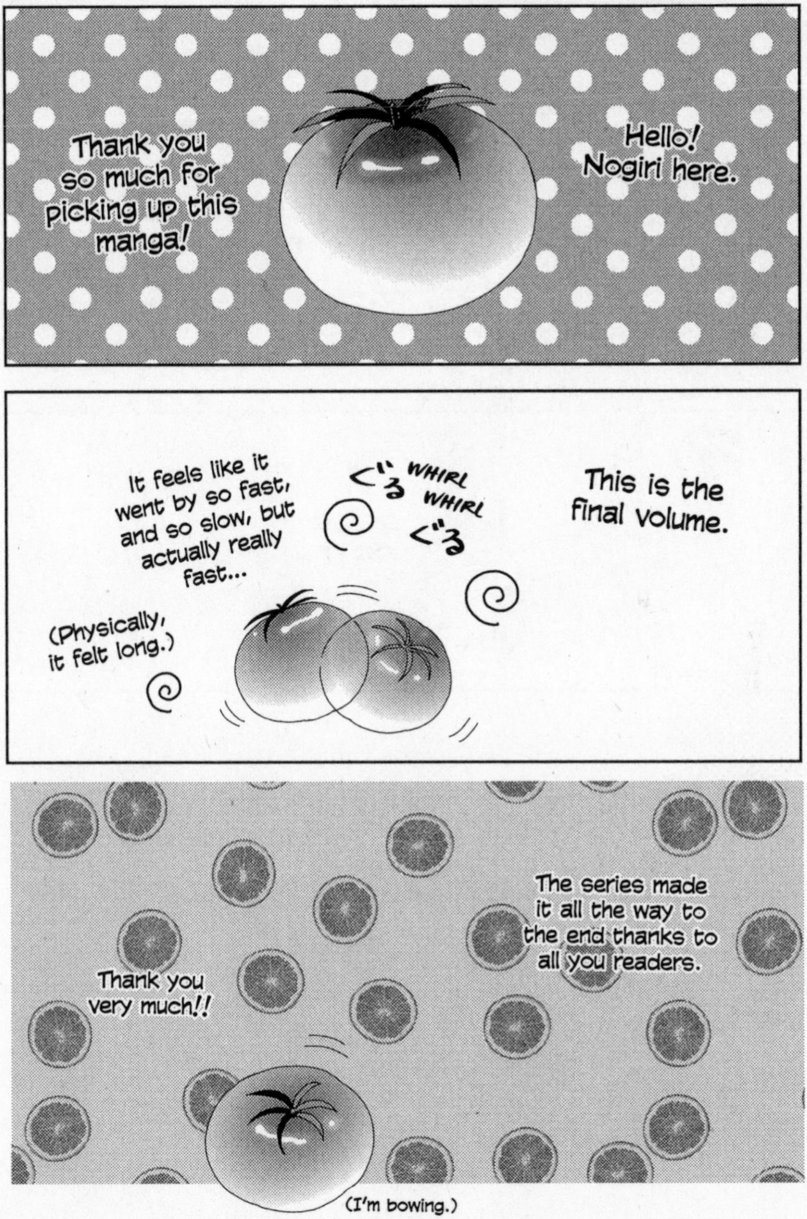
Hello! Nogiri here.
Thank you so much for picking up this manga!
This is the final volume.
ぐる WHIRL
ぐる WHIRL
It feels like it went by so fast, and so slow, but actually really fast...
(Physically, it felt long.)
The series made it all the way to the end thanks to all you readers.
Thank you very much!!
(I'm bowing.)

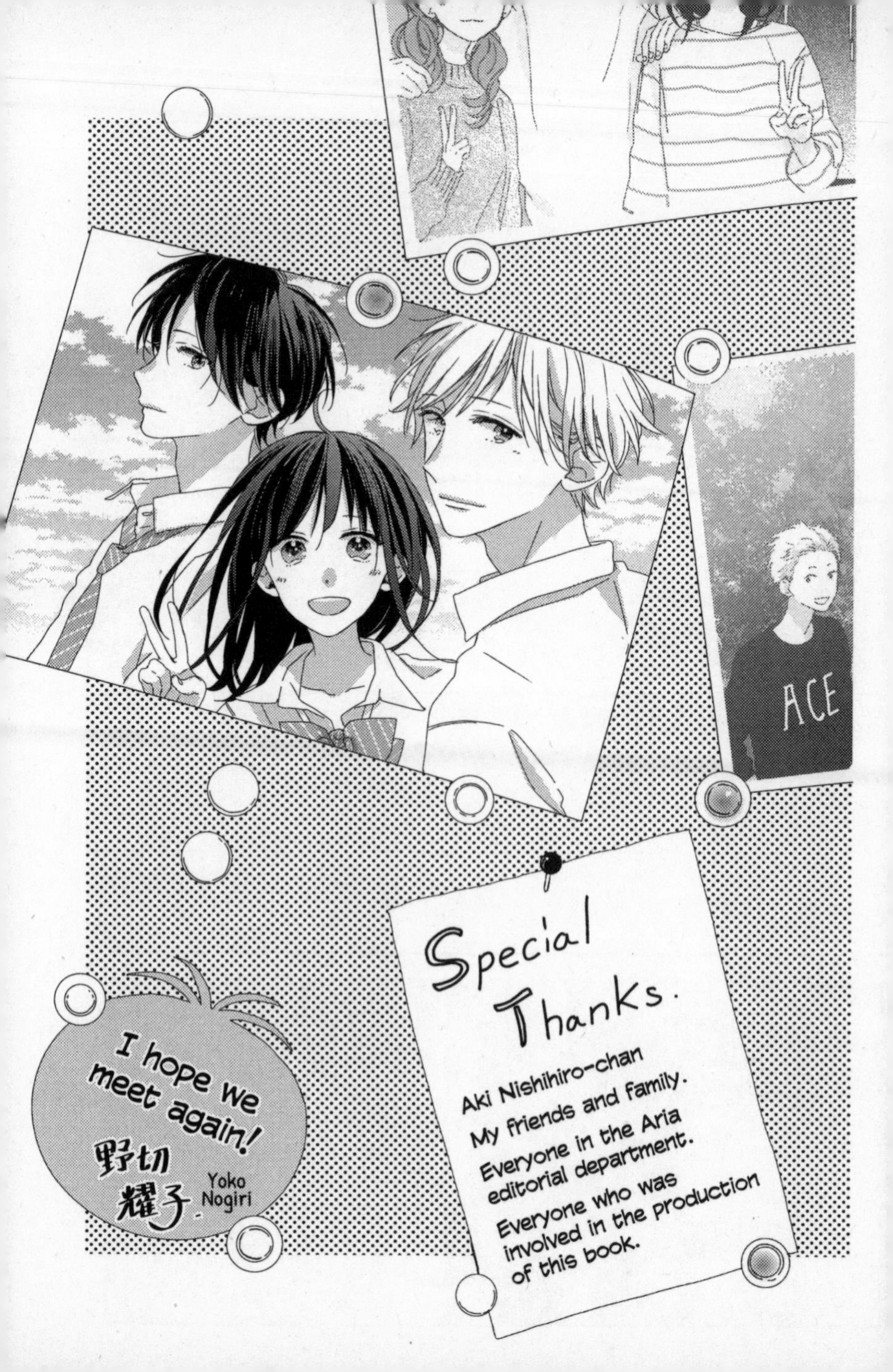
ACE
Special Thanks.
Aki Nishihiro-chan
My friends and family.
Everyone in the Aria editorial department.
Everyone who was involved in the production of this book.
I hope we meet again!
野切耀子.
Yoko Nogiri

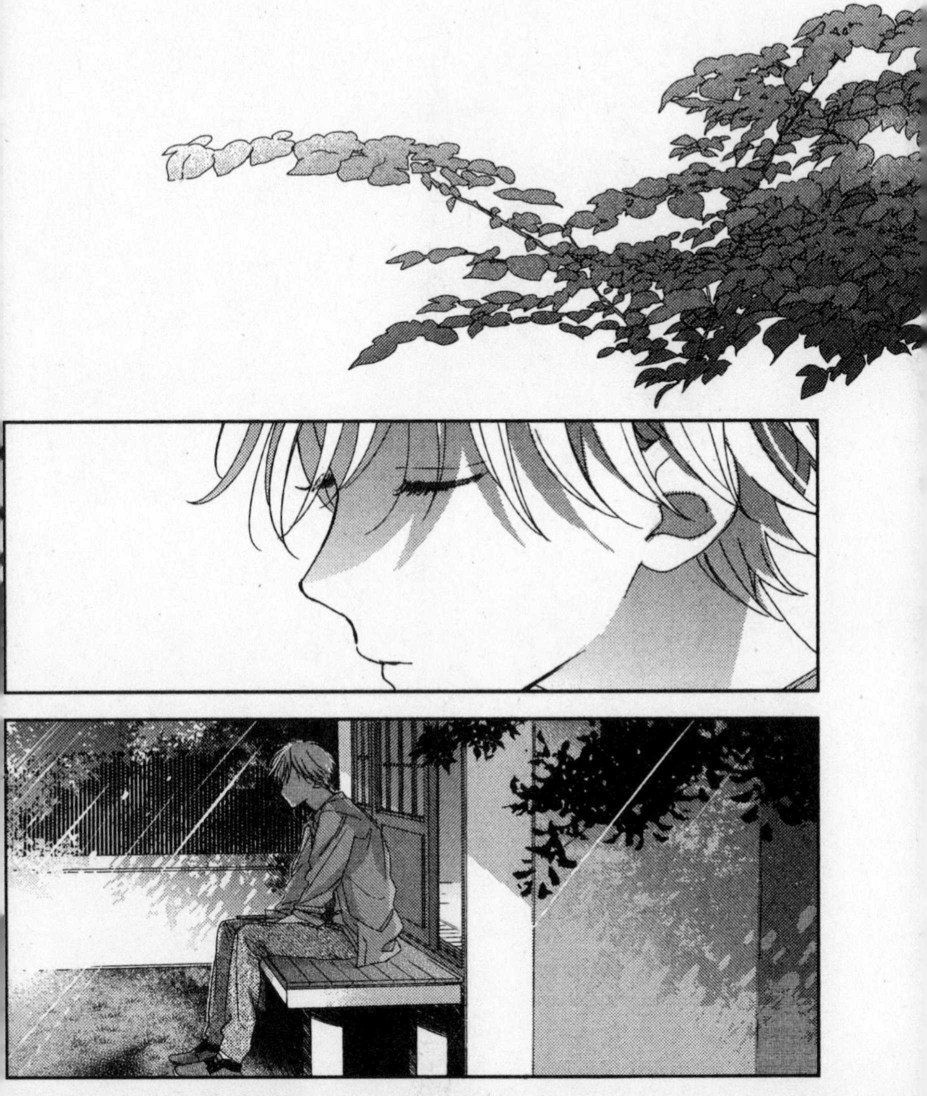

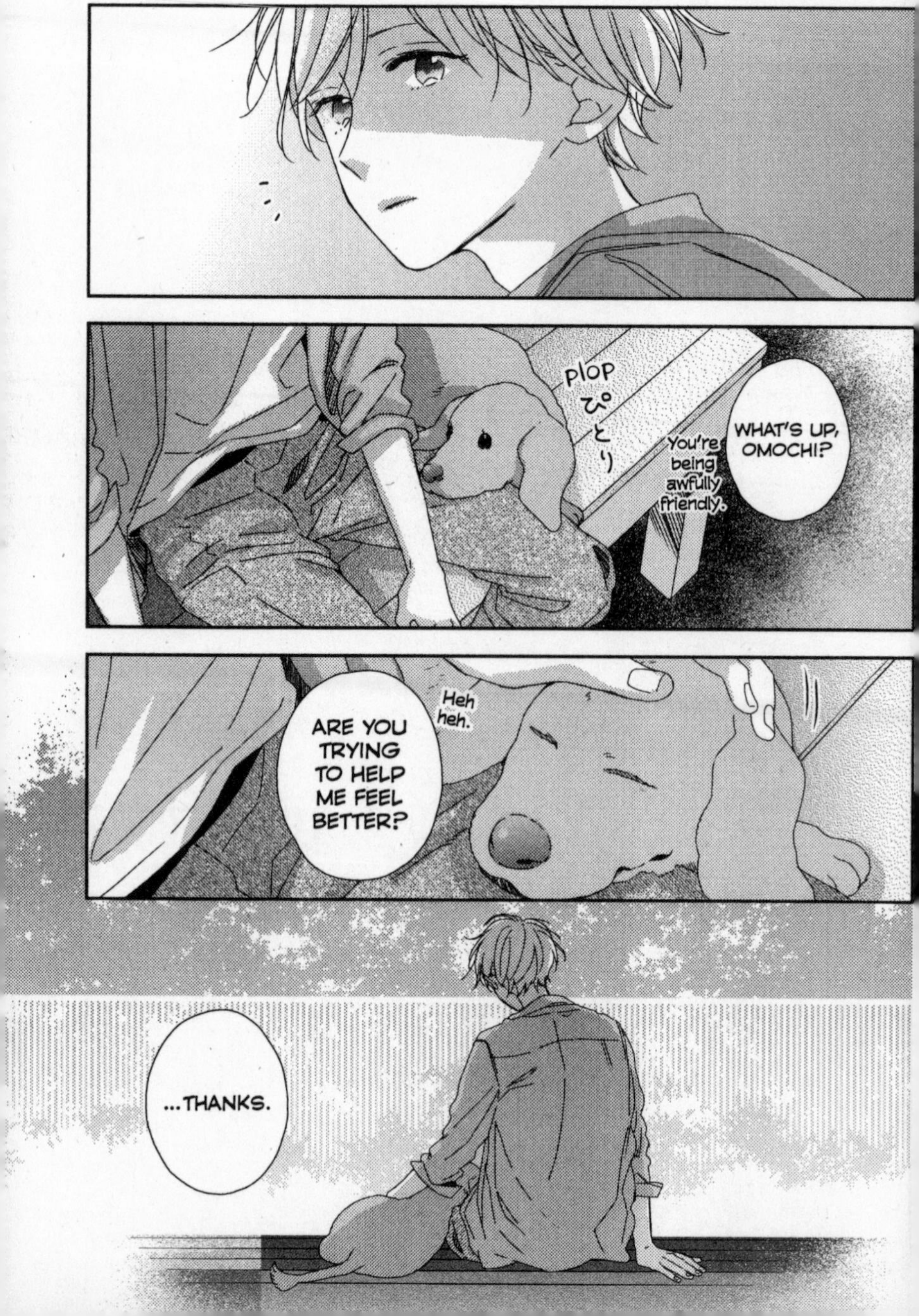
...
PLOP
ぴと
WHAT'S UP, OMOCHI?
You're being awfully friendly.
Heh heh.
ARE YOU TRYING TO HELP ME FEEL BETTER?
...THANKS.

LOVE IN FOCUS

Acclaimed screenwriter and director Mari Okada (*Maquia, anohana*) teams up with manga artist Nao Emoto (*Forget Me Not*) in this moving, funny, so-true-it's-embarrassing coming-of-age series!

When Kazusa enters high school, she joins the Literature Club, and leaps from reading innocent fiction to diving into the literary classics. But these novels are a bit more... *adult* than she was prepared for. Between euphemisms like fresh dewy grass and pork stew, crushing on the boy next door, and knowing you want to do that *one thing* before you die—discovering your budding sexuality is no easy feat! As if puberty wasn't awkward enough, the club consists of a brooding writer, the prettiest girl in school, an agreeable comrade, and an outspoken prude. Fumbling over their own discomforts, these five teens get thrown into chaos over three little letters: S...E...X...!

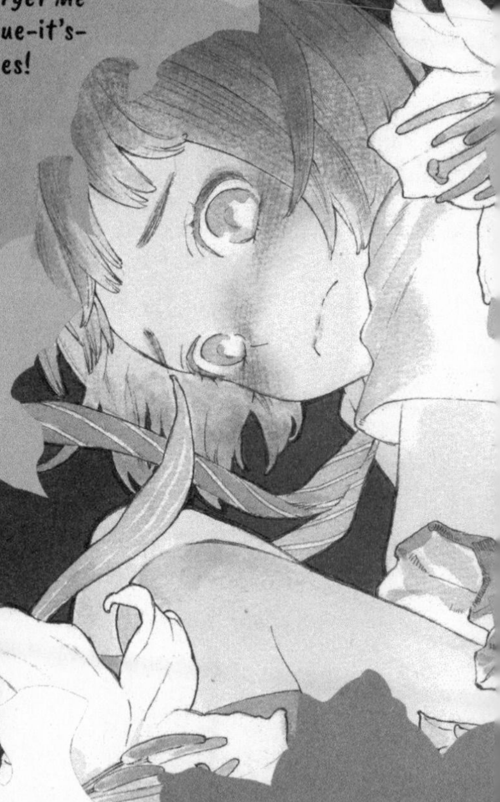

Anime coming soon!

O Maidens in your Savage Season

Mari Okada   Nao Emoto

WAITING FOR SPRING

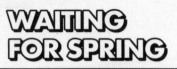

A sweet romantic story of a soft-spoken high school freshman and her quest to make friends. For fans of earnest, fun, and dramatic shojo like *Kimi ni Todoke* and *Say I Love You.*

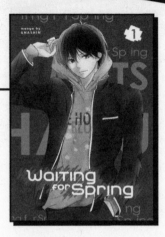

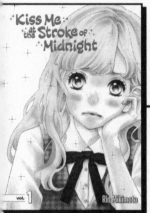

KISS ME AT THE STROKE OF MIDNIGHT

An all-new Cinderella comedy perfect for fans of *My Little Monster* and *Say I Love You!*

LOVE AND LIES

Love is forbidden. When you turn 16, the government will assign you your marriage partner. This dystopian manga about teen love and defiance is a sexy, funny, and dramatic new hit! Anime now streaming on Anime Strike!

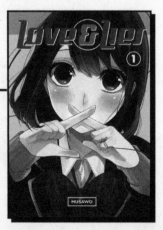

YOUR NEW FAVORITE ROMANCE MANGA IS WAITING FOR YOU!

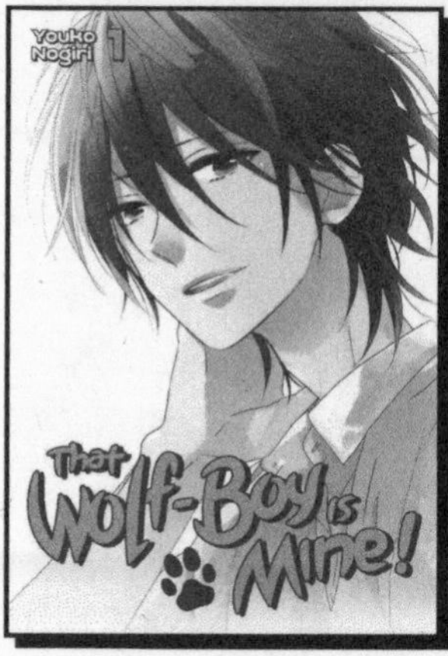
Youko Nogiri
1
That Wolf-Boy is Mine!

THAT WOLF-BOY IS MINE!

A beast-boy comedy and drama perfect for fans of *Fruits Basket*!

"A tantalizing, understated slice-of-life romance with an interesting supernatural twist."

- Taykobon

WAKE UP, SLEEPING BEAUTY

This heartrending romantic manga is not the fairy tale you remember! This time, Prince Charming is a teenage housekeeper, and Sleeping Beauty's curse threatens to pull them both into deep trouble.

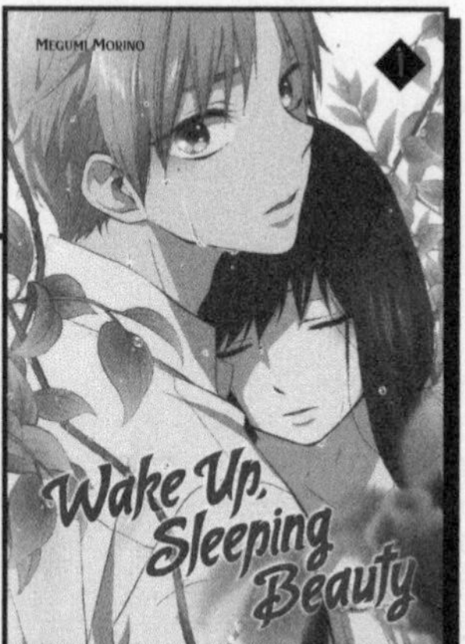
MEGUMI MORINO
1
Wake Up, Sleeping Beauty

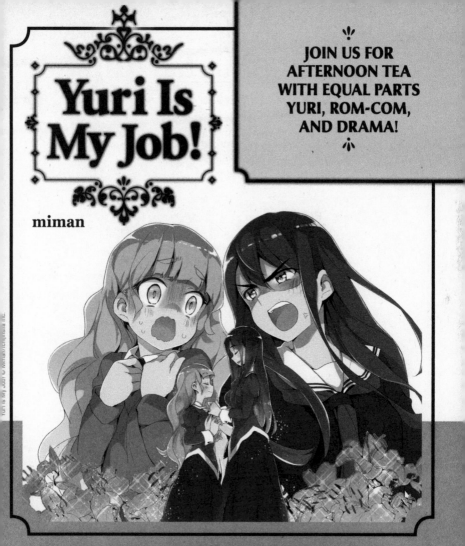

Yuri Is My Job!

miman

JOIN US FOR AFTERNOON TEA WITH EQUAL PARTS YURI, ROM-COM, AND DRAMA!

Hime is a picture-perfect high school princess, so when she accidentally injures a café manager named Mai, she's willing to cover some shifts to keep her façade intact. To Hime's surprise, the café is themed after a private school where the all-female staff always puts on their best act for their loyal customers. However, under the guidance of the most graceful girl there, Hime can't help but blush and blunder! Beneath all the frills and laughter, Hime feels tension brewing as she finds out more about her new job and her budding feelings...

KC KODANSHA COMICS

"A quirky, fun comedy series... If you're a yuri fan, or perhaps interested in getting into it but not sure where to start, this book is worth picking up."
— Anime UK News

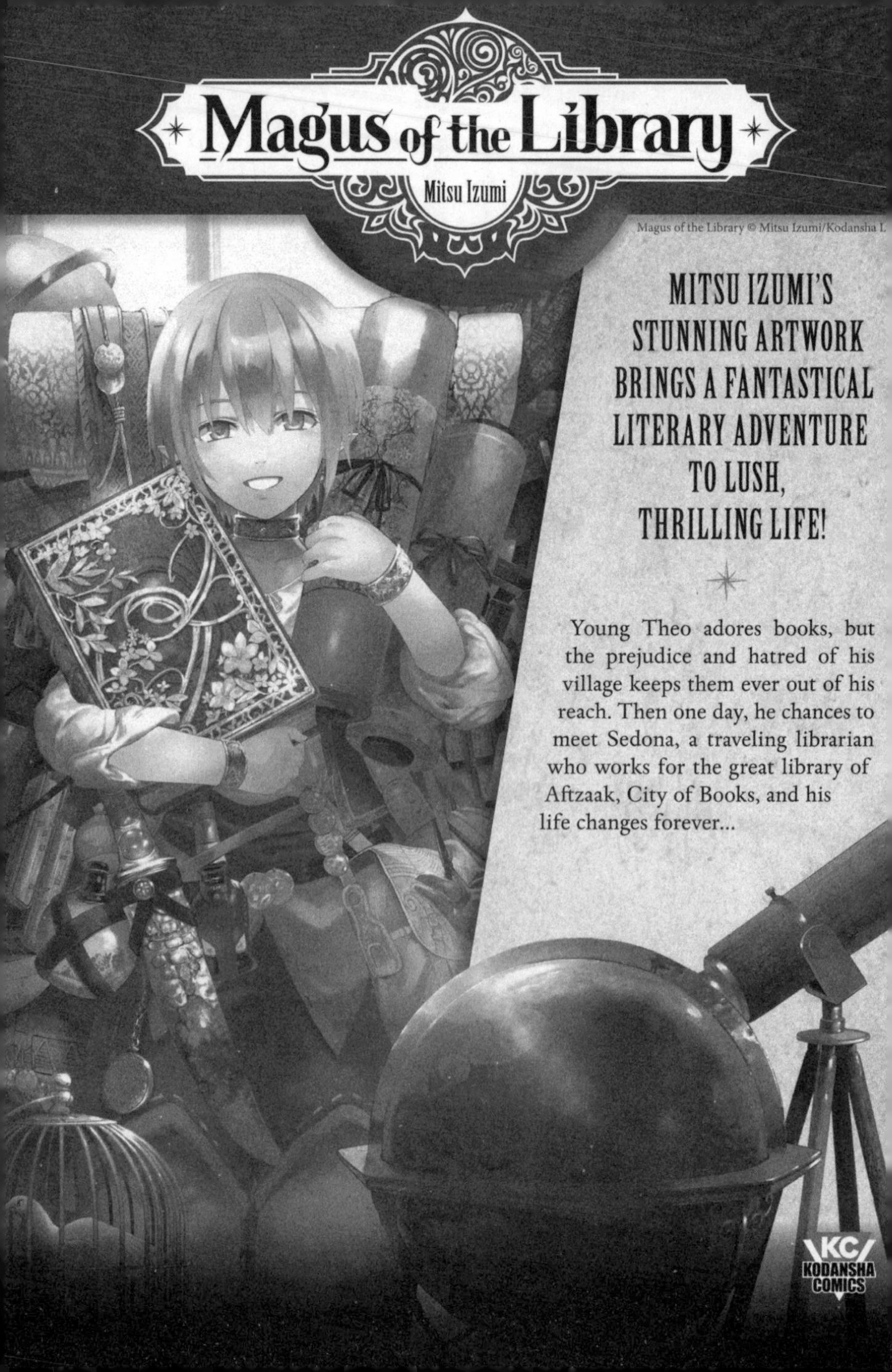
Magus of the Library
Mitsu Izumi
Magus of the Library © Mitsu Izumi/Kodansha L
MITSU IZUMI'S STUNNING ARTWORK BRINGS A FANTASTICAL LITERARY ADVENTURE TO LUSH, THRILLING LIFE!
Young Theo adores books, but the prejudice and hatred of his village keeps them ever out of his reach. Then one day, he chances to meet Sedona, a traveling librarian who works for the great library of Aftzaak, City of Books, and his life changes forever...
KC KODANSHA COMICS

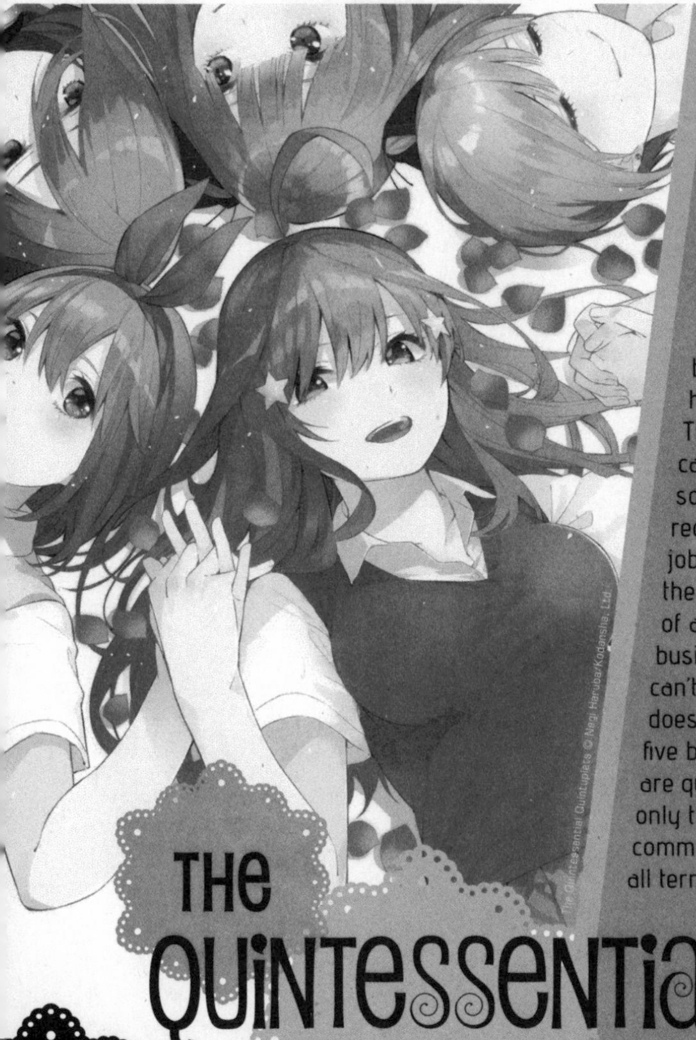

Futaro Uesugi is a second-year in high school, scraping to get by and pay off his family's debt. The only thing he can do is study, so when Futaro receives a part-time job offer to tutor the five daughters of a wealthy businessman, he can't pass it up. Little does he know, these five beautiful sisters are quintuplets, but the only thing they have in common...is that they're all terrible at studying!

The Quintessential Quintuplets © Negi Haruba/Kodansha, Ltd.

THE QUINTESSENTIAL QUINTUPLETS

negi haruba

ANIME OUT NOW!

KC
KODANSHA COMICS

The prestigious Dahlia Academy educates the elite of society from two countries; To the East is the Nation of Touwa; across the sea the other way, the Principality of West. The nations, though, are fierce rivals, and their students are constantly feuding—which means Romio Inuzuka, head of Touwa's first-year students, has a problem. He's fallen for his counterpart from West, Juliet Persia, and when he can't take it any more, he confesses his feelings.

Now Romio has two problems: A girlfriend, and a secret...

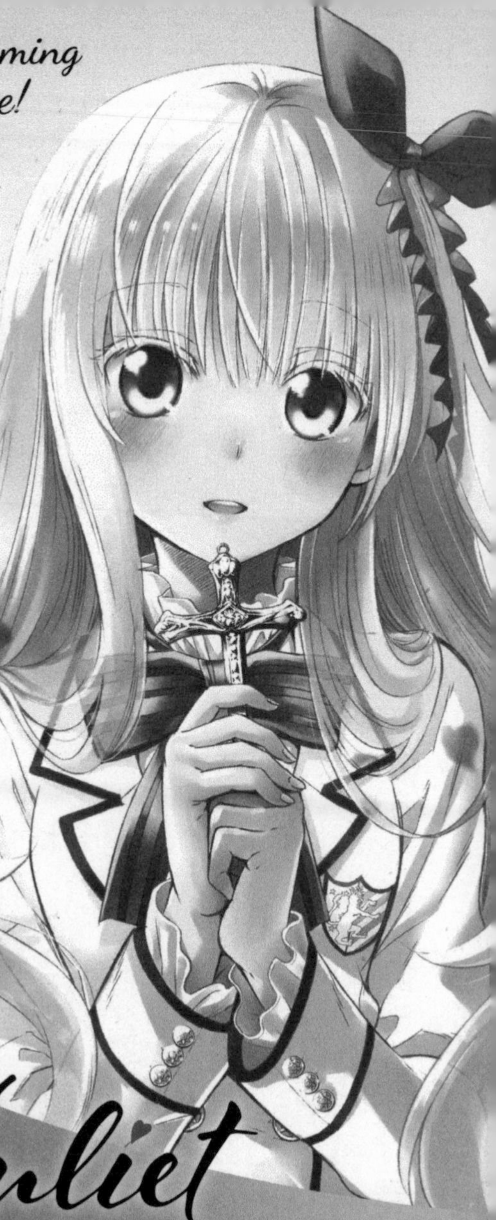

Boarding School *Juliet*

By Yousuke Kaneda

"A fine romantic comedy... The chemistry between the two main characters is excellent and the humor is great, backed up by a fun enough supporting cast and a different twist on the genre." –AiPT

KC KODANSHA COMICS

My Little Monster

OPPOSITES ATTRACT...MAYBE?

Haru Yoshida is feared as an unstable and violent "monster." Mizutani Shizuku is a grade-obsessed student with no friends. Fate brings these two together to form the most unlikely pair. Haru firmly believes he's in love with Mizutani and she firmly believes he's insane.

KC
KODANSHA COMICS

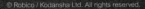

a Silent Voice

The New York Times bestselling manga and Eisner Award nominee—now available in a complete box set!

Now a feature-length animation from Kyoto Animation!

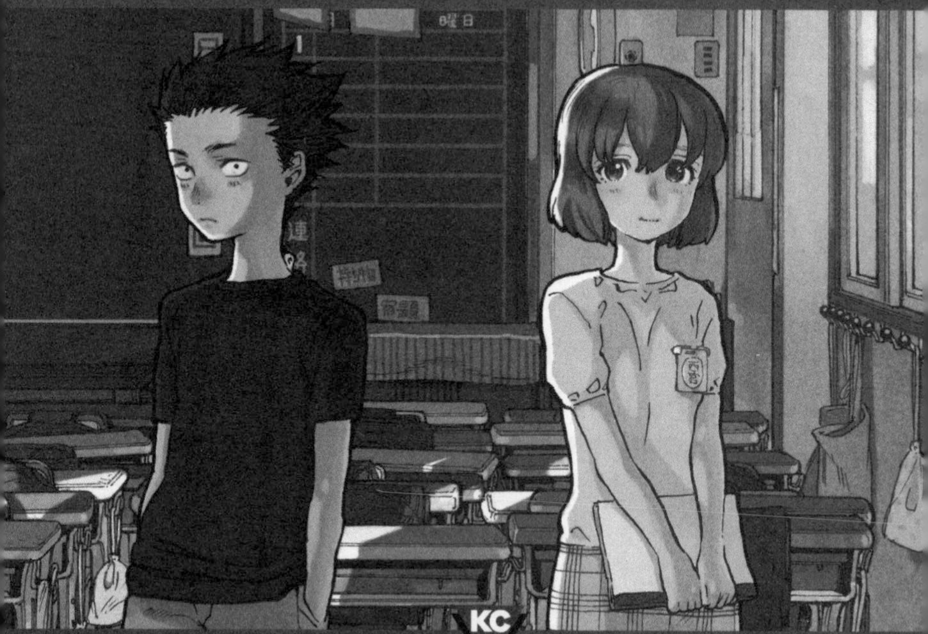

KC KODANSHA COMICS

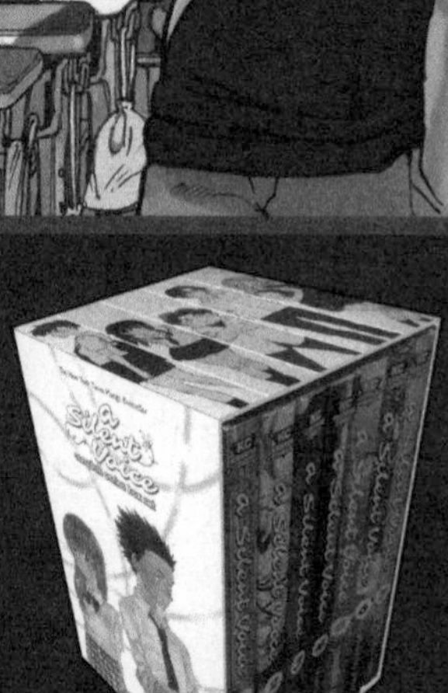

- Exclusive 2-sided poster
- Replica of Shoko's notebook
- Preview of Yoshitoki Oima's new series, To Your Eternity

Shoya is a bully. When Shoko, a girl who can't hear, enters his elementary school class, she becomes their favorite target, and Shoya and his friends goad each other into devising new tortures for her. But the children's cruelty goes too far. Shoko is forced to leave the school, and Shoya ends up shouldering all the blame. Six years later, the two meet again. Can Shoya make up for his past mistakes, or is it too late?

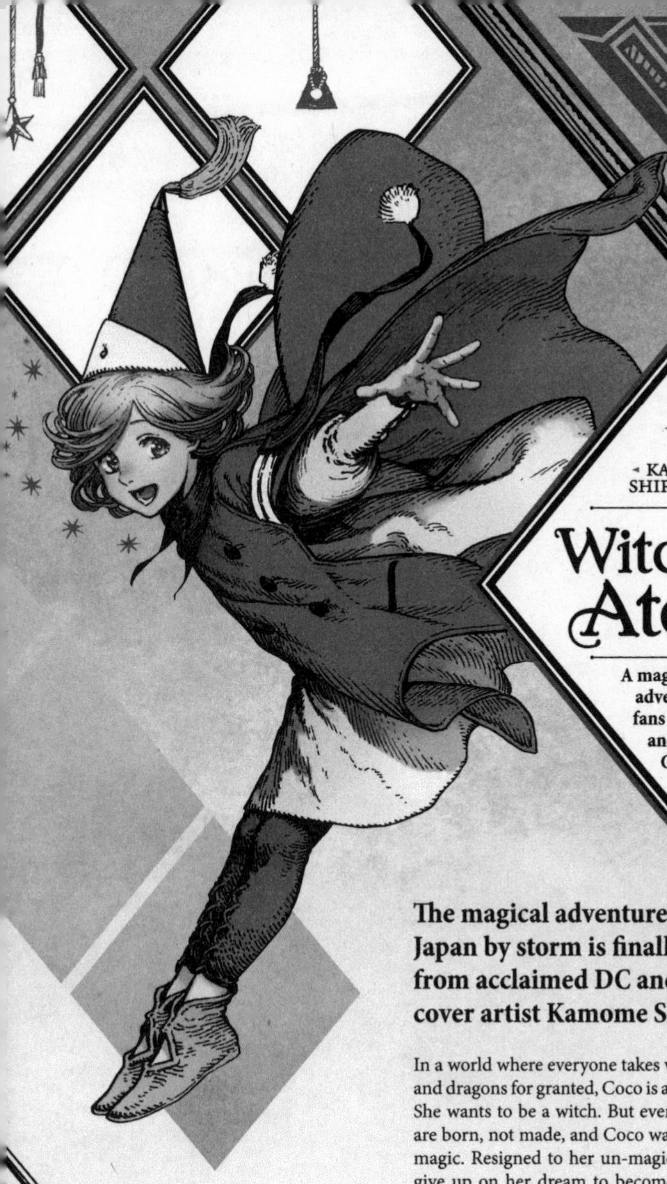

‹ KAMOME ›
SHIRAHAMA

Witch Hat Atelier

A magical manga
adventure for
fans of Disney
and Studio
Ghibli!

Witch Hat Atelier © Kamome Shirahama/Kodansha Ltd.

The magical adventure that took Japan by storm is finally here, from acclaimed DC and Marvel cover artist Kamome Shirahama!

In a world where everyone takes wonders like magic spells
and dragons for granted, Coco is a girl with a simple dream:
She wants to be a witch. But everybody knows magicians
are born, not made, and Coco was not born with a gift for
magic. Resigned to her un-magical life, Coco is about to
give up on her dream to become a witch...until the day
she meets Qifrey, a mysterious, traveling magician. After
secretly seeing Qifrey perform magic in a way she's never
seen before, Coco soon learns what everybody "knows"
might not be the truth, and discovers that her magical
dream may not be as far away as it may seem...

THE MAGICAL GIRL CLASSIC THAT BROUGHT A GENERATION OF READERS TO MANGA, NOW BACK IN A DEFINITIVE, HARDCOVER COLLECTOR'S EDITION!

CARDCAPTOR SAKURA
COLLECTOR'S EDITION
CLAMP

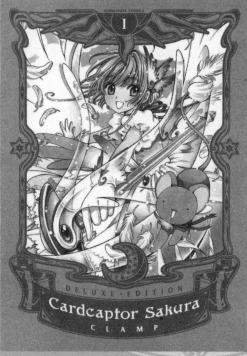

Ten-year-old Sakura Kinomoto lives a pretty normal life with her older brother, Tōya, and widowed father, Fujitaka— until the day she discovers a strange book in her father's library, and her life takes a magical turn...

- A deluxe large-format hardcover edition of CLAMP's shojo manga classic
- All-new foil-stamped cover art on each volume
- Comes with exclusive collectible art card

KC
KODANSHA
COMICS

EDENS ZERO
エデンズゼロ

HIRO MASHIMA IS BACK! JOIN THE CREATOR OF *FAIRY TAIL* AS HE TAKES TO THE STARS FOR ANOTHER THRILLING SAGA!

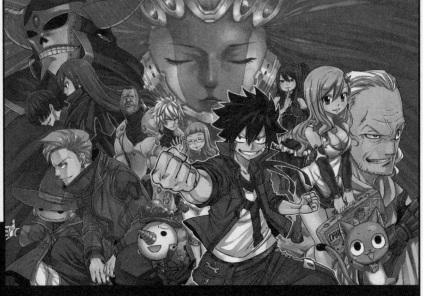

A high-flying space adventure! All the steadfast friendship and wild fighting you've been waiting for...IN SPACE!

At Granbell Kingdom, an abandoned amusement park, Shiki has lived his entire life among machines. But one day, Rebecca and her cat companion Happy appear at the park's front gates. Little do these newcomers know that this is the first human contact Granbell has had in a hundred years! As Shiki stumbles his way into making new friends, his former neighbors stir at an opportunity for a robo-rebellion... And when his old homeland becomes too dangerous, Shiki must join Rebecca and Happy on their spaceship and escape into the boundless cosmos.

KC KODANSHA COMICS

THE STORY STARTS **HERE!**

Again!!

アゲイン!!

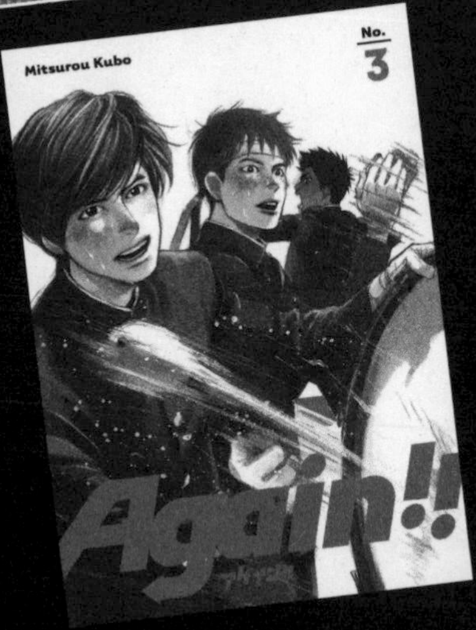

Mitsurou Kubo
No. 3
Again!!

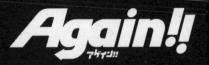

Kinichiro Imamura isn't a bad guy, really, but on the first day of high school his narrow eyes and bleached blonde hair made him look so shifty that his classmates assumed the worst. Three years later, without any friends or fond memories, he isn't exactly feeling bittersweet about graduation. But after an accidental fall down a flight of stairs, Kinichiro wakes up three years in the past... on the first day of high school! School's starting again—but it's gonna be different this time around!

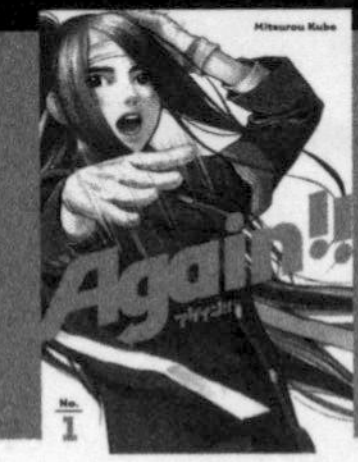

Mitsurou Kubo
Again!!
No. 1

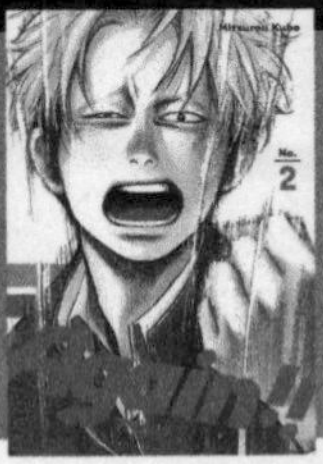

Mitsurou Kubo
No. 2

Vol. 1-3 now available in **PRINT** and **DIGITAL**!
Vol. 4 coming August 2018!

Find out **MORE** by visiting:
kodanshacomics.com/MitsurouKubo

ABOUT MITSUROU KUBO

Mitsurou Kubo is a manga artist born in Nagasaki prefecture. Her series *3.3.7 Byoshi!!* (2001-2003), *Tokkyu!!* (2004-2008), and *Again!!* (2011-2014) were published in *Weekly Shonen Magazine*, and *Moteki* (2008-2010) was published in the seinen comics magazine *Evening*. After the publication of *Again!!* concluded, she met Sayo Yamamoto, director of the global smash-hit anime ***Yuri!!! on ICE***. Working with Yamamoto, Kubo contributed the original concept, original character designs, and initial script for ***Yuri!!! on ICE***. *Again!!* is her first manga to be published in English.

KC KODANSHA COMICS

Kodansha COMICS

Love in Focus volume 3 is a work of fiction. Names, characters, places, and incidents are the products of the author's imagination or are used fictitiously. Any resemblance to actual events, locales, or persons, living or dead, is entirely coincidental.

A Kodansha Comics Trade Paperback Original

Published in the United States by Kodansha Comics, an imprint of Kodansha USA Publishing, LLC, New York.

Publication rights for this English edition arranged through Kodansha Ltd, Tokyo.

ISBN 978-1-63236-796-9

Printed in the United States of America.

www.kodanshacomics.com

9 8 7 6 5 4 3 2 1
Translation: Alethea and Athena Nibley
Lettering: Sara Linsley
Editing: Haruko Hashimoto
Kodansha Comics edition cover design by Phil Balsman